적중100

영어 기출 문제집

중**3**

시사 | 송미정

Best Collection

구성과 특징

교과서의 주요 학습 내용을 중심으로 학습 영역별 특성에 맞춰 단계별로 다양한 학습 기회를 제공하여
단원별 학습능력 평가는 물론 중간 및 기말고사 시험 등에 완벽하게 대비할 수 있도록 내용을 구성

Words & Expressions

Step1   Key Words 단원별 핵심 단어 설명 및 풀이
         Key Expression 단원별 핵심 숙어 및 관용어 설명
         Word Power 반대 또는 비슷한 뜻 단어 배우기
         English Dictionary 영어로 배우는 영어 단어

Step2   실력평가 단원별 수시평가 대비 주관식, 객관식 문제풀이

Step3   서술형 대비 학업성취도 및 수행능력평가 대비 서술형 문제풀이

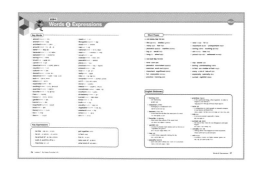

Conversation

Step1   핵심 의사소통 소통에 필요한 주요 표현 방법 요약
         핵심 Check 기본적인 표현 방법 및 활용능력 확인

Step2   대화문 익히기 교과서 대화문 심층 분석 및 확인

Step3   교과서 확인학습 빈칸 채우기를 통한 문장 완성 능력 확인

Step4   기본평가 시험대비 기초 학습 능력 평가

Step5   실력평가 단원별 수시평가 대비 주관식, 객관식 문제풀이

Step6   서술형 대비 학업성취도 및 수행능력평가 대비 서술형 문제풀이

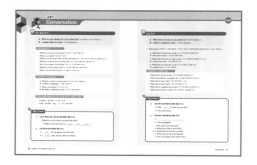

Grammar

Step1   주요 문법 단원별 주요 문법 사항과 예문을 알기 쉽게 설명
         핵심 Check 기본 문법사항에 대한 이해 여부 확인

Step2   기본평가 시험대비 기초 학습 능력 평가

Step3   실력평가 단원별 수시평가 대비 주관식, 객관식 문제풀이

Step4   서술형 대비 학업성취도 및 수행능력평가 대비 서술형 문제풀이

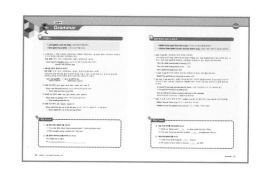

Reading

Step1   구문 분석 단원별로 제시된 문장에 대한 구문별 분석과 내용 설명
         확인문제 문장에 대한 기본적인 이해와 인지능력 확인

Step2   확인학습A 빈칸 채우기를 통한 문장 완성 능력 확인

Step3   확인학습B 제시된 우리말을 영어로 완성하여 작문 능력 키우기

Step4   실력평가 단원별 수시평가 대비 주관식, 객관식 문제풀이

Step5   서술형 대비 학업성취도 및 수행능력평가 대비 서술형 문제풀이
         교과서 구석구석 교과서에 나오는 기타 문장까지 완벽 학습

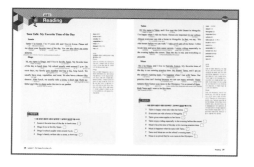

Composition

|영역별 핵심문제|

단어 및 어휘, 대화문, 문법, 독해 등 각 영역별 기출문제의 출제 유형을 분석하여 실전에 대비하고 연습할 수 있도록 문제를 배열

|단원별 예상문제|

기출문제를 분석한 후 새로운 시험 출제 경향을 더하여 새롭게 출제될 수 있는 문제를 포함하여 시험에 완벽하게 대비할 수 있도록 준비

|서술형 실전 및 창의사고력 문제|

학교 시험에서 점차 늘어나는 서술형 시험에 집중 대비하고 고득점을 취득하는데 만전을 기하기 위한 학습 코너

|단원별 모의고사|

영역별, 단계별 학습을 모두 마친 후 실전 연습을 위한 모의고사

INSIGHT on the textbook

교과서 파헤치기

- **단어Test1~3** 영어 단어 우리말 쓰기, 우리말을 영어 단어로 쓰기, 영영풀이에 해당하는 단어와 우리말 쓰기
- **대화문Test1~2** 대화문 빈칸 완성 및 전체 대화문 쓰기
- **본문Test1~5** 빈칸 완성, 우리말 쓰기, 문장 배열연습, 영어 작문하기 복습 등 단계별 반복 학습을 통해 교과서 지문에 대한 완벽한 습득
- **구석구석지문Test1~2** 지문 빈칸 완성 및 전문 영어로 쓰기

Lesson 3

Healthy Living, a Happy Life

 의사소통 기능

- 강조하기
  A: I think it's important to eat a good breakfast.
  B: I think so, too.

- 안타까움, 후회 표현하기
  A: Your bag is too small.
  B: Yes. I should have brought a bigger one.

 언어 형식

- 'the 비교급, the 비교급'
  The more sun you get, **the more** "happy hormone" the brain produces.

- It is ... that 강조 구문
  It is calcium **that** builds strong bones and teeth.

Words & Expressions

Key Words

- **already** [ɔːlrédi] 부 이미, 벌써
- **arrive** [əráiv] 동 도착하다
- **avoid** [əvɔ́id] 동 피하다
- **benefit** [bénəfit] 명 이득 동 이득을 보다
- **blanket** [blǽŋkit] 명 이불, 담요
- **bone** [boun] 명 뼈
- **brain** [brein] 명 뇌
- **calcium** [kǽlsiəm] 명 칼슘
- **calming** [kɑ́ːmiŋ] 형 진정시키는
- **check** [tʃek] 동 점검하다
- **clearly** [klíərli] 부 또렷하게
- **create** [kriéit] 동 만들어 내다, 창조하다
- **decide** [disáid] 동 결심하다, 결정하다
- **direct** [dirékt] 형 직접적인, (열기나 빛이) 직접 닿는
- **effect** [ifékt] 명 효과
- **exercise** [éksərsàiz] 동 운동하다
- **finally** [fáinəli] 부 마침내
- **flight** [flait] 명 항공편, 비행
- **fortunately** [fɔ́ːrtʃənətli] 부 다행스럽게도
- **grade** [greid] 명 성적
- **hang** [hæŋ] 동 걸다
- **healthy** [hélθi] 형 건강한
- **hormone** [hɔ́ːrmòun] 명 호르몬
- **interestingly** [íntərəstiŋli] 부 흥미롭게도
- **journal** [dʒə́ːrnl] 명 일지, 일기
- **leave** [liːv] 동 떠나다
- **level** [lévəl] 명 수준, 수치
- **mood** [muːd] 명 기분, 감정
- **moreover** [mɔːróuvər] 부 게다가
- **nature-friendly** 형 자연친화적인
- **outdoors** [áutdɔrz] 부 야외에서
- **peak** [piːk] 형 절정의, 최고조의 명 절정, 최고조
- **produce** [prədjúːs] 동 만들어 내다
- **properly** [prápərli] 부 제대로
- **protect** [prətékt] 동 보호하다
- **reach** [riːtʃ] 동 도달하다
- **regret** [rigrét] 동 후회하다
- **regularly** [régjulərli] 부 규칙적으로
- **review** [rivjúː] 동 복습하다
- **role** [roul] 명 역할
- **safely** [séifli] 부 안전하게
- **serotonin** [serətóunin] 명 세로토닌
- **shine** [ʃain] 동 빛나다
- **skin** [skin] 명 피부
- **sunlight** [sʌ́nlait] 명 햇살
- **sunscreen** [sʌ́nskrìːn] 명 자외선 차단제
- **sunshine** [sʌ́nʃain] 명 햇볕, 햇빛
- **vitamin** [váitəmin] 명 비타민
- **weather** [wéðər] 명 날씨
- **wet** [wet] 형 젖은

Key Expressions

- **be good for** ~에 유익하다
- **both A and B** A와 B 둘 다
- **full of** ~로 가득 찬
- **get sleep** 잠자다
- **go up** 높아지다
- **have a snack** 간식을 먹다
- **keep ~ in mind** ~을 명심하다
- **make a world of difference** 큰 차이를 만들다
- **on time** 제시간에
- **play an important role in** ~에 중요한 역할을 하다
- **put on** 착용하다, 바르다
- **put out** 내놓다
- **should have p.p.** ~했어야 했는데
- **stay healthy** 건강을 유지하다
- **stay up** 깨어 있다
- **surf the Internet** 인터넷 검색을 하다
- **too ~ to ...** 너무 ~해서 …할 수 없다

Word Power

※ 서로 비슷한 뜻을 가진 어휘

- □ **arrive** 도착하다 : **reach** 도착하다
- □ **exercise** 운동하다 : **work out** 운동하다
- □ **fortunately** 다행스럽게도 : **luckily** 운 좋게도
- □ **leave** 떠나다 : **depart** 떠나다
- □ **protect** 보호하다 : **cover** 보호하다

- □ **benefit** 이점 : **advantage** 이점, 장점
- □ **finally** 마침내 : **ultimately** 결국
- □ **grade** 성적 : **degree** 점수
- □ **properly** 제대로 : **suitably** 적절하게
- □ **role** 역할 : **part** 배역

※ 서로 반대되는 뜻을 가진 어휘

- □ **avoid** 피하다 ↔ **face** 마주하다
- □ **direct** 직접적인 ↔ **indirect** 간접적인
- □ **wet** 젖은 ↔ **dry** 건조한

- □ **clearly** 또렷하게 ↔ **vaguely** 모호하게
- □ **healthy** 건강한 ↔ **unhealthy** 건강하지 못한
- □ **regularly** 규칙적으로 ↔ **irregularly** 불규칙하게

※ 동사 – 명사

- □ **arrive** 도착하다 – **arrival** 도착
- □ **decide** 결심하다 – **decision** 결심
- □ **protect** 보호하다 – **protection** 보호

- □ **avoid** 피하다 – **avoidance** 회피
- □ **produce** 만들어 내다 – **production** 생산

English Dictionary

- □ **benefit** 이득을 보다
  → to take advantages from something
  무엇인가로부터 이득을 얻다
- □ **blanket** 이불, 담요
  → a large piece of cloth used as a covering for warmth
  따뜻하도록 덮개로 사용되는 큰 천
- □ **bone** 뼈
  → the hard part of the body that forms a framework inside people or animals
  사람이나 동물의 내부에서 골격을 형성하는 신체의 단단한 부분
- □ **brain** 뇌
  → the organ inside the head that control movements and feelings
  움직임과 감정을 조절하는 머리 속에 있는 기관
- □ **go up** 올라가다
  → to become higher or greater 더 높거나 크게 되다
- □ **journal** 일지, 일기
  → a book in which people regularly write about what has happened to them
  자신들에게 일어난 일을 규칙적으로 기록하는 책

- □ **mood** 기분, 감정
  → a temporary state of mind 일시적인 마음의 상태
- □ **peak** 절정, 최고조
  → the highest level or degree of excellence, quantity, activity, etc. 탁월함, 수량, 활동 등의 가장 높은 수준이나 정도
- □ **regularly** 규칙적으로
  → at the same time every day, week, month, or year
  매일, 매주, 매달, 매년 똑같은 시간에
- □ **role** 역할
  → the part assumed to be played by a person
  사람에 의해 수행되도록 떠맡겨지는 배역
- □ **skin** 피부
  → the outer layer of a person's or animal's body
  사람이나 동물 신체의 가장 바깥 층
- □ **sunshine** 햇빛
  → light and heat from the sun 태양으로부터의 빛과 열
- □ **wet** 젖은
  → covered or touched with water or another liquid
  물이나 다른 액체로 덮여 있거나 접촉한

01 다음 밑줄 친 부분과 의미가 가장 가까운 것을 고르시오.

> As you can see, sunshine has many <u>benefits</u>, but how can you enjoy its benefits safely?

① impacts　② favors　③ joys
④ events　⑤ advantages

02 다음 문장의 빈칸에 들어갈 단어를 사용하여 문장을 자연스럽게 완성할 수 있는 것은?

> What are the positive and negative _____ of social networking sites?

① A letter _____ for you this morning.
② He tends to _____ all physical contact.
③ He has cracked a _____ in his arm.
④ The drug has some bad side _____.
⑤ People need _____ to have strong bones.

03 다음 빈칸에 공통으로 들어가기에 알맞은 것은?

> • Look at my face. I should have _____ on some sunscreen.
> • I _____ the blanket out in the sun this morning.

① got　② had　③ put
④ let　⑤ left

서답형

04 〈보기〉와 같은 관계가 되도록 빈칸에 알맞은 말을 쓰시오.

> ┤ 보기 ├
> avoid : face

(1) wet : _____
(2) regular : _____

05 다음 중 밑줄 친 부분의 뜻풀이가 바르지 <u>않은</u> 것은?

① One of the <u>benefits</u> of a smartphone is that you can reach someone quickly in an emergency. (이점)
② This exercise helps increase growth <u>hormone</u>. (호르몬)
③ Some research has shown us that our sports ability is also related to our <u>brains</u>. (뇌)
④ This steak was cooked with <u>direct</u> heat. (즉각적인)
⑤ The house has a reasonable price. <u>Moreover</u>, the location is very good. (게다가)

06 다음 중 〈보기〉에 있는 단어를 사용하여 자연스러운 문장을 만들 수 <u>없는</u> 것은? (대 · 소문자 무시)

> ┤ 보기 ├
> difference　mood　outdoors　fortunately

① _____, the typhoon weakened before getting to my town.
② When you are cold, wearing a muffler will make a world of _____.
③ This book talks about how to get out of a bad _____.
④ Children enjoy playing _____.
⑤ When is the _____ hour for electricity use?

[01~02] 빈칸에 공통으로 들어갈 단어를 쓰시오.

01

> • A walk in the sun is good _____ both your mind and your body.
> • I have decided to exercise on the weekend _____ my health.

 02

> • It's important to arrive at school _____ time.
> • Serotonin helps you focus better _____ what you are doing.

03 밑줄 친 부분과 의미가 가장 가까운 단어를 주어진 철자로 시작하여 쓰시오.

> I am not really <u>suitably</u> dressed for a party.

➡ p_____

 04 주어진 단어를 이용해 빈칸을 완성하시오.

> We apologize for the late _____ of the train.

➡ _____ (arrive)

05 다음 짝지어진 단어의 관계가 같도록 빈칸에 알맞은 말을 쓰시오.

> healthy : unhealthy = direct : _____

 06 빈칸에 알맞은 단어를 〈보기〉에서 골라 쓰시오. (어형 변화 가능)

> ┤ 보기 ├
> skin   produce   role   properly

(1) This factory _____ car parts.
(2) Managing your time _____ is the key to success.
(3) Sue has an important _____ in our group.
(4) I need to buy a facial cream for dry _____.

07 다음 우리말에 맞게 빈칸에 알맞은 말을 쓰시오.

(1) Davis 박사는 햇살이 피부에 끼치는 영향을 연구 중이다.
  ➡ Dr. Davis is studying the action of _____ on the skin.
(2) 그는 아시아 횡단 여행에 대해 일기를 썼다.
  ➡ He kept a _____ of his travels across Asia.
(3) 75점 이상의 점수에 대해서는 A 학점을 받는다.
  ➡ You get an A _____ for scores of 75 and over.
(4) 제가 한 말을 유의하시기 바랍니다.
  ➡ I hope you'll keep in _____ what I've told you.

Conversation

1 강조하기

> **A** I think it's important to eat a good breakfast. 아침을 잘 먹는 것이 중요하다고 생각해.
>
> **B** I think so, too. 나도 역시 그렇게 생각해.

■ 전달하고자 하는 내용을 강조하는 표현은 다양하다. to부정사를 사용하여 부정사 부분을 강조할 때는 "It's important to V" 구문으로 나타내고, 절을 강조할 때에는 "It's important that S+V"의 형태를 취하고, "I think it's important to ~" 또는 "I think it's important that S+V"의 형태가 되기도 한다.

■ "It's important to + 동사원형~"은 "~하는 것은 중요하다"라는 의미이고, 이 표현에서 it은 가주어이고 "to부정사"가 진주어이다. 이 표현은 to부정사 부분을 강조하는 표현이다. "It's important that S+V"의 형태에서는 that절이 강조되는 내용이다.

■ to부정사를 강조할 때는 "important" 대신 necessary(필요한), essential(필수적인), crucial(중요한, 치명적인) 등을 이용하여 "It is necessary/important/essential/crucial to ~" 또는 "It is important/essential/crucial that S+V ~"라고 할 수도 있다.

■ 그 외에 강조하는 표현으로는 강조할 내용에 따라, 동사를 강조할 때는 강조의 조동사 do, does, did를 사용하고, 문장의 어느 한 성분을 강조할 때는 "It is ~ that" 강조구문을 사용할 수 있다.

강조를 나타내는 표현

- It is important[necessary] to/that ~. ~하는 것이 중요/필요하다
- I want to stress that ~. ~을 강조하고 싶다
- It is essential to ~. ~하는 것이 필수적이다
- It's crucial[critical] to V ~. ~하는 것이 중요하다
- It's significant to V ~. ~하는 것이 중요하다

핵심 Check

1. 다음 밑줄 친 우리말에 해당하는 표현으로 적절하지 <u>않은</u> 것은?

   G: How can we stay healthy?

   B: Well, <u>아침을 잘 먹는 것이 중요해.</u>

   ① I think it's important to eat a good breakfast
   ② it's important that you should eat a good breakfast
   ③ I want to stress that you eat a good breakfast
   ④ I think I will have a good breakfast, too
   ⑤ it's significant to have a good breakfast

② 안타까움, 후회 표현하기

> **A** Your bag is too small. 네 가방이 너무 작아.
>
> **B** Yes. I should have brought a bigger one. 맞아. 나는 더 큰 것을 가지고 왔어야 했는데.

- 과거의 행위에 대한 안타까움, 후회 또는 유감을 나타낼 때는 "should have+과거분사"의 표현을 사용한다. "should have+과거분사"는 "~했어야 했는데(하지 못해 유감이다)"의 의미로 과거와 반대되는 상황을 나타내기 위하여 사용할 수 있다.

- 이 표현에서는 "should"를 "ought to"로 바꾸어 "ought to have+과거분사"로 표현할 수 있다. "~하지 말았어야 했는데 (했다)"의 의미는 "should not have+과거분사" 또는 "ought not to have+과거분사"로 나타낸다.

- 안타까움, 후회를 나타내는 비슷한 표현으로 "I had to ~, but I didn't.", "I (really) regret ~." 등이 있고, sorry를 사용하여 "I'm sorry that 주어+과거동사 ~"로 나타내기도 한다. "should have+과거분사"는 과거 사실에 대한 가정의 표현으로 "~했어야 했는데 (하지 않았다)"의 의미를 나타내어 과거에 하지 않은 일에 대해 후회하는 표현이다. should 대신 could를 사용하여 "could have+과거분사"가 되면 "~할 수 있었는데"의 의미가 될 수 있다.

- "should have p.p."는 과거에 했어야 하는 일이나 하지 못한 일에 대한 후회, 유감, 안타까움을 표현하며 "~했어야 했는데 (못했다)"의 의미로 사용되고, "could/would have p.p."는 과거의 일에 대한 유감을 의미하여 "~할 수 있었는데(못했다), ~했어야 했는데(못했다)"의 의미로 가정법에 주로 사용된다. "must have p.p."는 과거에 대한 강한 추측을 나타내어 "~이었음에 틀림없다"의 의미로 사용되고, 그에 반해, "may have p.p."는 과거에 대한 약한 추측을 나타내어 "~했을지도 모른다"의 의미로 사용된다.

안타까움, 후회 표현하기

• 주어+should[shouldn't] have+과거분사 ~	~했어야[하지 말았어야] 했는데
• 주어+ought[ought not] to have+과거분사 ~	~했어야[하지 말았어야] 했는데
• I (really) regret (that) 주어+과거동사 ~	~한 것이 유감이다/후회한다
• I'm sorry that 주어+과거동사 ~	~한 것이 유감이다

핵심 Check

2. 다음 밑줄 친 말 대신 쓰기에 적절한 것은?

G: Aren't you cold?

B: Yes. <u>I should have worn a jacket.</u>

① Everything will be all right.　　② You ought to wear a jacket.

③ I must have worn a jacket.　　④ I am sorry that you wear a jacket.

⑤ I regret that I didn't wear a jacket.

 Real-Life Zone

G: Ben, you look full of energy today!

B: Do I? Maybe ❶that's because I finally got a good night's sleep last night.

G: Why? Don't you usually get enough sleep?

B: No, ❷I know it's really important to get a good night's sleep, but I always stay up late surfing the Internet or playing with my phone.

G: That sometimes happens to me too.

B: After I do that, I regret it the next morning and say, "I should have gone to bed earlier last night."

G: How was yesterday different?

B: Well, yesterday afternoon I climbed the mountain with my dad. I was really tired when I got home. I went to sleep right after I went to bed.

G: Outdoor activities are a great way ❸to help you get a good night's sleep.

G: 벤, 너 오늘 기운 차 보여!
B: 내가 그래? 그건 아마 내가 지난밤 마침내 잠을 잘 잤기 때문일 거야.
G: 왜? 평소에 충분한 잠을 자지 못하니?
B: 응. 잠을 잘 자는 것이 정말 중요하다는 것은 알지만 나는 언제나 인터넷 검색을 하거나 휴대폰을 가지고 놀면서 늦게까지 깨어 있어.
G: 그건 나에게도 가끔 일어나는 일이야.
B: 그러고 난 뒤에, 나는 다음 날 아침 후회하고 "지난밤에 더 일찍 잠들었어야 했는데."라고 말해.
G: 어제는 어떻게 달랐니?
B: 음, 어제 오후에 나는 아빠와 등산을 했어. 집에 왔을 때 나는 매우 피곤했어. 나는 침대에 가자마자 바로 잠들었어.
G: 야외 활동은 네가 잠을 잘 자도록 돕는 훌륭한 방법이구나.

❶ "that's because ~"는 "그것은 ~이기 때문이다"라는 뜻으로 이어지는 내용이 앞에 나온 것에 대한 이유가 된다.
❷ "I know" 뒤에는 명사절을 유도하는 접속사 that이 생략되어 있다.
❸ "to help"는 명사 way를 수식하는 형용사적 용법의 to부정사이다.

Check(√) True or False

(1) The boy didn't get a good night's sleep last night.　　　T ☐ F ☐

(2) Yesterday afternoon the boy climbed the mountain with his dad.　　　T ☐ F ☐

 Wrap Up 1

W: Oh, your blanket is wet from the rain! I should have checked the weather.

B: Did you wash it?

W: No. ❶I just put it out in the sun this morning.

B: Why didn't you wash it?

W: Hanging a blanket in the sun is ❷a nature-friendly way to keep the blanket clean.

B: Oh, I didn't know that. I'll remember that.

W: And it's also important to remember to do it regularly.

W: 오, 네 이불이 비에 젖었어! 내가 날씨를 확인했어야 했는데.
B: 그것을 빨았어요?
W: 아니. 오늘 아침에 그냥 햇볕에 널어놓았어.
B: 왜 빨지 않았어요?
W: 햇볕에 이불을 널어놓는 것은 이불을 깨끗하게 유지하는 친환경적인 방법이야.
B: 오, 저는 그것을 몰랐어요. 기억해 둘게요.
W: 그리고 정기적으로 그렇게 하는 것을 기억하는 것 또한 중요해.

❶ "put ~ out"은 "~을 밖에 내놓다"의 의미를 가진다.
❷ "a nature-friendly way to keep the blanket clean"에서 to keep은 way를 수식하는 형용사적 용법이다.

Check(√) True or False

(3) The woman regrets that she didn't wash the blanket.　　　T ☐ F ☐

(4) It is important to remember to wash a blanket regularly.　　　T ☐ F ☐

Listen & Speak 1 Listen

1. **G:** How can we stay healthy?
   B: Well, ❶it's important to eat a good breakfast.
2. **B:** What can we do to get good grades?
   G: It's important to review every day.
3. **G:** ❷I think it's important to write a journal after reading.
   B: I agree.
4. **B:** It's important to write down ❸what you spend your money on.
   G: I think so, too.

❶ "it's important to ～"에서 it은 가주어이고, to ～는 진주어이다.
❷ 강조하는 의미의 "It's important to ～"는 "I think it's important to ～"라고 할 수 있다.
❸ "what you spend ～"는 "무엇에 돈을 쓰는지"의 의미로 간접의문문이다.

Listen & Speak 1 A-1

B: What did you do on the weekend?
G: I played tennis. ❶I have decided to exercise on the weekend for my health.
B: Good for you. It's important to exercise regularly.
G: Right. ❷How about playing tennis with me?
B: Why not?

❶ 동사 decided의 목적어는 to부정사이다.
❷ "How about ～ing ?"는 "～하는 것이 어때?"의 의미로 상대에게 제안하는 표현이다.

Listen & Speak 1 A-2

M: John, you are late again.
B: I'm sorry. ❶I took the wrong bus.
M: ❷I think you need to leave home a little earlier.
B: I think so, too. Next time I won't be late.
M: It's important to arrive at school on time.

❶ take the wrong bus = 버스를 잘못 타다
❷ 동사 think의 목적어 역할을 하는 명사절에서 접속사 that이 생략되어 있다.

Listen & Speak 2 Listen

1. **G:** Your bag is too small.
   B: Yes. I should have brought a bigger one.

2. **G:** Aren't you cold?
   B: ❶Yes. I should have worn a jacket.
3. **B:** We ❷missed our flight.
   G: Oh, no. We should have come earlier.
4. **G:** Look at my face. I should have put on some sunscreen.
   B: Yes. You're right.

❶ "Aren't you ～?"에 해당하는 부정의 질문에 대한 대답은 대답이 긍정이면 Yes, 부정이면 No이다.
❷ miss flight = 항공편을 놓치다

Listen & Speak 2 A-1

B: Mina, ❶how was the movie?
G: I didn't enjoy it. It was boring.
B: What was bad about it?
G: I already knew the ending. I ❷shouldn't have read about it before seeing it.
B: Oh, I'm sorry you didn't like it.

❶ "how was the movie?"는 영화가 만족스러운지를 묻는 질문이다.
❷ "shouldn't have+과거분사"는 "～하지 말았어야 했는데"의 의미로 과거 사실에 대한 유감이나 후회를 나타낸다.

Listen & Speak 2 A-2

B: We still have 30 minutes ❶to go before we reach the top of the mountain. Let's sit down over there and have a snack.
G: Oh, I brought only water. I should have brought some snacks.
B: That's okay. I brought a lot. We can share.
G: I'll keep ❷it in mind to bring some snacks next time.

❶ "to go ～"는 minutes를 수식하는 형용사적 용법이다.
❷ it은 가목적어이고, to bring이 진목적어이다.

Wrap Up 2

G: Ryan, ❶are you okay? You look tired.
B: I couldn't sleep well last night.
G: Why is that? Did you have too much homework?
G: No. I ❷watched a movie on TV, and it didn't end until after 2:00.
G: Oh, you should have gone to bed earlier.

❶ "are you okay?"는 상대의 안부를 묻는 말이다.
❷ "watch a movie on TV"는 "TV로 영화를 보다"의 뜻이다.

● 다음 우리말과 일치하도록 빈칸에 알맞은 말을 쓰시오.

Listen & Speak 1 Listen

1. **G:** How _____ we _____ healthy?
   B: _____, it's _____ to eat a good _____.

2. **B:** _____ can we _____ to get good _____?
   G: It's _____ to review every day.

3. **G:** I _____ it's important to _____ a _____ after reading.
   B: I agree.

4. **B:** It's important to _____ _____ what you _____ your money _____.
   G: I _____ so, too.

해석

1. G: 우리는 어떻게 건강을 유지할 수 있을까?
   B: 음, 든든한 아침 식사를 하는 것이 중요해.
2. B: 좋은 점수를 받기 위해 우리는 무엇을 할 수 있을까?
   G: 매일 복습하는 것이 중요해.
3. G: 나는 독서 후에 일기를 쓰는 것이 중요하다고 생각해.
   B: 나도 동의해.
4. B: 네가 돈을 어디에 썼는지 적는 것은 중요해.
   G: 나도 그렇게 생각해.

Listen & Speak 1 A

1. **B:** _____ did you _____ on the _____?
   G: I _____ tennis. I have _____ to _____ on the weekend _____ my health.
   B: Good for _____. It's _____ to exercise _____.
   G: _____. How _____ playing tennis _____ me?
   B: Why not?

2. **M:** John, you are _____ again.
   B: I'm sorry. I _____ the wrong _____.
   M: I _____ you need to _____ home a little _____.
   B: I think so, _____. Next time I _____ be late.
   M: It's important to _____ at school _____ time.

1. B: 주말에 뭐 했니?
   G: 나는 테니스를 쳤어. 나는 건강을 위해 주말에 운동을 하기로 결정했어.
   B: 잘했어. 규칙적으로 운동하는 것은 중요해.
   G: 맞아. 나와 테니스 치는 것은 어때?
   B: 왜 안 되겠어?
2. M: 존, 또 지각이구나!
   B: 죄송해요. 버스를 잘못 탔어요.
   M: 나는 네가 집에서 좀 더 빨리 출발할 필요가 있다고 생각한단다.
   B: 저도 그렇게 생각해요. 다음번에는 늦지 않을 게요.
   M: 학교에 제시간에 오는 것은 중요하단다.

Listen & Speak 2

1. **G:** Your bag is _____ small.
   B: Yes. I _____ have _____ a bigger _____.

2. **G:** Aren't you _____?
   B: Yes. I should _____ worn a jacket.

3. **B:** We _____ our flight.
   G: Oh, no. We should _____ come _____.

4. **G:** _____ at my face. I _____ have _____ _____ some sunscreen.
   B: Yes. You're _____.

1. G: 네 가방은 정말 작아.
   B: 응. 난 더 큰 것을 가져왔어야 했어.
2. G: 춥지 않니?
   B: 응. 나는 재킷을 입었어야 했어.
3. B: 우리 비행기를 놓쳤어.
   G: 오, 안 돼. 우리는 더 빨리 왔어야 했어.
4. G: 내 얼굴 좀 봐. 나는 자외선 차단제를 발랐어야 했어.
   B: 그래. 네 말이 맞아.

Listen & Speak 2 A

1. **B:** Mina, _____ was the _____?

   G: I didn't _____ it. It _____ boring.

   B: _____ was bad _____ it?

   G: I already _____ the ending. I shouldn't _____ read about it _____ seeing it.

   B: Oh, I'm _____ you didn't _____ it.

2. **B:** We _____ have 30 _____ to go _____ we reach the _____ of the mountain. Let's sit _____ over there _____ have a _____.

   G: Oh, I _____ only water. I should have _____ some snacks.

   B: That's _____. I brought a lot. We can _____.

   G: I'll _____ it in _____ to bring _____ snacks next _____.

Real-Life Zone

G: Ben, you _____ full of _____ today!

B: Do I? Maybe that's _____ I finally _____ a good night's sleep _____ night.

G: Why? Don't you _____ get _____ sleep?

B: No, I _____ it's really _____ to get a good _____ sleep, but I _____ stay _____ late _____ the Internet or _____ with my _____.

G: That _____ happens to _____ too.

B: _____ I do that, I _____ it the next _____ and say, "I should _____ gone to bed _____ last night."

G: How was yesterday _____?

B: Well, yesterday afternoon I _____ the mountain with my _____. I was really _____ when I got _____. I went to _____ right _____ I went to bed.

G: _____ activities _____ a great _____ to help you _____ a good night's sleep.

Wrap Up 1

W: Oh, your _____ is _____ from the rain! I should have _____ the weather.

B: Did you _____ it?

W: No. I just _____ it out in the _____ this morning.

B: _____ didn't you _____ it?

W: Hanging a _____ in the sun is a nature-friendly _____ to _____ the blanket _____.

B: Oh, I didn't _____ that. I'll _____ that.

W: And it's also _____ to _____ to do it _____.

해석

1. **B:** 미나야, 영화 어땠니?

   G: 나는 그것을 즐기지 못했어. 지루했어.

   B: 무엇이 별로였니?

   G: 나는 이미 결말을 알고 있었어. 보기 전에 그것에 대해 읽지 말았어야 했는데.

   B: 오, 네가 좋아하지 않다니 유감이야.

2. **B:** 우리는 산 정상에 도착하기까지 아직 30분은 더 가야 해. 저기서 앉아서 간식 먹고 가자.

   G: 오, 난 물만 가져왔어. 간식을 가져왔어야 했는데.

   B: 괜찮아. 내가 많이 가져왔어. 우리는 같이 먹을 수 있어.

   G: 다음번에는 간식을 가져올 것을 명심할게.

G: 벤, 너 오늘 기운 차 보여!

B: 내가 그래? 그건 아마 내가 지난밤 마침내 잠을 잘 잤기 때문일 거야.

G: 왜? 평소에 충분한 잠을 자지 못하니?

B: 응, 잠을 잘 자는 것이 정말 중요하다는 것은 알지만 나는 언제나 인터넷 검색을 하거나 휴대폰을 가지고 놀면서 늦게까지 깨어 있어.

G: 그건 나에게도 가끔 일어나는 일이야.

B: 그러고 난 뒤에, 나는 다음 날 아침 후회하고 "지난밤에 더 일찍 잠들었어야 했는데."라고 말해.

G: 어제는 어떻게 달랐니?

B: 음, 어제 오후에 나는 아빠와 등산을 했어. 집에 왔을 때 나는 매우 피곤했어. 나는 침대에 가자마자 바로 잠들었어.

G: 야외 활동은 네가 잠을 잘 자도록 돕는 훌륭한 방법이구나.

W: 오, 네 이불이 비에 젖었어! 내가 날씨를 확인했어야 했는데.

B: 그것을 빨았어요?

W: 아니. 오늘 아침에 그냥 햇볕에 널어놓았어.

B: 왜 빨지 않았어요?

W: 햇볕에 이불을 널어놓는 것은 이불을 깨끗하게 유지하는 친환경적인 방법이야.

B: 오, 저는 그것을 몰랐어요. 기억해 둘게요.

W: 그리고 정기적으로 그렇게 하는 것을 기억하는 것 또한 중요해.

[01~02] 다음 대화의 빈칸에 들어갈 말로 알맞은 것은?

01

> B: What did you do on the weekend?
> G: I played tennis. I have decided to exercise on the weekend for my health.
> B: Good for you. It's important to exercise regularly.
> G: Right. _____ playing tennis with me?
> B: Why not?

① How about   ② Will you avoid   ③ Do you like
④ Are you   ⑤ Why do you enjoy

02

> M: John, you are late again.
> B: I'm sorry. _____
> M: I think you need to leave home a little earlier.
> B: I think so, too. Next time I won't be late.
> M: It's important to arrive at school on time.

① I won't leave home early.
② Will you say that again?
③ I'm sure you will be all right.
④ I can drive a car myself.
⑤ I took the wrong bus.

03 다음 대화에 이어지기에 적절하게 배열된 순서를 고르시오.

> B: Mina, how was the movie?
> G: I didn't enjoy it. It was boring.
>
> (A) I already knew the ending. I shouldn't have read about it before seeing it.
> (B) Oh, I'm sorry you didn't like it.
> (C) What was bad about it?

① (A) – (C) – (B)   ② (B) – (A) – (C)   ③ (B) – (C) – (A)
④ (C) – (A) – (B)   ⑤ (C) – (B) – (A)

Conversation 시험대비 실력평가

01 다음 빈칸에 적절한 말은?

> B: It's important to write down what you spend your money on.
> G: _____, too.

① You heard it
② I don't know
③ I think so
④ We will do it
⑤ They are ready

[02~03] 다음 대화를 읽고 물음에 답하시오.

> B: What did you do on the weekend?
> G: I played tennis. I have decided to _____(A)_____ for my health.
> B: Good for you. It's important to exercise regularly.
> G: Right. How about playing tennis with me?
> B: Why not?

02 빈칸 (A)에 들어가기에 적절한 것은?

① be ready for my finals
② invite you to my house
③ watch a tennis match
④ exercise on the weekend
⑤ write down how much I spend

03 위 대화를 읽고 알 수 없는 것은?

① The boy asked the girl what she did on the weekend.
② The girl played tennis on the weekday.
③ The girl decided to play tennis for the health.
④ The boy thinks it's important to exercise regularly.
⑤ The boy will play tennis with the girl.

[04~06] 다음 대화를 읽고 물음에 답하시오.

> G: Ben, you look full of energy today!
> B: Do I? Maybe that's because I finally got a good night's sleep last night.
> G: Why? Don't you usually get enough sleep?
> B: No, I know it's really important to get a good night's sleep, but I always _____ late surfing the Internet or playing with my phone. (A)
> G: That sometimes happens to me too.
> B: After I do that, I regret it the next morning and say, "I should have gone to bed earlier last night." (B)
> G: How was yesterday different? (C)
> B: Well, yesterday afternoon I climbed the mountain with my dad. (D) I went to sleep right after I went to bed.
> G: Outdoor activities are a great way to help you get a good night's sleep. (E)

04 위 대화의 빈칸에 들어가기에 가장 적절한 것은?

① make bed
② wake up
③ stay up
④ call you
⑤ work out

05 (A)~(E) 중에서 다음 주어진 문장이 들어가기에 적절한 곳은?

> I was really tired when I got home.

① (A)　② (B)　③ (C)　④ (D)　⑤ (E)

06 위 대화의 내용과 일치하지 <u>않는</u> 것은?

① Ben feels very good today.

② Ben slept well last night.

③ Ben will surf the Internet late at night.

④ Yesterday Ben climbed the mountain with his father.

⑤ Ben slept early last night.

[07~09] 다음 대화를 읽고 물음에 답하시오.

> B: ⓐMina, how was the movie?
>
> G: _____(A)_____ ⓑIt was boring.
>
> B: ⓒWhat was bad about it?
>
> G: I already knew the ending. ⓓI should have read about it before seeing it.
>
> B: ⓔOh, I'm sorry you didn't like it.

07 다음 중 빈칸 (A)에 들어가기에 적절한 것은?

① I didn't enjoy it.

② Do you like it?

③ How was the ending?

④ The story was very good.

⑤ Did you like it?

08 ⓐ~ⓔ 중에서 대화의 내용상 <u>어색한</u> 것은?

① ⓐ   ② ⓑ   ③ ⓒ   ④ ⓓ   ⑤ ⓔ

09 Which one CANNOT be answered from the dialogue above?

① What are they talking about right now?

② How did the girl think about the movie?

③ Did the girl know the ending of the movie?

④ Did the girl read about the movie?

⑤ Why didn't the boy like the movie?

[10~12] 다음 대화를 읽고 물음에 답하시오.

> B: We still have 30 minutes to go before we reach the top of the mountain. Let's sit down over there and have a snack.
>
> G: Oh, I brought only water. (A)I should bring some snacks.
>
> B: That's okay. I brought a lot. We can ___(B)___.
>
> G: I'll ___(C)___ it in mind to bring some snacks next time.

10 위 대화의 밑줄 친 (A)를 흐름상 알맞은 문장으로 고치시오.

➡ _____

11 위 대화의 빈칸 (B), (C)에 들어가기에 적절한 것은?

	(B)		(C)
①	share	–	keep
②	take	–	make
③	keep	–	get
④	share	–	have
⑤	help	–	keep

12 위 대화의 내용과 일치하지 <u>않는</u> 것은?

① They are going up the mountain.

② They are going to take some rest.

③ They don't have enough snacks.

④ The girl didn't bring any snacks.

⑤ The girl says she will bring some snacks next time.

Conversation 서술형 시험대비 Step6

01 다음 우리말을 영어로 쓰시오.

> G: Aren't you cold?
> B: Yes. 나는 재킷을 입었어야 했어.

➡ _____

02 다음 대화의 순서를 올바르게 배열하시오.

> G: Ryan, are you okay? You look tired.
> B: I couldn't sleep well last night.
> (A) Oh, you should have gone to bed earlier.
> (B) Why is that? Did you have too much homework?
> (C) No. I watched a movie on TV, and it didn't end until after 2:00.

➡ _____

[03~05] 다음 대화를 읽고 물음에 답하시오.

> B: What did you do on the weekend?
> G: I played tennis. I have decided to __(A)__ on the weekend for my health.
> B: Good for you. (B)규칙적으로 운동하는 것은 중요해.
> G: Right. How about (C)(play) tennis with me?
> B: Why not?

03 주어진 영영풀이를 참고하여 빈칸 (A)에 철자 e로 시작하는 단어를 쓰시오.

> to do physical activities in order to make yourself stronger and healthier

➡ _____

04 (B)에 주어진 우리말에 해당하는 영어 문장을 쓰시오.

➡ _____

05 (C)에 주어진 단어의 올바른 형태를 쓰시오.

➡ _____

[06~08] 다음 대화를 읽고 물음에 답하시오.

> B: Mina, how was the movie?
> G: I didn't enjoy it. It was boring.
> B: What was good about it?
> G: I already knew the ending. (A)(read, it, I shouldn't, before, have, seeing, about, it.)
> B: Oh, ____(B)____ you didn't like it.

06 위 대화에서 (A)의 괄호 안에 주어진 단어를 적절하게 배열하시오.

➡ _____

07 내용상 빈칸 (B)에 들어가기에 적절한 표현을 쓰시오. (2 words)

➡ _____

08 위 대화에서 흐름상 어색한 한 단어를 찾아 쓰고 적절한 단어로 바꾸시오.

➡ _____ ➡ _____

Grammar

1 the 비교급, the 비교급

> • **The more** sun you get, **the more** "happy hormone" the brain produces.
> 여러분이 햇빛을 많이 쬐면 쬘수록 뇌는 행복 호르몬을 더 만들어 냅니다.
>
> • **The stronger** will you have, **the more** you will learn.
> 의지가 더 강하면 강할수록 더 많이 배울 것이다.

■ the 비교급+주어+동사 ~, the 비교급+주어+동사 …
  • 의미: ~하면 할수록 더 …하다
  • 형태: 'the 비교급+주어+동사 ~, the 비교급+주어+동사 …'

■ 'the 비교급+주어+동사 ~, the 비교급+주어+동사 …' 구문은 정도가 점점 더해지거나 덜해지는 것을 표현할 때 사용한다.
  • **The more, the better.** 많으면 많을수록 더 좋다.

■ 최상급이 아닌 비교급임에도 the를 쓰는 것에 주의해야 하며, be동사나 반복되는 어구는 종종 생략된다. 이 구문에 쓰이는 'the'는 정관사가 아니라 부사이다.
  • **The harder** you work, **the more** you get. 더 열심히 일할수록 더 많이 얻는다.
  • **The less** my hope, **the hotter** my love. 내 희망이 적을수록 내 사랑은 더 뜨겁다.

■ 'the 비교급+주어+동사 ~, the 비교급+주어+동사 …' 구문은 'As+주어+동사+비교급 ~, 주어+동사+비교급 …'으로 바꿔 쓸 수 있다.
  • **The higher** we go up, **the colder** the air becomes.
  = **As** we go up **higher**, the air becomes **colder**. 높이 올라가면 올라갈수록 공기가 더욱 더 차가워진다.

cf. '비교급 and 비교급'은 '점점 더 …하다'의 뜻이다
  • It is getting **colder and colder**. 날씨가 점점 더 추워지고 있다.

핵심 Check

1. 다음 괄호 안에서 알맞은 말을 고르시오.

(1) The (long / longer) the soup cooks, the thicker it gets.

(2) The more I want to get something done, the (less / least) I call it work.

❷ It is[was] ... that 강조 구문

- **It** is calcium **that** builds strong bones and teeth. 튼튼한 뼈와 치아를 만드는 것은 칼슘입니다.
- **It** was his family **that** Sam wanted to meet before he died.
  샘이 죽기 전에 만나보고 싶은 것은 바로 그의 가족이었다.

■ 'It + is/was + 강조어(구) + that ...'의 형태로 특정 부분을 강조하여 나타낼 때 사용한다. 강조하고자 하는 부분을 'It is/was'와 'that' 사이에 쓰고, 나머지 부분을 that 뒤에 써서 주어, 목적어인 명사, 부사(구/절) 등을 강조한다. 'be'동사는 문장의 시제에 맞춰 'is'나 'was'를 사용한다.

- His laughter broke the silence in the room.
  - → **It was** his laughter **that** broke the silence in the room. (주어 강조)
  - → **It was** the silence **that** his laughter broke in the room. (목적어인 명사 강조)
  - → **It was** in the room **that** his laughter broke the silence. (부사구 강조)

■ 'It is[was] ~ that ...' 강조 구문에서 강조하는 대상이 명사일 경우, that 대신에 관계대명사 who[whom](사람일 경우) 또는 which(사물이나 동물일 경우)로 바꿔 쓸 수 있으며, 시간 또는 장소의 부사(구/절)일 경우, when(시간) 또는 where(장소)로 바꿔 쓸 수 있다.

- I bought the brush at the shop yesterday. 나는 어제 그 가게에서 빗을 샀다.
  - → **It was** I **that**[**who**] bought the brush at the shop yesterday.
  - → **It was** the brush **that**[**which**] I bought at the shop yesterday.
  - → **It was** yesterday **that**[**when**] I bought the brush at the shop.
  - → **It was** at the shop **that**[**where**] I bought the brush yesterday.

■ 'It is[was] ~ that ...' 강조 구문에서 강조하는 대상이 부사(구/절)일 경우 that 다음에 완전한 절이 나오지만 그 외의 경우에는 불완전한 절이 나오는 것에 유의한다. 또한 강조되는 부분에 형용사나 동사는 올 수 없다.

- **It was** a new smartphone **that**[**which**] I wanted to buy. 내가 사고 싶었던 것은 바로 새 스마트폰이었다. (that 다음에 buy의 목적어가 없는 불완전한 절)
- **It was** at the library **that**[**where**] I studied math. 내가 수학을 공부한 곳은 바로 그 도서실에서였다. (that 다음에 완전한 절)
- It is beautiful that she is. (형용사 강조 ×)
- It was bought that I the books yesterday. (동사 강조 ×)

핵심 Check

2. 다음 괄호 안에서 알맞은 말을 고르시오.

(1) It is Minjun (that / what) is playing basketball.

(2) (It / That) was in the morning that I got a call from Samuel.

(3) It was he (whom / which) they wanted for a king.

01 다음 각 문장의 빈칸에 공통으로 들어갈 말로 알맞은 것은?

> • It is California _____ Layla comes from.
> • It was her wallet _____ Linda lost in the subway yesterday.

① where   ② when   ③ who
④ that   ⑤ what

02 다음 빈칸에 들어갈 말로 알맞은 것은?

> • The _____ you laugh, the happier you become!

① much   ② many   ③ more
④ few   ⑤ fewer

03 다음 중 어법상 바르지 <u>않은</u> 것은?

① It was Mike that stole the wallet.
② It was John which loved her.
③ It was Clair whom he met again.
④ It was in the library that we studied together.
⑤ It was on Friday when we had dinner together.

04 다음 우리말에 맞게 주어진 어휘를 바르게 배열하시오.

(1) 내가 사랑하는 건 바로 너야.
    (that, I, it, you, is, love)
    ➡ _____

(2) 튼튼한 뼈와 치아를 만드는 것은 칼슘입니다.
    (calcium, bones, teeth, that, it, builds, strong, is, and)
    ➡ _____

(3) 운동을 하면 할수록 나는 더 강해진다.
    (I, I, get, exercise, the, the, more, stronger)
    ➡ _____

(4) 많으면 많을수록 더 좋다.
    (the, the, better, more)
    ➡ _____

01 다음 중 어법상 어색한 것은?

① The more I read, the more I learn.
② The hot it gets, the hard it is to work.
③ The colder it gets, the more clothes you need.
④ It is the baby that she should take care of.
⑤ It was some flowers which he bought for her.

02 다음 중 어법상 옳은 것은?

① It was the shoes which Ted bought last Sunday.
② It was James which went to the shop to buy some bread.
③ It is on Sundays where Daniel and I meet.
④ The much I play, the much I want to play.
⑤ The older he gets, the wise he becomes.

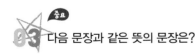
03 다음 문장과 같은 뜻의 문장은?

As I study harder, I learn more.

① Because I studied harder, I learned the more.
② I have studied the harder, so I have learned the more.
③ The hard I study, the much I learn.
④ The harder I study, the more I learn.
⑤ The hardest I study, the most I learn.

04 다음 밑줄 친 부분과 바꿔 쓸 수 있는 것은?

It was James <u>that</u> went to Amy's birthday party last Friday.

① whether   ② what
③ it   ④ which
⑤ who

[05~06] 다음 우리말을 알맞게 영작한 것을 모두 고르시오.

05
여러분이 햇볕을 쬘수록 뇌는 행복 호르몬을 더 만들어 냅니다.

① More sun you get, more "happy hormone" the brain produces.
② The most sun you get, the most "happy hormone" the brain produces.
③ The more sun you get, the more "happy hormone" the brain produces.
④ Because you get more sun, the brain produces the more "happy hormone".
⑤ As you get more sun, the brain produces more "happy hormone".

06
Tom이 매일 먹는 것은 바로 사과이다.

① It is an apple what Tom eats every day.
② It is an apple who Tom eats every day.
③ It is an apple which Tom eats every day.
④ It is an apple when Tom eats every day.
⑤ It is an apple where Tom eats every day.

07 다음 우리말과 일치하는 문장을 쓸 때, 빈칸에 알맞은 말은?

> 어두워질수록 우리의 두려움은 더 커졌다.
> = _____ it grew, the bigger our fear became.

① Dark
② Darker
③ Darkest
④ The darker
⑤ The darkest

08 다음 〈보기〉의 밑줄 친 that과 쓰임이 같은 것은?

> ┤ 보기 ├
> It was in the library that Ryan met Suho yesterday.

① He isn't that rich.
② It was the cookies that Amy made for me yesterday.
③ That's a nice tie you are wearing.
④ That the earth is round is common knowledge today.
⑤ That fifty dollars helped me greatly.

09 다음 문장의 빈칸 (A), (B)에 들어갈 말로 가장 적절한 것은?

> ____(A)____ she grows, ____(B)____ she becomes.

	(A)	(B)
①	The older	the prettier
②	The older	prettier
③	The old	the pretty
④	Older	the prettier
⑤	Older	prettier

10 다음 문장의 빈칸에 알맞은 말을 모두 고르시오.

> It was a book _____ Eric lent me in the library yesterday.

① that
② what
③ when
④ which
⑤ where

11 다음 문장과 비슷한 뜻이 되도록 비교급을 사용하여 바꿔 쓰시오.

(1) As I went up higher, the air was fresher.

➡ _____

(2) If you walk much, you will get tired.

➡ _____

12 다음 중 It ~ that 쓰임이 나머지와 <u>다른</u> 하나는?

① It was in the park that I played soccer with my friends.
② It is essential that you have some experience.
③ It was yesterday that I met him in the park.
④ It was math that I studied at the library.
⑤ It was when Kate came into the room that the phone rang.

13 다음 문장을 어법에 맞게 고쳐 쓰시오.

(1) This red dress looks prettier of the two.

➡ _____
_____

(2) More water we use, drier our well will become.

➡ _____
_____

(3) Much stress I get, much emotional I become.

➡ _____
_____

[14~15] 다음 중 어법상 올바른 문장을 고르시오.

14 ① That was a new smartphone which I wanted to buy.
② It is meet that Daniel and I on Sundays.
③ It was comfortable that you felt.
④ It is he who make decisions on the matter.
⑤ It is the blue shirt that Jay wants to buy.

15 ① The older the queen got, the ugly she got.
② The more slowly you drive, the more safe you are.
③ I believe the more often we laugh, the happier we will be.
④ My English is getting good and good.
⑤ My new computer was nicer of the two.

16 다음 문장에서 어법상 <u>어색한</u> 부분을 바르게 고치시오.

(1) It was because he was sick why we decided to return.

_____ ➡ _____

(2) It is a good breakfast who helps the brain work properly.

_____ ➡ _____

(3) It was July 26 when Gustav Jung was born.

_____ ➡ _____

17 괄호 안에서 알맞은 것을 고르시오.

(1) (The spicier / The spicy) the food is, (the more / the much) Kevin likes it.
(2) (The more / Much) Andy worked, (the more / much) money he earned.
(3) It was last Friday (which / when) James went to Amy's birthday party.
(4) It was under the bed (which / where) Tina found the wallet yesterday.
(5) It was William (whom / which) she wanted to see.

18 주어진 문장을 'the movie'를 강조하는 문장으로 바르게 고친 것은?

James watched the movie with his girl friend last night.

① It is the movie what James watched with his girl friend last night.
② It was the movie which James watched with his girl friend last night.
③ It is the movie whom James watched with his girl friend last night.
④ It is the movie when James watched with his girl friend last night.
⑤ It was the movie who James watched with his girl friend last night.

19 다음 빈칸에 들어갈 수 <u>없는</u> 것은?

The finer the weather is, _____ I become.

① the more gloomy   ② the happier
③ the brighter   ④ the merrier
⑤ the more excited

01 다음 두 문장을 〈보기〉와 같이 한 문장으로 완성하시오.

보기

- You get much sunlight.
- You feel happy and strong.
→ The more sunlight you get, the happier and stronger you feel.

(1) • A bird flies high.
   • It can see far.
   ➡ _____

(2) • They have much.
   • They want much.
   ➡ _____

02 다음 문장에서 어법상 어색한 것을 바르게 고쳐 다시 쓰시오.

(1) More stress I get, more emotional I become.
   ➡ _____

(2) Ryan thinks the much slowly he eats, the full he gets.
   ➡ _____

(3) Youngest you are, easiest it is to learn.
   ➡ _____

(4) This country is better of the two.
   ➡ _____

(5) It was Hamin which played basketball with Eric last Saturday.
   ➡ _____

(6) It is on Saturdays which there are lots of weddings.
   ➡ _____

(7) It was Hangang Park which Ms. Jones was at 2 p.m. last Saturday.
   ➡ _____

(8) It was Amy's house where James visited last Friday.
   ➡ _____

03 다음 그림을 보고 각 질문에 'It ~ that' 강조 구문을 사용하여 답하시오.

Jenny's family

(1) Who went to the beach last summer?
   ➡ _____

(2) Where did Jenny's family go last summer?
   ➡ _____

(3) When did Jenny's family go to the beach?
   ➡ _____

04 다음 문장과 비슷한 뜻이 되도록 비교급을 사용하여 바꿔 쓰시오.

(1) If I like her much, I will miss her much.

➡ _____

_____

(2) If you leave early, you will arrive there early.

➡ _____

_____

(3) As you study harder for the exam, you will do better.

➡ _____

_____

(4) As you are more careful, you will make fewer mistakes.

➡ _____

_____

05 다음 문장을 주어진 단어를 강조하는 문장으로 고쳐 쓰시오. that은 사용하지 말 것.

> Anna bought the dress on the Internet last Sunday.

(1) Anna

➡ _____

_____

(2) bought

➡ _____

_____

(3) the dress

➡ _____

_____

(4) on the Internet

➡ _____

_____

(5) last Sunday

➡ _____

_____

06 괄호 안에 주어진 어휘를 이용하여 빈칸에 알맞은 말을 쓰시오.

(1) The more you walk, _____

_____. (healthy, will, feel)

(2) The hotter the weather is, _____

_____. (hard, doing outdoor activities)

(3) The faster you drive, _____

_____. (dangerous, will, be)

07 다음 우리말과 일치하도록 괄호 안에 주어진 어휘를 이용하여 영작하시오.

(1) 공부를 많이 할수록, 너는 더 똑똑해질 것이다. (much, smart, become)

➡ _____

_____

(2) 당신이 돈을 덜 쓸수록, 당신은 당신의 계좌에 더 많은 돈을 갖게 될 것이다. (little, spend, have in your account)

➡ _____

_____

(3) Mr. Smith가 우리 아파트로 이사 온 것은 바로 5년 전이었다. (move to, apartment)

➡ _____

_____

(4) 내가 이 조리법을 배운 곳은 바로 그 이탈리아 식당이었다. (learned, this recipe)

➡ _____

_____

(5) Jack이 시장에서 잃어버린 것은 바로 그의 책 이었다. (lost, at the market)

➡ _____

_____

Reading

교과서

Enjoy the Sunshine

How much time do you spend every day out in the sun? Not much, right? Most people are too busy at school or at work to spend much time outdoors.
= Most people are so busy at school or at work that they cannot spend much time outdoors.
too ~ to부정사 = so ~ that 주어 cannot

However, the sun plays an important role in your health. It
play an important role in: ~에서 중요한 역할을 하다   = the sun

helps you stay healthy.
help+목적어+목적격보어(to부정사 또는 동사원형)

Everyone feels happier when the sun shines. This is because of
Everyone: 단수 취급, 단수 동사

serotonin, the body's happy hormone. The more sun you get, the more
동격의 콤마. the body's happy hormone = serotonin   the 비교급 ~, the 비교급 …: ~할수록 …하다

"happy hormone" the brain produces. When your serotonin level goes

up, you feel happier and stronger. This helps you fight everyday stress.
비교급 and 비교급   = to fight

Serotonin also has a calming effect, helping you focus better on what
분사구문. and it helps you   = the thing(s) which[that]

you are doing. Moreover, serotonin helps you get a good night's sleep
= to get

because it helps the brain produce a sleep hormone.
= serotonin   = to produce

sunshine 햇빛
outdoors 야외에서
role 역할
hormone 호르몬
brain 뇌
produce 만들어 내다. 생산하다
effect 효과
moreover 게다가
go up 올라가다

확인문제

● 다음 문장이 본문의 내용과 일치하면 T, 일치하지 않으면 F를 쓰시오.

1 Most people are so busy at school or at work that they cannot spend much time outdoors. ☐

2 The sun plays an insignificant role in your health. ☐

3 Everyone feels happier when the sun shines. ☐

4 As you get more sun, the brain produces less "happy hormone". ☐

5 Serotonin has a calming effect. ☐

6 Serotonin helps you get a good night's sleep because it helps the brain produce a calming hormone. ☐

Sunshine does not just make you feel and sleep better. It also
make(사역동사)+목적어+목적격보어(동사원형): ~에게 ...하게 하다

helps build strong bones. As you all know, it is calcium that builds
help가 준사역동사로 사용된   as: ~한 것처럼, ~하다시피(접속사)   'it ... that' 강조 구문: 강조하고자 하는 부분을 it과 that 사이에 쓰고,
문장으로, 목적어가 생략됨.   it 뒤에 오는 be동사는 문장의 시제에 맞춰 is나 was를 사용한다.

strong bones and teeth. However, for the body to use calcium properly,
for+목적격: to부정사의 의미상의 주어

it needs vitamin D. Interestingly, the skin creates vitamin D when

sunlight shines on it. The easiest way to make strong bones is to go
to부정사의 형용사적 용법   to부정사의 명사적 용법(보어)

outside and enjoy the sun.
enjoy 앞에 to가 생략된 것임.

As you can see, sunshine has many benefits, but how can you enjoy

its benefits safely? Fortunately, getting direct sunlight on your skin for
동명사 주어

10 to 20 minutes a day is enough to benefit from it. Try to go out into
하루에   enough+to부정사: ~하기에 충분한

the sun between classes or during lunch breaks and get sunshine on

your arms and hands. A walk in the sun, for just a few minutes every
= only

day, is good for both your mind and your body. However, avoid the
both A and B: 'A와 B 둘 다'. A와 B는 문법적으로 성격과 형식이 같은 요소가 와야 한다.

sun during peak summer hours, between 11 and 3, and use sunscreen

to protect your face and neck. Enjoy the sun safely and see how a little
to부정사의 부사적 용법(목적: ~하기 위해)

sunshine can make a world of difference in your health and your mood.
간접의문문(의문사+주어+동사). see의 목적어   a[the] world of: 산더미 같은, 막대한

bone 뼈

properly 제대로, 적절하게

vitamin 비타민

skin 피부

sunlight 햇빛, 햇살

benefit 이득; 이득을 보다

fortunately 다행스럽게도

direct (열기나 빛이) 직접 닿는

peak 절정의, 최고조의

sunscreen 자외선 차단제

mood 기분, 감정

확인문제

● 다음 문장이 본문의 내용과 일치하면 T, 일치하지 않으면 F를 쓰시오.

1 Sunshine helps build strong bones as well as makes you feel and sleep better. ☐

2 For the body to use vitamin D properly, it needs calcium. ☐

3 The easiest way to make strong bones is to go outside and enjoy the sun. ☐

4 Getting direct sunlight on your skin for 10 to 20 minutes a day isn't enough to benefit from it. ☐

5 A walk in the sun, for just a few minutes every day, is good for both your mind and your body. ☐

6 A little sunshine can make a little difference in your health and your mood. ☐

● 우리말을 참고하여 빈칸에 알맞은 말을 쓰시오.

1 Enjoy the _____

2 How much time do you spend every day _____ _____ _____ _____?

3 _____ _____, right?

4 Most people are _____ _____ at school or at work _____ _____ much time _____.

5 However, the sun _____ _____ _____ _____ in your health.

6 It helps you _____ _____.

7 Everyone _____ _____ when the sun shines.

8 This is because of serotonin, _____ _____ _____ _____.

9 _____ _____ _____ you get, _____ _____ "_____ _____" the brain produces.

10 When your serotonin level _____ _____, you feel happier and stronger.

11 This helps you _____ _____ _____.

12 Serotonin also has a _____ _____, helping you focus better on _____ _____ _____ _____.

13 _____, serotonin helps you get _____ _____ _____ _____ because it helps the brain produce a sleep hormone.

14 Sunshine does _____ _____ make you feel and sleep better.

---

1 햇빛을 즐기세요

2 여러분은 매일 햇빛 속에서 얼마나 많은 시간을 보내나요?

3 많지 않죠, 그렇죠?

4 대부분의 사람들은 학교와 직장에서 너무 바빠서 많은 시간을 야외에서 보내지 못합니다.

5 그러나 햇빛은 여러분의 건강에 중요한 역할을 합니다.

6 그것은 여러분이 건강을 유지하는 데 도움을 줍니다.

7 모든 사람들은 해가 비칠 때 더 행복하게 느낍니다.

8 이것은 몸의 행복 호르몬인 세로토닌 때문입니다.

9 여러분이 햇빛을 쬘수록 뇌는 행복 호르몬을 더 만들어 냅니다.

10 여러분의 세로토닌 수치가 높아지면, 여러분은 더 행복하고 더 건강하게 느낍니다.

11 이것은 여러분이 매일의 스트레스를 이겨 내는 데 도움을 줍니다.

12 세로토닌은 또한 진정 효과가 있고, 여러분이 하는 일에 더 잘 집중할 수 있도록 도와줍니다.

13 게다가, 세로토닌은 뇌가 수면 호르몬을 생성하도록 도와주기 때문에 여러분이 숙면을 취하도록 해 줍니다.

14 햇빛은 단지 여러분이 더 기분 좋게 느끼고 잠을 더 잘 자게 하는 것만은 아닙니다.

15 It _____ helps _____ _____ _____ .

16 _____ _____ _____ _____ , it is calcium that builds strong bones and teeth.

17 H o w e v e r , _____ _____ _____ _____ _____ calcium properly, it needs vitamin D.

18 Interestingly, the skin creates vitamin D _____ _____ _____ on it.

19 The easiest way to make strong bones is _____ _____ _____ and enjoy the sun.

20 _____ _____ _____ _____ , sunshine has many benefits, but how can you _____ _____ _____ _____ ?

21 Fortunately, _____ _____ _____ on your skin for 10 to 20 minutes a day is enough _____ _____ _____ _____ .

22 _____ _____ _____ _____ _____ the sun between classes or during lunch breaks and _____ _____ _____ your arms and hands.

23 A walk in the sun, _____ _____ _____ _____ _____ _____ , is good for both your mind and your body.

24 However, avoid the sun during peak summer hours, between 11 and 3, and use sunscreen _____ _____ _____ _____ _____ _____ .

25 Enjoy the sun safely and see how _____ _____ _____ can _____ _____ _____ _____ _____ in your health and your mood.

15 그것은 또한 튼튼한 뼈를 만드는 것을 돕습니다.

16 여러분 모두가 알다시피, 튼튼한 뼈와 치아를 만드는 것은 칼슘입니다.

17 그러나 몸이 칼슘을 적절하게 사용하기 위해서는 비타민 D가 필요합니다.

18 흥미롭게도, 피부는 햇빛이 피부에 비칠 때 비타민 D를 만들어 냅니다.

19 튼튼한 뼈를 만드는 가장 쉬운 방법은 밖으로 나가서 햇빛을 즐기는 겁니다.

20 보시다시피, 햇빛은 많은 이점이 있지만, 어떻게 그것의 이점을 안전하게 즐길 수 있을까요?

21 다행히도, 하루에 10분에서 20분 동안 피부에 직사광선을 쪼이는 것은 햇빛으로부터 이점을 얻는 데 충분합니다.

22 수업 시간 사이나 점심시간에 햇빛을 쬐러 밖으로 나가서 팔과 손에 햇빛을 쬐어 보세요.

23 매일 단 몇 분 동안 햇살을 쬐며 걷는 것은 여러분의 마음과 몸 모두에 좋습니다.

24 그러나 여름 절정 시간인 11시에서 3시 사이에는 햇빛을 피하고, 얼굴과 목을 보호하기 위해 자외선 차단제를 사용하세요.

25 태양을 안전하게 즐기고 적은 양의 햇빛이 여러분의 건강과 기분에 얼마나 큰 차이를 만들어 내는지 보세요.

● 우리말을 참고하여 본문을 영작하시오.

1 햇빛을 즐기세요

➡ _____

2 여러분은 매일 햇빛 속에서 얼마나 많은 시간을 보내나요?

➡ _____

3 많지 않죠, 그렇죠?

➡ _____

4 대부분의 사람들은 학교와 직장에서 너무 바빠서 많은 시간을 야외에서 보내지 못합니다.

➡ _____

5 그러나 햇빛은 여러분의 건강에 중요한 역할을 합니다.

➡ _____

6 그것은 여러분이 건강을 유지하는 데 도움을 줍니다.

➡ _____

7 모든 사람들은 해가 비칠 때 더 행복하게 느낍니다.

➡ _____

8 이것은 몸의 행복 호르몬인 세로토닌 때문입니다.

➡ _____

9 여러분이 햇빛을 쬘수록 뇌는 행복 호르몬을 더 만들어 냅니다.

➡ _____

10 여러분의 세로토닌 수치가 높아지면, 여러분은 더 행복하고 더 건강하게 느낍니다.

➡ _____

11 이것은 여러분이 매일의 스트레스를 이겨 내는 데 도움을 줍니다.

➡ _____

12 세로토닌은 또한 진정 효과가 있고, 여러분이 하는 일에 더 잘 집중할 수 있도록 도와줍니다.

➡ _____

13 게다가, 세로토닌은 뇌가 수면 호르몬을 생성하도록 도와주기 때문에 여러분이 숙면을 취하도록 해 줍니다.

➡ _____

14 햇빛은 단지 여러분이 더 기분 좋게 느끼고 잠을 더 잘 자게 하는 것만은 아닙니다.

➡ _____

15 그것은 또한 튼튼한 뼈를 만드는 것을 돕습니다.

➡ _____

16 여러분 모두가 알다시피, 튼튼한 뼈와 치아를 만드는 것은 칼슘입니다.

➡ _____

17 그러나 몸이 칼슘을 적절하게 사용하기 위해서는 비타민 D가 필요합니다.

➡ _____

18 흥미롭게도, 피부는 햇빛이 피부에 비칠 때 비타민 D를 만들어 냅니다.

➡ _____

19 튼튼한 뼈를 만드는 가장 쉬운 방법은 밖으로 나가서 햇빛을 즐기는 겁니다.

➡ _____

20 보시다시피, 햇빛은 많은 이점이 있지만, 어떻게 그것의 이점을 안전하게 즐길 수 있을까요?

➡ _____

21 다행히도, 하루에 10분에서 20분 동안 피부에 직사광선을 쪼이는 것은 햇빛으로부터 이점을 얻는 데 충분합니다.

➡ _____

_____

22 수업 시간 사이나 점심시간에 햇빛을 쪼러 밖으로 나가서 팔과 손에 햇빛을 쪼여 보세요.

➡ _____

_____

23 매일 단 몇 분 동안 햇살을 쪼이며 걷는 것은 여러분의 마음과 몸 모두에 좋습니다.

➡ _____

24 그러나 여름 절정 시간인 11시에서 3시 사이에는 햇빛을 피하고, 얼굴과 목을 보호하기 위해 자외선 차단제를 사용하세요.

➡ _____

_____

25 태양을 안전하게 즐기고 적은 양의 햇빛이 여러분의 건강과 기분에 얼마나 큰 차이를 만들어 내는지 보세요.

➡ _____

_____

[01~04] 다음 글을 읽고 물음에 답하시오.

How much time do you spend every day out in the sun? Not much, right? (A)[Almost / Most] people are too busy at school or at work to spend much time (B)[outdoor / outdoors]. ___ⓐ___, the sun plays an important ⓑrole in your health. It helps you stay (C)[healthy / healthily].

01 위 글의 빈칸 ⓐ에 들어갈 알맞은 말을 고르시오.

① Thus
② Moreover
③ For example
④ In other words
⑤ However

서답형

02 위 글의 괄호 (A)~(C)에서 문맥이나 어법상 알맞은 낱말을 골라 쓰시오.

➡ (A) _____ (B) _____ (C) _____

서답형

03 위 글의 밑줄 친 ⓑrole과 바꿔 쓸 수 있는 말을 쓰시오.

➡ _____

서답형

04 다음 문장에서 위 글의 내용과 <u>다른</u> 부분을 찾아서 고치시오.

Almost all the people spend much time outside a building or in the open air.

_____ ➡ _____

[05~06] 다음 글을 읽고 물음에 답하시오.

As you can see, sunshine has many benefits, but how can you enjoy its benefits safely? Fortunately, getting direct sunlight on your skin for 10 to 20 minutes a day is enough to benefit from it. Try to go out into the sun between classes or during lunch breaks and get sunshine on your arms and hands. A walk in the sun, for just a few minutes every day, is good for both your mind and your body. However, avoid the sun during peak summer hours, between 11 and 3, and use ___ⓐ___ to protect your face and neck. Enjoy the sun safely and see how a little sunshine can make a world of difference in your health and your mood.

중요

05 위 글의 제목으로 알맞은 것을 고르시오.

① Sunshine and Our Everyday Activity
② How to Enjoy Many Benefits of Sunshine Safely
③ How to Get Direct Sunlight?
④ Take Advantage of Spare Time to Enjoy the Sun
⑤ Make a Difference in Your Health and Your Mood!

서답형

06 주어진 영영풀이를 참고하여 빈칸 ⓐ에 철자 s로 시작하는 단어를 쓰시오.

a cream that protects your skin from the sun's rays, especially in hot weather

➡ _____

[07~10] 다음 글을 읽고 물음에 답하시오.

Sunshine does not just make you feel and sleep better. It also helps build strong bones. As you all know, ⓐ튼튼한 뼈와 치아를 만드는 것은 칼슘입니다. However, for the body ⓑto use calcium properly, it needs vitamin D. Interestingly, the skin creates vitamin D when sunlight shines on it. The easiest way to make strong bones is to go outside and enjoy the sun.

서답형

07 위 글의 밑줄 친 ⓐ의 우리말에 맞게 주어진 어휘를 이용하여 9 단어로 영작하시오.

> it, that, builds

➡ _____

08 아래 〈보기〉에서 위 글의 밑줄 친 ⓑto use와 to부정사의 용법이 다른 것의 개수를 고르시오.

> ┌─── 보기 ───┐
> ① I don't know how to use this machine.
> ② This machine is very simple to use.
> ③ Can you show me the way to use this machine?
> ④ It is easy to use this machine.
> ⑤ He is too old to use this machine.

① 1개　② 2개　③ 3개　④ 4개　⑤ 5개

중요

09 위 글의 주제로 알맞은 것을 고르시오.

① Sufficient calcium intake is very important to build strong bones.
② What's the nutritional value of vitamin D?
③ Are there any side effects caused by strong sunshine?
④ How much calcium is needed to build strong bones?

⑤ Sunshine is the easiest way to make strong bones.

서답형

10 What is necessary for the body to use calcium properly? Fill in the blanks with suitable words.

➡ _____ _____ is necessary.

[11~13] 다음 글을 읽고 물음에 답하시오.

As you can see, sunshine has many benefits, but how can you enjoy its benefits safely? (①) Fortunately, getting direct sunlight on your skin ___ⓐ___ 10 to 20 minutes a day is enough to benefit from it. (②) Try to go out into the sun between classes or during lunch (A)breaks and get sunshine on your arms and hands. (③) A walk ___ⓑ___ the sun, for just a few minutes every day, is good for both your mind and your body. (④) Enjoy the sun safely and see how a little sunshine can make a world of difference in your health and your mood. (⑤)

11 위 글의 빈칸 ⓐ와 ⓑ에 들어갈 전치사가 바르게 짝지어진 것은?

	ⓐ	ⓑ		ⓐ	ⓑ
①	for	– to	②	on	– in
③	for	– in	④	from	– to
⑤	from	– for			

중요

12 위 글의 흐름으로 보아, 다음 문장이 들어가기에 가장 적절한 곳은?

> However, avoid the sun during peak summer hours, between 11 and 3, and use sunscreen to protect your face and neck.

①　　　②　　　③　　　④　　　⑤

13 위 글의 밑줄 친 (A)breaks와 같은 의미로 쓰인 것을 고르시오.

① He breaks the chocolate in two.
② We could see the moon through breaks in the clouds.
③ He always breaks the speed limit.
④ Can you take coffee breaks whenever you want?
⑤ She breaks the silence by coughing.

[14~17] 다음 글을 읽고 물음에 답하시오.

Everyone feels happier when the sun shines. This is because of serotonin, the body's happy hormone. The more sun you get, the more "happy hormone" the brain produces. When your serotonin level goes up, you feel happier and stronger. This helps you fight everyday stress. Serotonin also has a calming effect, ⓐhelping you focus better on what you are doing. Moreover, serotonin helps you get a good night's sleep because ⓑit helps the brain produce a sleep hormone.

14 위 글의 밑줄 친 ⓐhelping과 문법적 쓰임이 같은 것을 모두 고르시오.

① Do you have a mentor helping you in your life?
② I will take pleasure in helping you.
③ I don't mind helping you if you can't find anyone else.
④ Jack listened to music, helping her sister do her homework.
⑤ Helping you has made my life meaningful.

서답형
15 위 글의 밑줄 친 ⓑit이 가리키는 것을 본문에서 찾아 쓰시오.

➡ _____

16 According to the passage, which is NOT true?

① Serotonin is the body's happy hormone.
② The brain produces more "happy hormone" as you get more sun.
③ If you want to feel happier and stronger, you had better lower your serotonin level.
④ Serotonin's calming effect helps you focus better on what you are doing.
⑤ Serotonin helps the brain produce a sleep hormone.

서답형
17 본문의 내용과 일치하도록 다음 빈칸 (A)와 (B)에 알맞은 단어를 쓰시오.

Thanks to (A)_____, you can have a good night's sleep. That's because it helps the brain produce a (B)_____ _____.

[18~20] 다음 글을 읽고 물음에 답하시오.

ⓐSunshine does not just make you feel and sleep better. ⓑIt also helps build strong bones. As you all know, it is calcium ⓒthat builds strong bones and teeth. However, for the body to use calcium properly, ⓓit needs vitamin D. Interestingly, the skin creates vitamin D when sunlight shines on it. The easiest way to make strong bones is to go outside and enjoy the sun.

서답형
18 위 글의 밑줄 친 ⓐ와 ⓑ를 as well as를 사용하여 한 문장으로 바꿔 쓰시오.

➡ _____
_____

19 위 글의 밑줄 친 ⓒthat과 문법적 쓰임이 같지 <u>않은</u> 것을 모두 고르시오.

① She was so tired <u>that</u> she couldn't think straight.

② It is you <u>that</u> are to blame.

③ What kind of work is it <u>that</u> you want?

④ It's possible <u>that</u> he has not received the letter.

⑤ It was an accident <u>that</u> changed my mind.

서답형

20 위 글의 밑줄 친 ⓓit이 가리키는 것을 본문에서 찾아 쓰시오.

➡ _____

[21~22] 다음 글을 읽고 물음에 답하시오.

ⓐ보시다시피, sunshine has many benefits, but how can you enjoy its benefits safely? Fortunately, getting direct sunlight on your skin for 10 to 20 minutes a day is enough to benefit from it. Try to go out into the sun between classes or during lunch breaks and get sunshine on your arms and hands. A walk in the sun, for just a few minutes every day, is good for both your mind and your body. However, avoid the sun during peak summer hours, between 11 and 3, and use sunscreen to protect your face and neck. Enjoy the sun safely and see how a little sunshine can make a world of difference in your health and your mood.

서답형

21 위 글의 밑줄 친 ⓐ의 우리말에 맞게 4 단어로 영작하시오.

➡ _____

22 다음 중 위 글의 내용을 바르게 이해하지 <u>못한</u> 사람을 고르시오.

① 진수: 햇빛의 이점들을 안전하게 즐길 수 있는 방법은 찾기 어려워.

② 영혜: 매일 단 몇 분 동안 햇빛을 쬐며 걷는 것은 우리의 마음과 몸 모두에 좋아.

③ 경호: 그러나 여름에 절정 시간인 11시에서 3시 사이에는 햇빛을 피해야 해.

④ 기철: 응, 그리고 얼굴과 목을 보호하기 위해 자외선 차단제를 사용해야 해.

⑤ 성미: 적은 양의 햇빛도 우리의 건강과 기분에 큰 차이를 만들어 낼 수 있어.

[23~24] 다음 글을 읽고 물음에 답하시오.

Everyone feels happier when the sun shines. This is because of serotonin, the body's happy hormone. The more sun you get, the more "happy hormone" the brain produces. When your serotonin level goes up, you feel happier and stronger. This helps you fight everyday stress. Serotonin also has a calming effect, ⓐ<u>helping you focus better on what you are doing.</u> Moreover, serotonin helps you get a good night's sleep because it helps the brain produce a sleep hormone.

서답형

23 위 글의 밑줄 친 ⓐhelping을 접속사를 사용하여 고쳐 쓰시오.

➡ _____

24 위 글의 제목으로 알맞은 것을 고르시오.

① What Makes You Feel Happy?

② The Difficulty of Increasing the Level of Serotonin

③ How to Fight Everyday Stress by Serotonin

④ Various Benefits of Serotonin

⑤ The Effect of Serotonin on Your Sleep Pattern

[01~03] 다음 글을 읽고 물음에 답하시오.

How much time do you spend every day out in the sun? Not much, right? ⓐMost people are too busy at school or at work to spend much time outdoors. However, the sun plays an important role in your health. ⓑIt helps you stay healthy.

01 위 글의 밑줄 친 ⓐ를 복문으로 고치시오.

➡ _____

_____

02 위 글의 밑줄 친 ⓑIt이 가리키는 것을 본문에서 찾아 쓰시오.

➡ _____

03 본문의 내용과 일치하도록 다음 빈칸 (A)와 (B)에 알맞은 단어를 쓰시오.

The sun has an important effect on your (A)_____, helping you to stay (B)_____.

[04~06] 다음 글을 읽고 물음에 답하시오.

Everyone feels happier when the sun shines. This is because of serotonin, the body's happy hormone. ⓐThe more sun you get, the more "happy hormone" the brain produces. When your serotonin level goes up, you feel happier and stronger. This helps you fight everyday stress. Serotonin also has a calming effect, ⓑ여러분이 하는 일에 더 잘 집중할 수 있도록 도와줍니다. Moreover, serotonin helps you get a good night's sleep because it helps the brain produce a sleep hormone.

04 위 글의 밑줄 친 ⓐ를 접속사 As를 사용하여, 고쳐 쓰시오.

➡ _____

_____

05 위 글의 밑줄 친 ⓑ의 우리말에 맞게 한 단어를 보충하여, 주어진 어휘를 알맞게 배열하시오.

better / helping / what / doing / are / you / focus / you

➡ _____

06 본문의 내용과 일치하도록 다음 빈칸 (A)와 (B)에 알맞은 단어를 쓰시오.

When you are in the sun, (A)_____ _____ produces serotonin, and in proportion to its level, you can feel happier. So, you can call serotonin the body's (B)_____ _____.

*in proportion to: …에 비례하여

[07~09] 다음 글을 읽고 물음에 답하시오.

Sunshine does not just make you feel and sleep better. It also helps build strong bones. As you all know, it is calcium that builds strong bones and teeth. ⓐTherefore, for the body to use calcium properly, it needs vitamin D. Interestingly, the skin creates vitamin D when sunlight shines on ⓑit. The easiest way to make strong bones is to go outside and enjoy the sun.

07 Write the three benefits of sunshine in English.

➡ (1) _____

(2) _____

(3) _____

08 위 글의 밑줄 친 ⓐ에서 흐름상 어색한 부분을 찾아 고치시오.

_____ ➡ _____

09 위 글의 밑줄 친 ⓑit이 가리키는 것을 본문에서 찾아 쓰시오.

➡ _____

[10~11] 다음 글을 읽고 물음에 답하시오.

Sunshine does not just make you feel and sleep better. It also helps build strong bones. As you all know, it is calcium that builds strong bones and teeth. However, for the body to use calcium properly, it needs vitamin D. Interestingly, the skin creates vitamin D when sunlight shines on it. The easiest way to make strong bones is to go outside and enjoy the sun.

10 위 글의 내용을 다음과 같이 정리하고자 한다. 빈칸 (A)~(C)에 들어갈 알맞은 단어를 본문에서 찾아 쓰시오.

The body needs (A)_____ _____ to use calcium properly, which builds strong bones. The skin creates vitamin D when (B)_____ shines on it, so the easiest way to make strong bones is to go outside and (C)_____ _____ _____.

11 다음 문장에서 위 글의 내용과 다른 부분을 찾아서 고치시오.

Sunshine does not make you feel and sleep better.

_____ ➡ _____

[12~13] 다음 글을 읽고 물음에 답하시오.

As you can see, sunshine has many benefits, but how can you enjoy its benefits safely? Fortunately, getting direct sunlight on your skin for 10 to 20 minutes a day is enough to benefit from it. Try to go out into the sun between classes or during lunch breaks and get sunshine on your arms and hands. A walk in the sun, for just a few minutes every day, is good for both your mind and your body. However, avoid the sun (A)[during / for] peak summer hours, between 11 and 3, and use sunscreen to (B)[prevent / protect] your face and neck. Enjoy the sun safely and see how a little sunshine can make (C)[a number of / a world of] difference in your health and your mood.

12 위 글의 괄호 (A)~(C)에서 문맥이나 어법상 알맞은 낱말을 골라 쓰시오.

➡ (A) _____ (B) _____ (C) _____

13 In order to benefit from sunlight, how long do you need to get direct sunlight? Fill in the blanks with suitable words.

We need to get direct sunlight on our skin for _____ _____ _____ minutes a day to benefit from it.

Communication Task

A: I think it's important to exercise every day. Do you exercise every day?

B: Yes, I do.

B: No, I don't. But I'll <u>try</u>.
"시도하다, 노력하다"

A: <u>Good for you.</u>
잘했다

A: Okay.

After You Read A

The Benefits of Sunshine

1. Sunshine helps you <u>deal with</u> stress and feel happier.
   = treat, handle
2. Sunshine helps you focus better on <u>what</u> you are doing.
   = the thing(s) which
3. If you <u>get</u> enough sunshine, you will sleep better at night.
   조건의 부사절에서 현재시제가 미래시제를 대신함.
4. When the sun shines on your skin, your skin produces vitamin D, <u>which</u> is
   that(×)
   needed for strong bones.

구문해설 • **benefit**: 혜택, 이득, 좋은 점 • **deal with**: 다루다 • **focus on**: ~에 주력하다, 초점을 맞추다
• **produce**: 생산하다

Writing Workshop

Health Comes First!

1. <u>Wash</u> your hands after <u>going</u> out. You will not catch a cold easily <u>if</u> you
   명령문   동명사(전치사 뒤)   조건의 접속사
   wash your hands well.

2. Get direct sunlight <u>for</u> 10 to 20 minutes every day. <u>The more sunlight you</u>
   ~ 동안
   <u>get, the happier and stronger you feel.</u>
   the 비교급+주어+동사 ~, the 비교급+주어+동사 …: ~할수록 …하다

3. <u>It is</u> a good breakfast <u>that</u> helps the brain <u>work</u> properly. <u>When</u> you eat a
   It is[was] ~ that …' 강조 구문   = which   = to work   ~하면(= If)
   good breakfast, you can focus more clearly on your work and remember
   things better.

구문해설 • **direct sunlight**: 직사광선 • **focus on**: ~에 집중하다

해석

A: 나는 매일 운동하는 것이 중요하다고 생각해. 너는 매일 운동하니?

B: 네, 그렇습니다.

A: 잘했다.

B: 아니요. 하지만 노력하겠습니다.

A: 알았어.

햇빛의 좋은 점

1. 햇빛은 여러분이 스트레스를 다루고 더 행복하게 느끼도록 돕는다.

2. 햇빛은 여러분이 하는 일에 더 잘 집중할 수 있도록 도와준다.

3. 햇빛을 충분히 쬐면 밤에 잠을 더 잘 잘 것이다.

4. 해가 여러분의 피부에 비칠 때, 여러분의 피부는 비타민 **D**를 만드는데, 그것은 튼튼한 뼈를 만드는 데 필요하다.

건강이 먼저야!

1. 외출 후에는 손을 씻어라. 손을 잘 씻으면 쉽게 감기에 걸리지 않을 것이다.

2. 매일 직사광선을 10~20분간 받아라. 햇빛을 더 많이 받을수록 더 행복하고 더 강하게 느낄 것이다.

3. 두뇌가 적절히 작동하도록 돕는 것은 좋은 아침식사이다. 좋은 아침을 먹으면, 일에 분명히 집중하고 더 잘 기억할 수 있다.

01 다음 빈칸에 들어가기에 적절한 단어를 고르시오.

> It was the most difficult _____ of her life.

① decision   ② decide   ③ decided

④ decisive   ⑤ deciding

02 다음 영영풀이에 해당하는 단어를 고르시오.

> the outer layer of a person's or animal's body

① knee   ② mood

③ cloth   ④ skin

⑤ production

03 다음 두 문장에 공통으로 알맞은 것을 고르시오.

> • The bus came right _____ time.
> • You'd better put _____ your coat in this cold weather.

① about   ② by   ③ for

④ with   ⑤ on

04 다음 밑줄 친 부분과 같은 뜻으로 쓰인 것은?

> What do you do to stay healthy?

① Where will you stay tomorrow?

② He will stay here for a month.

③ Will you stay there till he comes?

④ Remember to stay calm.

⑤ We enjoyed every minute of our stay.

[05~06] 다음 우리말과 일치하도록 빈칸에 알맞은 말을 쓰시오.

05
> M: John, you are late again.
> B: I'm sorry. I took the wrong bus.
> M: I think you need to leave home a little earlier.
> B: I think so, too. Next time I won't be late.
> M: _____.
> (학교에 제 시간에 도착하는 것이 중요하다.)
> (arrive, on time) (8 words)

➡ _____

06
> B: Mina, how was the movie?
> G: I didn't enjoy it. It was boring.
> B: What was bad about it?
> G: I already knew the ending. _____
> _____ before seeing it. (나는 영화를 보기 전에 그것에 관하여 읽지 말았어야 했는데.) (should) (6 words)
> B: Oh, I'm sorry you didn't like it.

➡ _____

07 다음 대화의 빈칸에 들어가기에 적절하지 <u>않은</u> 것은?

> B: We missed our flight.
> G: Oh, no. _____

① We ought to have come earlier.

② We should have come earlier.

③ I am sorry that we didn't come earlier.

④ I regret that we didn't come earlier.

⑤ We have to come earlier.

[08~10] 다음 대화를 읽고 물음에 답하시오.

> B: Mina, ⓐhow was the movie?
> G: I didn't ⓑenjoy it. It was ___(A)___.
> B: ⓒWhat was bad about it?
> G: I already knew the ending. I ⓓshouldn't have read about it before ⓔseen it.
> B: Oh, I'm sorry you didn't ___(B)___ it.

08 빈칸 (A), (B)에 들어가기에 알맞은 것을 〈보기〉에서 골라 쓰시오.

> ┌── 보기 ──┐
> exciting   boring   like   see   read

➡ (A) _____   (B) _____

09 위 대화의 밑줄 친 ⓐ~ⓔ 중에서 어법상 어색한 것을 고르시오.

① ⓐ   ② ⓑ   ③ ⓒ   ④ ⓓ   ⑤ ⓔ

10 위 대화를 통해서 알 수 있는 것은?

① Mina likes watching movies in her free time.
② The boy enjoyed the movie.
③ Mina has already read about the movie.
④ Mina thought the movie would be exciting.
⑤ The boy wants to read about the movie.

Grammar

11 다음 밑줄 친 부분과 바꿔 쓸 수 있는 것은?

> It was last week that Mr. Miller asked me to attend the meeting.

① what   ② when   ③ who
④ where   ⑤ which

12 주어진 단어가 알맞은 형태로 바르게 짝지어진 것은?

> • _____ we got to the fire, the warmer we felt. (close)
> • _____ you ride a mountain bike, the more you will enjoy it. (much)

① Close – Much
② Closer – Much
③ Closer – The more
④ The close – The much
⑤ The closer – The more

13 다음 중 어법상 올바른 것은?

① Which one is the bigger of the two?
② The high the top of a mountain, the good the view.
③ More I got to know her, more I liked her.
④ The more angrier she got, the more loudly she yelled.
⑤ The older David gets, the wiser becomes.

14 다음 문장을 각각의 주어진 단어를 강조하는 문장으로 바꿔 쓰시오.

> Tina bought a camera at the shop yesterday.

(1) Tina
➡ _____

(2) bought
➡ _____

(3) a camera

➡ _____

_____

(4) at the shop

➡ _____

_____

(5) yesterday

➡ _____

_____

15 다음 중 어법상 올바른 문장을 고르시오.

① It was my uncle what bought this smartphone for me on my birthday.

② It is Brian where broke the door.

③ It was his room which Kevin cleaned this morning.

④ It is the new car that my son wants to buy it.

⑤ It was on the day where I met her.

16 다음 밑줄 친 부분의 쓰임이 적절한 것은?

① More we exercise, the healthier we will get.

② More you study, better scores you will get in the test.

③ Much she gets to know him, the more she will like him.

④ The higher the bird flied up, the more it could see.

⑤ The old Ronald grew, the wise he became.

17 다음 괄호 안에서 어법상 알맞은 것을 고르시오.

(1) (The healthier / Healthier) one's mind is, (the healthier / healthier) one's body will be.

(2) I think (the much / the more) time I spend without her, (the sad / the sadder) I will become.

(3) It was getting (the darker and the darker / darker and darker), so we hurried to the shore.

(4) It was in the park (which / where) he left his car.

(5) It is the phone (which / when) I am looking for.

18 밑줄 친 말을 강조할 때, 빈칸에 알맞은 말을 쓰시오.

He had to reserve many seats <u>at the restaurant</u>.

→ _____ _____ at the restaurant _____ he had to reserve many seats.

Reading

[19~20] 다음 글을 읽고 물음에 답하시오.

Everyone feels happier when the sun shines. This is because of serotonin, the body's happy hormone. The more sun you get, the more "happy hormone" the brain produces. When your serotonin level goes up, you feel happier and stronger. This helps you fight everyday stress. Serotonin also has a calming effect, helping you focus better on what you are doing. ___ⓐ___, serotonin helps you get a good night's sleep because it helps the brain produce a sleep hormone.

19 위 글의 빈칸 ⓐ에 들어갈 알맞은 말을 고르시오.

① For example
② That is
③ Therefore
④ Moreover
⑤ However

20 According to the passage, which is NOT true about serotonin?

① Because of it, everyone feels happier when the sun shines.
② You can feel happier and stronger by raising your serotonin level.
③ Raising your serotonin level can help you fight everyday stress.
④ Its calming effect helps us focus better on what we are doing.
⑤ Serotonin has nothing to do with a good night's sleep.

[21~22] 다음 글을 읽고 물음에 답하시오.

　Sunshine does not just make you feel and sleep better. It also helps build strong bones. As you all know, it is calcium that builds strong bones and teeth. However, for the body to use calcium properly, it needs vitamin D. Interestingly, the skin creates vitamin D when sunlight shines on it. The easiest way to make strong bones is ⓐto go outside and enjoy the sun.

21 위 글의 밑줄 친 ⓐto go와 to부정사의 용법이 같은 것을 모두 고르시오.

① Why do you want to go outside?
② He likes to go outside.
③ She was pleased to go outside.
④ It's time for you to go outside.
⑤ You must be joking to go outside in this weather.

22 위 글의 제목으로 알맞은 것을 고르시오.

① Enjoying the Sun, the Easiest Way to Make Strong Bones!
② Various Usages of Vitamin D
③ How to Use Calcium Properly for Your Teeth
④ The Nutritional Value of Calcium
⑤ Too Much Sunshine and Your Skin Health

[23~25] 다음 글을 읽고 물음에 답하시오.

　As you can see, sunshine has many benefits, but how can you enjoy its benefits safely? Fortunately, getting direct sunlight on your skin ⓐ하루에 10분에서 20분 동안 is enough to benefit from it. Try to go out into the sun between classes or during lunch breaks and get sunshine on your arms and hands. A walk in the sun, for just a few minutes every day, is good for both your mind and your body. However, avoid the sun during peak summer hours, ___ⓑ___ 11 and 3, and use sunscreen to protect your face and neck. Enjoy the sun safely and see how a little sunshine can make a world of difference in your health and your mood.

23 위 글의 밑줄 친 ⓐ의 우리말에 맞게 7 단어로 영작하시오.

➡ _____

24 위 글의 빈칸 ⓑ에 알맞은 말을 쓰시오.

➡ _____

25 Which question CANNOT be answered after reading the passage?

① Is there any way to enjoy the benefits of sunshine safely?

② On what ground is getting direct sunlight on your skin for 10 to 20 minutes a day enough to benefit from it?

③ When is it that the writer advises you to go out into the sun?

④ When is it that you need to avoid the sun?

⑤ How can you protect your face and neck during peak summer hours?

[26~29] 다음 글을 읽고 물음에 답하시오.

Health Comes First!

1. Wash your hands after going out. You will not catch a cold easily if you wash your hands well.

2. Get direct sunlight for 10 to 20 minutes every day. ⓐThe more sunlight you get, the happier and stronger you feel.

3. It is a good breakfast that helps the brain work properly. When you eat a good breakfast, you can focus more clearly on your work and remember things better.

26 위 글의 밑줄 친 ⓐ를 접속사 As를 사용하여, 고쳐 쓰시오.

➡ _____

_____

27 According to the passage above, in order not to have a cold easily, what will be helpful? Fill in the blanks with suitable words.

If you _____ _____ _____ well after going out, you won't have a cold easily.

28 위 건강 홍보물의 내용과 일치하지 <u>않는</u> 것은?

① 외출한 다음에는 손을 씻어야 한다.

② 매일 10분에서 20분 동안 피부에 직사광선을 쐬는 것이 좋다.

③ 햇빛을 쐴수록 여러분은 더 행복하고 더 건강하게 느낀다.

④ 좋은 아침 식사는 뇌가 올바르게 작동하는 데 도움이 된다.

⑤ 아침 식사를 거르면 당신의 일에 더 잘 집중할 수 있고 사물들을 더 잘 기억할 수 있다.

29 본문의 내용과 일치하도록 다음 빈칸에 알맞은 단어를 쓰시오.

A _____ _____ helps you focus more clearly on your work and remember things better.

출제율 95%

01 짝지어진 단어의 관계가 같도록 빈칸에 알맞은 말을 쓰시오.

> wet : dry = regularly : _____

출제율 90%

02 다음 빈칸에 들어갈 말로 적절한 것은?

> Enjoy the sun safely and see how a little sunshine can make a _____ of difference in your health and your mood.

① word   ② sky   ③ world
④ light   ⑤ sunshine

출제율 95%

03 다음 빈칸에 들어가기에 적절한 것은?

> • When I have spare time, I usually _____ the Internet.
> • The sun _____ an important role in your health.

① play – tries   ② play – grows
③ surf – relaxes   ④ surf – plays
⑤ keep – gets

출제율 100%

04 다음 제시된 단어로 자연스러운 문장을 만들 수 없는 것은?

> ┤ 보기 ├
> flight   effect   journal   grade

① You will see the positive _____ of the advice.
② My _____ was an hour late because of bad weather.
③ He got the best _____ on the midterm exam.
④ He kept a _____ of his travels across Asia.
⑤ I came to _____ my rude remarks.

[05~07] 다음 대화를 읽고 물음에 답하시오.

> B: We still have 30 minutes to go before we ___(A)___ the top of the mountain. Let's sit down over there and have a snack.
> G: Oh, I brought only water. (B)내가 간식을 좀 가지고 왔어야 했는데.
> B: That's okay. I brought a lot. We can share.
> G: I'll keep it in mind to bring some snacks next time.

출제율 90%

05 빈칸 (A)에 들어가기에 알맞은 것은?

① go   ② work   ③ reach
④ arrive   ⑤ walk

출제율 90%

06 밑줄 친 (B)에 우리말을 바르게 영작한 것은?

① I will have to bring some snacks.
② I should have brought some snacks.
③ I ought to have some snacks to bring.
④ I must have brought some snacks.
⑤ I should have to bring some snacks.

출제율 95%

07 Which one of the following is NOT true according to the dialogue above?

① They have been climbing the mountain for 30 minutes.
② They will reach the top of the mountain in half an hour.
③ The girl has brought no snacks.
④ The boy has brought enough snacks for the two.
⑤ The girl will bring enough snacks next time.

G: Ben, you look full of energy today!

B: Do I? Maybe that's because I finally got a good night's sleep last night.

G: Why? Don't you usually get enough sleep?

B: No, I know it's really important to get a good night's sleep, but I always stay ___(A)___ late surfing the Internet or playing with my phone.

G: That sometimes happens to me too.

B: After I do that, I regret it the next morning and say, "I _____(B)_____ to bed earlier last night."

G: How was yesterday different?

B: Well, yesterday afternoon I climbed the mountain with my dad. I was really tired when I got home. I went to sleep right after I went to bed.

G: Outdoor activities are a great way to help you get a good night's sleep.

🖋 출제율 90%

08 위 대화의 빈칸 (A)에 알맞은 것은?

① up   ② on   ③ to
④ with   ⑤ from

🖋 출제율 95%

09 빈칸 (B)에 알맞은 것은?

① must go   ② will go
③ should go   ④ must have gone
⑤ should have gone

🖋 출제율 90%

10 밑줄 친 부분을 강조하는 문장으로 고쳐 쓰시오.

(1) We are pretty much unsure about <u>the whole thing</u>.

➡ _____

_____

(2) She went to the movies <u>with her friends</u> last Sunday.

➡ _____

_____

(3) A friend of mine bought a luxurious car <u>yesterday</u>.

➡ _____

_____

🖋 출제율 95%

11 다음 중 어법상 <u>어색한</u> 것은?

① The more things I have to do, the more tired I feel.

② The smarter the journalists are, the better off our society is.

③ I think the more you know a musical, the more you will enjoy it.

④ The red the apples are, the sweet they taste.

⑤ The more, the merrier.

🖋 출제율 100%

12 다음 중 어법상 올바른 문장을 <u>모두</u> 고르시오. (정답 2개)

① The high I went up, the foggy it became.

② Of the two boys, Simon is taller.

③ The lower the grade is, the worse Noah feels.

④ It is too costly that buying new furniture may prove.

⑤ It was my dad that suggested I do mountain biking.

⑥ It was played that he basketball at the playground.

⑦ It was last Friday where Bill lost his smartphone.

13 괄호 안에 주어진 어휘를 활용하여 글자 수에 맞게 다음 우리말을 영작하시오.

(1) 우리는 주의할수록, 실수를 더 적게 한다.
(few, much, make, careful, mistakes, 10 단어)

➡ _____

_____

(2) 외출 전에 네가 발라야 하는 것은 자외선 차단제이다. (put on, should, that, go out, sunscreen, 12 단어)

➡ _____

_____

[14~16] 다음 글을 읽고 물음에 답하시오.

Everyone feels happier when the sun shines. ⓐThis is because of serotonin, the body's happy hormone. (①) The more sun you get, the more "happy hormone" the brain produces. (②) This helps you fight everyday stress. (③) Serotonin also has a calming effect, helping you focus better on what you are doing. (④) Moreover, serotonin helps you get a good night's sleep because it helps the brain produce a sleep hormone. (⑤)

14 위 글의 흐름으로 보아, 주어진 문장이 들어가기에 가장 적절한 곳은?

When your serotonin level goes up, you feel happier and stronger.

①   ②   ③   ④   ⑤

15 위 글의 밑줄 친 ⓐThis가 가리키는 것을 본문에서 찾아 쓰시오.

➡ _____

16 위 글의 주제로 알맞은 것을 고르시오.

① the kinds of happy hormones in our body
② the influence of sunlight on our stress
③ the roles of the beneficial hormone, serotonin
④ the way to focus on what you're doing
⑤ the happy hormone versus the sleep hormone

[17~18] 다음 글을 읽고 물음에 답하시오.

Sunshine does not just make you feel and sleep better. It also helps build strong bones. ⓐAs you all know, it is calcium that builds strong bones and teeth. However, for the body to use calcium properly, it needs vitamin D. Interestingly, the skin creates vitamin D when sunlight shines on it. The easiest way to make strong bones is to go outside and enjoy the sun.

17 위 글의 밑줄 친 ⓐAs와 같은 의미로 쓰인 것을 고르시오.

① Sumi is not as pretty as Mary.
② As spring comes, the birds move northward.
③ As rust eats iron, so care eats the heart.
④ As she was tired, she didn't go there.
⑤ His anger grew as he talked.

18 According to the passage, which is NOT true?

① Sunshine makes you feel and sleep better.
② Sunshine helps build strong bones.
③ Calcium builds strong bones and teeth.

④ The body needs calcium to use vitamin D properly.

⑤ When sunlight shines on the skin, it creates vitamin D.

[19~21] 다음 글을 읽고 물음에 답하시오.

ⓐAs you can see, sunshine has many benefits, but how can you enjoy its benefits safe? Fortunately, getting direct sunlight on your skin for 10 to 20 minutes a day is enough to benefit from it. Try to go out into the sun between classes or during lunch breaks and get sunshine on your arms and hands. A walk in the sun, for just a few minutes every day, is good for both your mind and your body. However, avoid the sun during peak summer hours, between 11 and 3, and use sunscreen to protect your face and neck. Enjoy the sun safely and see how a little sunshine can make a world of difference in your health and your mood.

출제율 95%

19 위 글의 밑줄 친 ⓐ에서 어법상 틀린 부분을 찾아 고치시오.

_____ ➡ _____

출제율 90%

20 When do you need to avoid the sun? Fill in the blanks with suitable words.

> We need to avoid the sun during (A)_____ _____ _____ between 11 and 3.

출제율 100%

21 다음 중 본문에 소개된 '햇빛의 많은 이점을 즐길 수 있는 방법'에 해당하지 않는 것을 고르시오.

① 하루에 10분에서 20분 동안 피부에 직사광선을 쬔다.

② 수업 시간 사이나 점심시간에 햇빛을 쬐러 밖으로 나가서 팔과 손에 햇빛을 쬔다.

③ 매일 단 몇 분 동안 햇살을 쬐며 걷는다.

④ 얼굴과 목을 보호하기 위해 자외선 차단제를 사용한다.

⑤ 매일 많은 양의 햇빛을 쬐어 자신의 건강과 기분에 큰 차이를 만들어 낸다.

[22~24] 다음 글을 읽고 물음에 답하시오.

Good morning. Welcome to the ___ⓐ___. I'm Hana Kim. Here's today's weather for three cities in different parts of the world. The sun is shining and it's warm in Seoul. In the afternoon, there may be a shower. In New York, the rain stopped early this morning. It's cloudy now. In Paris, it'll be cloudy today with a chance of showers. ⓑIf you're in Seoul or Paris, take your sunscreen. Have a wonderful day.

출제율 95%

22 위 글의 빈칸 ⓐ에 들어갈 알맞은 말을 고르시오.

① Book Report ② Today's Article

③ Weather Report ④ Movie Review

⑤ Cool Travel Essay

출제율 90%

23 위 글의 밑줄 친 ⓑ에서 흐름상 어색한 부분을 찾아 고치시오.

_____ ➡ _____

출제율 100%

24 위 글의 내용과 일치하지 않는 것은?

① 서울은 현재 화창하고 따뜻하다.

② 오후에 서울에는 비가 내릴 수 있다.

③ 뉴욕은 오늘 아침 일찍 비가 그쳤다.

④ 뉴욕은 현재 날씨가 화창하다.

⑤ 파리는 오후에 흐리고 비가 내릴 가능성이 있다.

[01~03] 다음 대화를 읽고 물음에 답하시오.

> G: Ben, ①you look full of energy today!
>
> B: Do I? Maybe that's because (A)마침내 나는 지난밤에 잠을 잘 잤다. (got, good)
>
> G: Why? ②Don't you usually get enough sleep?
>
> B: No, I know it's really important to get a good night's sleep, but I always stay up late surfing the Internet or playing with my phone.
>
> G: ③That sometimes happens to me too.
>
> B: After I do that, I regret it the next morning and say, "I should have gone to bed earlier last night."
>
> G: ④How was yesterday the same?
>
> B: Well, yesterday afternoon I climbed the mountain with my dad. ⑤I was really tired when I got home. I went to sleep right after I went to bed.
>
> G: (B)   activities are a great way to help you get a good night's sleep.

01 밑줄 친 ①~⑤ 중에서 내용상 어색한 문장을 찾아 번호를 쓰고 적절한 내용으로 바꾸어 다시 쓰시오.

➡ _____, _____

02 밑줄 친 (A)의 우리말에 해당하는 영어 문장을 쓰시오. (9 words)

➡ _____

03 빈칸 (B)에 적절한 한 단어를 쓰시오.

➡ _____

04 어법상 어색한 것을 찾아 바르게 고쳐 문장을 다시 쓰시오.

(1) I think the old Sue gets, the wise she becomes.

➡ _____

_____

(2) Few the words, the good the prayer.

➡ _____

_____

(3) It was the library that he lent me the book yesterday.

➡ _____

_____

(4) It was last year where my family traveled to Busan.

➡ _____

_____

(5) It was because she lost her mother who the girl was confused.

➡ _____

_____

05 다음 그림을 보고, 'It ~ that ···' 강조 구문과 주어진 어휘를 활용하여 빈칸에 알맞게 쓰시오.

➡ _____ is the bus that _____ _____ to go to the theater. (be, wait, in the rain)

[06~07] 다음 글을 읽고 물음에 답하시오.

Everyone feels happier when the sun shines. This is because of serotonin, the body's happy hormone. The more sun you get, the more "happy hormone" the brain produces. When your serotonin level goes (A)[down / up], you feel happier and stronger. This helps you fight everyday stress. Serotonin also has a (B)[calming / calmed] effect, (C)[helps / helping] you focus better on what you are doing. Moreover, serotonin helps you get a good night's sleep because it helps the brain produce a sleep hormone.

06 위 글의 괄호 (A)~(C)에서 문맥이나 어법상 알맞은 낱말을 골라 쓰시오.

➡ (A) _____ (B) _____ (C) _____

07 본문의 내용과 일치하도록 다음 빈칸 (A)와 (B)에 알맞은 단어를 쓰시오.

If you need to fight (A)_____ _____, you may as well raise your (B)_____ _____, because it can help you feel happier and stronger.

[08~10] 다음 글을 읽고 물음에 답하시오.

As you can see, sunshine has many benefits, but how can you enjoy its benefits safely? Fortunately, getting direct sunlight on your skin for 10 to 20 minutes a day is enough to benefit from ⓐit. Try to go out into the sun between classes or during lunch breaks and get sunshine on your arms and hands. A walk in the sun, for just a few minutes every day, is good for both your mind and your body. However, avoid the sun during peak summer hours, between 11 and 3, and use sunscreen to protect your face and neck. Enjoy the sun safely and ⓑ적은 양의 햇빛이 여러분의 건강과 기분에 얼마나 큰 차이를 만들어 내는지 보세요.

08 위 글의 밑줄 친 ⓐit이 가리키는 것을 본문에서 찾아 쓰시오. (1 word)

➡ _____

09 위 글의 밑줄 친 ⓑ의 우리말에 맞게 주어진 어휘를 알맞게 배열하시오.

your mood / your health / how / difference / can / see / and / in / a little sunshine / a world of / make

➡ _____
_____

10 본문의 내용과 일치하도록 다음 빈칸 (A)~(C)에 알맞은 단어를 쓰시오.

You can enjoy (A)_____ _____ of sunshine in a (B)_____ way by getting direct sunlight on your skin for 10 to 20 minutes a day. You must also avoid the sun during peak summer hours, between 11 and 3, and use (C) _____ to protect your face and neck.

01 빈칸에 알맞은 낱말을 골라 햇빛의 좋은 점을 완성해 봅시다.

The Benefits of Sunshine

1. Sunshine helps you deal with _____ and feel _____.
2. Sunshine helps you _____ better on what you are doing.
3. If you get enough sunshine, you will _____ better at night.
4. When the sun shines on your skin, your skin produces _____, which is needed for strong _____.

| stress   vitamin D   focus   bones   happier   sleep |

02 다음 그림을 보고, 'It ~ that ...' 강조 구문을 활용하여 자유롭게 영작하시오.

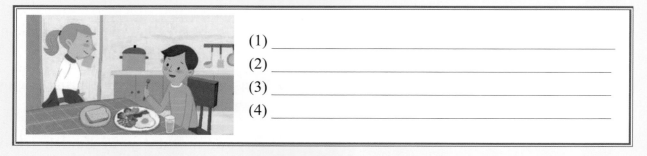

(1) _____
(2) _____
(3) _____
(4) _____

03 다음 내용을 바탕으로 나만의 건강 홍보물을 만드시오.

건강을 위한 습관 중 실천하지 못하고 있는 것
• Washing your hands after going out
• Getting direct sunlight for 10 to 20 minutes a day
• Eating a good breakfast

Health Comes First!

1. Wash your hands (A)_____. You will not catch a cold easily if you (B)_____ well.
2. Get (C)_____ for (D)_____ every day. The more sunlight you get, the happier and stronger you feel.
3. It is a good breakfast that helps the brain work properly. When you eat (E)_____, you can focus more clearly on your work and remember things better.

단원별 모의고사

01 다음 짝지어진 두 단어의 관계가 같도록 빈칸에 알맞은 말을 쓰시오.

> wide : narrow = healthy : _____

02 다음 영영풀이에 해당하는 단어로 적절한 것은?

> a book in which people regularly write about what has happened to them

① novel
② comic book
③ journal
④ poem
⑤ newspaper

03 다음 빈칸에 들어갈 말로 적절한 것은?

> Layla always applies _____ before she goes outside.

① sunlight
② sunshine
③ sunset
④ sunrise
⑤ sunscreen

04 다음 문장의 빈칸에 알맞은 것을 〈보기〉에서 찾아 쓰시오.

> ┌─ 보기 ─┐
> properly   outdoors   mood   peak

(1) He's always in a bad _____.
(2) The rain prevented them from eating _____.
(3) The hotels are always full during the _____ season.
(4) The television isn't working _____.

[05~07] 다음 대화를 읽고 물음에 답하시오.

W: Oh, your blanket is wet from the rain! I should _____ (가) _____.
B: Did you wash it? (A)
W: No. I just put it out in the sun this morning. (B)
B: Why didn't you wash it? (C)
W: Hanging a blanket in the sun is a nature-friendly way to keep the blanket clean.
B: Oh, I didn't know that. (D)
W: And it's also important to remember to do it regularly. (E)

05 빈칸 (가)에 들어가기에 적절한 것은?

① watch weather report
② have checked the weather
③ call the weather reporter
④ have known about the blanket
⑤ expect the sun

06 (A)~(E) 중에서 다음 문장이 들어가기에 적절한 곳은?

> I'll remember that.

① (A)   ② (B)   ③ (C)   ④ (D)   ⑤ (E)

07 Which one is NOT true according to the dialogue?

① The boy's blanket is wet from the rain.
② The woman didn't check the weather.
③ The woman washed the blanket this morning.
④ The woman hung the blanket in the sun.
⑤ The boy didn't know the nature-friendly way to keep the blanket clean.

[08~10] 다음 대화를 읽고 물음에 답하시오.

> G: Ben, you look full of energy today!
> B: Do I? Maybe that's ⓐbecause I finally got _____(A)_____ last night.
> G: Why? Don't you usually get enough sleep?
> B: No, I know it's really important to get a good night's sleep, but I always stay up late surfing the Internet or ⓑplay with my phone.
> G: That sometimes happens to me too.
> B: After I do that, I regret it the next morning and say, "I ⓒshould have gone to bed earlier last night."
> G: How was yesterday different?
> B: Well, yesterday afternoon I ⓓclimbed the mountain with my dad. I was really tired when I ⓔgot home. I went to sleep right after I went to bed.
> G: Outdoor activities are a great way to help you get a good night's sleep.

08 빈칸 (A)에 적절한 것은?

① a good night's sleep
② a long sleeping
③ a poor sleeping condition
④ a quiet room
⑤ a full stomach

09 밑줄 친 ⓐ~ⓔ 중에서 어법상 어색한 것은?

① ⓐ ② ⓑ ③ ⓒ ④ ⓓ ⑤ ⓔ

10 Which one of the following CANNOT be answered according to the dialogue above?

① Does Ben look full of energy today?
② What does Ben usually do before going to bed?
③ Does Ben usually get enough sleep?
④ With whom did Ben climb the mountain yesterday?
⑤ What outdoor activities does Ben like most?

11 빈칸을 채워 주어진 문장과 같은 의미의 문장을 쓰시오.

(1) I do not think that the richer I become, the happier I am.
= I do not think that as _____ _____.

(2) The bigger the magnet is, the stronger it is.
= As _____.

(3) The more you practice, the better your English speaking skills are.
= As _____ _____.

12 다음 문장의 밑줄 친 부분을 강조하는 문장으로 바꿔 쓰시오.

(1) You should put away your smartphone.
➡ _____ _____

(2) I did not learn Hangeul until I came to Korea.
➡ _____ _____

(3) Jina had a chocolate cake for dessert.
➡ _____ _____

(4) Minji and Jian want to join the art club.
➡ _____ _____

13 다음 문장의 빈칸에 들어갈 수 없는 말을 고르시오.

> The _____, the better.

① sooner   ② faster   ③ less
④ bitter   ⑤ more

14 다음 중 어법상 어색한 것을 모두 고르시오.

① The more Dan practices, the more skillful he is.
② The fast you go, the early you will reach your grandma's house.
③ It is on Sundays when Daniel and I meet.
④ It was the window what John broke.
⑤ The more Jay read this book, the more interested he is in it.
⑥ It was played that Harry the violin yesterday.
⑦ It was thoughtfully that I walked towards the train.

15 다음 우리말을 주어진 어휘를 이용하여 영작하시오.

(1) 국물을 오래 끓일수록 맛이 좋아진다. (I, taste, boil, long, good, it)
→ _____

(2) 날씨가 좋을수록, 나는 기분이 더 좋다. (good, the weather, feel)
→ _____

(3) Layla가 Jinho를 만난 곳은 바로 학교였다. (at)
→ _____

(4) Ella가 가장 존경하는 사람은 바로 그녀의 아버지이다. (respect, the most)
→ _____
_____

[16~18] 다음 글을 읽고 물음에 답하시오.

Everyone feels happier when the sun shines. This is because of serotonin, the body's happy hormone. (A)여러분이 햇빛을 쬘수록 뇌는 행복 호르몬을 더 만들어 냅니다. When your serotonin level goes up, you feel happier and stronger. (B)This helps you fight everyday stress. Serotonin also has a calming effect, helping you focus better on ___ⓐ___ you are doing. Moreover, serotonin helps you get a good night's sleep because it helps the brain produce a sleep hormone.

16 위 글의 빈칸 ⓐ에 들어갈 알맞은 말을 고르시오.

① that   ② what   ③ when
④ which   ⑤ where

17 위 글의 밑줄 친 (A)의 우리말에 맞게 주어진 어휘를 이용하여 12 단어로 영작하시오.

> sun, get, happy, produce

→ _____
_____

18 위 글의 밑줄 친 (B)가 가리키는 것을 본문에서 찾아 쓰시오.

→ _____
_____

[19~21] 다음 글을 읽고 물음에 답하시오.

As you can see, sunshine has many benefits, but how can you enjoy its benefits safely? Fortunately, ⓐgetting direct sunlight on your skin for 10 to 20 minutes a day is enough to benefit from it. Try to go out into the sun between classes or during lunch breaks and get sunshine on your arms and hands. A walk in the sun, for just a few minutes every day, is good for both your mind and your body. However, avoid the sun during peak summer hours, between 11 and 3, and use sunscreen to protect your face and neck. Enjoy the sun safely and see how a little sunshine can make a world of difference in your health and your mood.

19 위 글의 밑줄 친 ⓐgetting과 문법적 쓰임이 같은 것을 모두 고르시오.

① My dream is getting ahead of him.
② Did she give up getting the job?
③ It's getting warmer and warmer.
④ Is there any advantage in getting there early?
⑤ The nights are getting longer.

20 위 글의 주제로 알맞은 것을 고르시오.

① many benefits of walking
② the proper amount of getting direct sunlight on your skin
③ the way to enjoy many benefits of sunshine safely
④ the time to avoid the sun
⑤ the right way to use sunscreen to protect your face and neck

21 According to the passage, which is NOT true?

① Sunshine has many benefits.
② To get direct sunlight on your skin for 10 to 20 minutes a day isn't enough to benefit from it.
③ A walk in the sun, for just a few minutes every day, is good for both your mind and your body.

④ It's necessary to avoid the sun during peak summer hours, between 11 and 3.
⑤ It's possible to enjoy the sun safely and see how a little sunshine can make lots of difference in your health and your mood.

[22~23] 다음 글을 읽고 물음에 답하시오.

The ___ⓐ___ of Sunshine
1. Sunshine helps you deal with stress and feel happier.
2. Sunshine helps you focus better on what you are doing.
3. If you get enough sunshine, you will sleep better at night.
4. When the sun shines on your skin, your skin produces vitamin D, which is needed for strong bones.

22 주어진 영영풀이를 참고하여 빈칸 ⓐ에 철자 B로 시작하는 단어를 쓰시오.

the helps that you get from something or the advantages that results from something

➡ _____

23 다음 중 햇빛의 좋은 점에 해당하지 않는 것을 고르시오.

① 여러분이 스트레스를 다루고 더 행복하게 느끼도록 돕는다.
② 여러분이 하는 일에 더 잘 집중할 수 있도록 도와준다.
③ 햇빛을 충분히 쬐면 밤에 잠을 잘 잘 수 없다.
④ 해가 여러분의 피부에 비칠 때, 여러분의 피부는 비타민 D를 만든다.
⑤ 비타민 D는 튼튼한 뼈를 만드는 데 필요하다.

Lesson 4

Safety First

의사소통 기능

- 의무 표현하기
  A: You have to watch out for bees.
  B: Okay, I will.

- 가능성 정도 표현하기
  A: You should do some warm-up exercises.
  B: Why?
  A: Jumping into cold water can be dangerous.

언어 형식

- 접속사 'although'
  Although camping trips can create sweet memories for many people, they can also be occasions when bad things happen.

- seem to
  They **seem to** know what to do to make their camping trip safe and fun.

Words & Expressions

Key Words

- **accident**[ǽksidənt] 명 사고
- **although**[ɔːlðóu] 접 비록 ~이긴 하지만
- **apply**[əplái] 동 (크림 등을) 바르다
- **attention**[əténʃən] 명 주의, 집중
- **avoid**[əvɔ́id] 동 피하다
- **burn**[bə́ːrn] 동 (불이) 타다
- **burner**[bə́ːrnər] 명 (취사용) 버너, 가열 기구
- **by**[bai] 전 ~ 옆에
- **cause**[kɔːz] 동 ~을 야기하다
- **clear**[kliər] 형 (하늘이) 맑은, 청명한
- **create**[kriéit] 동 창조하다
- **deep**[diːp] 형 깊은
- **earthquake**[ə́ːrθkweik] 명 지진
- **electricity**[ilektrísəti] 명 전기
- **enough**[inʌ́f] 형 충분한
- **entrance**[éntrəns] 명 (출)입구, 문
- **explode**[iksplóud] 동 폭발하다
- **fall**[fɔːl] 동 넘어지다
- **feed**[fiːd] 동 먹이를 주다
- **flat**[flæt] 형 평평한
- **flooding**[flʌ́diŋ] 명 홍수, 범람
- **fit**[fit] 동 ~에 맞다
- **garlic**[gɑ́ːrlik] 명 마늘
- **guess**[ges] 동 추측하다, 짐작하다
- **hang**[hæŋ] 동 걸다, 매달다
- **inform**[infɔ́ːrm] 동 알리다, 통지하다
- **lightning**[láitiŋ] 명 번개
- **location**[loukéiʃən] 명 장소
- **memory**[méməri] 명 기억, 추억
- **mosquito**[məskíːtou] 명 모기
- **nature-friendly**[néitʃərfréndli] 형 자연 친화적인
- **occasion**[əkéiʒən] 명 (특정한) 때, 경우
- **overeat**[òuvəríːt] 동 과식하다
- **overflow**[òuvərflóu] 동 흘러넘치다, 범람하다
- **overuse**[òuvərjúːz] 동 남용하다, 너무 많이 사용하다
- **overwork**[òuvərwɔ́rk] 동 과로하다, 혹사하다
- **oxygen**[ɑ́ksidʒen] 명 산소
- **pack**[pæk] 동 (짐을) 꾸리다
- **pan**[pæn] 명 (손잡이가 달린 얕은) 냄비, 팬
- **path**[pæθ] 명 길, 통로
- **peel**[piːl] 명 (과일 또는 채소의) 껍질
- **place**[pleis] 동 놓다, 두다
- **prepare**[pripέər] 동 준비하다, 대비하다
- **protect**[prətékt] 동 보호하다
- **reach**[riːtʃ] 동 ~에 이르다, 도달하다
- **regularly**[régjulərli] 부 규칙적으로
- **report**[ripɔ́ːrt] 명 보도, 기사
- **rub**[rʌb] 동 문지르다, 비비다
- **safety**[séifti] 명 안전, 안전성
- **seem**[siːm] 동 ~인 것 같다
- **several**[sévərəl] 형 몇몇의, 각각의
- **sink**[siŋk] 명 싱크대
- **spill**[spil] 동 흘리다
- **strike**[straik] 동 (세게) 치다
- **sunscreen**[sʌ́nskrìːn] 명 자외선 차단제, 선크림
- **traffic**[trǽfik] 명 교통
- **trip**[trip] 동 걸려 넘어지다, (발이) 걸리다
- **uncomfortable**[ənkʌ́mfərtəbəl] 형 불편한
- **warm-up**[wɔ́rmʌp] 명 몸 풀기, 준비
- **wet**[wet] 형 젖은
- **weather**[wéðər] 명 날씨

Key Expressions

- **by -ing** ~함으로써
- **close to** ~에 가까운
- **do one's best** 최선을 다하다
- **hang out** 어울리다
- **instead of** ~ 대신에
- **keep away** ~을 접근하지 못하게 하다
- **keep ~ in mind** ~을 명심하다
- **keep -ing** 계속 ~하다
- **pass out** 의식을 잃다, 기절하다
- **put on** ~을 바르다
- **put up** 설치하다, 세우다
- **stay up** 안 자다, 깨어 있다
- **try to부정사** ~하려고 노력하다, ~하려고 애쓰다
- **use up** ~을 다 써버리다

Word Power

※ 서로 반대되는 뜻을 가진 어휘

- **popular**(인기 있는) ↔ **unpopular**(인기 없는)
- **available**(구할 수 있는) ↔ **unavailable**(구할 수 없는)
- **healthy**(건강한) ↔ **unhealthy**(건강하지 않은)
- **whole**(전체의) ↔ **partial**(일부분의)
- **nervous**(초조한) ↔ **calm**(차분한)
- **top**(맨 위의) ↔ **bottom**(밑바닥의)

※ 동사 – 명사

- **avoid**(피하다) – **avoidance**(회피)
- **attend**(주의를 기울이다) – **attention**(주의)
- **prepare**(준비하다) – **preparation**(준비)
- **create**(창조하다) – **creation**(창조)
- **explode**(폭발하다) – **explosion**(폭발)
- **inform**(알리다, 통지하다) – **information**(전달, 통지)
- **protect**(보호하다) – **protection**(보호)
- **memorize**(기억하다) – **memory**(기억)

※ 동사 – over+동사

- **act** (행동하다) → **overact** (과장된 행동을 하다)
- **cook** (요리하다) → **overcook** (너무 오래 익히다)
- **do** (하다) → **overdo** (지나치게 하다)
- **flow** (흐르다) → **overflow** (흘러넘치다, 범람하다)
- **eat** (먹다) → **overeat** (과식하다)
- **use** (사용하다) → **overuse** (남용하다)
- **work** (일하다) → **overwork** (과로하다, 혹사하다)
- **sleep** (잠자다) → **oversleep** (늦잠 자다)

English Dictionary

- **apply** (크림 등을) 바르다
  → to put or spread something such as paint, cream, etc. onto a surface
  페인트, 크림 등과 같은 것을 표면에 바르거나 펴 바르다

- **earthquake** 지진
  → a sudden, violent shaking of the earth's surface
  지구 표면의 갑작스럽고 격렬한 흔들림

- **entrance** (출)입구, 문
  → a door, gate, passage, etc. used for entering a room, building, or place
  방, 건물 또는 장소에 들어갈 때 사용하는 문, 대문, 통로 등

- **explode** 폭발하다
  → to burst, or to make something burst, loudly and violently, causing damage
  폭발하거나 무언가를 터지게 하여, 크고 격렬하게 피해를 입히다

- **flooding** 홍수, 범람
  → a situation in which water from a river or from rain covers large areas of land
  강물이나 빗물이 넓은 지역의 땅을 덮고 있는 상황

- **lightning** 번개
  → the bright flashes of light that you see in the sky during a storm
  폭풍우가 칠 때 여러분이 하늘에서 보는 밝은 빛

- **memory** 기억, 추억
  → something that you remember
  기억하고 있는 것

- **mosquito** 모기
  → a small flying insect that bites the skin of people and animals and sucks their blood
  사람과 동물의 피부를 물고 피를 빨아먹는 작은 날벌레

- **peel** (과일 또는 채소의) 껍질
  → the skin of a fruit
  과일의 껍질

- **rub** 문지르다, 비비다
  → to press and move your hands or an object over a surface
  손이나 물체를 어떤 표면 위로 누르고 움직이다

- **strike** (세게) 치다
  → to hit someone or something hard or with force
  누군가나 뭔가를 세게 때리거나 힘을 가해서 때리다

- **sunscreen** 자외선 차단제, 선크림
  → a cream that you can rub onto your skin to stop it from being burned by the sun
  햇빛에 타는 것을 막기 위해 피부에 비벼도 되는 크림

서답형

01 다음 짝지어진 단어의 관계가 같도록 빈칸에 알맞은 말을 쓰시오.

> wet : dry = entrance : _____

02 다음 영영풀이가 가리키는 것은?

> a situation in which water from a river or from rain covers large areas of land

① path   ② accident
③ weather   ④ earthquake
⑤ flooding

서답형

03 다음 우리말과 같도록 빈칸에 알맞은 말을 쓰시오.

> 내일 정원 주위에 울타리를 설치하자.

➡ Let's _____ _____ a fence around the garden tomorrow.

중요

04 다음 문장에 공통으로 들어갈 알맞은 것은?

> • He finished in third _____.
> • Please _____ the book on my desk.

① set   ② place
③ lay   ④ feed
⑤ prize

중요

05 다음 중 밑줄 친 부분의 뜻풀이가 바르지 않은 것은?

① This river flows in the East Sea. (흐르다)
② You should apply the cream to the sunburned area. (신청하다)
③ I will pack my things for a trip to Vietnam. (꾸리다)
④ His eyes got red after he rubbed them. (문지르다)
⑤ He walks a path through the forest every week. (길)

06 다음 빈칸에 알맞은 말이 바르게 짝지어진 것은?

> • When I was hit on the head, I almost _____ out.
> • Jiho has _____ up my phone's battery playing games.

① took – used   ② took – put
③ passed – used   ④ passed – put
⑤ passed – needed

서답형

07 다음 우리말에 맞게 빈칸에 알맞은 말을 쓰시오.

(1) 너는 과식하지 않는 편이 좋겠다.
   ➡ You had better not _____.
(2) 그 폭탄은 큰 소음을 내며 폭발했다.
   ➡ The tomb _____ with a loud noise.
(3) 너는 연설에 집중해야 한다.
   ➡ You should pay _____ to the speech.

01 다음 짝지어진 단어의 관계가 같도록 빈칸에 알맞은 말을 쓰시오.

> comfortable : uncomfortable
> = regularly : _____

02 다음 영영풀이에 해당하는 단어를 〈보기〉에서 찾아 쓰시오.

┌── 보기 ──┐
lightning earthquake memory
└──────────┘

(1) a sudden, violent shaking of the earth's surface: _____
(2) something that you remember: _____
(3) the bright flashes of light that you see in the sky during a storm: _____

03 다음 빈칸에 알맞은 말을 〈보기〉에서 골라 쓰시오.

┌── 보기 ──┐
safety entrance overflow apply
└──────────┘

(1) We should _____ sunscreen on our skin before we go out.
(2) We must put _____ before anything else.
(3) As it is raining a lot, the river can _____.
(4) Lots of people were waiting at the _____ to the baseball park.

04 다음 우리말에 맞게 주어진 단어를 바르게 배열하시오.

> 내가 말했던 것을 명심하세요.
> (what / you / keep / told / in / I / mind)

➡ _____

05 다음 문장의 빈칸에 다음 영어 설명에 해당하는 단어를 써 넣으시오.

> Do not _____ your eyes with dirty hands.

> <영어 설명> to press and move your hands or an object over a surface

➡ _____

06 다음 우리말에 맞게 빈칸에 알맞은 말을 쓰시오.

(1) 집에 거미가 접근하지 못하게 하는 방법을 알고 있니?
➡ Do you know how to _____ spiders _____ from your home?
(2) 그녀는 출산 후 기절했다.
➡ She _____ _____ after giving birth.
(3) 이 크림을 바르는 것이 도움이 될 것이다.
➡ It will be helpful to _____ _____ this cream.
(4) 내가 실수로 내 가방 대신에 네 가방을 가져갔어.
➡ I took your bag _____ _____ mine by mistake.

Conversation

1 의무 표현하기

> A: You have to watch out for bees. 너는 벌들을 조심해야 해.
> B: Okay, I will. 알았어, 그럴게.

- '~해야 한다'라는 의미로 의무를 나타낼 때는 'have to+동사원형'을 쓴다. 비슷한 표현으로는 'must', 'should', 'need to(~할 필요가 있다)' 등이 있다.

  - We must watch out for bees. 우리는 벌들을 조심해야만 해.
  - We should watch out for bees. 우리는 벌들을 조심해야만 해.
  - We need to watch out for bees. 우리는 벌들을 조심할 필요가 있어.

- 'must(~해야 한다)'는 'have to'보다 의미가 강하고, should는 'have to'보다 약한 의미로 도덕적 의무나 비강제적 의무를 나타낼 때 쓸 수 있다.

- '~해서는 안 된다'는 'must not'이나 'should not'으로 표현할 수 있다. 'do not have[need] to'는 '~할 필요가 없다'는 뜻임에 주의한다.

  - You must[should] not run from here. 너는 여기서부터 뛰면 안 된다.
  - You don't have[need] to run from here. 너는 여기서부터 뛰지 않아도 된다.

핵심 Check

1. 다음 우리말과 일치하도록 빈칸에 알맞은 말을 쓰시오.

   A: Can we go this way? It looks nice.

   B: No. We _____ _____ go straight if we want to get to the top.

   (정상에 가기를 원한다면 우리는 똑바로 가야 해.)

2. 다음 주어진 어구를 사용하여 대화를 완성하시오.

   A: Oh, the stairs are wet.

   B: Then _____.

   (the stairs / walk / to / we / slowly / down / have)

② 가능성 정도 표현하기

> A: You should do some warm-up exercises. 너는 준비 운동을 해야 해.
>
> B: Why? 왜?
>
> A: Jumping into cold water can be dangerous. 차가운 물에 뛰어드는 것은 위험할 수 있어.

■ 'can[may]+동사원형'은 '~할 수도 있다'라는 뜻으로 어떤 일이 발생할 수 있다는 가능성을 나타낸다.

　• The trip can be canceled because of the earthquake. 지진 때문에 여행이 취소될 수 있다.

　• It's cloudy. You may need your umbrella in the afternoon. 날씨가 흐려. 너는 오후에 우산이 필요할 수도 있어.

■ can이 일반적이고 이론적인 가능성을 나타낸다면 'may', 'could', 'might'는 그보다 가능성의 정도가 적은 경우에 사용할 수 있다.

■ 'can'은 '~할 수 있다(능력)', '~해도 된다(허가, 허락)' 등의 의미로도 쓸 수 있다.

　• Sumi can play the guitar. 수미는 기타를 연주할 수 있다.

　• Can I use this table? 제가 이 탁자를 사용해도 될까요?

핵심 Check

3. 다음 주어진 말을 사용하여 대화를 완성하시오.

　A: Can I swim right after eating?

　B: Swimming with a full stomach ＿＿＿＿ ＿＿＿＿ ＿＿＿＿＿.
　　(uncomfortable, be)

4. 다음 대화의 순서를 바르게 배열하시오.

　(A) If we don't leave now, we may not get to the concert in time.

　(B) Not, not yet. I have to check if I turned off the gas.

　(C) Mina, are you ready to leave?

　➡ ＿＿＿＿＿＿＿＿＿＿＿

Real-Life Zone

B: Uncle John, look at my new bike. What do you think?

M: It's really nice. Where are you going?

B: ❶To the park to meet a friend.

M: Where's your helmet?

B: ❷I don't have one. It's just a short ride.

M: Put on your helmet. ❸You may hurt yourself.

B: ❹But I see a lot of people riding bikes without helmets.

M: ❺You have to wear a helmet. It protects your head in an accident.

B: Okay. I'll get my dad's helmet.

M: No. You have to wear a helmet that fits you. ❻If not, it cannot protect your head.

B: I guess I'll have to buy one for myself.

B: 존 삼촌. 제 새로운 자전거 좀 보세요. 어떻게 생각하세요?
M: 아주 멋지구나. 어디를 가고 있니?
B: 친구 만나러 공원에요.
M: 네 헬멧이 어디 있니?
B: 저는 헬멧이 없어요. 그냥 잠깐 타는 거예요.
M: 헬멧을 쓰렴. 다칠 수 있단다.
B: 하지만 저는 헬멧 없이 자전거를 타는 많은 사람들을 봐요.
M: 너는 헬멧을 써야만 한단다. 그것은 사고가 났을 때 네 머리를 보호해 줘.
B: 알았어요. 아빠의 헬멧을 가져올게요.
M: 아니. 너는 네게 맞는 헬멧을 써야 해. 그렇지 않으면 그것은 네 머리를 보호해 줄 수 없어.
B: 저를 위한 헬멧을 사야겠어요.

---

❶ 'to meet'은 to부정사의 부사적 용법 중 목적(~하기 위해)으로 쓰였다.
❷ one은 부정대명사로 'a helmet'을 대신하여 쓰였다.
❸ may는 '~할 수도 있다, ~일 수도 있다'라는 뜻으로 'could'나 'might'로 바꿔 쓸 수 있다.
❹ see+목적어+목적격 보어: ~가 …하는 것을 보다
❺ have to는 '~해야 한다, ~할 필요가 있다'라는 뜻으로 must, should, need to 등으로 바꿔 쓸 수 있다.
❻ If not은 If you don't wear a helmet that fits you를 대신하는 말이다.

Check(√) True or False

(1) The boy is riding a bicycle with his uncle.   T ☐ F ☐

(2) The boy will buy a helmet for himself.   T ☐ F ☐

 Listen & Speak 1 A-1

G: Mom, can I play outside this afternoon?

W: Sure. ❶Don't forget to put on sunscreen before you go out.

G: But it's cloudy today. ❷Do I have to put on sunscreen?

W: Yes, you have to wear sunscreen every day.

G: Okay. ❸Then I'll put some on now.

G: 엄마, 오후에 밖에서 놀아도 될까요?
W: 물론이지. 나가기 전에 선크림 바르는 것을 잊지 말아라.
G: 그렇지만 오늘은 흐려요. 선크림을 발라야 하나요?
W: 그럼, 매일 선크림을 발라야 한단다.
G: 알겠어요. 그러면 지금 바를게요.

---

❶ Don't forget to ~.: ~할 것을 잊지 마라. / put on: ~을 바르다
❷ have to: ~해야 한다
❸ some은 부정대명사로 some sunscreen을 가리킨다. 구동사의 목적어로 대명사가 쓰이는 경우 대명사는 부사 사이에 위치한다.

Check(√) True or False

(3) The girl will not put on sunscreen before going outside.   T ☐ F ☐

(4) The weather is cloudy today.   T ☐ F ☐

Listen & Speak 1 Listen

1. B: ❶We have to watch out for bees.
   G: Oh, there are bees. Run!
2. G: Can we go this way? ❷It looks nice.
   B: No. ❸We have to go straight if we want to get to the top.
3. B: Oh, the stairs are wet.
   G: Then we have to walk down the stairs slowly.
4. G: Let's climb some more. I want to reach the top of the mountain.
   B: First we have to check the weather. ❹Oh, it says it's going to rain. We should go down.

❶ have to=must, should, need to
❷ look+형용사: ~하게 보이다
❸ get to: ~에 도착하다, ~에 이르다
❹ It says ~.: ~라고 한다.

Listen & Speak 1 A-2

B: ❶Let's go bowling.
G: I'm sorry, I can't. ❷I have to go see a doctor.
B: ❸Oh, what's wrong?
G: I don't know, but my stomach hurts.

❶ go -ing: ~하러 가다
❷ go see a doctor: 병원에 가다
❸ What's wrong?은 What's the matter?, What's the problem? 등으로 바꿔 쓸 수 있다.

Listen & Speak 2 Listen

1. M: Don't run. ❶You may fall.
   B: Okay, I won't run.
2. B: ❷Jumping into cold water without warming up can be dangerous.
   G: Oh, okay. I will warm up.
3. G: Mom, I want to swim here.
   W: ❸Okay, but first you should check how deep the water is. It may be deeper than you think.
4. B: ❹Can I swim right after eating?
   G: Swimming with a full stomach can be uncomfortable.

❶ may는 '~할 수도 있다, ~일 수도 있다'는 의미로 가능성을 나타낸다.
❷ without -ing: ~하지 않고, ~하지 않은 채로
❸ should는 '~해야 한다, ~하는 게 좋겠다'는 의미로 충고를 나타낸다.
❹ can은 '~해도 된다'는 뜻의 허가의 의미로 쓰였다.

Listen & Speak 2 A-1

M: Flooding can cause big problems. ❶ However, you may not know what to do when it happens. There are several things you have to do. First, you have to turn off the water and the electricity. Second, pack water and food when you leave the house. ❷Finally, you have to move to a high and safe place and keep listening to the weather report.

❶ may not: ~하지 않을 수도 있다 / what to do: 무엇을 해야 할지
❷ keep -ing: 계속 ~하다

Listen & Speak 2 A-2

B: Mina, are you ready to leave?
G: No, not yet. ❶I have to check if I turned off the gas.
B: ❷If we don't leave now, we may not get to the concert in time.
G: Okay, but I have to check the gas first. ❸It will only take a minute.

❶ if: ~인지 아닌지
❷ in time: 제 시간에, 늦지 않게
❸ take: 시간이 걸리다

Wrap Up

B: Here comes the bus!
G: ❶Oh, but first I have to finish drinking my tea.
B: ❷Why don't you just take it with you? ❸I'm sure that it will be okay if you are careful.
G: No. If the bus stops suddenly. I may spill it.
B: ❹Okay, then I can just wait for you to finish your drink. I'm sure another bus will come soon.
G: Thanks.

❶ finish는 동명사를 목적어로 취한다.
❷ Why don't you ~?: ~하는 게 어때?
❸ I'm sure that ~.: 나는 ~라고 확신한다.
❹ wait for+목적어+to부정사: …가 ~하는 것을 기다리다

● 다음 우리말과 일치하도록 빈칸에 알맞은 말을 쓰시오.

Listen & Speak 1 Listen

1. **B:** We _____ _____ _____ _____ for bees.
   G: Oh, there are bees. Run!
2. **G:** Can we go this way? It _____ _____.
   B: No. We have to go straight if we want _____ _____ the top.
3. **B:** Oh, the stairs are _____.
   G: Then we _____ _____ _____ _____ the stairs slowly.
4. **G:** _____ _____ some more. I want to reach the _____ of the mountain.
   B: First we _____ _____ _____ the weather. Oh, it says it's _____ _____ _____. We _____ go down.

Listen & Speak 1 A

1. **G:** Mom, can I _____ _____ this afternoon?
   W: Sure. _____ _____ _____ put on sunscreen before you go out.
   G: But it's _____ today. Do I _____ _____ _____ _____ sunscreen?
   W: Yes, you have to _____ sunscreen _____ _____.
   G: Okay. Then I'll _____ some _____ now.
2. **B:** Let's _____ _____.
   G: I'm sorry, I can't. I have to _____ _____ _____ _____.
   B: Oh, what's _____?
   G: I don't know, but my stomach _____.

Listen & Speak 2 Listen

1. **M:** Don't run. You _____ _____.
   B: Okay, I _____ _____.
2. **B:** Jumping _____ cold water _____ _____ _____ can be dangerous.
   G: Oh, okay. I will warm up.
3. **G:** Mom, I want _____ _____ here.
   W: Okay, but first you should check _____ _____ _____ _____ _____. It may be _____ _____ you think.
4. **B:** Can I swim _____ after eating?
   G: Swimming _____ a full stomach can be _____.

Listen & Speak 2 A

1. **M:** Flooding _____ _____ big problems. However, you may not know _____ _____ _____ when it happens. There are several things you _____ _____ _____. First, you _____ _____ _____ _____ the water and the electricity. Second, _____ water and food when you leave the house. _____, you have to move to a high and _____ _____ and _____ _____ _____ the weather report.

2. **B:** Mina, are you _____ _____ leave?
   G: No, not _____. I have to check _____ I _____ _____ _____ the gas.
   B: If we don't leave now, we _____ _____ _____ _____ the concert _____ _____.
   G: Okay, but I _____ _____ _____ the gas first. It will only take a minute.

Real-Life Zone

B: Uncle John, _____ _____ my new bike. _____ do you _____?
M: It's really nice. Where _____ you _____?
B: To the park _____ _____ a friend.
M: Where's your helmet?
B: I don't have _____. It's just a _____ _____.
M: _____ _____ your helmet. You may hurt _____.
B: But I see a lot of people _____ bikes _____ helmets.
M: You _____ _____ _____ a helmet. It _____ your head in an accident.
B: Okay. I'll get my dad's helmet.
M: No. You have to wear a helmet that _____ you. If _____, it cannot protect your head.
B: I guess I'll _____ _____ _____ one for myself.

Wrap Up

B: Here comes the bus!
G: Oh, but first I have to _____ _____ my tea.
B: _____ _____ you just take it with you? I'm _____ _____ it will be okay if you are careful.
G: No. If the bus stops _____, I _____ _____ it.
B: Okay, then I can just _____ _____ you to finish your drink. I'm sure _____ will come soon.
G: Thanks.

해석

1. **M:** 홍수는 큰 문제들을 일으킬 수 있습니다. 그러나, 당신은 홍수가 발생할 때 무엇을 해야 하는지 모를 수도 있습니다. 당신이 해야 하는 몇 가지 것들이 있습니다. 첫째, 수도와 전기를 꺼야 합니다. 둘째, 집을 떠날 때 물과 음식을 꾸려야 합니다. 마지막으로, 높고 안전한 곳으로 이동하여 일기 예보를 계속 들어야 합니다.

2. **B:** 미나야, 떠날 준비됐니?
   G: 아니, 아직. 가스를 껐는지 확인해야 해.
   B: 만약 우리가 지금 떠나지 않으면, 제 시간에 콘서트에 도착하지 못할 수도 있어.
   G: 알았어. 하지만 나는 우선 가스를 확인해야 해. 잠깐이면 될 거야.

B: 존 삼촌. 제 새로운 자전거 좀 보세요. 어떻게 생각하세요?
M: 아주 멋지구나. 어디를 가고 있니?
B: 친구 만나러 공원에요.
M: 네 헬멧이 어디 있니?
B: 저는 헬멧이 없어요. 그냥 잠깐 타는 거예요.
M: 헬멧을 쓰렴. 다칠 수 있단다.
B: 하지만 저는 헬멧 없이 자전거를 타는 많은 사람들을 봐요.
M: 너는 헬멧을 써야만 한단다. 그것은 사고가 났을 때 네 머리를 보호해 줘.
B: 알았어요. 아빠의 헬멧을 가져올게요.
M: 아니. 너는 네게 맞는 헬멧을 써야 해. 그렇지 않으면 그것은 네 머리를 보호해 줄 수 없어.
B: 저를 위한 헬멧을 사야겠어요.

B: 버스가 온다!
G: 오, 그렇지만 나는 우선 차 마시는 것을 끝내야 해.
B: 그냥 그것을 가지고 타는 것은 어때? 네가 조심한다면 괜찮을 거라고 확신해.
G: 아니, 만약 버스가 갑자기 멈춘다면, 나는 차를 흘릴 수도 있어.
B: 알았어, 그러면 난 네가 음료를 다 마실 때까지 기다릴 수 있어. 곧 다른 버스가 올 것이라고 확신해.
G: 고마워.

01 다음 대화의 밑줄 친 말의 의도로 알맞은 것은?

> A: Oh, the stairs are wet.
> B: Then we have to walk down the stairs slowly.

① 강조하기　　　② 요청하기　　　③ 의무 표현하기
④ 오해 지적하기　　⑤ 가능성 표현하기

02 다음 대화가 자연스럽게 이어지도록 순서대로 배열하시오.

> (A) Oh, what's wrong?
> (B) Let's go bowling.
> (C) I don't know, but my stomach hurts.
> (D) I'm sorry, I can't. I have to go see a doctor.

➡ _____

[03~04] 다음 대화를 읽고, 물음에 답하시오.

> B: Mina, are you ready to leave?
> G: No, not yet. I have to check ___(A)___ I turned off the gas.
> B: If we don't leave now, (B)우리는 제 시간에 콘서트에 도착하지 못할 수도 있어.(in, may, to)
> G: Okay, but I have to check the gas first. It will only take a minute.

03 위 대화의 빈칸 (A)에 알맞은 것은?

① that　　　　② if　　　　③ which
④ what　　　　⑤ who

04 위 대화의 밑줄 친 (B)의 우리말을 주어진 단어를 이용하여 영어로 쓰시오.

➡ _____

[01~04] 다음 대화를 읽고 물음에 답하시오.

B: Uncle John, look at my new bike. What do you think?

M: It's really nice. Where are you going?

B: To the park to meet a friend. (①)

M: Where's your helmet?

B: I don't have one. It's just a short ride. (②)

M: _____(A)_____ your helmet. You may hurt yourself.

B: But I see a lot of people riding bikes without helmets. (③)

M: You have to wear a helmet. (④)

B: Okay. I'll get my dad's helmet. (⑤)

M: No. You _____(B)_____ wear a helmet that fits you. If not, it cannot protect your head.

B: I guess I'll have to buy one for myself.

01 위 대화의 ①~⑤ 중 주어진 문장이 들어갈 알맞은 것은?

> It protects your head in an accident.

①   ②   ③   ④   ⑤

서답형
02 위 대화의 빈칸 (A)에 알맞은 말을 두 단어로 쓰시오.

➡ _____

03 위 대화의 빈칸 (B)에 알맞은 말을 <u>모두</u> 고르시오.

① can   ② should

③ might   ④ need to

⑤ have to

04 위 대화를 읽고 답할 수 <u>없는</u> 질문은?

① What does Uncle John think about the boy's new bike?

② Where is the boy going?

③ Does the boy have his own helmet?

④ Why is the boy going to the park?

⑤ When will the boy buy his helmet?

[05~07] 다음 대화를 읽고 물음에 답하시오.

G: Mom, can I play outside this afternoon?

B: Sure. _____(A)_____ sunscreen before you go out.

G: But it's cloudy today. (B)제가 선크림을 발라야 하나요? (have, put)

W: Yes, you have to wear sunscreen every day.

G: Okay. Then I'll put (C)some on now.

05 위 대화의 빈칸 (A)에 들어갈 말로 알맞은 것은?

① Remember to remove

② Make sure that you bring

③ Don't forget to put on

④ Be careful not to wear

⑤ Don't forget wearing

서답형
06 위 대화의 밑줄 친 (B)의 우리말을 주어진 단어를 이용하여 영어로 쓰시오.

➡ _____

서답형
07 위 대화의 밑줄 친 (C)가 가리키는 것을 쓰시오.

➡ _____

[08~10] 다음 대화를 읽고 물음에 답하시오.

> B: Here comes the bus!
> G: Oh, but first I have to finish drinking my tea.
> B: Why don't you just take it with you? I'm sure that it will be okay if you are careful.
> G: No. If the bus stops suddenly, I __(A)__ spill it.
> B: Okay, then I can just wait for you to finish your drink. I'm sure another bus will come soon.
> G: Thanks.

08 위 대화의 빈칸 (A)에 알맞은 것은?

① may ② will
③ must ④ should
⑤ have to

서답형

09 위 대화에서 다음 영영풀이에 해당하는 단어를 찾아 쓰시오

> to cause or allow something to fall, flow, or run over the edge of a container usually in an accidental way

➡ _____

10 위 대화의 내용과 일치하지 않는 것은?

① They are waiting for the bus.
② The girl is drinking tea.
③ The girl will take her tea and get on the bus.
④ The girl thinks she may spill her tea in the bus.
⑤ They decided to take the next bus.

11 다음 짝지어진 대화 중 어색한 것은?

① A: You have to check the weather.
  B: Okay, I will.
② A: Can I swim right after eating?
  B: Swimming with a full stomach can be comfortable.
③ A: Don't run. You may fall.
  B: Okay, I won't run.
④ A: Jumping into cold water without warming up can be dangerous.
  B: Oh, okay. I will warm up.
⑤ A: Do we have to close the windows before leaving?
  B: Yes, we have. The rain may start to pour.

[12~14] 다음 대화를 읽고 물음에 답하시오.

> B: (A)Let's go bowling.
> G: I'm sorry, I can't. (B)나는 병원에 가야 하거든.(see, have, doctor)
> B: Oh, what's wrong?
> G: I don't know, but my stomach hurts.

서답형

12 위 대화의 밑줄 친 (A)를 다음과 같이 바꿔 쓸 때 빈칸에 알맞은 말을 쓰시오.

> _____ _____ _____ go bowling?

서답형

13 위 대화의 밑줄 친 (B)의 우리말을 주어진 단어를 이용하여 영어로 쓰시오. (7 words)

➡ _____

서답형

14 Why does the girl have to go to the hospital? Answer in English. (4 words)

➡ _____

01 다음 대화가 자연스럽게 이어지도록 순서대로 배열하시오.

> (A) Mina, are you ready to leave?
> (B) If we don't leave now, we may not get to the concert in time.
> (C) Okay, but I have to check the gas first. It will only take a minute.
> (D) No, not yet. I have to check if I turned off the gas.

➡ _____

[02~04] 다음 대화를 읽고 물음에 답하시오.

B: Here comes the bus!
G: Oh, but first 나는 내 차 마시는 것을 끝내야 해.
B: Why don't you just take it with you? I'm sure that it will be okay (A)[if / that] you are careful.
G: No. If the bus (B)[stops / will stop] suddenly, I may spill it.
B: Okay, then I can just wait for you to finish your drink. I'm sure (C)[other / another] bus will come soon.
G: Thanks.

02 위 대화의 밑줄 친 우리말을 주어진 단어를 이용하여 영어로 쓰시오. (7 words)

> (to / my / I / drink / tea / finish)

➡ _____

03 위 대화의 괄호 (A)~(C)에서 알맞은 것을 골라 쓰시오.

(A) _____ (B) _____ (C) _____

04 위 대화의 내용에 맞게 다음 빈칸에 알맞은 말을 쓰시오.

> After the talk, the boy will _____ until the girl _____ her tea.

[05~07] 다음 대화를 읽고 물음에 답하시오.

B: Uncle John, look at my new bike. What do you think?
M: It's really nice. Where are you going?
B: ___(A)___ the park to meet a friend.
M: Where's your helmet?
B: I don't have one. It's just a short ride.
M: Put ___(B)___ your helmet. You may hurt yourself.
B: But I see a lot of people riding bikes without helmets.
M: You have to wear a helmet. It protects your head in an accident.
B: Okay. I'll get my dad's helmet.
M: No. (C)너는 네게 맞는 헬멧을 써야 해. If not, it cannot protect your head.
B: I guess I'll have to buy (D)one for myself.

05 위 대화의 빈칸 (A)와 (B)에 알맞은 말을 쓰시오.

(A) _____ (B) _____

06 위 대화의 밑줄 친 (C)의 우리말을 주어진 단어를 모두 배열하여 영작하시오.

> (a / you / that / you / helmet / to / fits / wear / have)

➡ _____

07 위 대화의 밑줄 친 (D)가 가리키는 것을 쓰시오.

➡ _____

Grammar

① 접속사 although

> - **Although** camping trips can create sweet memories for many people, they can also be occasions when bad things happen.
>   캠핑 여행은 많은 사람들에게 좋은 추억을 만들어 주기도 하지만, 나쁜 일이 일어나는 때가 될 수도 있습니다.

- although는 '비록 ~이지만'의 뜻으로 종속절을 이끈다.

  - **Although** I am not good at English, I love studying it.
    나는 영어를 잘 못하지만, 영어 공부하는 것을 아주 좋아한다.
    = I love studying English **although** I am not good at it.

- although 대신 though, even though, even if를 쓸 수 있다.

  - **Even though** dinosaurs were large, no dinosaur was over 165 feet long.
    비록 공룡은 거대했지만, 어떤 공룡도 165피트 이상으로 길지는 않았다.
  - **Though** the teacher was patient, he was hurt by the student's behavior.
    그 교사는 참을성이 있었지만, 그 학생의 행동에 상처받았다.
  - **Even if** you don't like cheesecake, try a piece of this.
    설령 네가 치즈케이크를 싫어한다 하더라도, 이것을 한 조각 먹어 봐라.

- 부사절을 이끄는 although, though, even though, even if는 접속사를 중심으로 앞뒤 내용이 대조적 의미를 갖는다.

  - **Although** Annie is not tall, she wants to be a model.
    비록 Annie는 키가 크지 않지만, 모델이 되고 싶어 한다.

- even though 뒤에는 이미 일어난 일이나 현실에 대한 사실을 말하는 문장이 오고, even if 뒤에는 명확한 사실이 아니거나 아직 일어나지 않은 일을 가정하는 문장이 온다.

  - I like her, **even though** she can be annoying at times. 가끔 짜증낼 수도 있지만 난 그녀를 좋아해.
  - I've got to get home **even if** it means flying the plane myself.
    내가 직접 비행기를 조종하게 되더라도 난 집에 가야 한다.

- although와 같은 뜻을 지닌 전치사로 despite(~임에도 불구하고)가 있다. despite은 전치사이므로 바로 뒤에 명사가 이어진다.

  - **Despite** the opposition, the policy was changed. 반대에도 불구하고 정책이 바뀌었습니다.

핵심 Check

1. 다음 괄호 안에서 알맞은 것을 고르시오.

   (1) I wasn't late for school (because / although) I got up late.
   (2) Even though Samantha (to eat / eats) almost all vegetables, she doesn't eat cucumbers.

② seem to

- They **seem to** know what to do to make their camping trip safe and fun.
그들은 그들의 캠핑 여행을 안전하고 재미있게 만들기 위해 무엇을 해야 하는지 알고 있는 것 같습니다.

- You **seem to** be a little busy these days. 요즘 너는 약간 바빠 보이는구나.

■ '주어+seem+to부정사'의 형태로 쓰인다.

- Two friends **seem to** like each other. 두 친구들은 서로를 좋아하는 것처럼 보인다.

■ 부정은 '주어 don't/didn't seem to부정사'이다.

- She doesn't **seem to** be OK. 그녀는 괜찮아 보이지 않아.

- They didn't **seem to** have a good idea. 그들은 좋은 생각을 갖고 있는 것 같지 않았다.

■ it을 써서 'It seems/seemed that+주어+동사' 구문으로 바꿔 쓸 수 있다. 이 때 seem to의 동사 시제가 현재인지 과거인지에 따라 'It seems/seemed that절' 구문으로 변환 시 that절 안의 동사의 시제를 일치 시켜 주어야 한다.

- The teacher **seems to** understand me. 선생님은 나를 이해하는 것처럼 보인다.
  = **It seems that** the teacher understands me.

- The teacher **seemed to** understand me. 선생님은 나를 이해하는 것처럼 보였다.
  = **It seemed that** the teacher understood me.

■ '주어+seem/seems/seemed+완료부정사(to have+과거분사)'는 that절 안의 동사의 시제가 앞설 경우이다.

- He **seems to have been** rich when he was young.
  = **It seems that he was** rich when he was young.
  그는 젊었을 때 부자였던 것처럼 보인다. (지금 그가 과거에 부자였던 것처럼 보이는 것을 의미한다.)

- He **seemed to have been** rich.
  = **It seemed that he had been** rich.
  그는 부자였던 것처럼 보였었다. (예전에 그가 부자였던 것처럼 과거에 그렇게 보였던 것을 의미한다.)

핵심 Check

2. 다음 문장을 it을 이용하여 바꿔 쓰시오.

(1) You seem to dance very well.

   ➡ _____

(2) Sara seems to like you

   ➡ _____

(3) You seem to be angry.

   ➡ _____

01 다음 문장에서 어법상 <u>어색한</u> 부분을 바르게 고쳐 쓰시오.

(1) Besides Yumin is famous in Korea, many Americans do not know her.

_____ ➡ _____

(2) Although Maria is almost 50, she seems to is 30 years old.

_____ ➡ _____

(3) You seem to enjoying playing computer games.

_____ ➡ _____

(4) It seems to Mina disagrees with the suggestion.

_____ ➡ _____

02 두 문장을 한 문장으로 쓰시오. (접속사 even though를 사용할 것)

> • I have a lot to do.
> • I am doing nothing.

➡ _____

➡ _____

03 be가 들어갈 곳으로 적절한 곳을 고르시오.

> • That car ① seems ② to ③ new because ④ there ⑤ are no scratches on it.

04 다음 우리말에 맞게 주어진 단어를 활용하여 영작하시오.

(1) 이 컵은 아름답지만 옆에 금이 가 있다. (even though, beautiful, crack)

➡ _____

➡ _____

(2) Rose는 잠자리에 늦게 든 것처럼 보였다. (seem)

➡ _____

➡ _____

(3) Alex는 요즘 우울한 것처럼 보인다. (seem, depressed)

➡ _____

➡ _____

서답형

01 다음 문장에서 어법상 틀린 부분을 찾아 바르게 고쳐 쓰시오.

> Despite it was pretty cold, the girl wasn't wearing a jacket.

_____ ➡ _____

02 다음 빈칸에 공통으로 들어갈 말로 알맞은 것을 고르시오.

> • It seems _____ Jay knows the answer.
> • It seems _____ he is leaving soon.

① with　　　　② at
③ to　　　　④ in
⑤ that

서답형

03 괄호 안의 단어와 조건을 참고하여 우리말에 맞게 영작하시오.

(1) 그는 외로워 보인다. (lonely)
➡ (to부정사 사용) _____
➡ (It seems/seemed that 사용)
_____

(2) 그녀는 행복해 보인다. (happy)
➡ (to부정사 사용) _____
➡ (It seems/seemed that 사용)
_____

(3) Sally는 바쁜 것 같아 보인다. (in a hurry)
➡ (to부정사 사용) _____
➡ (It seems/seemed that 사용)
_____

(4) 컴퓨터가 전혀 작동하지 않는 것처럼 보였다.
(work, at)
➡ (It seems/seemed that 사용)
_____

중요

04 다음 중 어색한 문장을 고르시오.

① My father seems to be angry.
② It seems that they will get back soon.
③ Kidson doesn't seem like her new hairstyle.
④ He doesn't seem to have any plans.
⑤ It seems that she misses her family.

05 다음 문장을 뜻이 같은 문장으로 바르게 고쳐 쓴 것을 고르시오.

> It seems that he was very busy.

① He seems to have been busy.
② He doesn't seem to be busy.
③ He didn't seem to be busy.
④ He seemed to be busy.
⑤ It seemed that he wasn't busy.

06 다음 빈칸에 들어갈 말로 적절한 것은?

> _____ he's ninety, his mental faculties remain unimpaired.
> *faculty: 기능, *unimpaired: 손상되지 않은

① Although　　　② Because
③ Due to　　　④ However
⑤ Despite

07 다음 중 빈칸에 공통으로 들어갈 단어로 알맞은 것을 고르시오. (대·소문자 무시)

> • Even _____ you run, you'll still be late.
>
> • _____ it may sound strange, I was pleased the game was over.

① though   ② although   ③ so
④ if   ⑤ that

서답형

08 although로 시작하고, 괄호 안의 단어를 활용하여 영작하시오.

(1) 많이 시끄러웠지만 아기는 깨지 않았다.
   (a loud noise, wake up)
   ➡ _____
   _____

(2) 그는 영화를 싫어하지만 여자 친구를 즐겁게 해 주기 위해 그녀와 함께 영화를 보러 갔다.
   (dislike, go, movies, please)
   ➡ _____
   _____

중요

09 다음 두 문장의 의미가 같지 <u>않은</u> 것은?

① They seem to know what to do to make their camping trip safe.
   = It seems that they know what to do to make their camping trip safe.

② They seem to have known what to do to make their camping trip safe.
   = It seems that they knew what to do to make their camping trip safe.

③ They seemed to know what to do to make their camping trip safe.
   = It seemed that they knew what to do to make their camping trip safe.

④ They seemed to have known what to do to make their camping trip safe.

= It seemed that they have known what to do to make their camping trip safe.

⑤ They seem to be a little busy these days.
   = It seems that they are a little busy these days.

서답형

10 다음 괄호 안에서 알맞은 것을 고르시오.

(1) They seem (to be / being) close friends.
(2) It seems (that / to be) she likes him.

11 다음 문장의 빈칸에 알맞은 말은?

> Harry and Catherine _____ to love each other.

① seem like   ② seems
③ seem   ④ look
⑤ looks

서답형

12 종속절과 주절 간에 대조적 의미를 담고 있는 부분을 찾으시오.

(1) Although she is three years old, she can read and write.
   ➡ 종속절: _____
   ➡ 주절: _____

(2) I think they're fantastic, even though they haven't won any games this season.
   ➡ 종속절: _____
   ➡ 주절: _____

(3) You're still going to be cold even if you put on two or three jumpers.
   ➡ 종속절: _____
   ➡ 주절: _____

13 다음 빈칸에 들어갈 말로 알맞은 것은?

> He seems to _____ an honest man.

① be   ② is
③ been   ④ was
⑤ being

14 다음 우리말을 옮긴 것으로 알맞은 것을 <u>모두</u> 고르시오.

> 돈이 많았지만 나는 행복하지 않았다.

① Although I had much money, I was not happy.
② Though I had much money, I was not happy.
③ I had much money although I was not happy.
④ I had much money though I was not happy.
⑤ Although I hadn't much money, I am happy.

15 다음 빈칸에 들어갈 말로 바르게 짝지어진 것을 고르시오.

> • _____ seems that she worries about everything.
> • Kevin seems _____ like his new school.
> • The children seemed to _____ hungry.

① She – that – was   ② She – that – be
③ It – to – be   ④ It – that – be
⑤ It – to – was

16 다음 문장을 같은 뜻으로 바꿔 쓸 때 <u>어색한</u> 것을 <u>모두</u> 고르시오.

① The jacket seems to have a hidden pocket.
= It seems that the jacket had a hidden pocket.
② You seem to have a fever.
= It seems that you have a fever
③ I seem to have picked up the wrong set of keys.
= It seemed that I had picked up the wrong set of keys.
④ You seem to know a lot of these rumors.
= It seems that you know a lot of these rumors.
⑤ He doesn't seem to agree with this suggestion.
= It doesn't seem that he agrees with this suggestion.

17 우리말에 맞게 괄호 안의 어휘들을 배열하여 영작할 때, 주어진 조건에 맞게 쓰시오.

(1) 5번째, 8번째 단어를 쓰시오.
• 그는 부자라 하더라도, 나는 그와 결혼하지 않을 거야. (he, rich, is, though, even, him, not, I will, marry)

➡ _____

(2) 4번째 단어를 쓰시오.
• 난 감기에 걸린 것 같아. (have, seem, I, to, cold, a)

➡ _____

(3) 4번째 단어를 쓰시오.
• 난 무언가 잊어버린 것 같아. (something, have, I, forgotten, to, seem)

➡ _____

(4) 8번째 단어를 쓰시오
• 악천후에도 불구하고 그들은 동물원에서 즐거운 하루를 보냈다. (enjoyed, day, their, they, the, despite, at, zoo, weather, the, bad)

➡ _____

Grammar 서술형 시험대비

01 우리말에 맞게 괄호 안의 단어를 활용하여 빈칸을 채우시오.

(1) 그들은 항상 우는 것 같아. (cry all the time)

➡ They _____ .

➡ It _____ .

(2) 그녀가 나쁜 남자들하고 어울려 다니는 것 같아.
(get along with, guys)

➡ She _____ .

➡ It _____ .

(3) 너는 그 영화를 재미있게 보는 것 같지 않았다.
(enjoy)

➡ You _____ .

(4) 올해에는 아무것도 그 팀을 멈추지 못할 듯이
보였다. (nothing, this year)

➡ It _____
_____ .

(5) 그녀는 실망한 것처럼 보였다.

➡ It _____ .

02 괄호 안의 단어와 조건을 보고 문장을 완성하시오.

(1) 그는 아픈 것 같다. (ill)

➡ (to부정사 사용) _____

➡ (It seems/seemed that 사용)
_____

(2) 그들은 무엇이든지 알고 있는 것 같다.
(know everything)

➡ (to부정사 사용) _____

➡ (It seems/seemed that 사용)
_____

(3) 그는 거기에 없었던 것 같다. (there)

➡ (It seems/seemed that 사용)
_____

(4) 그는 독살된 것 같다. (poison)

➡ (It seems/seemed that 사용)
_____

03 그림을 참고하여 우리말과 같도록 괄호 안의 단어를 활용하여 영작하시오.

차량 충돌 사고가 있었지만, 인명 피해는 없었다.
(although, crash, be lost)

➡ _____
_____

04 다음 그림을 참고하고 괄호 안의 단어를 사용하여 문장을 완성하시오.

(seem, enjoy themselves)

➡ They _____ .

05 to부정사를 활용하여 문장을 완성하시오.

(1) 그녀는 피곤해 보여.
➡ She _____ tired.

(2) 그들은 좋은 아이디어가 있는 것 같아.
➡ They _____ a good idea.

(3) 너는 경제학에 대해 많이 알고 있는 것 같다.
➡ You _____ a lot about economics.

(4) 난 선글라스를 제자리에 두지 않은 것 같아.
➡ I _____ misplaced my sunglasses.

06 'It seems/seemed that'을 활용하여 문장을 완성하시오.

(1) 나는 그녀에게 친절하지 못했던 것 같다.
➡ _____ I was unkind to her.

(2) 이것은 큰 문제인 것 같다.
➡ _____ this is a big problem.

07 다음 문장을 같은 뜻으로 바꿔 쓰시오.

(1) She seems to have been angry last night.
➡ _____

(2) It seems that he fell in love with the girl.
➡ _____

08 그림에 맞게 괄호 안의 단어를 활용하여 5 단어로 영작하시오.

(seem, cold)

➡ It _____ .

09 괄호 안의 단어를 활용하여 우리말에 맞게 영작하시오.

(1) 비가 내렸지만 그들은 밖에서 축구를 했다.
(although, rain, it, soccer)
➡ _____
_____

(2) 내 남동생은 음식을 먹었지만 여전히 배가 고팠다.
(eat, younger, be)
➡ _____
_____
_____

(3) 어젯밤 잠을 많이 못 잤는데도 피곤하지 않다.
(although, sleep, be)
➡ _____
_____
_____

(4) 그녀는 바빴지만, 절대 도움을 요청하려고 하지 않았다. (although, would, ask for)
➡ _____
_____
_____

10 though와 괄호 안의 단어를 활용하여 우리말에 맞게 빈칸을 채우시오.

나는 그를 좋아하지 않지만, 그가 좋은 매너를 가졌다는 건 인정해. (like, agree)

➡ _____ I _____ _____ him, I _____ that he has good manners. 또는 I _____ that he has good manners _____ I _____ _____ him.

Safe Camping

Although camping trips can create sweet memories for many people,
양보의 부사절을 이끄는 접속사
they can also be occasions when bad things happen. If you plan to go
= camping trips   선행사 occasions를 수식하는 관계부사
camping with family or friends this summer, you need to keep several
                                            to부정사의 명사적 용법
things in mind for your safety.

Listen to Yumin's family talk about their camping trip. They seem to
목적보어(원형부정사)   ~인 것처럼 보인다
know what to do to make their camping trip safe and fun.
= what they should do   목적보어

Yumin: Dad, why don't we put up our tent over here by this river?
우리 ~하는 게 어때요?   이쪽 강 옆에

Dad: I don't think that's a good idea. If it starts to rain, the river might
                                                        = may(~일지도 모른다)
overflow.

Yumin: I know, but the sky is clear. I really like the sound of the water!

Dad: The weather can change quickly in the mountains. You never

know when it might start to rain.
간접의문문(know의 목적어)

Yumin: Okay. Safety first! Let's find another place.
another+단수명사

When you set up a tent, choose a flat, sunny area. Avoid places too

close to big trees that might be struck by lightning.
= which   조동사가 있는 수동태

Hajun: Mom, I'm hungry. What's for lunch?

Mom: I'm cooking Samgyepsal.

---

safe 안전한
create 만들다, 창조하다
memory 추억
occasion 때, 경우
happen (사건 등이) 일어나다
keep ~ in mind ~을 명심하다
safety 안전
fun 재미있는
put up (텐트 등을) 치다, 세우다
overflow 범람하다
sound 소리, 음
weather 날씨
flat 평평한
sunny 햇볕이 잘 드는
avoid 피하다
strike 치다
lightning 번개

📎 **확인문제**

● 다음 문장이 본문의 내용과 일치하면 T, 일치하지 않으면 F를 쓰시오.

1 Bad things cannot happen when we go camping. ☐

2 There are several things to remember when you go camping. ☐

3 Yumin wants to put up a tent by the river. ☐

4 It is a good idea to put up a tent by the river. ☐

5 When we set up a tent, we should choose a flat, sunny area. ☐

Hajun: Mom, that's not enough for all of us. Can we cook <u>more</u> in a bigger pan?

Mom: I'm going to cook more, but we <u>have to</u> use this small pan.

Hajun: Why do we have to use a small pan?

Mom: Because the pan should not be bigger than the burner. If you use a big pan, it <u>sends the heat back</u> to the burner, and the gas can <u>explode</u>!

Hajun: Oh, I didn't know <u>that</u>.

Here is one more tip about fire when you go camping. Never use a gas heater or burner inside a tent. Your tent may catch fire, or you <u>might</u> pass out because the fire will use up the oxygen in the tent <u>as</u> it burns.

Yumin: Ouch! Mosquitoes!

Mom: Oh, I <u>forgot</u> to tell you to apply some bug spray. Here.

Yumin: Thanks, Mom. Oh, <u>you know what?</u> We can rub orange peels on our skin instead of <u>applying</u> bug spray. It is a nature-friendly way <u>to keep</u> mosquitoes away.

Mom: That's interesting!

Garlic can also keep bugs away. You can place <u>pieces of</u> garlic at the entrance to the tent, <u>and</u> bugs will not come inside.

pick 고르기, 선택	
enough 충분한	
pan 팬, 냄비	
burner 버너	
send back ~을 다시 돌려보내다	
explode 폭발하다	
tip 팁, 조언	
inside ~ 안에서	
catch fire 불이 붙다	
pass out 의식을 잃다	
use up ~을 다 쓰다	
oxygen 산소	
burn 타다	
ouch 앗	
mosquito 모기	
apply 바르다, 뿌리다	
bug 벌레, 곤충	
spary 스프레이	
nature-friendly 자연 친화적인	
keep away ~을 접근하지 못하게 하다	
garlic 마늘	
entrance 입구	

확인문제

● 다음 문장이 본문의 내용과 일치하면 T, 일치하지 <u>않으면</u> F를 쓰시오.

1 Hajun wanted his mom to cook more in a bigger pan. ☐

2 Hajun's mom will cook more in a bigger pan. ☐

3 The pan should not be bigger than the burner. ☐

4 It is dangerous to use a gas heater or burner inside a tent. ☐

5 We must not apply some bug spray. ☐

6 We can rub orange peels on our skin to keep mosquitoes away. ☐

● 우리말을 참고하여 빈칸에 알맞은 말을 쓰시오.

Safe Camping

1 Although camping trips can _____ sweet _____ for many people, they can also be occasions _____ bad things _____.

2 If you _____ _____ go camping with family or friends this summer, you _____ to keep several things _____ _____ for your safety.

3 Listen to Yumin's family _____ about their _____ _____.

4 They _____ to know _____ _____ do to make their camping trip _____ and fun.

5 Yumin: Dad, _____ _____ we _____ _____ our tent over here _____ this river?

6 Dad: I don't _____ that's a good _____.

7 If it _____ _____ rain, the river _____ overflow.

8 Yumin: I know, _____ the sky is _____.

9 I really like the _____ of the water!

10 Dad: The _____ can _____ quickly in the mountains.

11 You _____ know _____ it _____ start to rain.

12 Yumin: Okay. _____ first! Let's find _____ place.

13 When you _____ _____ a tent, _____ a flat, sunny area.

14 _____ places too _____ to big trees that might _____ _____ by lightning.

15 Hajun: Mom, I'm _____. What's _____ lunch?

16 Mom: I'm _____ Samgyepsal.

17 Hajun: Mom, that's not _____ for _____ of us. Can we cook _____ in a bigger pan?

안전한 캠핑

1 캠핑 여행이 많은 사람들에게 좋은 추억을 만들어 주기도 하지만, 나쁜 일이 일어나는 때가 될 수도 있습니다.

2 여러분이 이번 여름에 가족이나 친구들과 함께 캠핑을 하려고 계획하고 있다면, 여러분은 여러분의 안전을 위해서 몇 가지 사항을 명심해야 합니다.

3 유민이의 가족이 그들의 캠핑 여행에 대해 이야기하는 것을 들어 보세요.

4 그들은 그들의 캠핑 여행이 안전하고 재미있게 하기 위해 무엇을 해야 하는지 알고 있는 것 같습니다.

5 유민: 아빠, 이 강 근처 이쪽에 텐트를 치면 어때요?

6 아빠: 그건 좋은 생각 같지 않구나.

7 만약 비가 내리기 시작하면, 강이 범람할지도 몰라.

8 유민: 저도 알아요. 하지만 하늘이 맑잖아요.

9 저는 물소리를 정말 좋아한단 말이에요!

10 아빠: 산속의 날씨는 곧 바뀔 수 있어.

11 언제 비가 올지 절대 알 수 없는 일이지.

12 유민: 알겠어요. 안전이 우선이지요! 다른 곳을 찾아봐요.

13 텐트를 칠 때는 평평하고 햇볕이 잘 드는 장소를 고르세요.

14 번개를 맞을지도 모르는 키 큰 나무에 너무 가까운 장소는 피해야 합니다.

15 하준: 엄마, 저 배고파요. 점심이 뭐예요?

16 엄마: 삼겹살을 요리하고 있단다.

17 하준: 엄마, 그건 우리 모두가 먹기에 충분하지 않아요. 우리 더 큰 팬에 더 많이 요리하면 안 돼요?

18 Mom: I'm _____ _____ cook more, but we _____ _____ use this small pan.

19 Hajun: _____ do we _____ to use a small pan?

20 Mom: _____ the pan _____ _____ be bigger than the burner.

21 _____ you use a big pan, it _____ the heat _____ to the burner, and the gas can _____!

22 Hajun: Oh, I didn't _____ that.

23 _____ is one more _____ about fire _____ you go camping.

24 _____ use a gas heater or burner _____ a tent.

25 Your tent _____ catch fire, _____ you might _____ out because the fire will _____ up the _____ in the tent as it burns.

26 Yumin: Ouch! Mosquitoes!

27 Mom: Oh, I _____ _____ tell you to _____ some bug spray. Here.

28 Yumin: Thanks, Mom. Oh, you know _____?

29 We can _____ orange peels _____ our skin _____ of _____ bug spray.

30 It is a nature-friendly way _____ _____ mosquitoes _____.

31 Mom: That's _____!

32 Garlic can also _____ bugs _____.

33 You can place _____ _____ garlic at the _____ to the tent, and bugs will not _____ _____.

18 엄마: 더 굽긴 할 거야. 하지만 우리는 이 작은 팬을 써야 해.

19 하준: 왜 우리는 작은 팬을 써야 하죠?

20 엄마: 왜냐하면 팬이 버너보다 더 크면 안 되기 때문이야.

21 만약 큰 팬을 사용하면, 팬이 열을 버너로 다시 돌려보내서, 가스가 폭발할 수 있어!

22 하준: 오, 그것은 몰랐어요.

23 캠핑할 때 불을 사용하는 것에 대한 또 하나의 팁이 있습니다.

24 텐트 안에서 가스난로나 버너를 절대 쓰지 마세요.

25 여러분의 텐트에 불이 붙거나, 불이 타면서 텐트 내 산소를 다 써 버려서 여러분이 의식을 잃을 수도 있습니다.

26 유민: 앗! 모기!

27 엄마: 아, 벌레 퇴치 스프레이를 뿌리라고 네게 말하는 걸 잊었구나. 여기 있단다.

28 유민: 고마워요, 엄마. 아, 그거 아세요?

29 벌레 퇴치 스프레이를 뿌리는 것 대신에 오렌지 껍질을 피부에 문질러도 돼요.

30 모기가 접근하지 못하게 하는 자연 친화적인 방법이에요.

31 엄마: 그거 재미있구나!

32 마늘 또한 벌레가 접근하지 못하게 막을 수 있습니다.

33 마늘 조각을 텐트 입구에 놓아두면, 벌레가 안으로 들어오지 않을 것입니다.

● 우리말을 참고하여 본문을 영작하시오.

Safe Camping

1 캠핑 여행이 많은 사람들에게 좋은 추억을 만들어 주기도 하지만, 나쁜 일이 일어나는 때가 될 수도 있습니다.

➡ _____

2 여러분이 이번 여름에 가족이나 친구들과 함께 캠핑을 하려고 계획하고 있다면, 여러분은 여러분의 안전을 위해서 몇 가지 사항을 명심해야 합니다.

➡ _____
_____

3 유민이의 가족이 그들의 캠핑 여행에 대해 이야기하는 것을 들어 보세요.

➡ _____

4 그들은 그들의 캠핑 여행이 안전하고 재미있게 하기 위해 무엇을 해야 하는지 알고 있는 것 같습니다.

➡ _____

5 유민: 아빠, 이 강 근처 이쪽에 텐트를 치면 어때요?

➡ _____

6 아빠: 그건 좋은 생각 같지 않구나.

➡ _____

7 만약 비가 내리기 시작하면, 강이 범람할지도 몰라.

➡ _____

8 유민: 저도 알아요. 하지만 하늘이 맑잖아요.

➡ _____

9 저는 물소리를 정말 좋아한단 말이에요!

➡ _____

10 아빠: 산속의 날씨는 곧 바뀔 수 있어.

➡ _____

11 언제 비가 올지 절대 알 수 없는 일이지.

➡ _____

12 유민: 알겠어요. 안전이 우선이지요! 다른 곳을 찾아봐요.

➡ _____

13 텐트를 칠 때는 평평하고 햇볕이 잘 드는 장소를 고르세요.

➡ _____

14 번개를 맞을지도 모르는 키 큰 나무에 너무 가까운 장소는 피해야 합니다.

➡ _____

15 하준: 엄마, 저 배고파요. 점심이 뭐예요?

➡ _____

16 엄마: 삼겹살을 요리하고 있단다.

➡ _____

17 하준: 엄마, 그건 우리 모두가 먹기에 충분하지 않아요. 우리 더 큰 팬에 더 많이 요리하면 안 돼요?

➡ _____

18 엄마: 더 굽긴 할 거야. 하지만 우리는 이 작은 팬을 써야 해.

➡ _____

19 하준: 왜 우리는 작은 팬을 써야 하죠?

➡ _____

20 엄마: 왜냐하면 팬이 버너보다 더 크면 안 되기 때문이야.

➡ _____

21 만약 큰 팬을 사용하면, 팬이 열을 버너로 다시 돌려보내서, 가스가 폭발할 수 있어!

➡ _____

22 하준: 오, 그것은 몰랐어요.

➡ _____

23 캠핑할 때 불을 사용하는 것에 대한 또 하나의 팁이 있습니다.

➡ _____

24 텐트 안에서 가스난로나 버너를 절대 쓰지 마세요.

➡ _____

25 여러분의 텐트에 불이 붙거나, 불이 타면서 텐트 내 산소를 다 써 버려서 여러분이 의식을 잃을 수도 있습니다.

➡ _____

➡ _____

26 유민: 앗! 모기!

➡ _____

27 엄마: 아, 벌레 퇴치 스프레이를 뿌리라고 네게 말하는 걸 잊었구나. 여기 있단다.

➡ _____

28 유민: 고마워요, 엄마. 아, 그거 아세요?

➡ _____

29 벌레 퇴치 스프레이를 뿌리는 것 대신에 오렌지 껍질을 피부에 문질러도 돼요.

➡ _____

30 모기가 접근하지 못하게 하는 자연 친화적인 방법이에요.

➡ _____

31 엄마: 그거 재미있구나!

➡ _____

32 마늘 또한 벌레가 접근하지 못하게 막을 수 있습니다.

➡ _____

33 마늘 조각을 텐트 입구에 놓아두면, 벌레가 안으로 들어오지 않을 것입니다.

➡ _____

[01~03] 다음 글을 읽고 물음에 답하시오.

Although camping trips can create sweet memories for many people, they can also be occasions __(A)__ bad things happen. If you plan to go camping with family or friends this summer, you need to keep several things __(B)__ mind for your safety.

Listen to Yumin's family talk about their camping trip. They seem to know what to do to make their camping trip safe and fun.

01 빈칸 (A)에 들어갈 말로 적절한 것은?

① why   ② who
③ what   ④ when
⑤ which

서답형
02 위 글의 빈칸 (B)에 적절한 전치사를 쓰시오.

➡ _____

중요
03 다음 중 위 글의 내용으로 보아 알 수 <u>없는</u> 것은?

① 캠핑 여행은 많은 사람들에게 즐거운 추억을 남긴다.
② 캠핑을 갈 때는 위험한 일이 일어날 수 있다.
③ 캠핑을 갈 때는 안전에 유의해야 한다.
④ 유민의 가족은 자주 캠핑을 간다.
⑤ 유민의 가족은 캠핑 여행이 어떻게 하면 안전하고 즐거울 수 있는 지 아는 것 같다.

[04~06] 다음 글을 읽고 물음에 답하시오.

Yumin: Dad, why don't we put up our tent over here by this river? (①)
Dad: (②) I don't think (A)that's a good idea. If it starts to rain, the river might overflow.
Yumin: I know, but the sky is clear. I really like the sound of the water! (③)
Dad: (④) You never know when it might start to rain.
Yumin: Okay. _____(B)_____ Let's find another place. (⑤)

04 위 문장의 ①~⑤ 중 다음 주어진 문장이 들어갈 알맞은 곳은?

The weather can change quickly in the mountains.

①   ②   ③   ④   ⑤

서답형
05 밑줄 친 (A)That이 가리키는 것을 우리말로 쓰시오.

➡ _____

중요
06 빈칸 (B)에 들어갈 말로 가장 적절한 것은?

① Time is money!
② Hurry up.
③ Safety first!
④ Charity begins at home.
⑤ Health is above wealth!

[07~10] 다음 글을 읽고 물음에 답하시오.

Hajun: Mom, I'm hungry. What's for lunch?

Mom: I'm cooking Samgyepsal.

Hajun: Mom, that's not enough ___ⓐ___ all of us. Can we cook more in a bigger pan?

Mom: I'm going to cook more, (A)(so, but) we have to use this small pan.

Hajun: Why do we have to use a (B)(big, small) pan?

Mom: Because the pan should not be bigger than the burner. (C)(If, Though) you use a big pan, it sends the heat back to the burner, and the gas can ___ⓑ___!

Hajun: Oh, I didn't know that.

07 빈칸 ⓐ에 들어갈 말로 적절한 것은?

① at   ② for
③ on   ④ with
⑤ from

서답형

08 다음과 같이 풀이되는 말을 위 글의 빈칸 ⓑ에 쓰시오.

> something bursts loudly and with great force, often causing damage or injury

➡ _____

09 (A)~(C)에서 글의 흐름상 올바른 것으로 짝지어진 것은?

① but – small – If
② so – big – If
③ but – big – If
④ so – small – Though
⑤ but – small – Though

중요

10 다음 중 위 글의 내용으로 보아 질문에 답할 수 없는 것은?

① Why is Hajun hungry?
② What is Hajun's mom cooking?
③ Why is Hajun's mom using a small pan?
④ Is Hajun's mom going to cook more?
⑤ Why should the burner be bigger than the pan?

[11~13] 다음 글을 읽고 물음에 답하시오.

Here is one more tip about fire when you go ⓐcamp. Never use a gas heater or burner inside a tent. Your tent may catch fire, or you ⓑmight pass out because the fire will use ___ⓒ___ the oxygen in the tent as it burns.

서답형

11 밑줄 친 ⓐcamp를 알맞은 형으로 고치시오.

➡ _____

12 밑줄 친 ⓑmight와 의미가 다른 것을 모두 고르시오.

① I might be wrong.
② Might I leave now?
③ I thought that she might be angry.
④ She said that I might go home.
⑤ Ted said that it might rain.

서답형

13 빈칸 ⓒ에 알맞은 말을 쓰시오.

➡ _____

[14~18] 다음 글을 읽고 물음에 답하시오.

Yumin: Ouch! Mosquitoes!

Mom: Oh, I forgot (A)(to tell, telling) you to apply some bug spray. Here.

Yumin: Thanks, Mom. Oh, you know __(B)__ ? We can rub orange peels on our skin instead of applying bug spray. It is a nature-friendly way ⓐto keep mosquitoes away.

Mom: That's interesting!

Garlic can also keep bugs away. You can place pieces of garlic at the entrance to the tent, and bugs will not come inside.

서답형

14 괄호 (A)에서 알맞은 것을 고르시오.

➡ _____

15 빈칸 (B)에 들어갈 말로 적절한 것은?

① it　　　　② this

③ that　　　④ what

⑤ which

16 밑줄 친 ⓐto keep과 to부정사의 용법이 같은 것을 고르시오.

① They want to be friends with us.

② There is nothing to worry about.

③ Kathy came to Korea to be a K-pop singer.

④ She was pleased to hear of my success.

⑤ It is our duty to obey laws.

중요

17 다음 중 위 글의 내용으로 보아 알 수 없는 것은?

① There were some mosquitoes.

② Yumin's mom applied some bug spray.

③ We can rub orange peels on our skin to keep mosquitoes away.

④ Garlic can keep bugs away.

⑤ Bugs don't like garlic.

서답형

18 Where can you place pieces of garlic? Answer in Korean.

➡ _____

[19~23] 다음 글을 읽고 물음에 답하시오.

__(A)__ camping trips can create sweet memories for many people, they can also be occasions when bad things happen. If you plan to go camping with family or friends this summer, you need to keep several things __(B)__ mind for your (C)safe.

Listen to Yumin's family talk about their camping trip. (D)They seem to know what to do to make their camping trip safe and fun.

19 다음 중 위 글의 빈칸 (A)에 들어갈 말과 다른 것이 들어가는 것은?

① _____ he's nearly 90, he is still very active.

② _____ the sun was shinning, it wasn't very warm.

③ _____ it was very cold, the boy wasn't wearing a coat.

④ _____ it smells bad, it's probably not safe to eat.

⑤ _____ it rained a lot, they played soccer outside.

20 빈칸 (B)에 들어갈 말로 적절한 것은?

① in   ② at

③ to   ④ for

⑤ with

서답형

21 밑줄 친 (C)safe를 알맞은 형으로 고치시오.

➡ _____

서답형

22 밑줄 친 (D)와 같은 뜻이 되도록 빈칸에 알맞은 말을 쓰시오.

> They seem to know what _____
> _____ _____ to make their camping
> trip safe and fun.

중요

23 다음 중 위 글의 내용을 잘못 이해한 사람은?

① Amelia: Camping trips can create sweet memories for many people.

② Brian: When you go on camping trips, bad things may happen.

③ Chris: When we go on camping trips, we should take care of our safety.

④ David: I think Yumin's family will go on a camping trip.

⑤ Eden: I'm afraid Yumin's family may have an accident while camping.

[24~26] 다음 글을 읽고 물음에 답하시오.

> Yumin: (①) Dad, why ⓐdon't we put up our tent over here by this river?
> Dad: (②) If it starts to rain, the river ⓑmight overflow.
> Yumin: I know, ⓒbut the sky is clear. I really like the sound of the water! (③)
> Dad: The weather can change quickly in the mountains. (④) You never know when it might start to rain.
> Yumin: (⑤) Okay. Safety first! Let's find ⓓ other place.
>   When you set up a tent, choose a flat, sunny area. Avoid places too close to big trees that ⓔmight be struck by lightning.

24 위 글의 ①~⑤ 중 다음 주어진 문장이 들어갈 알맞은 곳은?

> I don't think that's a good idea.

①   ②   ③   ④   ⑤

25 밑줄 친 ⓐ~ⓔ 중 어법상 올바르지 않은 것은?

① ⓐ   ② ⓑ   ③ ⓒ   ④ ⓓ   ⑤ ⓔ

중요

26 다음 중 위 글을 읽고 답할 수 없는 것은?

① Why does Yumin want to put up their tent by this river?

② Does Yumin's dad agree to her idea?

③ Does Yumin like the sound of the water?

④ Why can the weather change quickly in the mountains?

⑤ Why should we avoid places too close to big trees?

[01~04] 다음 글을 읽고 물음에 답하시오.

> Hajun: Mom, I'm ___(A)___ . What's for lunch?
>
> Mom: I'm cooking Samgyepsal.
>
> Hajun: Mom, that's not enough for all of us. Can we cook more in a bigger pan?
>
> Mom: (B)나는 더 요리할 거야, 하지만 우리는 이 작은 팬을 사용해야 해.
>
> Hajun: Why do we have to use a small pan?
>
> Mom: ___(C)___ the pan should not be bigger than the burner. If you use a big pan, it sends the heat back to the burner, and the gas can explode!
>
> Hajun: Oh, I didn't know (D)that.

01 빈칸 (A)에 다음 영영풀이에 해당하는 단어를 쓰시오.

> wanting some food because you have not eaten for some time and have an uncomfortable or painful feeling in your stomach

➡ _____

02 주어진 단어를 활용하여 밑줄 친 우리말 (B)를 영어로 쓰시오. (중요)

> (go / much / have / pan)

➡ _____

03 빈칸 (C)에 알맞은 접속사를 쓰시오.

➡ _____

04 밑줄 친 (D)that이 구체적으로 가리키는 것을 우리말로 쓰시오. (중요)

➡ _____

_____

[05~06] 다음 글을 읽고 물음에 답하시오.

> (A)여기 캠핑을 갈 때 불에 관한 조언이 하나 더 있다. Never use a gas heater or burner inside a tent. Your tent may ___(B)___ fire, or you might pass out because the fire will use up the oxygen in the tent as it burns.

05 주어진 단어를 활용하여 밑줄 친 우리말 (A)를 영어로 쓰시오.

> (here / much / tip / when / go)

➡ _____

06 빈칸 (B)에 문맥상 알맞은 단어를 쓰시오.

➡ _____

[07~09] 다음 글을 읽고 물음에 답하시오.

Yumin: Ouch! Mosquitoes!

Mom: Oh, I forgot to tell you to apply some bug spray. Here.

Yumin: Thanks, Mom. Oh, you know what? We can rub orange peels on our skin instead __(A)__ applying bug spray. It is a nature-friendly way to keep mosquitoes away.

Mom: (B)That is interesting!

Garlic can also keep bugs away. You can place pieces __(C)__ garlic at the entrance to the tent, and bugs will not come inside.

07 빈칸 (A)와 (C)에 공통으로 들어갈 말을 쓰시오.

➡ _____

08 밑줄 친 (B)That이 가리키는 것을 우리말로 쓰시오.

➡ _____
_____

09 What did Yumin's mom forget to do? Answer in English with a full sentence.

➡ _____

[10~13] 다음 글을 읽고 물음에 답하시오.

Although camping trips can create sweet __(A)__ for many people, (B)they can also be occasions when bad things happen. If you plan to go camping with family or friends this summer, you need to keep several things in mind for your safety.

Listen to Yumin's family talk about their camping trip. (C)They seem to know what to do to make their camping trip safe and fun.

10 빈칸 (A)에 다음 영영풀이에 해당하는 단어를 알맞은 형으로 쓰시오.

something that you remember from the past

➡ _____

11 밑줄 친 (B)와 같은 의미가 되도록 빈칸을 완성하시오.

they can also be occasions _____ _____ bad things happen

12 밑줄 친 (C)와 같은 의미가 되도록 빈칸을 완성하시오.

It _____ _____ they _____ what to do to make their camping trip safe and fun.

13 What do Yumin's family seem to know? Answer in Korean.

➡ _____
_____

구석구석

Before You Read

Welcome to Our Sky Camping Trip!

We have prepared many activities for the two-day camping trip. Because we
현재완료 용법 중 완료   숫자+단위명사는 단수형으로 쓴다.
always think about your safety first, we do our best to prepare for anything
do one's best: 최선을 다하다   to부정사의 부사적 용법 중 목적(~하기 위하여)
bad that may happen. We help people have a comfortable stay by placing a
help+목적어+(to) 동사원형: ~가 …하도록 돕다   by -ing: ~함으로써
can of bug spray in each tent so you can avoid getting bitten by mosquitoes.
avoid+동명사
We hope everyone takes home good memories of the trip!

구문해설 • prepare: 준비하다 • safety: 안전 • happen: 발생하다 • comfortable: 편안한
• bite: 물다 • mosquito: 모기 • memory: 추억, 기억

Writing Workshop

Although you would think that you are free from an earthquake, that is not
although+주어+동사, 주어+동사(부사절과 주절이 대조를 이룸)
true. Then, what should you do when it strikes? There are several things you
= an earthquake   목적격 관계대명사 that 생략
need to keep in mind. First, stay inside and keep informed until the shaking

stops. It seems to be safe to go outside, but something might fall on you.
= It seems that to go outside is safe. It: 가주어. to go outside: 진주어   = may
Second, turn off the gas and the electricity. Third, get under the table and

cover your head with your arms. It is important to protect your head. Finally,
get과 병렬 관계   가주어   진주어
if you are outside, try to get as far away from buildings, trees, and streetlights

as possible. By following these tips, you can be safe from the earthquake.
by -ing: ~함으로써

구문해설 • keep in mind: 명심하다 • until: ~할 때까지

Wrap Up

My Camping Trip Diary

Location: Yeongwol   Date: September 12

Traveled with: my family

I went to Yeongwol with my family on September 12.
날짜 앞에는 전치사 on
During the trip, we enjoyed rafting and hiking. Although I was afraid of doing
during+기간을 나타내는 명사
rafting at first, it was really fun and exciting. I'll go rafting again if I have a

chance.

구문해설 • diary: 일기 • location: 위치, 장소 • date: 날짜 • rafting: 급류 타기
• be afraid of: ~을 무서워하다 • at first: 처음에 • chance: 기회

스카이 캠핑 여행에 오신 것을 환영합니다! 저희는 이틀간의 캠핑 여행을 위해 많은 활동들을 준비했습니다. 저희는 항상 여러분의 안전을 우선으로 생각하기 때문에, 발생할 수 있는 나쁜 일에 대비하기 위해 최선을 다합니다. 저희는 여러분이 모기에 물리는 것을 피할 수 있도록 각각의 텐트에 벌레 퇴치 스프레이를 한 통씩 비치해 둠으로써 여러분이 편안하게 머물도록 돕습니다. 저희는 모든 분들이 여행의 좋은 추억을 집으로 가져가시기를 바랍니다.

비록 여러분이 지진으로부터 자유롭다고 생각할 수 있지만, 사실은 그렇지 않습니다. 그러면 지진이 발생하면 여러분은 무엇을 해야 할까요? 여러분이 명심해야 할 것이 몇 가지 있습니다. 첫째, 흔들림이 멈출 때까지 안에서 머물며 계속 정보를 받아야 합니다. 밖으로 나가는 게 안전해 보이지만 무언가가 여러분에게 떨어질 수도 있습니다. 둘째, 가스와 전기를 끄십시오. 셋째, 테이블 아래로 들어가서 팔로 머리를 감싸세요. 여러분의 머리를 보호하는 것이 중요합니다. 마지막으로, 만일 여러분이 밖에 있다면, 가능한 한 건물이나 나무, 가로등으로부터 멀리 떨어지세요. 이 팁을 따름으로써 여러분은 지진으로부터 안전할 수 있습니다.
나의 캠핑 여행 일기
위치: 영월   날짜: 9월 12일
함께 여행한 사람: 나의 가족
나는 9월 12일에 나의 가족과 함께 영월에 갔다. 여행 중에 우리는 급류 타기와 하이킹을 즐겼다. 나는 처음에 급류 타기를 무서워했지만, 그것은 정말 재미있고 신났다. 기회가 있다면 나는 다시 급류 타기를 하러 갈 것이다.

01 다음 문장의 빈칸에 알맞은 것은?

> I called the police when I heard a bomb
> _____.

① avoid   ② rub   ③ apply

④ explode   ⑤ happen

02 다음 영영풀이에 해당하는 단어를 쓰시오.

> a plant like a small onion that is used in
> cooking to give a strong taste

➡ _____

03 다음 빈칸에 공통으로 들어갈 단어를 쓰시오.

> • Kate, _____ this lesson in mind.
> • She told him to do the dishes, so he
> couldn't _____ watching TV.

➡ _____

04 다음 빈칸에 알맞은 말을 〈보기〉에서 골라 쓰시오.

> ┤ 보기 ├
> up   on   away   out

(1) I often hang _____ with my friends
 after school.

(2) The fire will use _____ the oxygen in
 the tent as it burns.

(3) He warned Billy to keep _____ from
 his daughter.

(4) Before you go out, don't forget to put
 _____ sunscreen.

05 다음 빈칸에 들어갈 단어를 〈보기〉에서 골라 쓰시오.

> ┤ 보기 ├
> overeat   overuse   overwork

(1) It is not good to _____ computers.

(2) Think of your health and don't _____
 yourself.

(3) If you skip breakfast, you tend to
 _____ at lunch.

[06~08] 다음 대화를 읽고 물음에 답하시오.

> G: Mom, can I play outside this afternoon?
> W: Sure. (A)Don't forget to put on sunscreen
> before you go out.
> G: But it's cloudy today. _____ (B) _____
> W: Yes, you have to ___(C)___ sunscreen every
> day.
> G: Okay. Then I'll put some on now.

06 위 대화의 밑줄 친 (A)를 다음과 같이 바꿔 쓸 때 빈칸에 알맞은 말을 쓰시오.

> _____ to put on sunscreen before you
> go out.

07 위 대화의 빈칸 (B)에 들어갈 말로 나머지 넷과 의도가 다른 것은?

① Do I have to put on sunscreen?

② Must I put on sunscreen?

③ Should I put on sunscreen?

④ Do I need to put on sunscreen?

⑤ May I put on sunscreen?

08 위 대화의 빈칸 (C)에 위 대화에 나오는 어구와 같은 의미의 단어를 한 단어로 쓰시오.

➡ _____

[09~12] 다음 대화를 읽고 물음에 답하시오.

B: Uncle John, look at my new bike. What do you think?

M: It's really nice. Where are you going?

B: To the park to meet a friend. (①)

M: Where's your helmet?

B: I don't have (A)one. It's just a short ride.

M: Put on your helmet. You may hurt (a) yourself. (②)

B: But I see (b)a lot of people (c)riding bikes without helmets. (③)

M: You have to wear a helmet. It protects your head in an accident. (④)

B: Okay. I'll get my dad's helmet.

M: No. You have to wear a helmet that (d)fits you. (⑤)

B: I guess I'll have to buy one for (e)me.

09 위 대화의 밑줄 친 (A)one이 가리키는 것을 영어로 쓰시오.

➡ _____

10 위 대화의 ①~⑤ 중 주어진 문장이 들어갈 위치로 알맞은 것은?

If not, it cannot protect your head.

①   ②   ③   ④   ⑤

11 위 대화의 밑줄 친 (a)~(e) 중 어법상 틀린 것은?

① (a)   ② (b)   ③ (c)   ④ (d)   ⑤ (e)

12 위 대화의 내용과 일치하지 않는 것은?

① The boy is going to the park to meet a friend.

② The boy doesn't have a helmet.

③ The boy sees many people riding bikes without helmets.

④ The boy got hurt while riding a bike.

⑤ The boy will buy a helmet for himself.

Grammar

13 다음 문장에서 어법상 어색한 부분을 찾아 올바른 문장으로 고쳐 쓰시오.

(1) The tickets seemed to had got lost.

➡ _____

(2) Despite the sun was shining, it wasn't very warm.

➡ _____
_____

(3) The children always seem to are hungry.

➡ _____

(4) Because he's nearly 80, he is still very active.

➡ _____
_____

14 다음 중 어법상 올바른 문장을 고르시오.

① He's the best teacher, even though he has the least experience.

② She never took a taxi, even she could afford to.

③ Because I'm sad, I can't cry in front of them.

④ Even it were free, I wouldn't take it.

⑤ I wouldn't go if I could.

15 우리말과 같은 뜻이 되도록 괄호 안의 단어를 배열하여 영작하시오.

> 저는 그녀가 안 와도 상관없어요. (I로 시작할 것)
> (mind, if, don't, I, even, doesn't, she, come)

➡ _____

16 우리말에 맞게 괄호 안의 단어를 활용하여 영작하시오.

> 부엌이 작긴 하지만 설계가 잘 되어 있다.
> (although로 시작할 것)
> (although, small, well designed)

➡ _____

_____

17 괄호 안의 단어를 활용하여 우리말에 맞게 빈칸을 채우시오.

(1) 그녀는 그런 척하긴 했지만 그를 사랑하지 않았다. (though, love)
  ➡ She _____ she pretended to.   *pretend to: ~인 척하다

(2) Karen이 올지 확실히 알지 못하지만 Mike는 다음 주에 머무르러 올 것이다. (although, come)
  ➡ Mike _____ I'm not sure Karen is coming.

18 종속절과 주절 간에 대조적인 의미를 담고 있는 부분을 찾으시오.

> Although he is very young, he acts like an old man.

➡ 종속절: _____
➡ 주절: _____

19 그림을 보고 괄호 안의 단어를 활용하여 다음 빈칸을 채우시오.

> • The turtle _____ to win the race. (happy)
> • The rabbit _____ to lose the race. (sad)

20 괄호 안의 단어를 활용하여 우리말에 맞게 빈칸을 채우시오.

(1) 그는 백만장자임에도 불구하고, 아주 작은 집에서 산다. (millionaire, live in)
  ➡ Even though he is a _____, he _____ _____ a very small house.

(2) 비가 오고 있기는 하지만 우리는 외출을 했다. (go out, be)
  ➡ We _____ _____ although it _____ _____.

21 다음 우리말에 맞게 빈칸에 알맞은 말을 〈보기〉에서 고르시오.

> ┤ 보기 ├
> despite   although

> 그는 엉겁결에 웃어버렸다.
> ➡ He had to laugh _____ himself.

Reading

[22~25] 다음 글을 읽고 물음에 답하시오.

> **Yumin:** Dad, (A)why don't we put up our tent over here by this river?
>
> **Dad:** I don't think that's a good idea. If it starts to rain, the river (B)might overflow.
>
> **Yumin:** I know, but the sky is clear. I really like the sound of the water!
>
> **Dad:** The weather can change quickly in the mountains. You never know when it might start to rain.
>
> **Yumin:** Okay. Safety first! Let's find another place.

22 위 글의 밑줄 친 (A)와 같은 뜻이 되도록 다음 문장의 빈칸에 알맞은 말을 쓰시오.

> _____ put up our tent over here by this river.

23 위 글의 밑줄 친 ⓑmight와 의미가 다른 것을 모두 고르시오.

① The rumor might be false.
② Might I use your camera?
③ I think that Kathy might be wrong.
④ Jake said that she might use her cell phone.
⑤ Amy said that Ted might be innocent.

24 다음 중 위 글의 내용과 일치하지 않는 것은?

① Yumin wants to put up their tent by this river.
② Yumin's dad agrees to Yumin's idea.
③ Yumin likes the sound of the water.
④ The weather can change quickly in the mountains.
⑤ They will find another place to put up their tent.

25 Why doesn't Yumin's dad think Yumin's idea is good? Answer in Korean.

➡ _____

[26~29] 다음 글을 읽고 물음에 답하시오.

> Although you would think that you are free ①from an earthquake, (A)that is not true. Then, what should you do when it strikes? There are several things you need ②to keep in mind. First, stay inside and keep informed __(B)__ the shaking stops. It seems to be safe to go outside, but something might fall on you. Second, turn ③on the gas and the electricity. Third, get ④under the table and cover your head with your arms. It is important to protect your head. Finally, if you are outside, try to get as far away from buildings, trees, and streetlights as possible. By ⑤following these tips, you can be safe from the earthquake.

26 위 글의 밑줄 친 (A)가 구체적으로 가리키는 것을 우리말로 쓰시오.

➡ _____

27 다음 중 빈칸 (B)에 들어갈 말로 가장 적절한 것은?

① if ② when
③ until ④ though
⑤ while

28 밑줄 친 ①~⑤ 중 어법상 또는 문맥상 올바르지 <u>않은</u> 것은?

① ② ③ ④ ⑤

29 다음 중 지진이 일어날 때 해야 할 행동으로 알맞지 <u>않은</u> 것은?

① 흔들림이 멈출 때까지 집안에 머물며 지진에 대한 정보를 들어야 한다.
② 즉시 집밖으로 나가야 한다.
③ 가스와 전기를 꺼야 한다.
④ 테이블 밑으로 들어가 팔로 머리를 감싸야 한다.
⑤ 밖에 있을 때는 건물들이나 나무들 또는 가로등으로부터 가급적 멀리 떨어져 있어야 한다.

[30~33] 다음 글을 읽고 물음에 답하시오.

> My Camping Trip Diary
> ___(A)___ : Yeongwol
> Date: September 12
> Traveled with: my family
> I went to Yeongwol with my family on September 12. During the trip, we enjoyed rafting and hiking. Although I was afraid of doing rafting ___(B)___, it was really fun and (C)excite. I'll go rafting again if I have a chance.
>
> I=Yumi

30 위 글의 빈칸 (A)에 다음 영영풀이에 해당하는 단어를 쓰시오.

> the place where something happens or is situated

➡ _____

31 다음 중 빈칸 (B)에 들어갈 말로 가장 적절한 것은?

① at first ② at last
③ above all ④ in the end
⑤ on the contrary

32 위 글의 밑줄 친 (C)를 알맞은 형으로 고치시오.

➡ _____

33 다음 중 위 글의 내용과 일치하지 <u>않는</u> 것은?

① 유미의 가족은 영월로 캠핑 여행을 갔다.
② 유미의 가족은 9월 12일에 여행을 갔다.
③ 유미는 여행 중에 하이킹을 했다.
④ 급류 타기는 처음에는 무서웠지만, 정말 재미있었다.
⑤ 유미의 가족은 곧 다시 캠핑 여행을 갈 것이다.

01 다음 짝지어진 단어의 관계가 같도록 빈칸에 알맞은 말을 쓰시오.

출제율 90%

safety : danger = deep : _____

02 다음 빈칸에 공통으로 들어갈 말을 쓰시오.

출제율 95%

(1)

- They also use _____ our natural resources.
- They put _____ a tent in the backyard and slept there.

(2)

- I will _____ in mind your favorite saying, "Think big."
- Parents should _____ hot pans away from children.

03 다음 영영풀이에 해당하는 단어를 쓰시오.

출제율 90%

to flow over the edge or top of something

➡ _____

04 다음 빈칸 (A)와 (B)에 들어갈 말로 알맞은 것끼리 짝지어진 것을 고르시오.

출제율 95%

- I drank coffee (A)_____ tea this morning.
- (B)_____ she has lots of money, she isn't happy.

① except for – In spite of
② except for – Despite
③ instead of – Although
④ instead of – Despite
⑤ instead of – In spite of

05 다음 빈칸에 알맞은 단어를 <보기>에서 골라 쓰시오.

출제율 95%

┌─ 보기 ─┐
put   stay   close   try

(1) Always _____ to do your best.
(2) Can I _____ up late tonight?
(3) I'll _____ on sunscreen now.
(4) I went to an aquarium _____ to my house.

06 다음 중 밑줄 친 부분의 뜻풀이가 바르지 않은 것은?

출제율 100%

① My mother washes the dishes in the sink. (싱크대)
② Do not swim here. The water is too deep. (깊은)
③ You have to dress properly for the occasion.(경우, 때)
④ A flooding often destroys animals' shelters. (가뭄)
⑤ I spilled some of the tea when going up the stairs. (흘렸다)

[07~08] 다음 대화를 읽고 물음에 답하시오.

B: Mina, are you ready to leave?
G: No, not yet. I have to check if I ___(A)___ the gas.
B: If we don't leave now, we may not ___(B)___ to the concert in time.
G: Okay, but I have to check the gas first. It will only take a minute.

07 위 대화의 빈칸 (A)에 들어갈 말로 적절한 것은?

출제율 95%

① pick up   ② put off
③ turn on   ④ turn down
⑤ turn off

08 위 대화의 빈칸 (B)에 알맞은 것은?

① get　　　　② make　　　　③ do
④ have　　　　⑤ take

[09~11] 다음 대화를 읽고 물음에 답하시오.

> B: Here comes the bus!
> G: Oh, but first I have to finish (A)drink my tea.
> B: Why don't you just take it with you? I'm sure that it will be okay if you are ___(B)___ .
> G: No. If the bus stops suddenly, I may spill it.
> B: Okay, then I can just wait for you to finish your drink. (C)곧 다른 버스가 올 것이라고 확신해.
> G: Thanks.

09 위 대화의 밑줄 친 (A)를 알맞은 형태로 고쳐 쓰시오.

➡ _____

10 위 대화의 빈칸 (B)에 들어갈 말로 적절한 것은?

① terrible　　　　② serious
③ careful　　　　④ strange
⑤ wonderful

11 위 대화의 밑줄 친 (C)의 우리말을 주어진 단어를 이용하여 영작하시오. (8 words)

(soon, sure)

➡ _____

[12~14] 다음 글을 읽고 물음에 답하시오.

> M: ___(A)___ can ①cause big problems. However, you may not know what to do when it happens. (B)당신이 해야 할 몇 가지 것들이 있습니다. First, you have to ②turn off the water and the electricity. Second, ③unpack water and food when you leave the house. Finally, you have to move to a ④high and safe place and keep listening to the ⑤weather report.

12 위 글은 어떤 상황에 관한 행동 요령인지 빈칸 (A)에 알맞은 말을 주어진 철자로 시작하여 쓰시오.

➡ F_____

13 위 글의 밑줄 친 ①~⑤ 중 문맥상 어울리지 않는 것은?

①　　　　②　　　　③　　　　④　　　　⑤

14 위 글의 밑줄 친 (B)의 우리말을 주어진 단어를 이용하여 영어로 쓰시오. (8 words)

(several, there, have)

➡ _____

출제율 95%

15 보기에서 알맞은 단어를 골라 빈칸을 채우시오.

┌─── 보기 ───┐
│ although   despite │
└─────────────┘

(1) _____ I studied hard, I failed to pass the exam.

(2) _____ the bad weather, we decided to carry out the plan to go on a picnic.

(3) _____ Jay got up early, he left home later than usual.

(4) _____ Jay brought an umbrella, he still got wet.

(5) _____ our worries, everything turned out well.

(6) _____ his cries, no one came to his assistance.

출제율 90%

16 괄호 안의 단어를 사용하여 우리말에 맞게 영작하시오.

┌─────────────────────────┐
│ Jamin은 열심히 공부했지만 시험을 잘 치지 못 │
│ 했다. (study, do well) (although로 시작할 것) │
└─────────────────────────┘

➡ _____

_____

출제율 100%

17 다음 중 어색한 문장을 고르시오.

① Although it is cheap, I will really buy it.

② Although I failed the test, I will never give up.

③ Despite hot weather, you are wearing a coat.

④ Although he lost everything, I still love him.

⑤ Despite the recession, demand is growing.

*recession: 불경기

출제율 95%

18 괄호 안의 조건과 단어를 활용하여 우리말에 맞게 영작하시오.

(1) 그는 그 시험 결과를 아는 듯이 보인다.
(know, test, to부정사 사용)

➡ _____

(2) 그들은 그 시험 결과에 만족하는 듯이 보인다.
(satisfied with, it 사용)

➡ _____

(3) 모두 내 얼굴을 보고 있는 듯이 보인다.
(everyone, be, it 사용)

➡ _____

(4) Suji는 매일 아침 식사를 하는 것처럼 보인다.
(have, to부정사 사용)

➡ _____

[19~22] 다음 글을 읽고 물음에 답하시오.

Hajun: Mom, I'm hungry. (①) What's for lunch?

Mom: I'm cooking Samgyepsal.

Hajun: Mom, that's not enough for all of us. (②)

Mom: I'm going to cook ___(A)___, but we have to use this small pan. (③)

Hajun: Why do we have to use a small pan? (④)

Mom: (⑤) Because the pan should not be ___(B)___ than the burner. If you use a big pan, it sends the heat back to the burner, and the gas can explode!

Hajun: Oh, I didn't know (C)that.

출제율 95%

19 위 글의 ①~⑤ 중 다음 주어진 문장이 들어갈 알맞은 곳은?

┌─────────────────────────┐
│ Can we cook more in a bigger pan? │
└─────────────────────────┘

①   ②   ③   ④   ⑤

20 빈칸 (A)에 much, (B)에 big를 어법에 맞게 쓰시오.

출제율 90%

(A) _____   (B) _____

출제율 90%

21 밑줄 친 (C)that이 가리키는 것을 우리말로 구체적으로 쓰시오.

➡ _____

_____

출제율 100%

22 다음 중 위 글의 내용과 일치하지 <u>않는</u> 것은?

① Hajun is hungry now.
② Hajun's mom is cooking Samgyepsal.
③ Hajun's mom has to use a small pan.
④ Hajun's mom isn't going to cook more.
⑤ The burner should be bigger than the pan.

[23~26] 다음 글을 읽고 물음에 답하시오.

_____(A)_____ you would think that you are free from an earthquake, that is not true. Then, what should you do when ⓐit strikes? There are several things you need to keep in mind. First, stay inside and keep informed until the shaking stops. It seems to be safe to go outside, _____(B)_____ something might fall on you. Second, turn off the gas and the electricity. Third, get under the table and cover your head with your arms. It is important to protect your head. Finally, if you are outside, ⓑtry to get as far away from buildings, trees, and streetlights as possible. By following these tips, you can be _____(C)_____ from the earthquake.

出제율 100%

23 위 글의 빈칸 (A)와 (B)에 들어갈 말이 알맞게 짝지어진 것은?

① While – or
② If – and
③ Although – but
④ Unless – and
⑤ Because – for

출제율 95%

24 다음 중 빈칸 (C)에 들어갈 말로 가장 적절한 것은?

① hurt   ② sick
③ safe   ④ healthy
⑤ dangerous

출제율 90%

25 밑줄 친 ⓐit이 가리키는 것을 영어로 쓰시오.

➡ _____

출제율 95%

26 밑줄 친 ⓑ와 같은 뜻이 되도록 다음 문장의 빈칸에 알맞은 말을 쓰시오.

try to get as far away from buildings, trees, and streetlights as _____ _____

[01~04] 다음 대화를 읽고 물음에 답하시오.

> B: Uncle John, look at my new bike. What do you think?
>
> M: It's really nice. Where are you going?
>
> B: To the park to meet a friend.
>
> M: Where's your helmet?
>
> B: I don't have one. It's just a short ride.
>
> M: ____(A)____ your helmet. You may hurt yourself.
>
> B: But (B)저는 헬멧 없이 자전거 타는 많은 사람들을 봐요.
>
> M: You have to wear a helmet. It protects your head in an accident.

01 위 대화의 빈칸 (A)에 다음 영영풀이에 해당하는 말을 두 단어로 쓰시오.

> to have something on your body as clothing, decoration, or protection

➡ _____

02 위 대화의 밑줄 친 (B)의 우리말과 같도록 주어진 어구를 바르게 배열하시오.

> bikes / see / people / without / a lot of / helmets / I / riding

➡ _____

03 Why is the boy going to the park?

➡ _____

04 Write the reason why you have to wear a helmet when riding a bike. Answer in English

➡ _____

05 seem과 괄호 안의 단어를 활용하여 문장을 완성하시오.

(1) 그들은 서로를 사랑하는 것 같다. (love)

➡ _____

➡ _____

(2) 그들은 서로를 사랑했던 것 같다. (loved)

➡ _____

➡ _____

(3) Reina는 집에 고양이 한 마리를 키우는 것처럼 보인다. (raise)

➡ _____

➡ _____

(4) Reina는 집에 고양이 한 마리를 키웠던 것처럼 보인다. (raised)

➡ _____

➡ _____

06 그림을 보고 〈보기〉의 단어를 활용하여 빈칸을 채우시오.

(1)

> | 보기 |
> although   headache

> • _____ he slept well last night, he
>   _____ _____ _____.
> • He _____ _____ _____ _____
>   he slept well last night.

(2)

보기
seem   prepare

- They _____ the food.
- It _____ the food.

[07~10] 다음 글을 읽고 물음에 답하시오.

My Camping Trip Diary

Location: Yangpyeong
Date: May 10
Traveled with: middle school friends

I went to Yangpyeong with my friends on May 10. (A)(During, While) the trip, we baked potatoes, and played a board game. Although we tried to stay ____(B)____ all night, we were not able to do it. (C)나는 우리가 얼마나 즐겁게 지냈는지 결코 잊지 못할 것이다.

I=Yumin

07 괄호 (A)에서 알맞은 것을 고르시오.

➡ _____

08 빈칸 (B)에 알맞은 부사를 쓰시오.

➡ _____

09 밑줄 친 우리말 (C)를 주어진 어구를 이용해서 영어로 옮기시오.

never, how, fun, have

➡ _____

10 According to the passage, what did they bake? Answer in English with a full sentence.

➡ _____

[11~13] 다음 글을 읽고 물음에 답하시오.

Yumin: Ouch! Mosquitoes!
Mom: Oh, I forgot (A)(telling, to tell) you to apply some bug spray. Here.
Yumin: Thanks, Mom. Oh, you know what? We can rub orange peels on our skin instead of (B)apply bug spray. It is a nature-friendly way to keep mosquitoes away.
Mom: That's interesting!

Garlic can also keep bugs away. You can place pieces of garlic at the ____(C)____ to the tent, and bugs will not come inside.

11 괄호 (A)에서 알맞은 것을 고르시오.

➡ _____

12 밑줄 친 (B)apply를 알맞은 형으로 고치시오.

➡ _____

13 빈칸 (C)에 다음 영영풀이에 해당하는 단어를 쓰시오.

the way into a place, for example a door or gate

➡ _____

창의사고력 서술형 문제

01 다음 표를 참고하여 구매 후기를 완성하시오.

What I bought	a pair of running shoes
What I like about the product	They are very comfortable, so I wear them often.
What I don't like about the product	The color is white, so they get dirty easily.
Stars	( ) not satisfied (✓) satisfied ★★★★☆

A Pair of Running Shoes
This is what I bought. I'd like to begin with _____. _____
_____. Now, let me write _____ .
_____. All in all, I'm _____ the shoes,
and I give the product _____.

02 다음은 학교에서 지켜야 할 규칙에 대해 열거 되어 있다. 그림을 참고하여 순서에 맞게 문장을 배열하시오.

(1) First, do not just leave your bag on the floor.
(2) Here are three safety rules you should follow at school.
(3) You might fall and hurt yourself.
(4) Someone can trip over it.
(5) You might bump into someone.
(6) Second, do not run in the hallway.
(7) Third, do not jump on desks or chairs.
(8) Keep these rules in mind so that everyone can be safe.

단원별 모의고사

01 다음 빈칸에 공통으로 들어갈 말을 쓰시오.

> • They _____ up hidden cameras.
> • She _____ sunscreen on her face.

➡ _____

[02~03] 다음 주어진 영어 설명에 해당하는 어휘를 빈칸에 쓰시오.

02
> Try not to _____ the medication.

> <영어 설명> to use something too much or too often

03
> I slipped and fell on a banana _____.

> <영어 설명> the skin of a fruit

04 다음 중 <보기>에 있는 단어를 사용하여 자연스러운 문장을 만들 수 없는 것은?

> ┌── 보기 ──┐
> avoid   pan   memory   flat

① The earth is not _____.
② Pour milk into the _____ and boil it.
③ As it is raining a lot, the river can _____.
④ Tell me about one happy _____ you have.
⑤ We have to hurry up to_____ rush hour.

05 다음 주어진 문장 다음에 이어질 대화의 순서를 바르게 배열하시오.

> Mom, can I play outside this afternoon?

(A) Okay. Then I'll put some on now.
(B) But it's cloudy today. Do I have to put on sunscreen?
(C) Sure. Don't forget to put on sunscreen before you go out.
(D) Yes, you have to wear sunscreen every day.

➡ _____

[06~08] 다음 글을 읽고 물음에 답하시오.

> M: Flooding can _____(A)_____ big problems. However, you may not know what to do when it happens. There are several things you have to do. First, you have to turn off the water and the electricity. Second, pack water and food when you leave the house. Finally, you have to move to a high and safe place and keep (B)listen to the weather report.

06 위 글의 빈칸 (A)에 다음 영영풀이에 해당하는 단어를 쓰시오.(주어진 철자로 시작할 것)

> to make something happen or exist

➡ c_____

07 위 글의 밑줄 친 (B)listen을 알맞은 형태로 고쳐 쓰시오.

➡ _____

08 홍수가 발생했을 때, 행동 요령 세 가지를 우리말로 쓰시오.

➡ _____

_____

_____

09 다음 빈칸에 공통으로 들어갈 단어를 고르시오. (대·소문자 무시)

• I'll get there _____ if I have to walk.
• _____ though he lied to me, I still trust him.

① as   ② although   ③ despite
④ even   ⑤ in

10 다음 빈칸에 들어갈 알맞은 것을 고르시오.

Even though I _____ in the USA, I'm having a hard time speaking English.

① live   ② lived
③ doesn't live   ④ have lived
⑤ had lived

11 다음 우리말에 맞게 빈칸에 알맞은 말을 쓰시오.

(1) 나는 바가지를 쓴 것 같아요.
➡ I _____ _____ be overcharged.
(2) 네 방은 더러워 보인다.
➡ Your room _____ _____ be dirty.
(3) 비록 여행은 짧았지만 나는 잊을 수 없는 많은 추억을 만들었다.
➡ _____ it was a short trip, I made many unforgettable memories.
(4) 우리는 밤을 꼬박 새려고 했지만 그렇게 할 수 없었다.
➡ _____ we tried to stay up all night, we were not able to do it.

12 even if를 사용하여 (A)와 (B)의 문장을 연결해 문장을 완성하시오.

(A)
• He gets accepted to Harvard.
• You should always exercise.
• The government survives this crisis.
• He's going to buy the farm.

(B)
• He won't be able to afford the tuition.
• It's only 10 minutes a day.
• They still face big problems.
• The government raises the price.

*tuition: 수업료

➡ _____

➡ _____

➡ _____

➡ _____

13 다음 중 어법상 어색한 것은?

① Even if he lies again, I'll forgive him.
② Even though she lied to me, we are still good friends.
③ His grades were up despite his bad behavior.
④ Despite she is beautiful, she lacks intellectual beauty.
⑤ I still look fat, even though I've been exercising regularly.

14 우리말에 맞게 괄호 안의 단어를 배열하시오.

> 미국에서 태어났지만 그는 대한민국의 아들이다.
> (he, he, even though, born, was, America, in, is, son, Korean, a) (even though로 시작할 것)

➡ _____

_____

15 다음 그림을 보고 괄호 안의 단어를 활용하여 빈칸을 채우시오.

> Although my mom _____ _____ (try) iron, it didn't work well. The iron seems _____ _____ _____ (be) broken.

[16~19] 다음 글을 읽고 물음에 답하시오.

> Listen to Yumin's family ①talk about their camping trip. They seem to know __(A)__ to do to make their camping trip ②safely and fun.
>
> **Yumin:** Dad, __(B)__ don't we put up our tent over here by this river?
>
> **Dad:** I don't think that's a good idea. If it starts ③to rain, the river might overflow.
>
> **Yumin:** I know, but the sky is clear. I really like the sound of the water!
>
> **Dad:** The weather can change ④quickly in the mountains. You never know when it might start to rain.

> **Yumin:** Okay. Safety first! Let's find ⑤another place.
>
> When you set up a tent, choose a flat, (C)sun area. Avoid places too close to big trees that might be struck by lightning.

16 밑줄 친 ①~⑤ 중 어법상 어색한 것은?

①   ②   ③   ④   ⑤

17 다음 중 빈칸 (A)와 (B)에 알맞은 것으로 짝지어진 것은?

① what – why   ② when – how
③ when – why   ④ which – what
⑤ what – how

18 밑줄 친 (C)를 알맞은 형으로 고치시오.

➡ _____

19 According to the passage, why should we avoid places too close to big trees? Answer in English by beginning with 'because'. (7 words)

➡ _____

[20~23] 다음 글을 읽고 물음에 답하시오.

Yumin: Ouch! Mosquitoes! (①)

Mom: (②) Oh, I forgot to tell you to apply some bug spray. Here.

Yumin: Thanks, Mom. (③) We can rub orange peels on our skin instead __(A)__ applying bug spray. It is a nature-friendly way ⓐto keep mosquitoes away. (④)

Mom: (⑤) ⓑThat's interesting!

Garlic can also keep bugs away. You can place pieces __(B)__ garlic at the entrance to the tent, and bugs will not come inside.

20 위 글의 ①~⑤ 중 다음 주어진 문장이 들어갈 알맞은 곳은?

> Oh, you know what?

①   ②   ③   ④   ⑤

21 위 글의 빈칸 (A)와 (B)에 공통으로 알맞은 전치사를 쓰시오.

➡ _____

22 밑줄 친 ⓐto keep과 용법이 같은 것은?

① I want to learn Chinese culture.
② Is there anything to eat in the fridge?
③ Were you glad to hear the news?
④ Love is to trust each other.
⑤ Her daughter grew up to be an actress.

23 밑줄 친 ⓑThat이 가리키는 것을 우리말로 쓰시오.

➡ _____
_____

[24~26] 다음 글을 읽고 물음에 답하시오.

Welcome to Our Sky Camping Trip!

We have prepared many activities for the ①two-days camping trip. Because we always think about your safety first, we do our best to prepare for ②anything bad that (A)may happen. We help people have a comfortable stay by ③placing a can of bug spray in each tent __(B)__ you can avoid ④getting bitten by mosquitoes. We hope everyone takes ⑤home good memories of the trip!

24 밑줄 친 ①~⑤ 중 어법상 어색한 것은?

①   ②   ③   ④   ⑤

25 다음 중 밑줄 친 (A)may와 같은 용법으로 쓰인 것은?

① You may come in if you wish.
② May she rest in peace!
③ The rumor may be false.
④ May I take a picture here?
⑤ You may stay at this hotel for a week.

26 빈칸 (B)에 알맞은 것은?

① in   ② to
③ with   ④ so
⑤ for

Special

Coach Carter

Words & Expressions

Key Words

- **accept** [əksépt] 통 받아들이다
- **actually** [æktʃuəli] 부 실제로, 정말로
- **allow** [əláu] 통 허락하다
- **attend** [əténd] 통 참석하다
- **bonus** [bóunəs] 명 보너스, 상여금
- **care** [kɛər] 통 마음을 쓰다, 걱정하다
- **championship** [tʃæmpiənʃip] 명 선수권 대회, 챔피언전
- **coach** [koutʃ] 명 (스포츠 팀의) 코치
- **college** [kálidʒ] 명 대학
- **contract** [kántrækt] 명 계약, 계약서
- **decide** [disáid] 통 결정하다
- **decision** [disíʒən] 명 결정, 판단
- **demand** [diménd] 명 요구
- **disappointed** [dìsəpɔ́intid] 형 실망한, 낙담한
- **either** [í:ðər] 부 (부정문에서) 역시, 또한
- **eventually** [ivéntʃuəli] 부 결국, 마침내
- **exactly** [igzǽktli] 부 정확히
- **except** [iksépt] 전 ~을 제외하고
- **famous** [féiməs] 형 유명한
- **follow** [fálou] 통 (충고 · 지시 등을) 따르다
- **future** [fjú:tʃər] 명 미래
- **grade** [greid] 명 성적
- **gym** [dʒim] 명 체육관

- **happen** [hǽpən] 통 일어나다, 발생하다
- **hard** [hɑːrd] 부 열심히 형 힘든, 어려운
- **imagine** [imǽdʒin] 통 상상하다
- **improve** [imprú:v] 통 향상하다, 향상시키다
- **life** [laif] 명 인생, 삶
- **lock** [lɑk] 통 잠그다
- **lose** [lu:z] 통 지다, 패하다
- **order** [ɔ́:rdər] 통 명령하다
- **pack** [pækt] 통 (짐을) 싸다, 꾸리다
- **part** [pɑ:rt] 명 역할, 부분
- **plan** [plæn] 명 계획 통 계획하다
- **practice** [prǽktis] 통 연습하다
- **principal** [prínsəpəl] 명 교장
- **promise** [prámis] 통 약속하다
- **realize** [rí:əlàiz] 통 깨닫다, 알아차리다
- **refuse** [rifjú:z] 통 거절하다
- **reopen** [rióupən] 통 다시 문을 열다, 다시 시작하다
- **rule** [ru:l] 명 규칙
- **send** [send] 통 보내다, 발송하다
- **seriously** [síəriəsli] 부 심각하게
- **sign** [sain] 통 서명하다
- **win** [win] 통 이기다, 얻다
- **winner** [wínər] 명 승리자

Key Expressions

- **A as well as B** B뿐만 아니라 A도
- **become used to -ing** ~하는 데 익숙해지다
- **by -ing** ~함으로써
- **carry out** 이행하다, 수행하다
- **find out** ~을 찾아보다
- **for the first time** 처음으로
- **from that point on** 그때 이후로

- **game after game** 경기마다
- **how+to부정사** ~하는 방법
- **in addition to** 게다가, ~에 더하여
- **one after another** 잇따라서
- **pay attention to** ~에 유의하다, ~에 관심을 가지다
- **take action** 조치를 취하다
- **to make matters worse** 설상가상으로

Word Power

※ 서로 반대되는 뜻을 가진 어휘

☐ **win** (이기다) ↔ **lose** (지다)

☐ **future** (미래) ↔ **past** (과거)

☐ **pack** ((짐을) 꾸리다) ↔ **unpack** ((짐을) 풀다)

☐ **lock** (잠그다) ↔ **unlock** (열다)

※ 서로 비슷한 뜻을 가진 어휘

☐ **famous** (유명한) – **well-known** (유명한, 잘 알려진)

☐ **refuse** (거절하다) – **reject** (거절하다)

☐ **actually** (정말로) – **really** (정말로)

☐ **exactly** (정확히) – **correctly** (정확하게)

☐ **hard** (어려운) – **difficult** (어려운)

☐ **allow** (허락하다) – **permit** (허락하다)

☐ **eventually** (결국, 마침내) – **finally** (결국, 마침내)

☐ **order** (명령하다) – **command** (명령하다)

English Dictionary

☐ **attend** 참석하다
→ to go to and be present at an event, meeting, etc.
행사, 모임 등에 참석하다

☐ **bonus** 상여금, 보너스
→ an extra amount of money that is given to an employee
고용인에게 주는 가외의 돈

☐ **coach** (스포츠 팀의) 코치
→ a person who teaches and trains an athlete
운동선수를 가르치고 훈련시키는 사람

☐ **contract** 계약서
→ a document on which the words of a contract are written
계약의 내용을 적은 서류

☐ **demand** 요구
→ a forceful statement in which you say that something must be done or given to you
어떤 것을 해야 한다거나 받아야 한다는 강력한 주장

☐ **gym** 체육관
→ a room or hall with equipment for doing physical exercise, for example in a school
예를 들어 학교에서 운동할 수 있는 장비가 있는 방이나 홀

☐ **improve** 향상시키다
→ to make something better
어떤 것을 더 나아지게 하다

☐ **order** 명령하다
→ to use your authority to tell someone to do something
권위를 사용하여 누군가에게 어떤 일을 하라고 시키다

☐ **pack** (짐을) 꾸리다, 싸다
→ to put something into a bag, suitcase, etc., so that you can take it with you
어떤 것을 가져갈 수 있도록 가방, 여행 가방 등에 넣다

☐ **principal** 교장
→ the person in charge of a school or college
학교나 대학의 책임자

☐ **refuse** 거절하다
→ to say that you will not do something that someone has asked you to do
누군가가 부탁한 일을 하지 않겠다고 말하다

☐ **rule** 규칙
→ a statement that tells you what is or is not allowed in a particular game, situation, etc.
특정한 게임, 상황 등에서 할 수 있는 일과 할 수 없는 일을 알려 주는 말

☐ **sign** 서명하다
→ to write your name on something
어떤 것에 이름을 쓰다

☐ **win** 이기다
→ to achieve victory in a fight, contest, game, etc.
싸움, 시합, 경기 등에서 승리를 거두다

Coach Carter

Welcome to *Movie Trip*. Today we're going to talk about the movie *Coach Carter*. Can you imagine a basketball coach who doesn't allow his players to practice? That's exactly what Coach Carter does. This moive is about a coach who cares more about his students than about winning games.

The basketball team at Richmond High School in Richmond, California, was having one losing season after another. The players became used to losing. To make matters worse, they had no plans for the future; they went to school only to play baskeball, and they did not do that very well. Then they got a new coach, Kenny Carter. Coach Carter wanted to change things. He wanted to teach kids how to play basketball well and win. But more than that, he wanted to give the players a future by sending them to college.

To carry out his plan, Coach Carter had the players sign a contract. They had to promise to study hard in addition to playing basketball. At first, students did not take his idea for a contract seriously.

coach (스포츠 팀의) 코치
allow 허락하다
exactly 정확하게
care 마음을 쓰다, 걱정하다
send 보내다, 발송하다
college 대학
sign 서명하다
contract 계약서
promise 약속하다
seriously 심각하게

확인문제

● 다음 문장이 본문의 내용과 일치하면 T, 일치하지 않으면 F를 쓰시오.

1 The name of the movie program is *Movie Trip*. ☐

2 The basketball team at Richmond High School kept winning. ☐

3 Before the new coach came, the players were used to losing. ☐

4 The players went to school to study hard for their future. ☐

5 Coach Carter had the players sign a contract to carry out his plan. ☐

6 The players took Carter's idea for a contract seriously. ☐

Carter: I'm going to give you a contract.

Cruz: "Attend all classes," "Get a C⁺ or higher," "Don't be late…."

부정명령문: Don't[Never]+동사원형 ~

What are all these rules about? Do I get a signing bonus for

전치사+동명사

signing this contract?

Carter: Yes. You will get a big bonus because you will become a

접속사: ~ 때문에

winner in the game of basketball as well as in the game of life.

A as well as B: B뿐만 아니라 A도

With hard work and a new game plan, the team began to win for

~으로 인해

the first time in many years. From that point on, they won game

그때 이후로 경기마다

after game. Everybody, except Coach Carter, was happy. The players

did not do the "study" part of their contract. Few of them actually

부정의 의미

believed∧they could go to college, so they paid little attention to their

접속사 that 생략 pay attention to: ~에 관심을 가지다

grades. Carter decided to take stronger action.

조치를 취하다

He locked the gym and refused to let them play basketball until their

사역동사+목적어+동사원형: ~가 …하도록 허락하다

grades improved, as promised in the contract. The players did not like

~한 대로

it. They told him that his actions were just for him, not for them.

명사절을 이끄는 접속사 that = Carter = the players

attend 참석하다
rule 규칙
bonus 상여금, 보너스
except ~을 제외하고
actually 실제로, 정말로
grade 성적
lock 잠그다
gym 체육관
refuse 거절하다
until ~할 때까지
improve 향상하다

확인문제

● 다음 문장이 본문의 내용과 일치하면 T, 일치하지 <u>않으면</u> F를 쓰시오.

1 Coach Carter was not happy when the team won game after game. ☐

2 Most of the players believed they could go to college. ☐

3 The players paid much attention to their grades. ☐

4 Coach Carter didn't allow the players to play basketball until their grades improved. ☐

5 The players complained when Coach Carter locked the gym. ☐

Worm: We're the basketball team. All∧we see is you on TV, getting
famous.

Carter: If you think so, go home and ask yourself, "Do I want a better
life?" If the answer is yes, I will do everything in my power to
help you. But you have to do your part.

The players' parents did not like Carter's decision either. At the
parents' demand, the principal ordered Carter to reopen the gym.
Disappointed, Carter decided to leave Richmond High. When he
entered the gym to pack his things, however, all of his players were
there.

We want you to enjoy the movie, so we won't tell you what happens
next. Find out for yourself by watching the movie *Coach Carter*.

famous 유명한
part 역할
decision 결정. 판단
demand 요구
principal 교장
order 명령하다
gym 체육관
pack (짐을) 싸다

확인문제

● 다음 문장이 본문의 내용과 일치하면 T, 일치하지 않으면 F를 쓰시오.

1 Carter required the players to do their part. ☐

2 Both the players and their parents did not like Carter's decision. ☐

3 At the parents' demand, the principal forced the players to take more classes. ☐

4 Satisfied with the result, Carter decided to leave Richmond High. ☐

5 When Carter entered the gym to pack his things, only the parents were there. ☐

● 우리말을 참고하여 빈칸에 알맞은 말을 쓰시오.

1 _____ _____ *Movie Trip*.

2 Today we're _____ _____ _____ about the movie *Coach Carter*.

3 Can you _____ a basketball coach who doesn't _____ his players _____ _____?

4 That's exactly _____ Coach Carter _____.

5 This movie is about a coach who _____ more _____ his students than _____ _____ _____.

6 The basketball team at Richmond High School in Richmond, California, was having _____ losing season _____ _____.

7 The players _____ _____ _____ _____.

8 _____ _____ matters _____, they had no plans for the future; they went to school _____ _____ _____ basketball, and they did not do that very well.

9 Then they got a _____ _____, Kenny Carter.

10 Coach Carter wanted _____ _____ things.

11 He wanted to teach kids _____ _____ _____ basketball well and win.

12 But _____ _____ that, he wanted to give the players a future _____ _____ them to college.

13 _____ _____ _____ his plan, Coach Carter had the players sign a _____.

1 「영화 여행」에 오신 것을 환영합니다.

2 오늘 우리는 영화 「코치 카터」에 대해 이야기할 것입니다.

3 선수들이 연습하는 것을 허락하지 않는 농구 코치를 상상할 수 있나요?

4 그것이 바로 카터 코치가 한 것입니다.

5 이 영화는 경기에서 이기는 것보다 학생들을 더 걱정하는 코치에 대한 영화입니다.

6 캘리포니아 리치몬드 지역의 리치몬드 고등학교 농구 팀은 연속해서 경기에서 지고 있었습니다.

7 선수들도 지는 것에 익숙하게 되었습니다.

8 설상가상으로 그들은 미래에 대한 계획도 없었습니다. 즉, 그들은 단지 농구하기 위해 학교에 갔고, 그것마저도 잘하지 못했습니다.

9 그때 그들은 케니 카터라는 새로운 코치를 선임했습니다.

10 카터 코치는 몇 가지를 바꾸고자 했습니다.

11 그는 아이들에게 어떻게 농구를 잘하고 이기는지를 가르치기를 원했습니다.

12 그러나 그것보다도, 그는 그들을 대학에 보냄으로써 선수들에게 미래를 주기를 원했습니다.

13 그의 계획을 실행하기 위해서, 카터 코치는 선수들에게 계약서에 서명하게 했습니다.

14 They _____ _____ promise to study hard _____ _____ _____ playing basketball.

15 _____ _____, students did not take his idea for a contract _____.

16 Carter: I'm going to _____ _____ _____ _____.

17 Cruz: "_____ all classes," "Get a C⁺ or higher," "Don't _____ _____...."

18 What are _____ _____ _____ about?

19 Do I get a _____ _____ for signing this contract?

20 Carter: Yes. You will get a big bonus _____ you will become a winner in the game of basketball _____ _____ _____ in the game of life.

21 _____ hard work and a new game plan, the team began to win for the first time _____ _____ _____.

22 _____ that _____ _____, they won game _____ game.

23 Everybody, _____ Coach Carter, was happy.

24 The players did not do the "study" _____ _____ their contract.

25 _____ _____ them actually believed they could go to college, so they _____ _____ _____ _____ their grades.

26 Carter decided to _____ stronger _____.

27 He locked the gym and refused to _____ them _____ basketball _____ their grades _____, _____ promised in the contract.

14 그들은 농구를 하는 것뿐만 아니라 열심히 공부할 것도 약속해야만 했습니다.

15 처음에는 학생들이 계약서에 대한 그의 생각을 심각하게 받아들이지 않았습니다.

16 카터: 내가 너희들에게 계약서를 줄 것이다.

17 크루즈: "모든 수업에 출석하라." "C 플러스 또는 그 이상 받아라." "지각하지 말아라."

18 이 모든 규칙들은 무엇이죠?

19 제가 이 계약서에 사인하면 사이닝 보너스를 받나요?

20 카터: 그래. 너는 큰 보너스를 받게 될 거야. 왜냐하면 인생의 게임에서뿐 아니라 농구 경기에서도 승리자가 될 것이기 때문이지.

21 맹연습과 새로운 경기 전략으로 그 팀은 몇 년 만에 처음으로 이기기 시작했습니다.

22 그때 이후로 경기마다 이겼습니다.

23 카터 코치를 제외한 모든 이들이 행복했습니다.

24 선수들은 그들 계약의 '학습' 부분을 하지 않았습니다.

25 그들 중 정말 그들이 대학을 갈 수 있다고 믿는 사람들은 거의 없었습니다. 그래서 그들은 성적에는 거의 관심을 두지 않았습니다.

26 카터는 더 강력한 조치를 취하기로 결심했습니다.

27 그는 체육관 문을 잠그고 계약서에서 약속한 대로 그들의 성적이 좋아질 때까지 농구를 못하게 했습니다.

116 **Special Lesson.** Coach Carter

28 The players did not like _____.

29 They told him _____ his actions were _____ for him, _____ for them.

30 Worm: We're the _____ _____.

31 _____ _____ _____ is you on TV, getting famous.

32 Carter: _____ you think so, go home and ask _____, "Do I want a _____ _____?"

33 If the answer is yes, I will do everything in my power _____ _____ you.

34 But you _____ _____ do your part.

35 The players' parents did not like Carter's decision _____.

36 At the parents' _____, the principal _____ Carter _____ _____ the gym.

37 _____, Carter _____ _____ leave Richmond High.

38 _____ he entered the gym _____ _____ his things, however, all of his players _____ there.

39 We want you to enjoy the movie, so we won't tell you _____ _____ _____.

40 _____ _____ for yourself _____ _____ the movie *Coach Carter*.

28 선수들은 그것을 좋아하지 않았습니다.

29 그들은 그에게 그의 행동들이 그들을 위한 것이 아닌 단지 카터 자신을 위한 것이라고 말했습니다.

30 웜: 우리는 농구 팀이에요.

31 우리가 보는 모든 것은 유명세를 타며 TV에 있는 당신이에요.

32 카터: 네가 그렇게 생각한다면, 집으로 가서 너 자신에게 물어봐. "나는 더 나은 삶을 원하는가?"

33 대답이 '맞다'라면, 나는 너를 돕기 위해 내 힘이 닿는 한 모든 것을 할 거야.

34 그러나 너는 네 역할을 해야만 해.

35 선수들의 부모들 역시 카터의 결정을 좋아하지 않았습니다.

36 부모들의 요구에 따라 교장은 카터에게 체육관을 다시 열도록 했습니다.

37 실망한 카터는 리치몬드 고등학교를 떠나기로 결심했습니다.

38 그가 짐을 싸기 위해 체육관으로 들어섰을 때, 그의 선수들 모두가 그곳에 있었습니다.

39 우리는 여러분이 이 영화를 즐기기 원합니다. 그래서 당신에게 다음에 무슨 일이 일어나는지 이야기하지 않을 것입니다.

40 영화 「코치 카터」를 보고 스스로 찾아보세요.

● 우리말을 참고하여 본문을 영작하시오.

1 「영화 여행」에 오신 것을 환영합니다.

➡ _____

2 오늘 우리는 영화 「코치 카터」에 대해 이야기할 것입니다.

➡ _____

3 선수들이 연습하는 것을 허락하지 않는 농구 코치를 상상할 수 있나요?

➡ _____

4 그것이 바로 카터 코치가 한 것입니다.

➡ _____

5 이 영화는 경기에서 이기는 것보다 학생들을 더 걱정하는 코치에 대한 영화입니다.

➡ _____

6 캘리포니아 리치몬드 지역의 리치몬드 고등학교 농구 팀은 연속해서 경기에서 지고 있었습니다.

➡ _____

_____

7 선수들도 지는 것에 익숙하게 되었습니다.

➡ _____

8 설상가상으로 그들은 미래에 대한 계획도 없었습니다. 즉, 그들은 단지 농구하기 위해 학교에 갔고, 그것마저도 잘하지 못했습니다.

➡ _____

_____

9 그때 그들은 케니 카터라는 새로운 코치를 선임했습니다.

➡ _____

10 카터 코치는 몇 가지를 바꾸고자 했습니다.

➡ _____

11 그는 아이들에게 어떻게 농구를 잘하고 이기는지를 가르치기를 원했습니다.

➡ _____

12 그러나 그것보다도, 그는 그들을 대학에 보냄으로써 선수들에게 미래를 주기를 원했습니다.

➡ _____

13 그의 계획을 실행하기 위해서, 카터 코치는 선수들에게 계약서에 서명하게 했습니다.
➡ _____

14 그들은 농구를 하는 것뿐만 아니라 열심히 공부할 것도 약속해야만 했습니다.
➡ _____

15 처음에는 학생들이 계약서에 대한 그의 생각을 심각하게 받아들이지 않았습니다.
➡ _____

16 카터: 내가 너희들에게 계약서를 줄 것이다.
➡ _____

17 크루즈: "모든 수업에 출석하라." "C 플러스 또는 그 이상 받아라." "지각하지 말아라."
➡ _____

18 이 모든 규칙들은 무엇이죠?
➡ _____

19 제가 이 계약서에 사인하면 사이닝 보너스를 받나요?
➡ _____

20 카터: 그래. 너는 큰 보너스를 받게 될 거야. 왜냐하면 인생의 게임에서뿐 아니라 농구 경기에서도 승리자가 될 것이기 때문이지.
➡ _____
_____

21 맹연습과 새로운 경기 전략으로 그 팀은 몇 년 만에 처음으로 이기기 시작했습니다.
➡ _____

22 그때 이후로 경기마다 이겼습니다.
➡ _____

23 카터 코치를 제외한 모든 이들이 행복했습니다.
➡ _____

24 선수들은 그들 계약의 '학습' 부분을 하지 않았습니다.
➡ _____

25 그들 중 정말 그들이 대학을 갈 수 있다고 믿는 사람들은 거의 없었습니다. 그래서 그들은 성적에는 거의 관심을 두지 않았습니다.
➡ _____
_____

26 카터는 더 강력한 조치를 취하기로 결심했습니다.
➡ _____

27 그는 체육관 문을 잠그고 계약서에서 약속한 대로 그들의 성적이 좋아질 때까지 농구를 못하게 했습니다.
➡ _____
_____

28 선수들은 그것을 좋아하지 않았습니다.

➡ _____

29 그들은 그에게 그의 행동들이 그들을 위한 것이 아닌 단지 카터 자신을 위한 것이라고 말했습니다.

➡ _____

30 웜: 우리는 농구 팀이에요.

➡ _____

31 우리가 보는 모든 것은 유명세를 타며 TV에 있는 당신이에요.

➡ _____

32 카터: 네가 그렇게 생각한다면, 집으로 가서 너 자신에게 물어봐. "나는 더 나은 삶을 원하는가?"

➡ _____

33 대답이 '맞다'라면, 나는 너를 돕기 위해 내 힘이 닿는 한 모든 것을 할 거야.

➡ _____

34 그러나 너는 네 역할을 해야만 해.

➡ _____

35 선수들의 부모들 역시 카터의 결정을 좋아하지 않았습니다.

➡ _____

36 부모들의 요구에 따라 교장은 카터에게 체육관을 다시 열도록 했습니다.

➡ _____

37 실망한 카터는 리치몬드 고등학교를 떠나기로 결심했습니다.

➡ _____

38 그가 짐을 싸기 위해 체육관으로 들어섰을 때, 그의 선수들 모두가 그곳에 있었습니다.

➡ _____

39 우리는 여러분이 이 영화를 즐기기 원합니다. 그래서 당신에게 다음에 무슨 일이 일어나는지 이야기하지 않을 것입니다.

➡ _____

40 영화 「코치 카터」를 보고 스스로 찾아보세요.

➡ _____

01 다음 짝지어진 단어의 관계가 같도록 빈칸에 알맞은 말을 쓰시오.

> win : lose = lock : _____

02 다음 문장의 빈칸에 들어갈 말을 〈보기〉에서 골라 쓰시오.

┌─ 보기 ─┐
take action / one after another /
carry out / for the first time
└───────┘

(1) Jane visited Korea _____.
(2) We should _____ his plans immediately.
(3) The company will _____ to prevent further damage.
(4) Many animals died _____.

03 다음 우리말에 맞게 빈칸에 알맞은 말을 쓰시오.

(1) 그는 즉시 그 문서에 서명해야 한다.
　➡ He has to _____ the document immediately.
(2) 당신은 계약서에서 세부사항을 확인할 수 있다.
　➡ You can see the details in the _____.
(3) 그 식당은 일요일을 제외하고 매일 영업한다.
　➡ The restaurant is open every day _____ Sundays.

04 다음 영영풀이에 알맞은 어휘를 〈보기〉에서 찾아 쓰시오.

┌─ 보기 ─┐
order　pack　improve　attend
└───────┘

(1) to make something better: _____
(2) to go to and be present at an event, meeting, etc.: _____
(3) to use your authority to tell someone to do something: _____
(4) to put something into a bag, suitcase, etc., so that you can take it with you: _____

05 다음 문장의 괄호 안에서 알맞은 것을 고르시오.

(1) Do you know (what, when, where) to come here again?
　➡ _____
(2) She ordered me (wash, washing, to wash) the dishes.
　➡ _____
(3) We were (too, so, enough) tired to walk anymore.
　➡ _____

06 다음 우리말에 맞게 주어진 어휘를 바르게 배열하시오.

(1) Brown 씨는 그의 아들이 파티에 가게 허락했다.
　(Mr. Brown, the party, his son, go, let, to)
　➡ _____
(2) 프로젝트 책임자는 우리를 오전 9시에 만나게 했다.
　(the project manager, us, had, meet, 9 a.m., at)
　➡ _____

(3) 그들은 내게 그 이야기 전체를 반복하게 만들었다.
(me, they, story, repeat, whole, made, the)

➡ _____

(4) 그녀는 내가 이 숙제를 끝낼 수 있도록 도와주었다.

(this assignment, she, me, complete, helped, to)

➡ _____

07 관계대명사 what을 사용하여 주어진 두 문장을 한 문장으로 바꾸시오.

(1) • I want to do something for the community.
    • It is to pick up trash.

➡ _____

_____

(2) • I liked the thing.
    • Yuna gave it to me last month.

➡ _____

(3) • Did you enjoy the movie?
    • We saw it at the movie theater last night.

➡ _____

_____

08 다음 두 문장을 괄호 안의 조건대로 한 문장으로 쓰시오.

> • He has knowledge. (well을 이용하여)
> • He has experience, too.

➡ _____

[09~10] 다음 글을 읽고, 물음에 답하시오.

> To carry ___ⓐ___ his plan, Coach Carter had the players sign a contract. They had to promise to study hard in addition ___ⓑ___ playing basketball. At first, students did not take his idea for a contract ⓒserious.

09 위 글의 빈칸 ⓐ와 ⓑ에 알맞은 단어를 쓰시오.

ⓐ _____ ⓑ _____

10 위 글의 밑줄 친 ⓒ를 알맞은 형으로 고치시오.

➡ _____

[11~12] 다음 글을 읽고, 물음에 답하시오.

> Welcome to *Movie Trip*. Today we're going to talk about the movie *Coach Carter*. Can you imagine a basketball coach who doesn't allow his players to practice? That's exactly ___ⓐ___ Coach Carter does. This movie is about a coach who cares more about his students than about ⓑwin games.

11 위 글의 빈칸 ⓐ에 알맞은 말을 쓰시오.

➡ _____

12 위 글의 밑줄 친 ⓑwin을 알맞은 형으로 고치시오.

➡ _____

[13~16] 다음 글을 읽고, 물음에 답하시오.

The basketball team at Richmond High School in Richmond, California, was having one losing season after another. The players became used to losing. ⓐ설상가상으로, they had no plans for the future; they went to school only to play basketball, and ⓑthey did not do that very well. Then they got a new coach, Kenny Carter. Coach Carter wanted to change things. He wanted to teach kids ⓒ_____ to play basketball well and win. But more than that, he wanted to give the players a future by sending them to college.

13 위 글의 밑줄 친 ⓐ를 주어진 단어를 써서 영어로 옮기시오.

(make, worse)

➡ _____

14 위 글의 밑줄 친 ⓑ가 do that의 의미가 구체적으로 들어나도록 우리말로 옮기시오.

➡ _____

15 위 글의 빈칸 ⓒ에 알맞은 의문사를 쓰시오.

➡ _____

16 Carter가 어떤 변화를 원했는지 우리말로 쓰시오.

(1) _____
(2) _____

[17~20] 다음 글을 읽고, 물음에 답하시오.

With hard work and a new game plan, the team began to win for the first time in many years. From that point on, they won game ⓐ_____ game. Everybody, except Coach Carter, was happy. The players did not do the "study" part of their contract. Few of them actually believed they could go to college, so they paid ⓑ(little / a little) attention to their grades. Carter decided to take stronger action. He locked the gym and refused to let them play basketball until their grades improved, as promised in the contract. The players did not like it. They told him that his actions were just for him, not for them.

17 위 글의 빈칸 ⓐ에 알맞은 단어를 쓰시오.

➡ _____

18 위 글의 괄호 ⓑ에서 알맞은 것을 고르시오.

➡ _____

19 Why wasn't Coach Carter happy? Answer in English by beginning with 'Because'. (12 words)

➡ _____

_____

20 Carter가 취한 더 강한 조치가 구체적으로 무엇인지 우리말로 쓰시오.

➡ _____

_____

01 출제율 95%

다음 문장의 빈칸에 들어갈 말을 〈보기〉에서 골라 쓰시오.

┌─ 보기 ─┐
coach / exactly / imagine /
lock / college
└─────┘

(1) Please describe _____ what you saw.
(2) If you shut the door, it will _____ automatically.
(3) She will graduate from _____ this year.
(4) The _____ is teaching him how to jump.
(5) Close your eyes and _____ that you are in a forest.

02 출제율 90%

다음 영영풀이에 해당하는 단어는?

┌──────────────────────┐
a document on which the words of a
contract are written
└──────────────────────┘

① grade   ② data
③ diagram   ④ contract
⑤ evidence

03 출제율 100%

다음 중 밑줄 친 부분의 뜻풀이가 바르지 <u>않은</u> 것은?

① Jack runs every day to <u>improve</u> his health. (향상시키다)
② They're waiting to <u>sign</u> the contract. (서명하다)
③ My mom will <u>allow</u> me to keep a dog. (허락하다)
④ I work every day <u>except</u> Monday. (~을 포함하여)
⑤ The store will <u>reopen</u> at 9 a.m. on 2 January. (다시 문을 열다)

04 출제율 95%

다음 짝지어진 두 단어의 관계가 같도록 빈칸에 알맞은 말을 쓰시오.

┌──────────────────────┐
decide : decision = refuse : _____
└──────────────────────┘

05 출제율 100%

다음 문장의 빈칸에 공통으로 들어갈 알맞은 것은?

┌──────────────────────┐
• I'd like to _____ Chinese food.
• I _____ you to leave here immediately!
└──────────────────────┘

① sign   ② pack
③ order   ④ allow
⑤ care

06 출제율 95%

다음 빈칸을 〈보기〉에 있는 어휘를 이용하여 채우시오.

┌─ 보기 ─┐
take   make   pay   carry
└─────┘

(1) She didn't _____ out her promise.
(2) My car broke down, and to _____ matters worse, it began to rain.
(3) Why don't you _____ attention to me when I speak to you?
(4) I asked him to _____ appropriate action.

07 출제율 90%

다음 영영풀이에 해당하는 단어를 쓰시오. (d로 시작할 것)

┌──────────────────────┐
a forceful statement in which you say
that something must be done or given to
you
└──────────────────────┘

➡ _____

Look Inside You

🎤 의사소통 기능

- 설명 요청하기

  A: What does "pull myself together" mean?

  B: It means "to calm down."

- 대안 묻기

  A: Are there any other sauces?

  B: Sorry. Those are the only two we have.

🎤 언어 형식

- 관계대명사 what

  What you draw and how you draw it are related to your personality.

- 현재완료진행형

  Doctors **have been using** various drawing tests to better understand people.

Words & Expressions

Key Words

- **above** [əbʌ́v] 전 ~ 위에
- **active** [ǽktiv] 형 활동적인
- **against** [əgénst] 전 ~에 반대하여
- **annoyed** [ənɔ́id] 형 짜증이 난
- **app** [æp] 명 앱, 응용 프로그램
- **article** [áːrtikl] 명 기사
- **attention** [əténʃən] 명 주의, 집중
- **below** [bilóu] 전 ~ 아래에
- **bright** [brait] 형 밝은, 긍정적인
- **calm** [kɑːm] 형 차분한
- **careful** [kɛ́ərfəl] 형 주의 깊은
- **cheerful** [tʃíərfəl] 형 발랄한, 쾌활한
- **closely** [klóusli] 부 면밀히, 밀접하게
- **comfortable** [kʌ́mfərtəbl] 형 편한, 편안한
- **creative** [kriéitiv] 형 창의적인
- **crowd** [kraud] 명 사람들, 군중
- **culture** [kʌ́ltʃər] 명 문화
- **curious** [kjúəriəs] 형 호기심이 있는
- **delay** [diléi] 동 미루다, 연기하다
- **dependent** [dipéndənt] 형 의존적인
- **detail** [ditéil] 명 세부 사항
- **difference** [dífərəns] 명 다름, 차이점
- **draw** [drɔː] 동 (그림을) 그리다, (관심 등을) 끌다
- **drop** [drɑp] 명 방울
- **emotion** [imóuʃən] 명 감정
- **express** [iksprés] 동 표현하다
- **focus** [fóukəs] 동 집중하다
- **future** [fjúːtʃər] 명 미래
- **friendly** [fréndli] 형 친절한
- **frightened** [fráitnd] 형 겁먹은, 두려워하는
- **heavy** [hévi] 형 심한, 거센
- **hold** [hould] 동 들다
- **hopeful** [hóupfəl] 형 희망찬
- **imagination** [imædʒənéiʃən] 명 상상, 상상력
- **independent** [ìndipéndənt] 형 독립적인, 자립심이 강한
- **language** [lǽŋgwidʒ] 명 언어
- **light** [lait] 형 가벼운
- **loudly** [láudli] 부 큰 소리로
- **magazine** [mǽgəzìːn] 명 잡지
- **means** [miːnz] 명 수단, 방법
- **meaning** [míːniŋ] 명 의미
- **nervous** [nə́ːrvəs] 형 불안해[초조해/두려워] 하는
- **opinion** [əpínjən] 명 의견
- **personality** [pə̀ːrsənǽləti] 명 성격
- **peaceful** [píːsfəl] 형 평화로운
- **popular** [pɑ́pjulər] 형 인기 있는
- **possible** [pɑ́səbl] 형 가능한
- **protection** [prətékʃən] 명 보호
- **raise** [reiz] 동 기르다
- **realistic** [rìːəlístik] 형 현실적인
- **reasonable** [ríːzənəbl] 형 합리적인
- **recipe** [résəpi] 명 조리[요리]법
- **reduce** [ridjúːs] 동 줄이다
- **relate** [riléit] 동 ~을 관련[연결]시키다
- **relax** [rilǽks] 동 (긴장을) 늦추다, 휴식을 취하다
- **scary** [skɛ́əri] 형 무서운, 겁나는
- **seat** [siːt] 명 자리, 좌석
- **shy** [ʃai] 형 수줍어하는
- **situation** [sìtʃuéiʃən] 명 상황, 환경
- **spicy** [spáisi] 형 매운
- **stressful** [strésfəl] 형 스트레스가 많은
- **study** [stʌ́di] 동 연구하다, 살피다
- **sweat** [swet] 명 땀, 식은땀
- **try** [trai] 동 (시험 삼아) 해 보다
- **type** [taip] 명 유형
- **useful** [júːsfəl] 형 유용한, 도움이 되는
- **various** [vɛ́əriəs] 형 여러 가지의, 다양한
- **zone** [zoun] 명 구역

Key Expressions

- **according to** ~에 따르면, ~에 따라
- **at the same time** 동시에, 함께
- **be ready to** ~할 준비가 되다
- **be related to** ~와 연관되다
- **deal with** ~을 다루다, ~을 처리하다
- **draw attention to oneself** 자신에게 관심을 끌다
- **for example** 예를 들어
- **get along** (사람들과) 잘 어울리다
- **have to do with** ~와 관련되다
- **in other words** 다시 말하면
- **on the other hand** 반면에, 한편으로는
- **participate in** ~에 참가하다
- **see A as B** A를 B로 보다
- **sold out** 매진된, 다 팔린

Word Power

※ 서로 비슷한 뜻을 가진 어휘

- □ **various** (여러 가지의) – **diverse** (여러 가지의)
- □ **scary** (무서운) – **horrifying** (무서운)
- □ **popular** (인기 있는) – **well-liked** (인기 있는)
- □ **personality** (성격) – **character** (성격)

- □ **useful** (도움이 되는) – **helpful** (도움이 되는)
- □ **reduce** (줄이다) – **lessen** (줄이다)
- □ **nervous** (걱정하는) – **anxious** (걱정하는)
- □ **reasonable** (합리적인) – **logical** (타당한)

※ 서로 반대의 뜻을 가진 어휘

- □ **above** (~ 위에) ↔ **below** (~ 아래에)
- □ **comfortable** (편안한) ↔ **uncomfortable** (불편한)
- □ **difference** (다름, 차이) ↔ **similarity** (유사, 비슷함)
- □ **dependent** (의존적인) ↔ **independent** (독립적인)

- □ **future** (미래) ↔ **past** (과거)
- □ **heavy** (무거운) ↔ **light** (가벼운)
- □ **hopeful** (희망찬) ↔ **hopeless** (절망적인)

※ 동사 → 명사

- □ **imagine** (상상하다) → **imagination** (상상)
- □ **create** (창조하다) → **creation** (창조)
- □ **attend** (주의를 기울이다) → **attention** (주의)

- □ **express** (표현하다) → **expression** (표현)
- □ **protect** (보호하다) → **protection** (보호)
- □ **relate** (관련시키다) → **relation** (관련)

English Dictionary

□ **attitude** 태도
→ the way you think and feel about someone or something
당신이 어떤 사람이나 사물에 대해 생각하거나 느끼는 방식

□ **calm** 차분한
→ not excited, nervous, or upset
흥분하거나 긴장하거나 화내지 않는

□ **difference** 다름, 차이점
→ something that makes one thing or person not the same as another thing or person
한 사물이나 사람을 다른 사물이나 사람과 같지 않게 만드는 것

□ **express** 표현하다
→ to show or make known a feeling, an opinion, etc. by words, looks or actions
말, 표정 또는 행동으로 감정, 의견 등을 표시하거나 알려주다

□ **frightened** 겁먹은, 두려워하는
→ feeling or showing fear
두려움을 느끼거나 드러내는

□ **hopeful** 희망찬
→ believing that something you want will happen
당신이 원하는 일이 일어날 것이라고 믿는

□ **independent** 독립적인, 자립심이 강한
→ not requiring or relying on other people for help or support
다른 사람에게 도움이나 지원을 구하거나 의지하지 않는

□ **personality** 성격
→ the set of emotional qualities, ways of behaving, etc., that makes a person different from other people
어떤 사람을 다른 사람과 구별시켜 주는 일련의 감정적인 특성, 행동 방식 따위

□ **reasonable** 합리적인
→ fair and sensible
타당하고 분별 있는

□ **reduce** 줄이다
→ to make something smaller in size, amount, number, etc.
어떤 것의 크기, 양, 수 등이 작아지게 하다

서답형

01 다음 짝지어진 단어의 관계가 같도록 빈칸에 알맞은 말을 쓰시오.

> future : past = dependent : _____

02 다음 영영풀이가 가리키는 것을 고르시오.

> the set of emotional qualities, ways of behaving, etc., that makes a person different from other people

① detail   ② expression

③ attitude   ④ opinion

⑤ personality

중요

03 다음 중 밑줄 친 부분의 뜻풀이가 바르지 <u>않은</u> 것은?

① The price was quite <u>reasonable</u>. (합리적인)

② Let me write a <u>recipe</u> for you. (조리법)

③ Please <u>hold</u> this box for a while. (들다)

④ Television is an effective <u>means</u> of communication. (의미)

⑤ You should <u>focus</u> more on your studies. (집중하다)

서답형

04 다음 우리말에 맞게 빈칸에 알맞은 말을 쓰시오. (2 단어)

> 표가 매진되어서 나는 그 콘서트에 갈 수 없었다.
>
> ➡ I couldn't go to the concert because the tickets were _____.

서답형

05 다음 영영풀이에 해당하는 단어를 쓰시오. (주어진 철자로 시작할 것)

> the way you think and feel about someone or something

➡ a_____

중요

06 다음 주어진 문장의 밑줄 친 express와 <u>다른</u> 의미로 쓰인 것은?

> In class, we learned how to <u>express</u> our opinions clearly.

① I <u>expressed</u> concern about the changes.

② Teenagers often have difficulty <u>expressing</u> themselves.

③ My twins <u>express</u> their feelings in the paintings.

④ I'm going to travel by <u>express</u>.

⑤ Words cannot <u>express</u> how happy I am now.

서답형

07 다음 우리말에 맞게 빈칸에 알맞은 단어를 쓰시오.

(1) 우리는 삼림 보호를 위한 법률을 만들어야 한다.

  ➡ We should make a law for the _____ of forests.

(2) 이 상황에서는 그것이 좋은 생각인 것 같다.

  ➡ In this _____, I think that would be a good idea.

(3) 이 두 단어 사이에는 의미상 차이가 없다.

  ➡ There's no _____ in meaning between these two words.

01 다음 짝지어진 두 단어의 관계가 같도록 빈칸에 알맞은 말을 쓰시오. (주어진 철자로 시작할 것)

> heavy : light = difference : s_____

02 다음 빈칸에 알맞은 단어를 〈보기〉에서 골라 쓰시오.

> ┌─ 보기 ─┐
> focus   opinion   raise   details

(1) His boss checked the _____ before the meeting.
(2) My personal _____ doesn't matter in this situation.
(3) You should take responsibility when you _____ a dog.
(4) You should _____ more on your studies.

03 다음 우리말에 맞게 빈칸에 알맞은 말을 쓰시오.

(1) 이 두 개의 버튼을 동시에 눌러 주세요.
  ➡ Please press these two buttons _____ _____ _____ _____.
(2) 후기들에 따르면, 이 영화는 흥미로울 것이 틀림없다.
  ➡ _____ _____ the reviews, this movie must be interesting.
(3) 이번 행사에 참여할 뜻이 있으면 언제든지 전화 주세요.
  ➡ Please call me anytime if you want to _____ _____ this event.

04 다음 제시된 의미에 맞는 단어를 주어진 철자로 시작하여 빈칸에 쓰고, 알맞은 것을 골라 문장을 완성하시오.

> • r_____ : fair and sensible
> • f_____ : feeling or showing fear
> • r_____ : to make something smaller in size, amount, number, etc.

(1) Ellen was _____ to speak in public.
(2) He is a very _____ man.
(3) We'll need to _____ the weight by half.

05 두 문장이 같은 의미가 되도록 빈칸을 채우시오.

> There are now several different types of cars which are eco-friendly.
> = There are now _____ cars which are eco-friendly.

06 다음 우리말과 일치하도록 주어진 단어를 모두 배열하여 영작하시오.

(1) Jake는 혼자 살 준비가 되지 않았다. (not / is / Jake / live / on / to / ready / own / his)
  ➡ _____
(2) Jane은 화가 난 개들을 다루는 방법을 안다. (knows / with / how / Jane / deal / to / dogs / angry)
  ➡ _____
(3) 그건 문화와 관련이 있을지도 모른다. (with / it / have / may / to / culture / do)
  ➡ _____

1 설명 요청하기

> A: What does "pull myself together" mean? 'pull myself together'가 무엇을 의미하니?
> B: It means "to calm down." 그것은 '진정하는 것'을 의미해.

- What does ~ mean?은 '~가 무엇을 의미하니?'라는 뜻으로 상대방에게 설명을 요청할 때 쓸 수 있는 표현이다. What is the meaning of ~?, What do you mean by ~?, 또는 Could[Can] you explain what ~ mean(s)?, Could[Can] you tell me the meaning of ~? 등으로 바꿔 쓸 수 있다.

- 상대방의 질문에 설명할 때는 It means ~.(그것은 ~을 의미한다.)로 답한다. 상대방이 질문한 것에 모른다고 답할 때는 I'm sorry, but I don't know what it means., Sorry, but I'm not sure what it means. 등으로 답할 수 있다.

- 상대방의 말을 듣고 더 설명해 달라고 할 때는 Could[Can] you tell me more about ~?이라고 한다. 좀더 공손하게 표현하여 Can 대신 Could나 Would를 사용할 수도 있다. tell 대신 explain을 써서 Could[Can] you explain that more, please?라고 할 수 있다.

설명 요청하기

- What does ~ mean? ~가 무엇을 의미하니?
- What is the meaning of ~? ~의 의미가 무엇이니?
- What do you mean by ~? ~의 의미가 무엇이니?
- Could[Can] you explain what ~ mean(s)? ~가 무슨 의미인지 설명해 줄 수 있니?
- Could[Can] you tell me the meaning of ~? ~의 의미를 설명해 줄 수 있니?

핵심 Check

1. 다음 대화의 순서를 바르게 배열하시오.

A: Hi, Jack! How are you doing?

(A) It means I'm really happy and excited.

(B) I'm on cloud nine! I got a concert ticket for my favorite band.

(C) What does 'on cloud nine' mean?

➡ _____

01 다음 중 짝지어진 대화가 <u>어색한</u> 것은?

① A: What does "have a long face" mean?
B: It means "to look sad."
② A: Are there any other sauces?
B: Sorry. Those are the only two we have.
③ A: What do you mean by that?
B: It means "to give up."
④ A: What does that mean?
B: He seems to understand you.
⑤ A: Let's watch this movie.
B: Are there any other movies?

[02~06] 다음 대화를 읽고 물음에 답하시오.

G: I took a personality test today. I had to draw a house.
B: A house?
G: Yeah. According to the test, you can tell a lot about a person ___(A)___ their drawing. Here's mine.
B: Interesting. So (B)what do these big windows mean?
G: (C)They mean I'm open to other people

02 위 대화의 빈칸 (A)에 알맞은 것은?

① on   ② by
③ into   ④ with
⑤ from

03 위 대화의 밑줄 친 (B)를 다음과 같이 바꿔 쓸 때 빈칸에 알맞은 말을 쓰시오.

what is the _____ of these big windows?

04 위 대화의 밑줄 친 (C)They가 가리키는 말을 쓰시오.

➡ _____

05 위 대화에서 다음 영영풀이에 해당하는 단어를 찾아 쓰시오.

expressing thoughts and feelings in a direct and honest way

➡ _____

06 위 대화의 내용과 일치하지 <u>않는</u> 것은?

① 소녀는 오늘 성격검사를 했다.
② 소녀는 성격검사에서 집을 그렸다.
③ 그림을 통해서 사람에 대해 많은 것을 알 수 있다.
④ 소녀는 큰 창문들을 그렸다.
⑤ 큰 창문들은 타인에 의해 괴롭힘을 당한다는 의미이다.

07 다음 대화가 자연스럽게 이어지도록 순서대로 배열하시오.

(A) Hi, Jack! How are you doing?
(B) It means I'm really happy and excited.
(C) What does "on cloud nine" mean?
(D) I'm on cloud nine! I got a concert ticket for my favorite band.

➡ _____

[08~10] 다음 대화를 읽고 물음에 답하시오.

B: Jane, what are you reading?
G: I'm reading an interesting magazine. (①)
B: That's surprising. (②)
G: Yes. (③) For example, the color red can help us focus better. (④)
B: 다른 어떤 유용한 색깔들이 있니? (useful / any / there)
G: Yes. The color blue helps people relax. (⑤)

08 위 대화의 ①~⑤ 중 다음 문장이 들어갈 위치로 알맞은 곳은?

It says colors can change people's feelings.

①   ②   ③   ④   ⑤

09 위 대화의 밑줄 친 우리말을 주어진 단어를 이용해 영작하시오.

➡ _____

10 위 대화의 내용과 일치하지 <u>않는</u> 것은?

① Jane은 흥미로운 잡지책을 읽고 있다.
② 잡지는 색깔과 사람들의 기분에 관한 것이다.
③ Jane은 이미 색깔이 어떻게 사람의 감정에 영향을 미치는지 알고 있었다.
④ 빨간색은 사람들이 보다 더 집중하도록 도와준다.
⑤ 사람들은 파란색으로 편안함을 느낄 수 있다.

[11~13] 다음 대화를 읽고 물음에 답하시오.

M: EDPI Test Center. Do you want to learn more about yourself? We have many kinds of personality tests. If there are ___(A)___ tests you want to learn more about, we are here to help you.
B: Hi, I'm calling to take a personality test. Can I do (B)one this afternoon?
M: Sure, you can come ___(C)___ before 5 o'clock.

11 위 대화의 빈칸 (A)와 (C)에 알맞은 말이 바르게 짝지어진 것은?

① another – any time
② any other – a little time
③ any more – some time
④ any other – any time
⑤ some more – any time

12 위 대화의 밑줄 친 (B)one이 가리키는 말을 찾아 쓰시오.

➡ _____

13 위 대화의 내용과 일치하지 <u>않는</u> 것은?

① M은 EDPI 적성검사 센터의 직원이다.
② 검사 센터에는 많은 종류의 검사가 있다.
③ B는 적성검사를 신청하기 위해 검사 센터를 방문했다.
④ B는 오늘 오후에 적성검사를 받고 싶어 한다.
⑤ B는 5시 이전에 아무 때나 센터에 방문하면 된다.

[01~04] 다음 대화를 읽고 물음에 답하시오.

Hajun: Look! I found this test on an app that tells what kind of person you are. Do you want to try (a)it?

Emma: Sure. Sounds like fun.

Hajun: Okay, listen. What are you afraid of? Choose one of (A)[this / these]: crowds, spiders, or dark places.

Emma: I hate dark places. I cannot sleep without a night light (B)[on /off]. What does that mean?

Hajun: It says you are full of imagination. That's why you fill dark places (C)[of / with] all kinds of scary things.

Emma: That's very interesting. What about you? Is there anything you are afraid of?

Hajun: I chose dark places too. But I don't think I have a big imagination.

Emma: This is fun. I want to do some more. (b)우리가 할 수 있는 다른 검사들이 있니? (take / there / any)

Hajun: Sure. This app has a lot of them.

01 위 대화의 밑줄 친 (a)it이 가리키는 말을 영어로 쓰시오.

➡ _____

02 위 대화의 (A)~(C)에서 어법상이나 문맥상 알맞은 단어를 골라 쓰시오.

(A) _____ (B) _____ (C) _____

03 위 대화의 밑줄 친 (b)의 우리말을 주어진 단어를 이용하여 영작하시오.

➡ _____

04 What does it mean to you if you hate dark places? Answer in English.

➡ _____

[05~08] 다음 대화를 읽고 물음에 답하시오.

B: What's your blood type?

G: Type A. Why?

B: I'm reading an article. It says that blood type tells something about your personality.

G: Wow. 그러면 A형은 무엇을 의미하니?

B: People with blood type A are calm. They are good listeners, too.

05 What are the boy and the girl talking about?

➡ _____

06 What's the girl's blood type?

➡ _____

07 Write down the personality of people with blood type A. Answer in Korean.

➡ _____

08 위 대화의 밑줄 친 우리말을 영어로 쓰시오.

➡ _____

Grammar

① 관계대명사 what

> • **What** you draw and how you draw it are related to your personality.
> 당신이 무엇을 그리는지 그리고 그것을 어떻게 그리는지는 당신의 성격과 관련이 있습니다.

■ 관계대명사 what은 '~인 것', '~하는 것'으로 해석한다.

• I know **what** you did yesterday. 나는 네가 어제 한 것을 알고 있다.

■ 선행사를 포함하는 관계대명사로 풀어서 표현하면 the thing(s) that[which]로 쓸 수 있다.

• I can't hear the thing. + You said the thing. 나는 그것을 들을 수 없다. + 너는 그것을 말했다.
= I can't hear the thing that you said.
= I can't hear **what** you said.

cf. The rain shows the stress the person **who** drew the picture is under. 비는 그림을 그린 사람이 받고 있는 스트레스를 보여 줍니다. (관계대명사 who의 선행사는 the person이고 who는 형용사절을 이끔.)

Tell me the story **which** you have heard. 당신이 들은 이야기를 나에게 말해 주세요.
(관계대명사 which의 선행사는 the story이고 which는 형용사절을 이끔.)

■ 관계대명사 what은 명사절로 주어, 목적어, 보어 역할을 한다.

• You can pick the thing. + You want the thing.
= You can pick the thing which you want.
(관계대명사 which의 선행사는 the thing이다.)
= You can pick **what** you want. 너는 네가 원하는 것을 고를 수 있다.
(관계대명사 what은 what 앞에 위치한 주절의 동사 pick의 목적어(명사)와 관계사절의 동사 want의 목적어 역할을 한다.)

• He wanted to have **what** they had found. 그는 그들이 발견한 것을 가지기를 원했다.

핵심 Check

1. 다음 괄호 안에서 알맞은 것을 고르시오.

(1) This is (that / what) made him happy.

(2) (That / What) she says is not important.

② 현재완료진행형

> • Doctors **have been using** various drawing tests to better understand people.
> 의사들은 사람들을 더 잘 이해하기 위해 다양한 그림 그리기 검사를 사용해 오고 있습니다.

■ 현재완료진행형은 현재완료(have/has+p.p.) + 현재진행형(be+~ing)으로 'have[has]+been+~ing'로 쓰고, '(과거부터 지금까지) ~해 오고 있다'로 해석한다.

  • Lisa **has been learning** English since she was ten. Lisa는 10살 때부터 영어를 배워오고 있다.

■ 과거에 시작되어 현재도 지속되는 일을 표현할 때 쓰고, 기간을 나타내기 위해 'for, how long, since' 등을 함께 쓸 수 있다.

  • He **has been playing** the guitar for two straight hours. 그는 2시간 연속으로 기타를 치고 있다.

  • My sister **has been playing** the piano since this morning. 언니는 오늘 아침부터 피아노를 치고 있다.

■ 현재완료진행형의 축약형은 "'ve['s]+been+~ing"로 쓴다.

  • We**'ve been waiting** for Paul for 50 minutes. 우리는 50분 동안 Paul을 기다리고 있다.

  • My dad**'s been looking** for his cellphone since yesterday evening.
  아버지는 어제 저녁부터 그의 휴대폰을 찾고 있다.

■ 부정문은 'have/has not been ~ing'로 쓴다.

  • She **hasn't been working** for two weeks. 그녀는 2주 동안 일을 하지 않고 있다.

■ 의문문은 'have/has+주어+been ~ing ~?'로 쓴다.

  • How long **have** you **been learning** Spanish? 당신은 얼마나 오랫동안 스페인어를 배우고 있나요?

■ 인식, 소유, 감정 등을 나타내는 동사는 현재완료진행형으로 쓰지 않는다.

  • I **have wanted** to meet you since I was young. 나는 어렸을 때부터 너를 만나고 싶었다.
    → I have been wanting to meet you since I was young. (✕)

핵심 Check

2. 다음 괄호 안에서 알맞은 말을 고르시오.

  (1) I (have been living / am living) in America for three years.

  (2) He (has drawing / has been drawing) a plan for the new city hall.

01 다음 문장에서 어법상 <u>어색한</u> 부분을 바르게 고쳐 쓰시오.

(1) We have been knowing each other for five years.

_____ ➡ _____

(2) I am learning French for four months.

_____ ➡ _____

(3) Which I want is to have a pet.

_____ ➡ _____

(4) I remember which I saw at the beach.

_____ ➡ _____

02 두 문장을 한 문장으로 쓰시오. (관계대명사 what을 사용할 것)

• You need the thing.
• You can tell me the thing.

➡ _____

03 다음 우리말에 맞게 괄호 안에 주어진 어구를 바르게 배열하시오.

(1) 점심때부터 내내 비가 내리고 있다. (be, since)

➡ _____

(2) 그들은 1시간 동안 달리고 있다. (be, run)

➡ _____

(3) Paul이 요리한 것은 피자였다. (what, cook)

➡ _____

(4) 나는 아들이 진짜로 필요한 것을 사줬다. (what, need)

➡ _____

(5) Suji는 1년 동안 영어를 공부하고 있다.

➡ _____

서답형

01 다음 문장에서 어법상 틀린 부분을 찾아 바르게 고쳐 쓰시오.

> My mom has cooking beef stew in the kitchen for two hours.

_____ ➡ _____

[02~03] 다음 글을 읽고 물음에 답하시오.

> I was not really good at English. (A)[That / What] I have done to improve it is to read a lot of books in English, and I could get better grades. Still, I _____(study) English at least one hour a day.

서답형

02 괄호 (A)에서 알맞은 것을 고르시오.

➡ _____

서답형

03 '공부해 오고 있는 중이다'라는 의미가 되도록 주어진 단어를 이용하여 빈칸을 채우시오.

➡ _____

 중요

04 다음 중 어색한 문장을 고르시오.

① He is the only person that I can trust.
② Sam and Son bought a swimming suit that could minimize resistance against water.
③ I don't care what people say.
④ I told you everything what I know.
⑤ The artists are drawing what they see.

*minimize: 최소화하다 *resistance: 저항

중요

05 다음 문장과 같은 뜻을 지닌 문장을 고르시오.

> The thing which he said is true.

① Which he said is true.
② What he said is true.
③ Who he said is true.
④ Whom he said is true.
⑤ That he said is true.

06 다음 빈칸에 들어갈 말로 알맞은 것을 고르시오.

> Jay is the most brilliant student _____ I've taught.

① that   ② what
③ which   ④ the thing
⑤ the thing which

서답형

07 다음 〈보기〉의 두 문장을 관계대명사를 사용하여 한 문장으로 영작하시오.

> ┤ 보기 ├
> • She bought a luxurious house.
> • It has a huge pool.

➡ _____

_____

[08~09] 다음 글을 읽고 물음에 답하시오.

> ___(A)___ I do when I'm stressed out is to watch comedy movies. I ___(B)___ (do) that since last month. It is a very helpful way to release my stress.

08 빈칸 (A)에 들어갈 적절한 단어는?

① Which ② What ③ When
④ How ⑤ That

서답형

09 괄호 안의 단어를 활용하여 빈칸 (B)에 현재완료진행형을 쓰시오.

➡ _____

서답형

10 다음 우리말과 같은 뜻이 되도록 괄호 안의 단어를 활용하여 현재완료진행 형태로 문장을 완성하시오.

> 3일 동안 비가 오고 있다. (rain)

➡ _____

중요

11 다음 우리말에 맞게 영작할 경우 어법상 어색한 것을 고르시오.

① 영어를 얼마나 오래 공부해 왔니?
  → How long have you been studying English?
② 나는 너를 찾고 있었어.
  → I have been looking for you.
③ 그녀는 3시간 동안 페인트칠을 하고 있다.
  → She painted for 3 hours.
④ 나는 2시간 동안 운동하고 있습니다.
  → I have been working out for 2 hours.
⑤ 그녀는 오늘 아침부터 기타를 치고 있습니다.
  → She has been playing the guitar since this morning.

12 우리말에 맞게 영작하고자 할 때 빈칸에 들어갈 말로 알맞은 것은?

> 나는 지난주부터 이 책을 읽고 있다.
> ➡ I _____ this book since last week.

① read ② was reading
③ reading ④ am reading
⑤ have been reading

13 다음 우리말을 바르게 영작한 것을 모두 고르시오.

> 내가 필요한 것은 바로 너의 도움이다.

① What I need is your help.
② Which I need is your help.
③ The thing which I need is your help.
④ That I need is your help.
⑤ Who I need is your help

중요

14 다음 빈칸에 들어갈 말로 바르게 짝지어진 것을 고르시오.

> • _____ makes me happy is to play soccer.
> • The book _____ he wrote was a big hit.

① That – that ② That – what
③ What – that ④ What – what
⑤ Which – that

서답형

15 우리말에 맞게 괄호 안의 어휘들을 배열하여 영작할 때, 8번째 단어를 쓰시오.

> John과 Paul이 먹고 싶은 것은 프라이드 치킨이다. (John, Paul, want, is, to, what, and, eat, fried chicken)

➡ _____

16 다음 우리말과 같은 뜻이 되도록 괄호 안의 단어를 활용하여 조건에 맞게 빈칸을 채우시오.

(1) 우리는 학교에서 많은 다양한 종류의 활동들을 하고 있다. (현재완료진행형)

➡ We _____ (do) a lot of different kinds of activities at school.

(2) 내 친구들이 나에 대해 말하는 것은 꽤 달랐다.

➡ _____ (what) about me was quite different.

(3) 나는 5년 동안 고양이를 키우고 있다. (현재완료진행형)

➡ I _____ (raise) a cat for five years.

(4) 3일 동안 눈이 오고 있다. (현재완료진행형)

➡ It _____ (snow) for three days.

(5) 내가 원하는 저녁식사는 중국 음식이다.

➡ _____ (what) for dinner is Chinese food.

(6) Jane과 Jay가 볼 것은 판타지 영화이다.

➡ _____ (what, see) is a fantasy movie.

17 다음 중 어법상 어색한 것을 고르시오.

① I have been planting trees with my friends since then.

② I've been living in Australia for 20 years.

③ Jason hasn't been feeling well since this morning.

④ She was working very hard recently.

⑤ I've been looking for this.

18 다음 중 어법상 올바른 것을 모두 고르시오.

① We have planting flowers regularly there.

② Harry has been waiting for the bus for 30 minutes.

③ Nathan worked on the project since 2019.

④ He has been watched TV since this morning.

⑤ She has been driving since she was 20.

19 다음 중 어색한 것을 고르시오.

① Don't forget that I said.

② She did what she had to do.

③ I will cook my daughter what she wants to eat.

④ What they needed was just a bottle of water.

⑤ The girl is watching a movie that makes her excited.

20 우리말에 맞게 괄호 안의 단어를 활용하여 빈칸을 채우시오. (현재완료진행형으로 쓸 것)

Tom은 2시간 동안 컴퓨터 게임을 하고 있다. (play)

➡ Tom _____ computer games for two hours.

01 우리말에 맞게 괄호 안의 단어를 활용하여 빈칸을 채우시오.

> 그림은 종종 당신의 마음속에 당신이 느끼고 있는 것과 밀접하게 관련되어 있다.
> ➡ A picture is often closely related to _____ (what, feel) in your mind.

02 밑줄 친 (A) 대신 들어갈 수 있는 것을 쓰시오.

> (A)The thing which I want to have is a computer.

➡ _____

03 관계대명사 what과 괄호 안의 단어를 활용하여 영작하시오.

(1) 나는 네가 원하는 것을 알아. (want, 5 단어)
➡ _____

(2) 이것이 바로 내가 의미하는 것이야. (mean, 5 단어)
➡ _____

(3) 내가 하는 것을 해 봐. (do, 4 단어)
➡ _____

(4) Suji가 영화관에 타고 갈 것은 버스이다. (take, 10 단어)
➡ _____

04 그림을 참고하여 우리말과 같도록 괄호 안의 단어를 활용하여 영작하시오.

> 그들은 30분 동안 치킨을 먹고 있다.
> (eat, for, 8 단어)

➡ _____

05 괄호 안의 단어를 활용하여 우리말에 맞게 영작하시오.

> 난 네가 지난여름에 한 일을 알고 있다. (know, do)

➡ _____

 06 다음 우리말을 괄호 안의 어휘를 활용하여 영작하시오.

> 나는 사람들이 말하는 것에 신경 쓰지 않는다. (care, say)

(1) (관계대명사 what을 사용할 것)
➡ _____

(2) (which를 사용할 것)
➡ _____

07 그림에 맞게 괄호 안의 단어를 활용하여 영작하시오.

(1) John은 2시간 동안 노래를 부르고 있다. (7 단어)

　➡ _____

　　(sing)

(2) 그들은 1시간 동안 다트 게임을 하고 있다.

　(8 단어)　　　　　　　　*darts: 다트 게임

　➡ _____

　　(play, darts)

(3) 그들이 원하는 것은 이야기하고 노는 것이다.

　(8 단어)

　➡ _____

　　(want, talk and play)

08 다음 우리말을 괄호 안에 주어진 어휘와 주어진 조건에 맞춰 영작하시오.

> 난 네가 요즘 무엇을 하고 있는지 알아.
> (know, do)

(1) (the thing which 사용)

　➡ _____

(2) (관계대명사 what 사용)

　➡ _____

09 괄호 안의 단어를 어법에 맞게 배열하시오.

> _____(I, to, what, finish, have) by three o'clock is an essay for homework. However, I do not have enough time to finish it. _____(have, writing, I, been) it for an hour, but I just wrote two sentences. I need more time!

10 괄호 안의 단어를 활용하여 우리말에 맞게 영작하시오.

> John이 Sally와 하고 싶은 것은 영화를 보는 것이다. (what, do, see)

➡ _____

11 다음 우리말에 맞게 괄호의 단어를 활용하여 빈칸을 채우시오.

(1) 나는 오늘 아침부터 숙제를 해오고 있는 중이다.

　➡ I _____(do) my homework since this morning.

(2) 나는 가까운 장래에 회사가 어떻게 될지 알고 있다.

　➡ I know _____ (what, become) in the near future.

Drawing the Mind

Everything you do says something about you. The language you use,
_{앞에 관계대명사 that 생략}
the clothes you wear, and even the pets you raise somehow show what
_{의문형용사 what으로 시작하는 간접의문문}
kind of person you are.

The things you draw are not much different. What you draw and how
_{별로}
you draw it are related to your personality. Doctors have been using
_{it=what you draw 동사} _{현재완료진행형}
various drawing tests to better understand people.
_{목적을 나타내는 부사적 용법}

One of those tests is the Draw-a-Person-in-the-Rain (DAPR) test.
Study the pictures below.
_{아래에, 밑에}

The person in Drawing A is holding an umbrella in a light rain. On
the other hand, the person in Drawing B is in a heavy rain and has no
umbrella. Also, there are dark clouds above the person in Drawing B.
_{~ 위에}
What can these differences mean?

First, the rain shows the stress the person who drew the picture is
_{앞에 관계대명사 that이나 which 생략}
under. The bigger the drops are or the more heavily the rain is falling,
_{the+비교급 ~, the+비교급 …: ~하면 할수록 더 …하다}
the bigger the stress is. The clouds mean problems waiting to happen,
_{현재분사: problems를 수식}
so a big cloud shows the drawer is not very hopeful about the future.
_{그래서}

---

even 심지어
raise 기르다
somehow 어떻게든, 왠지
be related to ~과 관련이 있다
personality 인격, 성격
various 다양한
light 가벼운
on the other hand 한편에
be under stress 스트레스를 받다

📎 **확인문제**

● 다음 문장이 본문의 내용과 일치하면 T, 일치하지 않으면 F를 쓰시오.

1 We can understand you by everything you do. ☐

2 The things you draw aren't related to your personality. ☐

3 A big cloud means the drawer's hope about the future. ☐

Second, the umbrella means the protection the person has in a
stressful situation. A big umbrella shows that the drawer has a lot of
plans or protection. If there's no umbrella in the drawing, the drawer
does not have any means to deal with difficult situations.

Third, the details in the drawing of the person have to do with the
drawer's attitude under stress. For example, someone who draws a
person without a face does not want to draw people's attention to
himself or herself. Someone who draws the person on the right side of
the paper is ready to meet the future. On the other hand, someone who
draws the person on the left side may be worried about things that have
happened in the past.

These are some of the possible meanings of each part of the
drawings. Now, go back and look at the two drawings. Try reading
them yourself. Can you understand what kind of person drew each
one? What's your opinion?

protection 보호

stressful 스트레스를 주는

means 수단

detail 상세

attitude 태도

deal with ~을 처리하다, 헤쳐 나가다

draw one's attention 사람의 주의를 끌다

happen 일어나다

possible 가능한

be ready to ~할 준비가 되다

확인문제

- 다음 문장이 본문의 내용과 일치하면 T, 일치하지 않으면 F를 쓰시오.

1　A small umbrella shows that the drawer has many plans. ☐

2　A big umbrella means more protection than a small umbrella. ☐

3　Someone who draws a person without a face wants to be well known. ☐

4　There are some of the possible meanings of each part of the drawings. ☐

● 우리말을 참고하여 빈칸에 알맞은 말을 쓰시오.

Drawing the Mind

1   Everything you do _____ _____ about you.

2   The language you _____, the clothes you _____, and _____ the pets you _____ somehow show _____ _____ _____ person you are.

3   The things you _____ are not _____ different.

4   _____ you draw and _____ you draw it _____ _____ _____ your personality.

5   Doctors have been using various drawing tests _____ _____ _____ people.

6   _____ of _____ _____ is the Draw-a-Person-in-the-Rain (DAPR) test.

7   Study the pictures _____.

8   The person in Drawing A is _____ an umbrella in a _____ rain.

9   On the _____ _____, the person in Drawing B is in a _____ rain and has _____ umbrella.

10 Also, there are dark clouds _____ the person in Drawing B.

11 What can these _____ _____?

12 First, the rain shows the stress the person _____ drew the picture is _____.

13 _____ _____ the drops are or _____ _____ _____ the rain is falling, _____ _____ the stress is.

14 The clouds mean problems _____ to _____, so a big cloud shows the drawer is not very _____ about the _____.

마음 그리기
1 당신이 하는 모든 행동은 당신에 대해 말해 줍니다.
2 당신이 사용하는 언어, 당신이 입는 옷, 그리고 당신이 기르는 애완동물까지도 당신이 어떤 종류의 사람인지 보여 줍니다.
3 당신이 그리는 그림도 마찬가지입니다.
4 당신이 무엇을 그리는지 그리고 그것을 어떻게 그리는지는 당신의 성격과 관련이 있습니다.
5 의사들은 사람들을 더 잘 이해하기 위해 다양한 그림 그리기 검사를 사용해 오고 있습니다.
6 이런 검사들 중 하나는 빗속의 사람 그리기 검사입니다.
7 아래의 그림들을 연구해 봅시다.
8 A 그림 속의 사람은 가벼운 빗속에서 우산을 들고 있습니다.
9 반면에, B 그림 속의 사람은 거센 빗속에서 우산을 가지고 있지 않습니다.
10 또한, 검은 구름들이 B 그림의 사람 머리 위에 있습니다.
11 이런 차이는 무엇을 의미하는 걸까요?
12 첫 번째, 비는 그림을 그린 사람이 받고 있는 스트레스를 보여 줍니다.
13 빗방울의 크기가 크면 클수록, 혹은 비가 더 세게 내리면 내릴수록 스트레스는 더 큽니다.
14 구름은 앞으로 벌어질 문제를 의미하기 때문에, 큰 구름은 그림을 그린 사람이 미래에 대해 그다지 희망적이지 않다는 것을 나타냅니다.

15 _____, the umbrella means the _____ the person has in a _____ situation.

16 A _____ umbrella _____ that the drawer has a lot of _____ or _____.

17 If there's no umbrella in the _____, the drawer does not have any _____ to _____ _____ difficult situations.

18 _____, the _____ in the drawing of the person _____ _____ _____ with the drawer's _____ under stress.

19 For _____, someone _____ draws a person _____ a face does not want to draw people's _____ to _____ or _____.

20 Someone _____ draws the person on the _____ side of the paper _____ _____ _____ meet the future.

21 On the other _____, someone who draws the person on the left side _____ be _____ about things that have _____ in the past.

22 These are some of the _____ _____ of each _____ of the drawings.

23 Now, go _____ and look _____ the two drawings.

24 Try _____ them _____.

25 Can you understand _____ _____ of person drew _____ _____?

26 What's your _____?

---

15 두 번째, 우산은 스트레스를 받는 상황에서 그 사람이 가지고 있는 보호 기제를 의미합니다.

16 큰 우산은 그림을 그린 사람이 많은 계획이나 보호 기제를 가지고 있음을 보여 줍니다.

17 만약 그림에 우산이 없다면, 그 그림을 그린 사람은 어려운 상황을 헤쳐 나갈 어떤 방법도 가지고 있지 않습니다.

18 세 번째, 그림 속 사람의 세부적인 것들은 그 그림을 그린 사람이 스트레스를 받을 때의 태도와 관련이 있습니다.

19 예를 들어, 얼굴이 없는 사람을 그린 사람은 사람들의 관심을 끌기를 원하지 않습니다.

20 사람을 종이의 오른쪽에 그린 사람은 미래를 맞이할 준비가 되어 있습니다.

21 반면에, 사람을 왼쪽에 그린 사람은 과거에 일어났던 일에 대해 걱정하고 있을 수도 있습니다.

22 이것들은 그림 각 부분의 가능한 의미 풀이 중 일부입니다.

23 이제, 돌아가서 두 그림을 보세요.

24 그 그림들을 스스로 읽으려고 시도해 보세요.

25 당신은 각 그림을 그린 사람이 어떤 사람인지 알 수 있나요?

26 당신의 의견은 어떤가요?

● 우리말을 참고하여 본문을 영작하시오.

Drawing the Mind

1 당신이 하는 모든 행동은 당신에 대해 말해 줍니다.

➡ _____

2 당신이 사용하는 언어, 당신이 입는 옷, 그리고 당신이 기르는 애완동물까지도 당신이 어떤 종류의 사람인지 보여 줍니다.

➡ _____

_____

3 당신이 그리는 그림도 마찬가지입니다.

➡ _____

4 당신이 무엇을 그리는지 그리고 그것을 어떻게 그리는지는 당신의 성격과 관련이 있습니다.

➡ _____

5 의사들은 사람들을 더 잘 이해하기 위해 다양한 그림 그리기 검사를 사용해 오고 있습니다.

➡ _____

6 이런 검사들 중 하나는 빗속의 사람 그리기 검사입니다.

➡ _____

7 아래의 그림들을 연구해 봅시다.

➡ _____

8 A 그림 속의 사람은 가벼운 빗속에서 우산을 들고 있습니다.

➡ _____

9 반면에, B 그림 속의 사람은 거센 빗속에서 우산을 가지고 있지 않습니다.

➡ _____

10 또한, 검은 구름들이 B 그림의 사람 머리 위에 있습니다.

➡ _____

11 이런 차이는 무엇을 의미하는 걸까요?

➡ _____

12 첫 번째, 비는 그림을 그린 사람이 받고 있는 스트레스를 보여줍니다.

➡ _____

13 빗방울의 크기가 크면 클수록, 혹은 비가 더 세게 내리면 내릴수록 스트레스는 더 큽니다.

➡ _____

14 구름은 앞으로 벌어질 문제를 의미하기 때문에, 큰 구름은 그림을 그린 사람이 미래에 대해 그다지 희망적이지 않다는 것을 나타냅니다.

➡ _____

_____

15 두 번째, 우산은 스트레스를 받는 상황에서 그 사람이 가지고 있는 보호 기제를 의미합니다.

➡ _____

16 큰 우산은 그림을 그린 사람이 많은 계획이나 보호 기제를 가지고 있음을 보여 줍니다.

➡ _____

17 만약 그림에 우산이 없다면, 그 그림을 그린 사람은 어려운 상황을 헤쳐 나갈 어떤 방법도 가지고
있지 않습니다.

➡ _____

_____

18 세 번째, 그림 속 사람의 세부적인 것들은 그 그림을 그린 사람이 스트레스를 받을 때의 태도와 관련이
있습니다.

➡ _____

19 예를 들어, 얼굴이 없는 사람을 그린 사람은 사람들의 관심을 끌기를 원하지 않습니다.

➡ _____

_____

20 사람을 종이의 오른쪽에 그린 사람은 미래를 맞이할 준비가 되어 있습니다.

➡ _____

21 반면에, 사람을 왼쪽에 그린 사람은 과거에 일어났던 일에 대해 걱정하고 있을 수도 있습니다.

➡ _____

_____

22 이것들은 그림 각 부분의 가능한 의미 풀이 중 일부입니다.

➡ _____

23 이제, 돌아가서 두 그림을 보세요.

➡ _____

24 그 그림들을 스스로 읽으려고 시도해 보세요.

➡ _____

25 당신은 각 그림을 그린 사람이 어떤 사람인지 알 수 있나요?

➡ _____

26 당신의 의견은 어떤가요?

➡ _____

[01~03] 다음 글을 읽고 물음에 답하시오.

(①) Everything you do says something about you. (②) The language you use, the clothes you wear, and even the pets you raise somehow show what kind of person you are. (③) _____ ⓐ you draw and _____ ⓑ you draw it are related to your personality. (④) Doctors have been using various drawing tests to better understand people. (⑤)

01 위 글의 ①~⑤ 중 다음 주어진 문장이 들어갈 알맞은 곳은?

> The things you draw are not much different.

①   ②   ③   ④   ⑤

서답형

02 위 글의 빈칸 ⓐ와 ⓑ에 알맞은 말을 쓰시오.

ⓐ _____ ⓑ _____

중요

03 위 글의 뒤에 이어질 내용으로 가장 알맞은 것은?

① 행동과 성격의 관계
② 집에서 기르는 애완동물의 종류
③ 취미로 그림 그리기
④ 나쁜 성격 고치기
⑤ 그림으로 사람의 성격을 이해하기

[04~07] 다음 글을 읽고 물음에 답하시오.

One of those tests is the Draw-a-Person-in-the-Rain (DAPR) test. Study the pictures below.

The person in Drawing A is holding an umbrella in a light rain. _____ ⓐ _____, the person in Drawing B is in a heavy rain and has no umbrella. Also, there are dark clouds above the person in Drawing B. What can these differences mean?

First, the rain shows the stress the person who drew the picture is _____ ⓑ _____. The bigger the drops are or the more heavily the rain is falling, the bigger the stress is. The clouds mean problems (A)wait to happen, so a big cloud shows the drawer is not very hopeful about the future.

04 위 글의 빈칸 ⓐ에 들어갈 말로 적절한 것은?

① At last   ② That is
③ On the whole   ④ For example
⑤ On the other hand

05 위 글의 빈칸 ⓑ에 들어갈 말로 적절한 것은?

① on   ② over
③ under   ④ across
⑤ among

서답형
06 위 글의 밑줄 친 (A)를 알맞은 형으로 고치시오.

➡ _____

중요
07 위 글의 내용과 일치하지 <u>않는</u> 것은?

① 그림 A에서는 비가 적게 오고 있다.
② 그림 B에서는 비가 많이 오고 있다.
③ 그림 B에 있는 사람의 머리 위에는 어두운 구름이 보인다.
④ 비가 많이 내릴수록 그림 속의 사람은 많은 스트레스를 받는다.
⑤ 그림 속의 큰 구름은 미래에 대한 도전을 나타낸다.

[08~10] 다음 글을 읽고 물음에 답하시오.

Second, the umbrella means the protection the person has in a ⓐstress situation. A big umbrella shows that the drawer has a lot of plans or protection. If there's no umbrella in the drawing, the drawer does not have any means ⓑto deal with difficult situations.

서답형
08 위 글의 밑줄 친 ⓐstress를 알맞은 형으로 고치시오.

➡ _____

09 위 글의 밑줄 친 ⓑ와 용법이 같은 것은?

① My hope is to work as a doctor in Africa.
② It's time to go to bed now.
③ My job is to report the news.
④ The boys hoped to find the hidden treasure.
⑤ Kate went to a shopping mall to buy clothes.

10 What does a big umbrella show? Answer in Korean.

➡ _____

[11~14] 다음 글을 읽고 물음에 답하시오.

Third, the details in the drawing of the person have to do ①with the drawer's attitude ②under stress. (A)(For example / On the other hand), someone who draws a person without a face does not want to draw people's attention ③at himself or herself. Someone who draws the person on the right side of the paper is ready to meet the ⓐ . (B)(For example / On the other hand), someone who draws the person on the left side ⓑmay be worried ④about things that have happened ⑤in the past.

11 위 글의 밑줄 친 전치사 ①~⑤ 중 어법상 어색한 것은?

① ② ③ ④ ⑤

서답형
12 위 글의 괄호 (A)와 (B)에서 각각 알맞은 것을 고르시오.

(A) _____
(B) _____

서답형

13 위 글의 빈칸 ⓐ에 본문에 나오는 단어의 반의어를 쓰시오.

➡ _____

중요

14 위 글의 밑줄 친 ⓑmay와 용법이 같은 것은?

① You <u>may</u> come in if you wish.

② <u>May</u> she rest in peace!

③ The rumor <u>may</u> be false.

④ <u>May</u> I take a picture here?

⑤ You <u>may</u> stay at this hotel for a week.

[15~16] 다음 글을 읽고 물음에 답하시오.

These are ①some of the possible meanings of each ②part of the drawings. Now, go back and look ③at the two drawings. Try ④to read them yourself. Can you understand ⑤what kind of person drew each ⓐone? What's your opinion?

15 위 글의 밑줄 친 ①~⑤ 중 어색한 것을 올바르게 바꾼 것은?

① any   ② parts

③ for   ④ reading

⑤ which

서답형

16 위 글의 밑줄 친 ⓐone이 가리키는 것을 영어로 쓰시오.

➡ _____

[17~20] 다음 글을 읽고 물음에 답하시오.

___(A)___ you do says ___(B)___ about you. The language you use, the clothes you wear, and even the pets you raise somehow show ⓐ당신이 어떤 종류의 사람인지. The things you draw are not much different. ___ⓑ___ you draw and how you draw it are related to your ⓒpersonal. Doctors have been using various drawing tests to better understand people.

중요

17 위 글의 빈칸 (A)와 (B)에 알맞은 것으로 짝지어진 것은?

① Everything – anything

② Everything – something

③ Nothing – something

④ Something – anything

⑤ Nothing – everything

서답형

18 위 글의 밑줄 친 ⓐ를 영어로 옮기시오. (6 words)

➡ _____

19 위 글의 빈칸 ⓑ에 알맞은 것은?

① What   ② That

③ Whom   ④ Why

⑤ Which

서답형

20 위 글의 밑줄 친 ⓒ를 알맞은 형으로 고치시오.

➡ _____

[21~26] 다음 글을 읽고 물음에 답하시오.

First, the rain shows the stress the person ___(A)___ drew the picture is under. ⓐThe bigger the drops are or the more heavily the rain is falling, the bigger the stress is. The clouds mean problems waiting to happen, ___(B)___ a big cloud shows the drawer is not very hopeful about the future.

Second, the umbrella means the protection the person has in a stressful situation. A big umbrella shows that the drawer has ⓑa lot of plans or protection. If there's no umbrella in the drawing, the drawer does not have any means to deal ___(C)___ difficult situations.

21 위 글의 빈칸 (A)에 알맞은 것은?

① what
② who
③ whom
④ how
⑤ which

서답형

22 밑줄 친 ⓐ와 같은 뜻이 되도록 다음 문장의 빈칸에 알맞은 말을 쓰시오.

> _____ the drops are _____
>
> _____.

23 위 글의 빈칸 (B)에 알맞은 것은?

① so
② or
③ but
④ for
⑤ because

서답형

24 위 글의 밑줄 친 ⓑ를 한 단어로 바꿔 쓰시오.

➡ _____

25 위 글의 빈칸 (C)에 알맞은 것은?

① at
② to
③ from
④ for
⑤ with

26 위 글의 내용과 일치하지 <u>않는</u> 것은?

① 비는 그림을 그린 사람이 받고 있는 스트레스를 보여 준다.
② 빗방울이 크면 스트레스도 더 크다.
③ 구름은 앞으로 벌어질 문제를 의미한다.
④ 우산은 스트레스를 받는 상황에서 그 사람이 가지고 있는 보호 기제를 의미한다.
⑤ 큰 우산은 그림을 그린 사람이 더 많은 문제를 가지게 될 것을 의미한다.

[27~28] 다음 글을 읽고 물음에 답하시오.

These are some of the possible meanings of each part of the drawings. Now, go back and look at the two drawings. Try reading ⓐthem yourself. ⓑCan you understand what kind of person drew each one? What's your opinion?

서답형

27 위 글의 밑줄 친 ⓐ가 가리키는 것을 영어로 쓰시오.

➡ _____

서답형

28 위 글의 밑줄 친 ⓑ를 우리말로 옮기시오.

➡ _____

_____

[01~04] 다음 글을 읽고 물음에 답하시오.

One of those tests is the Draw-a-Person-in-the-Rain (DAPR) test. Study the pictures below.

The person in Drawing A is holding an umbrella in a light rain. On the other ⓐ , the person in Drawing B is in a ⓑ rain and has no umbrella. Also, there are dark clouds above the person in Drawing B. What can these ⓒ mean?

01 위 글의 빈칸 ⓐ에 알맞은 말을 쓰시오.

➡ _____

02 위 글의 빈칸 ⓑ에 본문에 나오는 단어의 반의어를 쓰시오.

➡ _____

03 위 글의 빈칸 ⓒ에 different를 알맞은 어형으로 바꿔 쓰시오.

➡ _____

04 주어진 단어를 활용하여 다음 물음에 영어로 답하시오.

> Q: What are above the person in Drawing B? (there, 4 words)

➡ _____

[05~08] 다음 글을 읽고 물음에 답하시오.

Third, the details in the drawing of the person have to do ⓐ the drawer's attitude under stress. For example, someone who draws a person without a face does not want to draw people's attention to ⓑhim or her. Someone who draws the person on the right side of the paper is ready to meet the future. On the other hand, someone who draws the person on the left side may be worried about things that ⓒ(are happened / have happened) in the past.

05 위 글의 빈칸 ⓐ에 알맞은 전치사를 쓰시오.

➡ _____

06 위 글의 밑줄 친 ⓑ를 알맞게 고치시오.

➡ _____

07 위 글의 괄호 ⓒ에서 알맞은 것을 고르시오.

➡ _____

08 사람을 종이의 오른쪽에 그린 사람은 무엇을 맞이할 준비가 되었는지 우리말로 간단히 쓰시오.

➡ _____

[09~12] 다음 글을 읽고 물음에 답하시오.

(A)당신이 하는 모든 것은 당신에 대해 무엇인가를 말해 줍니다. The language you use, the clothes you wear, and even the pets you raise somehow show what kind of person you are. (B)The things you draw are not much different. What you draw and how you draw ⓐit are related to your personality. Doctors have been using various drawing tests to better understand people.

09 주어진 단어를 활용하여 밑줄 친 우리말 (A)를 영어로 쓰시오.

(everything, something, 7 words)

➡ _____

10 위 글의 밑줄 친 (B)가 구체적으로 의미하는 것을 우리말로 쓰시오.

➡ _____

11 위 글의 밑줄 친 ⓐit이 가리키는 것을 우리말로 쓰시오.

➡ _____

12 Why have doctors been using various drawing tests? Answer in English with a full sentence.

➡ _____

[13~15] 다음 글을 읽고 물음에 답하시오.

First, the rain shows the stress the person who drew the picture is under. (A)The bigger the drops are or the more heavily the rain is falling, bigger the stress is. The clouds mean problems (B)(waiting, waited) to happen, so a big cloud shows the drawer is not very hopeful about the future.

Second, the umbrella means the protection the person has in a (C)(stressed / stressful) situation. A big umbrella shows that the drawer has a lot of plans or protection. If there's no umbrella in the drawing, the drawer does not have any means to deal with difficult situations.

13 위 글의 밑줄 친 (A)에서 어법상 어색한 것을 고쳐 다시 쓰시오.

➡ _____

14 위 글의 괄호 (B)에서 알맞은 것을 고르시오.

➡ _____

15 위 글의 괄호 (C)에서 알맞은 것을 고르시오.

➡ _____

해석

Before You Read

A picture is often closely related to what you're feeling in your mind. When
　　　　　　　　　　　　　　　　　　관계대명사　　　　　　　　　　　　　　　　　시간 부사절
you draw a picture, it shows your feelings. In other words, your various

feelings can be expressed through pictures. Therefore, you can find out other
　　　　　조동사+be+p.p. 수동태
people's feelings if you pay careful attention to their drawings.

구문해설 • in other words: 다시 말해서 • pay attention to: ～에 관심을 기울이다

그림은 종종 네 마음속에 느끼고 있는 것과 밀접한 관계가 있다. 네가 그림을 그릴 때, 그것은 너의 감정들을 나타낸다. 다시 말해서, 너의 다양한 감정들은 그림들을 통해 표현될 수 있다. 그러므로 너는 다른 사람들의 그림에 주의 깊게 관심을 기울인다면 그들의 감정을 이해할 수 있다.

Writing Workshop

This year, we have been doing a lot of different kinds of activities at school.
　　　　　　　　현재완료진행형　　　= many
Today, we had to talk about our own personalities and then talk about a
　　　　　　　　　　　　　　　　　　　　　　　　　　　　　　had to에 연결되는 동사원형
friend's personality. I saw myself as shy and friendly. What my friend said
　　　　　　　　재귀목적어　　　　　　　　　선행사를 포함하는 관계대명사
about me was quite different. She said I am active and curious because I get

along well with others and am in lots of clubs.
　　　　　　　= other people

구문해설 • activity: 활동 • personality: 성격, 개성 • shy: 수줍은 • active: 활동적인
• curious: 호기심이 많은

올해, 우리는 학교에서 많은 다양한 종류의 활동들을 해오고 있다. 오늘 우리는 우리 자신의 성격과 친구의 성격에 대해 말해야 했다. 나는 내 자신이 수줍음이 많고 친절하다고 생각했다. 나에 대해 내 친구가 말한 것은 매우 달랐다. 그녀는 내가 활동적이고 호기심이 많다고 말했는데, 그 이유는 내가 다른 사람들과 잘 지내고 많은 동아리에 속해 있기 때문이라고 했다.

Wrap Up 3~4

G: I need to go to Daegu today, but there are no train tickets left. Are there any
　　～해야 한다　　　　　　　　　　　　　　　　　　　　　Are there any other ~?: 다른 ~가 있니?
other ways to get there?

B: You can take a bus. It's fast and comfortable.

G: That's a great idea. I'll do that.

구문해설 • take a bus: 버스를 타다 • comfortable: 편리한

G: 나는 오늘 대구에 가야 하지만 남아 있는 기차표가 없어. 거기로 가는 다른 방법이 있을까?
B: 버스를 탈 수 있어. 그것은 빠르고 편해.
G: 좋은 생각이야. 그렇게 할게.

Words & Expressions

01 다음 짝지어진 단어의 관계가 같도록 빈칸에 알맞은 말을 쓰시오.

> future : past = above : _____

02 다음 영영풀이에 해당하는 단어로 적절한 것은?

> not requiring or relying on other people for help or support

① dependent   ② realistic
③ reasonable   ④ hopeful
⑤ independent

03 다음 빈칸에 공통으로 들어갈 말로 적절한 것은?

> • A turtle is covered _____ a hard shell.
> • Counselors deal _____ many kinds of problems.

① on   ② in   ③ at
④ by   ⑤ with

04 다음 중 밑줄 친 부분의 뜻풀이가 바르지 <u>않은</u> 것은?

① The bakery had so many different <u>types</u> of cookies. (유형)
② Emma's hands were soaked in <u>sweat</u> during the test. (땀)
③ Many Koreans enjoy eating <u>spicy</u> food like *tteokbokki*. (매운)
④ The price of this chair is very <u>reasonable</u>. (합리적인)
⑤ Kevin's parents were <u>against</u> his plan to travel alone. (～에 찬성하는)

05 다음 빈칸에 들어갈 말로 적절한 것은?

> My friend is handsome and has a good _____.

① rest   ② personality
③ difference   ④ protection
⑤ situation

06 다음 문장에 공통으로 들어갈 말을 고르시오.

> • I _____ a hamster as my pet.
> • Please _____ your hand if you know the answer.

① hang   ② raise   ③ have
④ hold   ⑤ keep

07 다음 우리말과 같도록 빈칸에 알맞은 말을 〈보기〉에서 골라 쓰시오. (필요시 형태를 바꿀 것)

> ┤ 보기 ├
> have to do with / in other words /
> get along with

(1) Kate는 너무 친절하고 인기가 있어서 모든 사람과 잘 어울린다.
  ➡ Kate is so kind and popular that she _____ everyone.
(2) 다시 말하면, 각각의 색은 우리의 정신에 영향을 끼친다.
  ➡ _____, each color affects our mind.
(3) 그 음악은 오늘 축제와 관련이 있다.
  ➡ The music _____ the festival toady.

[08~09] 다음 대화를 읽고 물음에 답하시오.

> G: I took a personality test today. (①)
> B: A house? (②)
> G: Yeah. (③) According to the test, you can tell a lot about a person by their drawing. Here's mine. (④)
> B: Interesting. So (A)what do these big windows mean? (⑤)
> G: They mean I'm open to other people.

08 위 대화의 ①~⑤ 중 다음 문장이 들어갈 알맞은 곳은?

> I had to draw a house.

①   ②   ③   ④   ⑤

09 위 대화의 밑줄 친 (A)와 같은 의미가 되도록 괄호 안에 주어진 단어를 이용하여 문장을 완성하시오.

➡ _____ these big windows?
  (meaning / is)

➡ _____ these big windows?
  (by / mean)

[10~11] 다음 대화를 읽고 물음에 답하시오.

> G: I need to go to Daegu today, but there are no train tickets left. 거기로 가는 다른 방법이 있을까? (get / ways / there / other / are / any / to / there)
> B: You can take a bus. It's fast and comfortable.
> G: That's a great idea. I'll do that.

10 위 대화의 밑줄 친 우리말과 같은 뜻이 되도록 괄호 안의 단어를 알맞게 배열하시오.

➡ _____

11 How will the girl go to Daegu? Answer in English. (5 words)

➡ _____

[12~13] 다음 대화를 읽고 물음에 답하시오.

> B: What's your blood type?
> (A) Wow. Then what does type A mean?
> (B) Type A. Why?
> (C) (a)People with blood type A is calm. They are good listeners, too.
> (D) I'm reading an article. It says that blood type tells something about your personality.

12 위 대화의 (A)~(D)의 순서를 바르게 배열한 것은?

① (B) – (A) – (C) – (D)
② (B) – (D) – (A) – (C)
③ (C) – (B) – (D) – (A)
④ (D) – (B) – (A) – (C)
⑤ (D) – (B) – (C) – (A)

13 위 대화의 밑줄 친 (a)에서 어법상 틀린 부분을 찾아 바르게 고쳐 쓰시오.

_____ ➡ _____

[14~16] 다음 대화를 읽고 물음에 답하시오.

> M: EDPI Test Center. Do you want to learn more about yourself? We have many kinds of personality tests. If there are any other tests you want to learn more about, we are here (A)help you.
> B: Hi, I'm calling (B)take a personality test. Can I do one this afternoon?
> M: Sure, you can come any time before 5 o'clock.

14 When does the boy want to take a personality test? Answer in English.

➡ _____

15 위 대화의 밑줄 친 (A)와 (B)를 알맞은 형태로 쓰시오.

(A) _____ (B) _____

16 Write the purpose of the boy's telephone call. Answer in Korean.

➡ _____

Grammar

17 다음 우리말에 맞게 괄호 안의 단어를 활용하여 빈칸을 채우시오.

(1) 의사들은 사람들을 더 잘 이해하기 위해 다양한 그리기 검사를 사용하고 있다. (3 단어)
➡ Doctors _____(use) various drawing tests to better understand people.

(2) 좋은 친구를 사귀는 것이 나를 행복하게 하는 것이다.
➡ Having good friends is _____ _____(what).

(3) Fred는 2010년 이후로 서울에서 살고 있다. (3 단어)
➡ Fred _____(live) in Seoul since 2010.

(4) 이것이 내가 생활비를 벌기 위해서 할 수 있는 일이다.
➡ This is _____(what) to make a living. *make a living: 생활비를 벌다

18 다음 중 어법상 올바른 문장을 고르시오.

① What people want to see is the letter that Gogh wrote.
② They need a specialist what can handle the challenging situation. *specialist: 전문가
③ I used to wear the red shoes the thing which my cousin liked.
④ You can order that you want to eat.
⑤ I want to know that they did.

19 우리말과 같은 뜻이 되도록 괄호 안의 어휘를 배열하여 영작하시오.

그들이 원하는 것은 약간의 음식이다. (food, they, is, what, some, want)

➡ _____

20 다음 우리말에 맞게 괄호 안의 단어를 활용하여 빈칸을 6 단어로 채우시오.

이것이 내가 말하려고 하던 것이다.

➡ This is _____. (what)

21 다음 우리말과 같은 뜻이 되도록 괄호 안의 단어를 활용하여 문장을 완성하시오.

(1) 그것은 그들이 원했던 것이 아니다. (what을 이용하여 쓸 것.)
➡ That isn't _____ _____ _____.

(2) 우리는 5년 동안 서로를 알아 왔다. (완료형을 이용하여 쓸 것.)
➡ We _____ _____(know) each other for five years.

(3) 나는 작년부터 그 프로젝트를 작업해 오고 있
다. (진행형을 이용하여 쓸 것.)

➡ I _____ _____ _____ (work)
on the project since last year.

(4) 내가 하는 말을 믿으세요. (what을 이용하여
쓸 것.)

➡ Believe _____ _____ _____.

22 그림의 상황에 맞게 괄호 안의 단어를 활용하여 빈칸을 채
우시오.

I _____ (know) what I
can do first.

23 괄호 안의 단어를 활용하여 우리말에 맞게 빈칸을 채우시오.

(1) 나는 그가 하는 말을 믿을 수가 없다. (what)
➡ I can't believe _____ _____ _____.

(2) 나는 네가 발견했던 것을 알고 있었다. (know)
➡ _____ _____ _____ you had
found.

24 다음 두 문장을 관계대명사 what을 사용하여 한 문장으로
만드시오.

• Henry couldn't understand the thing.
• The teacher said it.

➡ _____

[25~28] 다음 글을 읽고 물음에 답하시오.

One of those tests is the Draw-a-Person-in-the-Rain (DAPR) test. Study the pictures below.

(①) The person in Drawing A is holding an umbrella in a ___ⓐ___ rain. (②) On the other hand, the person in Drawing B is in a heavy rain and has no umbrella. (③) What can these differences mean? (④)

First, the rain shows the stress the person who drew the picture is under. (⑤) The bigger the drops are or the more heavily the rain is falling, the bigger the stress is. The clouds mean problems waiting to happen, so a big cloud shows the drawer is not very ⓑhope about the future.

25 위 글의 ①~⑤ 중 다음 주어진 문장이 들어갈 알맞은 곳은?

Also, there are dark clouds above the person in Drawing B.

①   ②   ③   ④   ⑤

26 위 글의 빈칸 ⓐ에 본문에 나오는 단어의 반의어를 쓰시오.

➡ _____

27 위 글의 밑줄 친 ⓑhope를 알맞은 형으로 바꿔 쓰시오.

➡ _____

28 다음 중 위 글의 내용을 바르게 이해하지 <u>못한</u> 사람은?

① Amelia: 그림 A의 사람은 가벼운 빗속에서 우산을 들고 있어.

② Brian: 그림 B의 사람은 거센 빗속에서 우산을 가지고 있지 않아.

③ Chris: 검은 구름들이 그림 B의 사람 머리 위에 있어.

④ David: 비는 그림을 그린 사람이 받는 스트레스를 보여 줘.

⑤ Eden: 큰 구름은 그림을 그린 사람의 미래에 대한 도전 의식을 나타내.

[29~32] 다음 글을 읽고 물음에 답하시오.

Third, the details in the drawing of the person have to do with the drawer's attitude ___ⓐ___ stress. __(A)__ example, someone who draws a person without a face does not want to draw people's attention to himself or herself. Someone who draws the person on the right side of the paper is ready to meet the future. __(B)__ the other hand, someone who draws the person on the left side may be worried about things that have happened in the ___ⓑ___.

29 위 글의 빈칸 ⓐ에 적절한 것은?

① on   ② to
③ over   ④ among
⑤ under

30 위 글의 빈칸 (A)와 (B)에 적절한 것으로 짝지어진 것은?

① To – On   ② For – To
③ For – At   ④ For – On
⑤ With – To

31 위 글의 빈칸 ⓑ에 본문에 나오는 단어의 반의어를 쓰시오.

➡ _____

32 What is someone who draws the person on the right side of the paper ready to meet? Answer in English.

➡ _____

[33~35] 다음 글을 읽고 물음에 답하시오.

(①) This year, we have been doing a lot of different kinds of activities at school. (②) Today, we had to talk about our own personalities and then talk about a friend's personality. (③) ___ⓐ___ my friend said about me was quite different. (④) She said I am active and ___ⓑ___ because I get along well with others and am in lots of clubs. (⑤)

33 위 글의 ①~⑤ 중 다음 주어진 문장이 들어갈 알맞은 곳은?

I saw myself as shy and friendly.

①   ②   ③   ④   ⑤

34 위 글의 빈칸 ⓐ에 적절한 것은?

① That   ② How
③ Who   ④ What
⑤ Which

35 위 글의 빈칸 ⓑ에 다음 영영풀이에 해당하는 단어를 철자 c로 시작하여 쓰시오.

interested in something and wanting to know more about it

➡ _____

01 출제율 90%

다음 중 짝지어진 단어의 관계가 <u>다른</u> 하나는?

① heavy – light
② future – past
③ various – diverse
④ calm – excited
⑤ carefully – carelessly

02 출제율 95%

다음 빈칸에 알맞은 말이 바르게 짝지어진 것은?

> • I saw myself _____ shy and friendly.
> • I want to deal _____ two other issues.

① as – to   ② with – of
③ as – about   ④ with – as
⑤ as – with

03 출제율 90%

다음 문장의 빈칸에 〈영어 설명〉에 해당하는 알맞은 단어를 쓰시오. (주어진 철자로 시작할 것)

> The sky darkened and a few d_____ of rain fell.

> <영어 설명> a very small amount of liquid that falls in a rounded shape

04 출제율 95%

다음 밑줄 친 부분과 바꿔 쓸 수 있는 것은?

> They all burst out laughing <u>at the same time</u>.

① completely   ② carefully
③ significantly   ④ consequently
⑤ simultaneously

[05~06] 다음 대화를 읽고 물음에 답하시오.

> B: Jane, what are you reading?
> G: I'm reading an interesting magazine. (①)
> B: That's surprising. (②)
> G: Yes. For example, the color red can help us focus better. (③)
> B: Are there any other useful colors? (④)
> G: Yes. The color blue helps people relax. (⑤)

05 출제율 100%

위 대화의 ①~⑤ 중 다음 문장이 들어갈 위치로 알맞은 곳은?

> It says colors can change people's feelings.

①   ②   ③   ④   ⑤

06 출제율 90%

위 대화에서 다음 영영풀이에 해당하는 단어를 찾아 쓰시오.

> to become or make someone become calmer and less worried

➡ _____

07 출제율 90%

다음 대화의 빈칸에 주어진 말을 이용해서 쓰시오.

> G: What does "have a long face" mean?
> B: It means '_____'. (sad, 3 words)

➡ _____

G: I ___(A)___ a personality test today. I had to draw a house.
B: A house?
G: Yeah. ___(B)___ the test, you can tell a lot about a person by their drawing. Here's mine.
B: Interesting. So what do these big windows ___(C)___ ?
G: They mean I'm open to other people.

출제율 100%

08 위 대화의 빈칸 (A)와 (C)에 알맞은 말이 바르게 짝지어진 것은?

① made – have
② threw – mean
③ had – take
④ took – mean
⑤ had – have

출제율 90%

09 위 대화의 빈칸 (B)에 '~에 따르면'이라는 어구를 두 단어로 쓰시오. (철자 A로 시작할 것)

➡ _____

출제율 95%

10 What do the big windows that the girl drew mean? Answer in Korean.

➡ _____

출제율 95%

11 〈보기〉 중 알맞은 단어를 골라 빈칸을 채우시오.

┌─── 보기 ───┐
　　what　　that
└───────────┘

(1) Everybody _____ I know is honest and kind.
(2) He gave me _____ I wanted.

출제율 95%

12 괄호 안의 단어를 사용하여 우리말에 맞게 현재완료진행형 문장을 쓰시오.

┌─────────────────────────────┐
비가 3시간 동안 심하게 내리고 있다.
(rain, heavily)
└─────────────────────────────┘

➡ _____

출제율 100%

13 다음 중 어법상 어색한 문장을 고르시오.

① I have been knowing him since my childhood.
② She has been crying since last night.
③ I have been studying Spanish for 5 years.
④ I've been reading the book you lent me.
⑤ He has been collecting stamps since he was eight.

출제율 95%

14 괄호 안의 단어를 활용하여 우리말에 맞게 빈칸을 채우시오.

(1) 그것은 그들이 원했던 집이 아니다. (that)
　➡ That isn't the house _____ .
(2) 그 여인은 자기가 필요한 것을 말했다. (what)
　➡ The woman said _____ .
(3) 나는 지난해부터 여기에서 일하고 있는 중이다. (work)
　➡ I _____ here since last year.

15 다음 그림을 보고 괄호 안의 단어를 활용하여 빈칸을 채우시오. (현재완료진행형으로 쓸 것.)

출제율 95%

We ＿＿＿＿＿＿＿＿＿＿＿＿(discuss) the problems for one hour.

[16~17] 다음 글을 읽고 물음에 답하시오.

(A)이것들은 그림들 각 부분의 가능한 의미 풀이 중 일부입니다. Now, go back and look ①at the two drawings. Try ②reading them ③yourself. Can you understand ④what kind of person drew ⑤both one? What's your opinion?

출제율 90%

16 위 글의 밑줄 친 (A)를 주어진 단어를 이용하여 영어로 옮기시오.

some, possible, meanings, each, drawings

➡ ＿＿＿＿＿＿＿＿＿＿＿＿＿＿＿＿
＿＿＿＿＿＿＿＿＿＿＿＿＿＿＿＿

출제율 95%

17 위 글의 밑줄 친 ①~⑤ 중 어법상 어색한 것은?

① ② ③ ④ ⑤

[18~21] 다음 글을 읽고 물음에 답하시오.

This year, we have been doing ⓐa lot of different kinds of activities at school. Today, we had to talk about our own personalities and then talk about a friend's personality. I saw myself as shy and friendly. What my friend said about me was quite ＿ⓑ＿. She said I am active and curious because I get along well with others and am in lots of clubs.

I=Minsu

출제율 95%

18 위 글의 밑줄 친 ⓐ 대신 쓸 수 있는 것은?

① few ② little
③ enough ④ many
⑤ much

출제율 95%

19 위 글의 빈칸 ⓑ에 알맞은 것은?

① strange ② same
③ different ④ essential
⑤ important

출제율 100%

20 위 글의 내용과 일치하지 <u>않는</u> 것은?

① 민수의 학교에서는 많은 종류의 활동을 해 오고 있다.
② 그들은 자신의 성격과 친구의 성격을 말하는 활동을 가졌다.
③ 민수는 자신이 수줍음을 탄다고 생각했다.
④ 민수의 친구는 민수가 소극적인 성격이라고 말했다.
⑤ 민수는 많은 동아리에 가입하고 있다.

출제율 90%

21 Why did Minsu's friend say he is active and curious? Answer in English.

➡ _____

_____

[22~27] 다음 글을 읽고 물음에 답하시오.

First, the rain shows the stress the person who drew the picture is under. (A)As the drops are bigger or the rain is falling more heavily, the stress is bigger. The clouds mean problems waiting to happen, so a big cloud shows the drawer is not very ___(B)___ about the future.

Second, the umbrella means the protection the person has in a stressful situation. A big umbrella shows (C)that the drawer has a lot of plans or protection. ___(D)___ there's no umbrella in the drawing, the drawer does not have any means to deal with difficult situations.

출제율 90%

22 위 글의 밑줄 친 (A)를 'the+비교급 ~, the+비교급 ...' 구문을 써서 바꿔 쓰시오.

➡ _____

_____

출제율 95%

23 위 글의 빈칸 (B)에 알맞은 것은?

① careful　　　② promising

③ hopeful　　　④ essential

⑤ exciting

출제율 95%

24 위 글의 밑줄 친 (C)와 용법이 같은 것은?

① It is strange that she doesn't come.

② I know that you don't like cats.

③ Look at the trees that stand on the hill.

④ It was here that she first met Mike.

⑤ This is the doll that my mother made for me.

출제율 95%

25 위 글의 빈칸 (D)에 알맞은 것은?

① If　　　　　② As

③ Since　　　　④ While

⑤ Although

출제율 100%

26 위 글의 내용과 일치하지 않는 것은?

① 빗방울이 클수록 스트레스도 크다.

② 구름은 어떤 문제들이 발생할 것을 의미한다.

③ 큰 구름은 미래에 나쁜 일이 발생할 것을 나타낸다.

④ 우산은 스트레스를 주는 상황에서 사람을 보호해 준다는 것을 의미한다.

⑤ 우산을 가지고 있지 않은 사람은 어려운 상황을 극복할 용기가 있음을 나타낸다.

출제율 90%

27 What does a big umbrella show? Answer in Korean.

➡ _____

_____

01 다음 대화의 빈칸에 괄호 안의 단어를 이용하여 〈조건〉에 맞게 알맞은 말을 쓰시오.

(1)

> A: What does "feel blue" mean?
> B: It means '_____'. (sad, 3 words)

(2)

> A: What does "throw up one's hands" mean?
> B: It means '_____'. (give, 3 words)

[02~03] 다음 대화를 읽고 물음에 답하시오.

> B: Jane, what are you reading?
> G: I'm reading an interesting magazine. It says colors can change people's feelings.
> B: (A)That's surprising.
> G: Yes. For example, the color red can help us focus better.
> B: Are there any other useful colors?
> G: Yes. The color blue helps people relax.

02 What is the magazine about?

➡ _____

03 위 대화의 밑줄 친 (A)That이 가리키는 것을 우리말로 쓰시오.

➡ _____

04 괄호 안의 단어를 활용하여 문장을 완성하시오. (관계대명사 that이나 what을 사용할 것.)

(1) 그가 음악을 사랑하는 바로 그 사람이다. (the very)

➡ _____

(2) 당신이 원하는 것을 고르세요. (pick)

➡ Please _____.

(3) 그것은 그가 사랑하는 바로 그 음악이다. (the very)

➡ _____

(4) 네가 가지고 온 것을 보여 줘. (bring)

➡ Show me _____.

05 우리말에 맞게 〈보기〉의 단어를 활용하여 배열하시오.

> ┤ 보기 ├
> months, the, do, I, course, have, for, been, six

> 나는 6개월 동안 그 과정을 밟아 왔다.

➡ _____

06 다음 우리말에 맞게 괄호 안의 단어를 활용하여 영작하시오. (9 단어)

> 그는 2시간 동안 버스를 타고 있다. (take, for)

➡ _____

INSIGHT
on the textbook

교과서 파헤치기

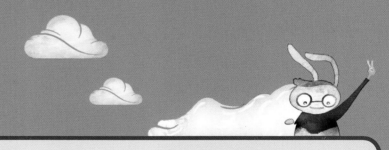

※ 다음 영어를 우리말로 쓰시오.

01 benefit	
02 moreover	
03 calming	
04 nature-friendly	
05 regret	
06 produce	
07 avoid	
08 finally	
09 blanket	
10 flight	
11 grade	
12 regularly	
13 brain	
14 fortunately	
15 calcium	
16 journal	
17 serotonin	
18 wet	
19 sunscreen	
20 mood	
21 properly	

22 shine	
23 protect	
24 already	
25 skin	
26 weather	
27 outdoors	
28 peak	
29 review	
30 safely	
31 direct	
32 effect	
33 bone	
34 healthy	
35 put on	
36 keep ~ in mind	
37 both A and B	
38 full of	
39 stay up	
40 should have p.p.	
41 put out	
42 too ~ to ...	
43 be good for	

※ 다음 우리말을 영어로 쓰시오.

01 이미

02 흥미롭게도

03 이득; 이득을 보다

04 게다가

05 건강한

06 진정시키는

07 햇살

08 자연친화적인

09 야외에서

10 피부

11 피하다

12 항공편, 비행

13 이불, 담요

14 다행스럽게도

15 점검하다

16 걸다

17 복습하다

18 뇌

19 마침내

20 햇볕, 햇빛

21 효과

22 날씨

23 일지, 일기

24 뼈

25 기분, 감정

26 절정의, 최고조의

27 만들어 내다

28 후회하다

29 규칙적으로

30 역할

31 젖은

32 제대로

33 보호하다

34 안전하게

35 ～로 가득 찬

36 착용하다, 바르다

37 ～에 유익하다

38 제시간에

39 A와 B 둘 다

40 내놓다

41 깨어 있다

42 ～을 명심하다

43 인터넷 검색을 하다

※ 다음 영영풀이에 알맞은 단어를 <보기>에서 골라 쓴 후, 우리말 뜻을 쓰시오.

1 _____ : the highest point: _____

2 _____ : a temporary state of mind: _____

3 _____ : light and heat from the sun: _____

4 _____ : to take advantages from something: _____

5 _____ : to become higher or greater: _____

6 _____ : to study or look at something again: _____

7 _____ : the part assumed to be played by a person: _____

8 _____ : the outer layer of a person's or animal's body: _____

9 _____ : covered or touched with water or another liquid: _____

10 _____ : a large piece of cloth used as a covering for warmth: _____

11 _____ : to produce or reflect light: _____

12 _____ : at the same time every day, week, month, or year: _____

13 _____ : the organ inside the head that control movements and feelings: _____

14 _____ : the hard part of the body that forms a framework inside people or animals: _____

15 _____ : a book in which people regularly write about what has happened to them: _____

16 _____ : to make sure that someone or something is not harmed, injured, damaged, etc.: _____

보기			
journal	peak	brain	go up
shine	blanket	mood	benefit
protect	regularly	review	skin
role	bone	sunshine	wet

※ 다음 우리말과 일치하도록 빈칸에 알맞은 말을 쓰시오.

Listen & Speak 1 Listen

1. **G:** How _____ we _____ _____?

   B: _____, it's _____ _____ _____ a good _____.

2. **B:** _____ can we _____ _____ _____ good _____?

   G: It's _____ to _____ every day.

3. **G:** I _____ it's important to _____ a _____ after reading.

   B: I agree.

4. **B:** It's important _____ _____ _____ what you _____ your money _____.

   G: I _____ so, _____.

Listen & Speak 1 A

1. **B:** _____ did you _____ on the _____?

   G: I _____ tennis. I have _____ _____ _____ on the weekend _____ my health.

   B: Good for _____. It's _____ to _____ _____.

   G: _____. How _____ _____ tennis _____ me?

   B: Why _____?

2. **M:** John, you are _____ again.

   B: I'm sorry. I _____ the _____ _____.

   M: I _____ you need to _____ home a little _____.

   B: I think so, _____. Next time I _____ _____ _____ _____.

   M: It's important to _____ at school _____ _____.

Listen & Speak 2

1. **G:** Your bag is _____ small.

   B: Yes. I _____ _____ _____ a bigger _____.

2. **G:** Aren't you _____?

   B: Yes. I _____ _____ _____ a jacket.

3. **B:** We _____ our _____.

   G: Oh, no. We should _____ come _____.

4. **G:** _____ my face. I _____ _____ _____ _____ _____ some sunscreen.

   B: Yes. You're _____.

1. **G:** 우리는 어떻게 건강을 유지할 수 있을까?
   B: 음, 든든한 아침 식사를 하는 것이 중요해.
2. **B:** 좋은 점수를 받기 위해 우리는 무엇을 할 수 있을까?
   G: 매일 복습하는 것이 중요해.
3. **G:** 나는 독서 후에 일기를 쓰는 것이 중요하다고 생각해.
   B: 나도 동의해.
4. **B:** 네가 돈을 어디에 썼는지 적는 것은 중요해.
   G: 나도 그렇게 생각해.

1. **B:** 주말에 뭐 했니?
   G: 나는 테니스를 쳤어. 나는 건강을 위해 주말에 운동을 하기로 결정했어.
   B: 잘했어. 규칙적으로 운동하는 것은 중요해.
   G: 맞아. 나와 테니스 치는 것은 어때?
   B: 왜 안 되겠어?
2. **M:** 존, 또 지각이구나!
   B: 죄송해요. 버스를 잘못 탔어요.
   M: 나는 네가 집에서 좀 더 빨리 출발할 필요가 있다고 생각한단다.
   B: 저도 그렇게 생각해요. 다음번에는 늦지 않을 게요.
   M: 학교에 제시간에 오는 것은 중요하단다.

1. **G:** 네 가방은 정말 작아.
   B: 응. 난 더 큰 것을 가져왔어야 했어.
2. **G:** 춥지 않니?
   B: 응. 나는 재킷을 입었어야 했어.
3. **B:** 우리 비행기를 놓쳤어.
   G: 오, 안 돼. 우리는 더 빨리 왔어야 했어.
4. **G:** 내 얼굴 좀 봐. 나는 자외선 차단제를 발랐어야 했어.
   B: 그래. 네 말이 맞아.

Listen & Speak 2 A

1. **B:** Mina, _____ was the _____?
   G: I didn't _____ it. It _____ _____.
   B: _____ was bad _____ it?
   G: I already _____ the _____. I shouldn't _____ read about it _____ _____ it.
   B: Oh, I'm _____ you didn't _____ it.
2. **B:** We _____ have 30 _____ to go _____ we reach the _____ of the mountain. Let's _____ _____ over there _____ have a _____.
   G: Oh, I _____ only water. I should have _____ some snacks.
   B: That's _____. I _____ a lot. We can _____.
   G: I'll _____ it in _____ to bring _____ snacks next _____.

Real-Life Zone

G: Ben, you _____ full of _____ today!
B: Do I? Maybe that's _____ I finally _____ a good night's sleep _____ night.
G: Why? Don't you _____ get _____ _____?
B: No, I _____ it's really _____ to get a good _____ sleep, but I _____ _____ _____ late _____ the Internet or _____ _____ my _____.
G: That _____ _____ to _____ too.
B: _____ I do that, I _____ it the next _____ and say, "I should _____ gone to bed _____ last night."
G: How was yesterday _____?
B: Well, yesterday afternoon I _____ the mountain with my _____. I was really _____ when I got _____. I went to _____ right _____ I _____ _____ _____.
G: _____ activities _____ a great _____ _____ _____ you _____ a good night's sleep.

Wrap Up 1

W: Oh, your _____ is _____ from the rain! I _____ _____ _____ the weather.
B: Did you _____ it?
W: No. I just _____ it _____ in the _____ this morning.
B: _____ didn't you _____ it?
W: Hanging a _____ in the sun is a nature-friendly _____ to _____ the blanket _____.
B: Oh, I didn't _____ that. I'll _____ that.
W: And it's also _____ to _____ to do it _____.

1. **B:** 미나야, 영화 어땠니?
   G: 나는 그것을 즐기지 못했어. 지루했어.
   B: 무엇이 별로였니?
   G: 나는 이미 결말을 알고 있었어. 보기 전에 그것에 대해 읽지 말았어야 했는데.
   B: 오, 네가 좋아하지 않다니 유감이야.
2. **B:** 우리는 산 정상에 도착하기까지 아직 30분은 더 가야 해. 저기서 앉아서 간식 먹고 가자.
   G: 오, 난 물만 가져왔어. 간식을 가져왔어야 했는데.
   B: 괜찮아. 내가 많이 가져왔어. 우리는 같이 먹을 수 있어.
   G: 다음번에는 간식을 가져올 것을 명심할게.

G: 벤, 너 오늘 기운 차 보여!
B: 내가 그래? 그건 아마 내가 지난밤 마침내 잠을 잘 잤기 때문일 거야.
G: 왜? 평소에 충분한 잠을 자지 못하니?
B: 응, 잠을 잘 자는 것이 정말 중요하다는 것은 알지만 나는 언제나 인터넷 검색을 하거나 휴대폰을 가지고 놀면서 늦게까지 깨어 있어.
G: 그건 나에게도 가끔 일어나는 일이야.
B: 그리고 난 뒤에, 나는 다음 날 아침 후회하고 "지난밤에 더 일찍 잠들었어야 했는데."라고 말해.
G: 어제는 어떻게 달랐니?
B: 음, 어제 오후에 나는 아빠와 등산을 했어. 집에 왔을 때 나는 매우 피곤했어. 나는 침대에 가자마자 바로 잠들었어.
G: 야외 활동은 네가 잠을 잘 자도록 돕는 훌륭한 방법이구나.

W: 오, 네 이불이 비에 젖었어! 내가 날씨를 확인했어야 했는데.
B: 그것을 빨았어요?
W: 아니. 오늘 아침에 그냥 햇볕에 널어놓았어.
B: 왜 빨지 않았어요?
W: 햇볕에 이불을 널어놓는 것은 이불을 깨끗하게 유지하는 친환경적인 방법이야.
B: 오, 저는 그것을 몰랐어요. 기억해 둘게요.
W: 그리고 정기적으로 그렇게 하는 것을 기억하는 것 또한 중요해.

※ 다음 우리말에 맞도록 대화를 영어로 쓰시오.

Listen & Speak 1 Listen

1. G: _____
   B: _____
2. B: _____
   G: _____
3. G: _____
   B: _____
4. B: _____
   G: _____

1. G: 우리는 어떻게 건강을 유지할 수 있을까?
   B: 음, 든든한 아침 식사를 하는 것이 중요해.
2. B: 좋은 점수를 받기 위해 우리는 무엇을 할 수 있을까?
   G: 매일 복습하는 것이 중요해.
3. G: 나는 독서 후에 일기를 쓰는 것이 중요하다고 생각해.
   B: 나도 동의해.
4. B: 네가 돈을 어디에 썼는지 적는 것은 중요해.
   G: 나도 그렇게 생각해.

Listen & Speak 1 A

1. B: _____
   G: _____
   B: _____
   G: _____
   B: _____
2. M: _____
   B: _____
   M: _____
   B: _____
   M: _____

1. B: 주말에 뭐 했니?
   G: 나는 테니스를 쳤어. 나는 건강을 위해 주말에 운동을 하기로 결정했어.
   B: 잘했어. 규칙적으로 운동하는 것은 중요해.
   G: 맞아. 나와 테니스 치는 것은 어때?
   B: 왜 안 되겠어?
2. M: 존, 또 지각이구나!
   B: 죄송해요. 버스를 잘못 탔어요.
   M: 나는 네가 집에서 좀 더 빨리 출발할 필요가 있다고 생각한단다.
   B: 저도 그렇게 생각해요. 다음번에는 늦지 않을 게요.
   M: 학교에 제시간에 오는 것은 중요하단다.

Listen & Speak 2

1. G: _____
   B: _____
2. G: _____
   B: _____
3. B: _____
   G: _____
4. G: _____
   B: _____

1. G: 네 가방은 정말 작아.
   B: 응. 난 더 큰 것을 가져왔어야 했어.
2. G: 춥지 않니?
   B: 응. 나는 재킷을 입었어야 했어.
3. B: 우리 비행기를 놓쳤어.
   G: 오, 안 돼. 우리는 더 빨리 왔어야 했어.
4. G: 내 얼굴 좀 봐. 나는 자외선 차단제를 발랐어야 했어.
   B: 그래. 네 말이 맞아.

Listen & Speak 2 A

1. B: _____

   G: _____

   B: _____

   G: _____

   B: _____

2. B: _____

   _____

   G: _____

   B: _____

   G: _____

Real-Life Zone

G: _____

B: _____

G: _____

B: _____

   _____

G: _____

B: _____

   _____

G: _____

B: _____

   _____

G: _____

Wrap Up 1

W: _____

B: _____

W: _____

B: _____

W: _____

B: _____

W: _____

1. B: 미나야, 영화 어땠니?
   G: 나는 그것을 즐기지 못했어. 지루했어.
   B: 무엇이 별로였니?
   G: 나는 이미 결말을 알고 있었어. 보기 전에 그것에 대해 읽지 말았어야 했는데.
   B: 오, 네가 좋아하지 않다니 유감이야.

2. B: 우리는 산 정상에 도착하기까지 아직 30분은 더 가야 해. 저기서 앉아서 간식 먹고 가자.
   G: 오, 난 물만 가져왔어. 간식을 가져왔어야 했는데.
   B: 괜찮아. 내가 많이 가져왔어. 우리는 같이 먹을 수 있어.
   G: 다음번에는 간식을 가져올 것을 명심할게.

G: 벤, 너 오늘 기운 차 보여!
B: 내가 그래? 그건 아마 내가 지난밤 마침내 잠을 잘 잤기 때문일 거야.
G: 왜? 평소에 충분한 잠을 자지 못하니?
B: 응, 잠을 잘 자는 것이 정말 중요하다는 것은 알지만 나는 언제나 인터넷 검색을 하거나 휴대폰을 가지고 놀면서 늦게까지 깨어 있어.
G: 그건 나에게도 가끔 일어나는 일이야.
B: 그러고 난 뒤에, 나는 다음 날 아침 후회하고 "지난밤에 더 일찍 잠들었어야 했는데."라고 말해.
G: 어제는 어떻게 달랐니?
B: 음, 어제 오후에 나는 아빠와 등산을 했어. 집에 왔을 때 나는 매우 피곤했어. 나는 침대에 가자마자 바로 잠들었어.
G: 야외 활동은 네가 잠을 잘 자도록 돕는 훌륭한 방법이구나.

W: 오, 네 이불이 비에 젖었어! 내가 날씨를 확인했어야 했는데.
B: 그것을 빨았어요?
W: 아니. 오늘 아침에 그냥 햇볕에 널어 놓았어.
B: 왜 빨지 않았어요?
W: 햇볕에 이불을 널어놓는 것은 이불을 깨끗하게 유지하는 친환경적인 방법이야.
B: 오, 저는 그것을 몰랐어요. 기억해 둘게요.
W: 그리고 정기적으로 그렇게 하는 것을 기억하는 것 또한 중요해.

※ 다음 우리말과 일치하도록 빈칸에 알맞은 것을 골라 쓰시오.

1 _____ the _____
A. Sunshine　　　B. Enjoy

2 How _____ time do you _____ every day _____ _____ the sun?
A. out　　　B. much　　　C. in　　　D. spend

3 _____ _____, right?
A. much　　　B. not

4 Most people are _____ _____ at school or at work to _____ much time _____.
A. outdoors　　　B. busy　　　C. spend　　　D. too

5 _____, the sun _____ an important _____ in your _____.
A. role　　　B. plays　　　C. health　　　D. however

6 It _____ you _____ _____.
A. stay　　　B. helps　　　C. healthy

7 Everyone _____ _____ when the sun _____.
A. happier　　　B. feels　　　C. shines

8 This is _____ of serotonin, the _____ _____ _____.
A. hormone　　　B. because　　　C. body's　　　D. happy

9 The _____ sun you get, the more "happy _____" the _____ _____.
A. brain　　　B. hormone　　　C. more　　　D. produces

10 _____ your serotonin level _____ _____, you feel happier and _____.
A. up　　　B. stronger　　　C. goes　　　D. when

11 This helps you _____ _____ _____.
A. stress　　　B. fight　　　C. everyday

12 Serotonin also has a _____ _____, helping you focus better on _____ you are _____.
A. effect　　　B. what　　　C. calming　　　D. doing

13 _____, serotonin helps you get a good _____ _____ because it helps the brain _____ a sleep hormone.
A. sleep　　　B. moreover　　　C. produce　　　D. night's

14 Sunshine does _____ _____ make you _____ and sleep _____.
A. just　　　B. better　　　C. not　　　D. feel

1 햇빛을 즐기세요

2 여러분은 매일 햇빛 속에서 얼마나 많은 시간을 보내나요?

3 많지 않죠, 그렇죠?

4 대부분의 사람들은 학교와 직장에서 너무 바빠서 많은 시간을 야외에서 보내지 못합니다.

5 그러나 햇빛은 여러분의 건강에 중요한 역할을 합니다.

6 그것은 여러분이 건강을 유지하는 데 도움을 줍니다.

7 모든 사람들은 해가 비칠 때 더 행복하게 느낍니다.

8 이것은 몸의 행복 호르몬인 세로토닌 때문입니다.

9 여러분이 햇빛을 쬘수록 뇌는 행복 호르몬을 더 만들어 냅니다.

10 여러분의 세로토닌 수치가 높아지면, 여러분은 더 행복하고 더 건강하게 느낍니다.

11 이것은 여러분이 매일의 스트레스를 이겨 내는 데 도움을 줍니다.

12 세로토닌은 또한 진정 효과가 있고, 여러분이 하는 일에 더 잘 집중할 수 있도록 도와줍니다.

13 게다가, 세로토닌은 뇌가 수면 호르몬을 생성하도록 도와주기 때문에 여러분이 숙면을 취하도록 해 줍니다.

14 햇빛은 단지 여러분이 더 기분 좋게 느끼고 잠을 더 잘 자게 하는 것만은 아닙니다.

15 It _____ helps _____ _____ _____.

   A. strong   B. also   C. bones   D. build

16 _____ you all know, it is calcium that _____ strong _____ and _____.

   A. bones   B. as   C. teeth   D. builds

17 However, _____ the _____ to _____ calcium _____, it needs vitamin D.

   A. properly   B. body   C. use   D. for

18 Interestingly, the skin _____ vitamin D _____ _____ _____ on it.

   A. shines   B. creates   C. sunlight   D. when

19 The _____ way to make strong _____ is to _____ _____ and enjoy the sun.

   A. outside   B. easiest   C. go   D. bones

20 _____ you can _____, sunshine has many _____, but how can you enjoy its benefits _____?

   A. benefits   B. safely   C. as   D. see

21 Fortunately, getting _____ _____ on your _____ for 10 to 20 minutes a day is enough to _____ from it.

   A. direct   B. benefit   C. sunlight   D. skin

22 Try to go out into the sun between _____ or during lunch _____ and get _____ on your _____ and hands.

   A. arms   B. sunshine   C. breaks   D. classes

23 A _____ in the sun, for just a _____ _____ every day, is good for both your _____ and your body.

   A. few   B. mind   C. walk   D. minutes

24 However, avoid the sun during _____ summer hours, between 11 and 3, and use sunscreen to _____ your _____ and _____.

   A. protect   B. neck   C. peak   D. face

25 Enjoy the sun _____ and see how a _____ sunshine can make a world of _____ in your health and your _____.

   A. difference   B. little   C. safely   D. mood

---

15 그것은 또한 튼튼한 뼈를 만드는 것을 돕습니다.

16 여러분 모두가 알다시피, 튼튼한 뼈와 치아를 만드는 것은 칼슘입니다.

17 그러나 몸이 칼슘을 적절하게 사용하기 위해서는 비타민 D가 필요합니다.

18 흥미롭게도, 피부는 햇빛이 피부에 비칠 때 비타민 D를 만들어 냅니다.

19 튼튼한 뼈를 만드는 가장 쉬운 방법은 밖으로 나가서 햇빛을 즐기는 겁니다.

20 보시다시피, 햇빛은 많은 이점이 있지만, 어떻게 그것의 이점을 안전하게 즐길 수 있을까요?

21 다행히도, 하루에 10분에서 20분 동안 피부에 직사광선을 쪼이는 것은 햇빛으로부터 이점을 얻는 데 충분합니다.

22 수업 시간 사이나 점심시간에 햇빛을 쬐러 밖으로 나가서 팔과 손에 햇빛을 쬐어 보세요.

23 매일 단 몇 분 동안 햇살을 쬐며 걷는 것은 여러분의 마음과 몸 모두에 좋습니다.

24 그러나 여름 절정 시간인 11시에서 3시 사이에는 햇빛을 피하고, 얼굴과 목을 보호하기 위해 자외선 차단제를 사용하세요.

25 태양을 안전하게 즐기고 적은 양의 햇빛이 여러분의 건강과 기분에 얼마나 큰 차이를 만들어 내는지 보세요.

※ 다음 우리말과 일치하도록 빈칸에 알맞은 말을 쓰시오.

1 _____ the _____

2 How much time do you _____ every day _____ _____ _____ _____?

3 _____ _____, right?

4 Most people are _____ _____ at school or _____ _____ _____ much time _____.

5 _____, the sun _____ _____ _____ _____ in your health.

6 It _____ you _____ _____ _____.

7 Everyone _____ _____ when the sun _____.

8 This is _____ _____ serotonin, _____ _____ _____ _____.

9 _____ _____ _____ you get, _____ _____ " _____ _____ " the brain _____.

10 When your serotonin level _____ _____, you _____ _____ and _____.

11 This _____ you _____ _____ _____ _____.

12 Serotonin also has a _____ _____, helping you _____ better on _____ _____ _____ _____ _____.

13 _____, serotonin helps you get _____ _____ _____ _____ because it _____ the brain _____ a sleep hormone.

14 Sunshine does _____ _____ make you feel and _____ _____.

1 햇빛을 즐기세요

2 여러분은 매일 햇빛 속에서 얼마나 많은 시간을 보내나요?

3 많지 않죠, 그렇죠?

4 대부분의 사람들은 학교와 직장에서 너무 바빠서 많은 시간을 야외에서 보내지 못합니다.

5 그러나 햇빛은 여러분의 건강에 중요한 역할을 합니다.

6 그것은 여러분이 건강을 유지하는 데 도움을 줍니다.

7 모든 사람들은 해가 비칠 때 더 행복하게 느낍니다.

8 이것은 몸의 행복 호르몬인 세로토닌 때문입니다.

9 여러분이 햇빛을 쬘수록 뇌는 행복 호르몬을 더 만들어 냅니다.

10 여러분의 세로토닌 수치가 높아지면, 여러분은 더 행복하고 더 건강하게 느낍니다.

11 이것은 여러분이 매일의 스트레스를 이겨 내는 데 도움을 줍니다.

12 세로토닌은 또한 진정 효과가 있고, 여러분이 하는 일에 더 잘 집중할 수 있도록 도와줍니다.

13 게다가, 세로토닌은 뇌가 수면 호르몬을 생성하도록 도와주기 때문에 여러분이 숙면을 취하도록 해 줍니다.

14 햇빛은 단지 여러분이 더 기분 좋게 느끼고 잠을 더 잘 자게 하는 것만은 아닙니다.

15 It _____ helps _____ _____ _____.

16 _____ _____ _____ _____, it is calcium that builds strong _____ and _____.

17 However, _____ _____ _____ _____ _____ calcium _____, it needs vitamin D.

18 _____, the skin _____ vitamin D _____ _____ _____ on it.

19 _____ _____ _____ _____ to make strong bones is _____ _____ _____ and enjoy the sun.

20 _____ _____ _____ _____, sunshine has many benefits, but how can you _____ _____ _____ _____?

21 Fortunately, _____ _____ _____ on your skin for 10 to 20 minutes a day is enough _____ _____ _____ _____.

22 _____ _____ _____ _____ _____ the sun _____ classes or _____ lunch breaks and _____ _____ _____ your arms and hands.

23 A walk in the sun, _____ _____ _____ _____ _____ _____ _____, is good for _____ your mind _____ your body.

24 However, _____ the sun during _____ summer hours, between 11 and 3, and use sunscreen _____ _____ _____ _____ _____ _____.

25 Enjoy the sun safely and see how _____ _____ _____ can _____ _____ _____ _____ _____ in your _____ and your _____.

---

15 그것은 또한 튼튼한 뼈를 만드는 것을 돕습니다.

16 여러분 모두가 알다시피, 튼튼한 뼈와 치아를 만드는 것은 칼슘입니다.

17 그러나 몸이 칼슘을 적절하게 사용하기 위해서는 비타민 D가 필요합니다.

18 흥미롭게도, 피부는 햇빛이 피부에 비칠 때 비타민 D를 만들어 냅니다.

19 튼튼한 뼈를 만드는 가장 쉬운 방법은 밖으로 나가서 햇빛을 즐기는 겁니다.

20 보시다시피, 햇빛은 많은 이점이 있지만, 어떻게 그것의 이점을 안전하게 즐길 수 있을까요?

21 다행히도, 하루에 10분에서 20분 동안 피부에 직사광선을 쪼이는 것은 햇빛으로부터 이점을 얻는 데 충분합니다.

22 수업 시간 사이나 점심시간에 햇빛을 쪼러 밖으로 나가서 팔과 손에 햇빛을 쪼여 보세요.

23 매일 단 몇 분 동안 햇살을 쪼이며 걷는 것은 여러분의 마음과 몸 모두에 좋습니다.

24 그러나 여름 절정 시간인 11시에서 3시 사이에는 햇빛을 피하고, 얼굴과 목을 보호하기 위해 자외선 차단제를 사용하세요.

25 태양을 안전하게 즐기고 적은 양의 햇빛이 여러분의 건강과 기분에 얼마나 큰 차이를 만들어 내는지 보세요.

※ 다음 문장을 우리말로 쓰시오.

1 Enjoy the Sunshine

➡ _____

2 How much time do you spend every day out in the sun?

➡ _____

3 Not much, right?

➡ _____

4 Most people are too busy at school or at work to spend much time outdoors.

➡ _____

5 However, the sun plays an important role in your health.

➡ _____

6 It helps you stay healthy.

➡ _____

7 Everyone feels happier when the sun shines.

➡ _____

8 This is because of serotonin, the body's happy hormone.

➡ _____

9 The more sun you get, the more "happy hormone" the brain produces.

➡ _____

10 When your serotonin level goes up, you feel happier and stronger.

➡ _____

11 This helps you fight everyday stress.

➡ _____

12 Serotonin also has a calming effect, helping you focus better on what you are doing.

➡ _____

13 Moreover, serotonin helps you get a good night's sleep because it helps the brain produce a sleep hormone.

➡ _____

14 ▶ Sunshine does not just make you feel and sleep better.

➡ _____

15 ▶ It also helps build strong bones.

➡ _____

16 ▶ As you all know, it is calcium that builds strong bones and teeth.

➡ _____

17 ▶ However, for the body to use calcium properly, it needs vitamin D.

➡ _____

18 ▶ Interestingly, the skin creates vitamin D when sunlight shines on it.

➡ _____

19 ▶ The easiest way to make strong bones is to go outside and enjoy the sun.

➡ _____

20 ▶ As you can see, sunshine has many benefits, but how can you enjoy its benefits safely?

➡ _____

21 ▶ Fortunately, getting direct sunlight on your skin for 10 to 20 minutes a day is enough to benefit from it.

➡ _____

22 ▶ Try to go out into the sun between classes or during lunch breaks and get sunshine on your arms and hands.

➡ _____

23 ▶ A walk in the sun, for just a few minutes every day, is good for both your mind and your body.

➡ _____

24 ▶ However, avoid the sun during peak summer hours, between 11 and 3, and use sunscreen to protect your face and neck.

➡ _____

25 ▶ Enjoy the sun safely and see how a little sunshine can make a world of difference in your health and your mood.

➡ _____

※ 다음 괄호 안의 단어들을 우리말에 맞도록 바르게 배열하시오.

1 (the / Enjoy / Sunshine)
➡ _____

2 (much / how / time / you / do / every / spend / out / day / in / sun? / the)
➡ _____

3 (much, / not / right?)
➡ _____

4 (people / most / too / are / at / busy / or / school / at / to / work / much / spend / outdoors. / time)
➡ _____

5 (the / however, / sun / an / plays / role / important / your / in / health.)
➡ _____

6 (helps / it / you / healthy. / stay)
➡ _____

7 (feels / everyone / when / happier / the / shines. / sun)
➡ _____

8 (is / this / of / because / serotonin, / body's / the / hormone. / happy)
➡ _____

9 (more / the / you / sun / get, / more / the / hormone" / "happy / the / produces. / brain)
➡ _____

10 (your / when / level / serotonin / up, / goes / feel / you / stronger. / and / happier)
➡ _____

11 (helps / this / fight / you / stress. / everyday)
➡ _____

12 (also / serotonin / a / has / effect, / calming / you / helping / better / focus / what / on / are / you / doing.)
➡ _____

13 (serotonin / moreover, / you / helps / a / get / night's / good / because / sleep / helps / it / brain / the / a / produce / hormone. / sleep)
➡ _____

14 (does / sunshine / just / not / you / make / feel / and / better. / sleep)
➡ _____

15 (also / it / build / helps / bones. / strong)

➡ _____

16 (you / as / know, / all / is / it / that / calcium / strong / builds / teeth. / and / bones)

➡ _____

17 (for / however, / body / the / use / to / properly, / calcium / it / vitamin / needs / D.)

➡ _____

18 (the / interestingly, / skin / vitamin / creates / when / D / sunlight / on / shines / it.)

➡ _____

19 (easiest / the / to / way / strong / make / is / bones / go / to / and / outside / the / enjoy / sun. / the)

➡ _____
_____

20 (you / as / see, / can / has / sunshine / benefits, / many / how / but / you / can / its / enjoy / safely? / benefits)

➡ _____
_____

21 (getting / fortunately, / sunlight / direct / your / on / for / skin / to / 10 / minutes / 20 / day / a / enough / is / benefit / to / it. / from)

➡ _____
_____

22 (to / try / out / go / into / sun / the / classes / between / or / lunch / during / breaks / and / sunshine / get / your / on / arms / hands. / and)

➡ _____
_____

23 (walk / a / in / sun, / the / just / for / a / minutes / few / day, / every / good / is / both / for / mind / your / and / body. / your)

➡ _____
_____

24 (avoid / however, / sun / the / peak / during / hours, / summer / between / 3, / and / 11 / use / and / to / sunscreen / protect / face / your / fance / neck. / and)

➡ _____
_____

25 (the / enjoy / sun / and / safely / see / a / how / little / can / sunshine / a / make / world / difference / of / your / in / health / and / mood. / your)

➡ _____
_____

---

15 그것은 또한 튼튼한 뼈를 만드는 것을 돕습니다.

16 여러분 모두가 알다시피, 튼튼한 뼈와 치아를 만드는 것은 칼슘입니다.

17 그러나 몸이 칼슘을 적절하게 사용하기 위해서는 비타민 D가 필요합니다.

18 흥미롭게도, 피부는 햇빛이 피부에 비칠 때 비타민 D를 만들어 냅니다.

19 튼튼한 뼈를 만드는 가장 쉬운 방법은 밖으로 나가서 햇빛을 즐기는 겁니다.

20 보시다시피, 햇빛은 많은 이점이 있지만, 어떻게 그것의 이점을 안전하게 즐길 수 있을까요?

21 다행히도, 하루에 10분에서 20분 동안 피부에 직사광선을 쪼이는 것은 햇빛으로부터 이점을 얻는 데 충분합니다.

22 수업 시간 사이나 점심시간에 햇빛을 쬐러 밖으로 나가서 팔과 손에 햇빛을 쬐어 보세요.

23 매일 단 몇 분 동안 햇살을 쬐며 걷는 것은 여러분의 마음과 몸 모두에 좋습니다.

24 그러나 여름 절정 시간인 11시에서 3시 사이에는 햇빛을 피하고, 얼굴과 목을 보호하기 위해 자외선 차단제를 사용하세요.

25 태양을 안전하게 즐기고 적은 양의 햇빛이 여러분의 건강과 기분에 얼마나 큰 차이를 만들어 내는지 보세요.

※ 다음 우리말을 영어로 쓰시오.

1 햇빛을 즐기세요

➡ _____

2 여러분은 매일 햇빛 속에서 얼마나 많은 시간을 보내나요?

➡ _____

3 많지 않죠, 그렇죠?

➡ _____

4 대부분의 사람들은 학교와 직장에서 너무 바빠서 많은 시간을 야외에서 보내지 못합니다.

➡ _____

5 그러나 햇빛은 여러분의 건강에 중요한 역할을 합니다.

➡ _____

6 그것은 여러분이 건강을 유지하는 데 도움을 줍니다.

➡ _____

7 모든 사람들은 해가 비칠 때 더 행복하게 느낍니다.

➡ _____

8 이것은 몸의 행복 호르몬인 세로토닌 때문입니다.

➡ _____

9 여러분이 햇빛을 쬘수록 뇌는 행복 호르몬을 더 만들어 냅니다.

➡ _____

10 여러분의 세로토닌 수치가 높아지면, 여러분은 더 행복하고 더 건강하게 느낍니다.

➡ _____

11 이것은 여러분이 매일의 스트레스를 이겨 내는 데 도움을 줍니다.

➡ _____

12 세로토닌은 또한 진정 효과가 있고, 여러분이 하는 일에 더 잘 집중할 수 있도록 도와줍니다.

➡ _____

13 게다가, 세로토닌은 뇌가 수면 호르몬을 생성하도록 도와주기 때문에 여러분이 숙면을 취하도록
해 줍니다.

➡ _____

_____

14 햇빛은 단지 여러분이 더 기분 좋게 느끼고 잠을 더 잘 자게 하는 것만은 아닙니다.

➡ _____

15 그것은 또한 튼튼한 뼈를 만드는 것을 돕습니다.

➡ _____

16 여러분 모두가 알다시피, 튼튼한 뼈와 치아를 만드는 것은 칼슘입니다.

➡ _____

17 그러나 몸이 칼슘을 적절하게 사용하기 위해서는 비타민 D가 필요합니다.

➡ _____

18 흥미롭게도, 피부는 햇빛이 피부에 비칠 때 비타민 D를 만들어 냅니다.

➡ _____

19 튼튼한 뼈를 만드는 가장 쉬운 방법은 밖으로 나가서 햇빛을 즐기는 겁니다.

➡ _____

20 보시다시피, 햇빛은 많은 이점이 있지만, 어떻게 그것의 이점을 안전하게 즐길 수 있을까요?

➡ _____

21 다행히도, 하루에 10분에서 20분 동안 피부에 직사광선을 쪼이는 것은 햇빛으로부터 이점을 얻는 데 충분합니다.

➡ _____

_____

22 수업 시간 사이나 점심시간에 햇빛을 쬐러 밖으로 나가서 팔과 손에 햇빛을 쬐어 보세요.

➡ _____

_____

23 매일 단 몇 분 동안 햇살을 쬐며 걷는 것은 여러분의 마음과 몸 모두에 좋습니다.

➡ _____

24 그러나 여름 절정 시간인 11시에서 3시 사이에는 햇빛을 피하고, 얼굴과 목을 보호하기 위해 자외선 차단제를 사용하세요.

➡ _____

_____

25 태양을 안전하게 즐기고 적은 양의 햇빛이 여러분의 건강과 기분에 얼마나 큰 차이를 만들어 내는지 보세요.

➡ _____

_____

※ 다음 우리말과 일치하도록 빈칸에 알맞은 말을 쓰시오.

Communication Task

1. A: I think _____ _____ _____ _____ every day. Do you _____ _____ _____?

2. B: _____, I _____. But I'll _____.

3. A: _____.

1. A: 나는 매일 운동하는 것이 중요하다고 생각해. 너는 매일 운동하니?
2. B: 아니, 하지만 노력할 거야.
3. A: 알았어.

After You Read A

1. The _____ of _____

2. Sunshine _____ you _____ _____ stress and _____ _____.

3. Sunshine _____ _____ _____ _____ you are doing.

4. If you _____ _____ _____, you _____ _____ _____ at night.

5. _____ the _____ _____ _____ _____ _____, your skin produces vitamin D, _____ _____ _____ for strong bones.

1. 햇빛의 좋은 점
2. 햇빛은 여러분이 스트레스를 다루고 더 행복하게 느끼도록 돕는다.
3. 햇빛은 여러분이 하는 일에 더 잘 집중할 수 있도록 도와준다.
4. 햇빛을 충분히 쬐면 밤에 잠을 더 잘 잘 것이다.
5. 해가 여러분의 피부에 비칠 때, 여러분의 피부는 비타민 D를 만드는데, 그것은 튼튼한 뼈를 만드는 데 필요하다.

Writing Workshop

1. _____ Comes _____!

2. _____ your hands _____ _____ _____ _____. You _____ _____ _____ _____ easily _____ you wash your hands well.

3. Get _____ _____ for 10 to 20 minutes _____ _____.

4. _____ _____ sunlight you get, the _____ and _____ _____ _____.

5. _____ is a good breakfast _____ helps the _____ _____ _____.

6. _____ you eat a good breakfast, you can _____ _____ _____ _____ _____ and _____ things _____.

1. 건강이 먼저야!
2. 외출 후에는 손을 씻어라. 손을 잘 씻으면 쉽게 감기에 걸리지 않을 것이다.
3. 매일 직사광선을 10∼20분간 받아라.
4. 햇빛을 더 많이 받을수록 더 행복하고 더 강하게 느낄 것이다.
5. 두뇌가 적절히 작동하도록 돕는 것은 좋은 아침식사이다.
6. 좋은 아침을 먹으면, 일에 분명히 집중하고 더 잘 기억할 수 있다.

※ 다음 우리말을 영어로 쓰시오.

Communication Task

1. A: 나는 매일 운동하는 것이 중요하다고 생각해. 너는 매일 운동하니?
➡ _____

2. B: 아니, 하지만 노력할 거야.
➡ _____

3. A: 좋아.
➡ _____

After You Read A

1. 햇빛의 좋은 점
➡ _____

2. 햇빛은 여러분이 스트레스를 다루고 더 행복하게 느끼도록 돕는다.
➡ _____

3. 햇빛은 여러분이 하는 일에 더 잘 집중할 수 있도록 도와준다.
➡ _____

4. 햇빛을 충분히 쬐면 밤에 잠을 더 잘 잘 것이다.
➡ _____

5. 해가 여러분의 피부에 비칠 때, 여러분의 피부는 비타민 D를 만드는데, 그것은 튼튼한 뼈를 만드는 데 필요하다.
➡ _____

Writing Workshop

1. 건강이 먼저야!
➡ _____

2. 외출 후에는 손을 씻어라. 손을 잘 씻으면 쉽게 감기에 걸리지 않을 것이다.
➡ _____

3. 매일 직사광선을 10~20분간 받아라.
➡ _____

4. 햇빛을 더 많이 받을수록 더 행복하고 강하게 느낄 것이다.
➡ _____

5. 두뇌가 적절히 작동하도록 돕는 것은 좋은 아침식사이다.
➡ _____

6. 좋은 아침을 먹으면, 일에 분명히 집중하고 더 잘 기억할 수 있다.
➡ _____

※ 다음 영어를 우리말로 쓰시오.

01	accident
02	overuse
03	although
04	path
05	uncomfortable
06	peel
07	regularly
08	overwork
09	earthquake
10	cause
11	electricity
12	overeat
13	pack
14	explode
15	feed
16	oxygen
17	garlic
18	lightning
19	location
20	memory
21	avoid

22	overflow
23	mosquito
24	nature-friendly
25	occasion
26	prepare
27	protect
28	entrance
29	sunscreen
30	apply
31	attention
32	flooding
33	fit
34	safety
35	use up
36	pass out
37	hang out
38	keep away
39	put up
40	by -ing
41	keep ~ in mind
42	put on
43	do one's best

※ 다음 우리말을 영어로 쓰시오.

01	불편한	_____
02	사고	_____
03	흘러넘치다, 범람하다	_____
04	마늘	_____
05	~에 맞다	_____
06	모기	_____
07	(과일 또는 채소의) 껍질	_____
08	비록 ~이긴 하지만	_____
09	(크림 등을) 바르다	_____
10	번개	_____
11	규칙적으로	_____
12	(출)입구, 문	_____
13	장소	_____
14	폭발하다	_____
15	과식하다	_____
16	지진	_____
17	과로하다, 혹사하다	_____
18	보호하다	_____
19	산소	_____
20	안전, 안전성	_____
21	남용하다, 너무 많이 사용하다	_____

22	평평한	_____
23	주의, 집중	_____
24	홍수, 범람	_____
25	걸다, 매달다	_____
26	자연 친화적인	_____
27	흘리다	_____
28	(특정한) 때, 경우	_____
29	(짐을) 꾸리다	_____
30	준비하다, 대비하다	_____
31	문지르다, 비비다	_____
32	(세게) 치다	_____
33	전기	_____
34	피하다	_____
35	~을 바르다	_____
36	~을 다 써버리다	_____
37	~을 명심하다	_____
38	어울리다	_____
39	~을 접근하지 못하게 하다	_____
40	안 자다, 깨어 있다	_____
41	~ 대신에	_____
42	의식을 잃다, 기절하다	_____
43	최선을 다하다	_____

※ 다음 영영풀이에 알맞은 단어를 <보기>에서 골라 쓴 후, 우리말 뜻을 쓰시오.

1 _____ : something that you remember: _____

2 _____ : to give food to someone or something: _____

3 _____ : a sudden, violent shaking of the earth's surface: _____

4 _____ : the skin of a fruit: _____

5 _____ : the bright flashes of light that you see in the sky during a storm:
_____

6 _____ : to hit someone or something hard or with force: _____

7 _____ : to press and move your hands or an object over a surface: _____

8 _____ : a door, gate, passage, etc. used for entering a room, building, or place:
_____

9 _____ : a place where something happens or exists; the position of something:
_____

10 _____ : a situation in which water from a river or from rain covers large areas of
land: _____

11 _____ : to put something into a bag, suitcase, etc., so that you can take it with
you: _____

12 _____ : to burst, or to make something burst, loudly and violently, causing
damage: _____

13 _____ : to put or spread something such as paint, cream, etc. onto a surface:
_____

14 _____ : a small flying insect that bites the skin of people and animals and sucks
their blood: _____

15 _____ : a cream that you can rub onto your skin to stop it from being burned by
the sun: _____

16 _____ : a vegetable of the onion family with a very strong taste and smell, used
in cooking to give flavor to food: _____

보기			
pack	location	rub	entrance
garlic	mosquito	feed	earthquake
flooding	explode	strike	lightning
apply	sunscreen	memory	peel

※ 다음 우리말과 일치하도록 빈칸에 알맞은 말을 쓰시오.

Listen & Speak 1 Listen

1. **B:** We _____ _____ _____ _____ for bees.
   G: Oh, there are bees. Run!
2. **G:** Can we go _____ _____? It _____ _____.
   B: No. We have to _____ _____ if we want _____ _____ _____ the top.
3. **B:** Oh, the _____ are _____.
   G: Then we _____ _____ _____ _____ the stairs slowly.
4. **G:** _____ _____ some more. I want to reach the _____ of the mountain.
   B: First we _____ _____ _____ the weather. Oh, it says it's _____ _____ _____. We _____ _____ _____.

Listen & Speak 1 A

1. **G:** Mom, can I _____ _____ this afternoon?
   W: Sure. _____ _____ _____ put on sunscreen before you _____ _____.
   G: But it's _____ today. Do I _____ _____ _____ _____ sunscreen?
   W: Yes, you have to _____ sunscreen _____ _____.
   G: Okay. Then I'll _____ some _____ now.
2. **B:** Let's _____ _____.
   G: I'm sorry, I can't. I have to _____ _____ _____ _____ _____.
   B: Oh, what's _____?
   G: I don't know, but my _____ _____.

Listen & Speak 2 Listen

1. **M:** _____ run. You _____ _____.
   B: Okay, I _____ _____.
2. **B:** Jumping _____ cold water _____ _____ _____ can _____ _____.
   G: Oh, okay. I will _____ _____.
3. **G:** Mom, I want _____ _____ here.
   W: Okay, but first you should check _____ _____ _____ _____ _____. It may be _____ _____ you think.
4. **B:** Can I swim _____ _____ _____?
   G: Swimming _____ a full stomach can be _____.

해석

1. **B:** 우리는 벌들을 조심해야만 해.
   G: 오, 벌들이다. 뛰어!
2. **G:** 이쪽으로 갈 수 있을까? 좋아 보여.
   B: 아니. 정상에 가기를 원한다면 우리는 똑바로 가야 해.
3. **B:** 오, 계단이 젖었어.
   G: 그러면 우리는 계단을 천천히 내려가야 해.
4. **G:** 조금 더 올라가 보자. 나는 산 정상에 닿고 싶어.
   B: 우리는 먼저 날씨를 확인해야 해. 오, 비가 내릴 예정이래. 우리는 내려가야 해.

1. **G:** 엄마, 오후에 밖에서 놀아도 될까요?
   W: 물론이지. 나가기 전에 선크림 바르는 것을 잊지 말아라.
   G: 그렇지만 오늘은 흐려요. 선크림을 발라야 하나요?
   W: 그럼, 매일 선크림을 발라야 한단다.
   G: 알겠어요. 그러면 지금 바를게요.

2. **B:** 볼링 치러 가자.
   G: 미안해. 갈 수 없어. 병원에 가야 하거든.
   B: 오, 무슨 문제 있니?
   G: 몰라, 하지만 배가 아파.

1. **M:** 뛰지 마. 넘어질 수도 있단다.
   B: 알겠어요, 뛰지 않을게요.
2. **B:** 준비 운동을 하지 않고 차가운 물로 뛰어드는 것은 위험할 수 있어.
   G: 오, 알았어. 준비 운동할게.
3. **G:** 엄마, 여기에서 수영하고 싶어요.
   W: 그래, 하지만 우선 물이 얼마나 깊은지 확인해야 한단다. 네가 생각하는 것보다 물이 깊을 수 있어.
4. **B:** 먹고 난 후에 바로 수영해도 될까?
   G: 배가 부른 채로 수영하는 것은 불편할 수 있어.

Listen & Speak 2 A

1. **M:** Flooding _____ _____ big problems. However, you may not know _____ _____ _____ when it happens. There are several things you _____ _____ _____. First, you _____ _____ _____ _____ the water and the electricity. Second, _____ water and food when you leave the house. _____, you have to move to a high and _____ _____ and _____ _____ _____ the weather report.

2. **B:** Mina, are you _____ _____ _____?
   G: No, not _____. I _____ _____ check _____ I _____ _____ the gas.
   B: If we don't leave now, we _____ _____ _____ _____ the concert _____ _____.
   G: Okay, but I _____ _____ _____ the gas first. It will only take a _____.

Real-Life Zone

B: Uncle John, _____ _____ my new bike. _____ do you _____?
M: It's really nice. Where _____ you _____?
B: To the park _____ _____ a friend.
M: Where's your helmet?
B: I _____ _____ _____. It's just a _____ _____.
M: _____ _____ your helmet. You may _____ _____.
B: But I see a _____ of people _____ bikes _____ helmets.
M: You _____ _____ _____ a helmet. It _____ your head in an accident.
B: Okay. I'll get my dad's helmet.
M: No. You _____ _____ _____ a helmet that _____ you. If _____, it cannot protect your head.
B: I guess I'll _____ _____ _____ one for myself.

Wrap Up

B: Here _____ the bus!
G: Oh, but first I have to _____ _____ my tea.
B: _____ _____ you just take it with you? I'm _____ _____ it will be okay if you are _____.
G: No. If the bus stops _____, I _____ _____ _____ it.
B: Okay, then I can just _____ _____ you _____ your drink. I'm sure _____ _____ will come soon.
G: Thanks.

1. **M:** 홍수는 큰 문제들을 일으킬 수 있습니다. 그러나, 당신은 홍수가 발생할 때 무엇을 해야 하는지 모를 수도 있습니다. 당신이 해야 하는 몇 가지 것들이 있습니다. 첫째, 수도와 전기를 꺼야 합니다. 둘째, 집을 떠날 때 물과 음식을 꾸려야 합니다. 마지막으로, 높고 안전한 곳으로 이동하여 일기 예보를 계속 들어야 합니다.

2. **B:** 미나야, 떠날 준비됐니?
   G: 아니, 아직. 가스를 껐는지 확인해야 해.
   B: 만약 우리가 지금 떠나지 않으면, 제 시간에 콘서트에 도착하지 못할 수도 있어.
   G: 알았어. 하지만 나는 우선 가스를 확인해야 해. 잠깐이면 될 거야.

B: 존 삼촌. 제 새로운 자전거 좀 보세요. 어떻게 생각하세요?
M: 아주 멋지구나. 어디를 가고 있니?
B: 친구 만나러 공원에요.
M: 네 헬멧이 어디 있니?
B: 저는 헬멧이 없어요. 그냥 잠깐 타는 거예요.
M: 헬멧을 쓰렴. 다칠 수 있단다.
B: 하지만 저는 헬멧 없이 자전거를 타는 많은 사람들을 봐요.
M: 너는 헬멧을 써야만 한단다. 그것은 사고가 났을 때 네 머리를 보호해 줘.
B: 알았어요. 아빠의 헬멧을 가져올게요.
M: 아니. 너는 네게 맞는 헬멧을 써야 해. 그렇지 않으면 그것은 네 머리를 보호해 줄 수 없어.
B: 저를 위한 헬멧을 사야겠어요.

B: 버스가 온다!
G: 오, 그렇지만 나는 우선 차 마시는 것을 끝내야 해.
B: 그냥 그것을 가지고 타는 것은 어때? 네가 조심한다면 괜찮을 거라고 확신해.
G: 아니, 만약 버스가 갑자기 멈춘다면, 나는 차를 흘릴 수도 있어.
B: 알았어, 그러면 난 네가 음료를 다 마실 때까지 기다릴 수 있어. 곧 다른 버스가 올 것이라고 확신해.
G: 고마워.

※ 다음 우리말에 맞도록 대화를 영어로 쓰시오.

 해석

Listen & Speak 1 Listen

1. **B:** _____
   G: _____

2. **G:** _____
   B: _____

3. **B:** _____
   G: _____

4. **G:** _____
   B: _____
   _____

1. **B:** 우리는 벌들을 조심해야만 해.
   G: 오, 벌들이다. 뛰어!
2. **G:** 이쪽으로 갈 수 있을까? 좋아 보여.
   B: 아니. 정상에 가기를 원한다면 우리는 똑바로 가야 해.
3. **B:** 오, 계단이 젖었어.
   G: 그러면 우리는 계단을 천천히 내려가야 해.
4. **G:** 조금 더 올라가 보자. 나는 산 정상에 닿고 싶어.
   B: 우리는 먼저 날씨를 확인해야 해. 오, 비가 내릴 예정이래. 우리는 내려가야 해.

Listen & Speak 1 A

1. **G:** _____
   W: _____
   G: _____
   W: _____
   G: _____

2. **B:** _____
   G: _____
   B: _____
   G: _____

1. **G:** 엄마, 오후에 밖에서 놀아도 될까요?
   W: 물론이지. 나가기 전에 선크림 바르는 것을 잊지 말아라.
   G: 그렇지만 오늘은 흐려요. 선크림을 발라야 하나요?
   W: 그럼, 매일 선크림을 발라야 한단다.
   G: 알겠어요. 그러면 지금 바를게요.

2. **B:** 볼링 치러 가자.
   G: 미안해. 갈 수 없어. 병원에 가야하거든.
   B: 오, 무슨 문제 있니?
   G: 몰라, 하지만 배가 아파.

Listen & Speak 2 Listen

1. **M:** _____
   B: _____

2. **B:** _____
   G: _____

3. **G:** _____
   W: _____
   _____

4. **B:** _____
   G: _____

1. **M:** 뛰지 마. 넘어질 수도 있단다.
   B: 알겠어요, 뛰지 않을게요.
2. **B:** 준비 운동을 하지 않고 차가운 물로 뛰어드는 것은 위험할 수 있어.
   G: 오, 알았어. 준비 운동할게.
3. **G:** 엄마, 여기에서 수영하고 싶어요.
   W: 그래, 하지만 우선 물이 얼마나 깊은지 확인해야 한단다. 네가 생각하는 것보다 물이 깊을 수 있어.
4. **B:** 먹고 난 후에 바로 수영해도 될까?
   G: 배가 부른 채로 수영하는 것은 불편할 수 있어.

Listen & Speak 2 A

1. M: _____
   _____
   _____
   _____
   _____

2. B: _____
   G: _____
   B: _____
   G: _____

Real-Life Zone

B: _____
M: _____
B: _____
M: _____
B: _____
M: _____
B: _____
M: _____
B: _____
M: _____
B: _____

Wrap Up

B: _____
G: _____
B: _____
G: _____
B: _____
G: _____

1. M: 홍수는 큰 문제들을 일으킬 수 있습니다. 그러나, 당신은 홍수가 발생할 때 무엇을 해야 하는지 모를 수도 있습니다. 당신이 해야 하는 몇 가지 것들이 있습니다. 첫째, 수도와 전기를 꺼야 합니다. 둘째, 집을 떠날 때 물과 음식을 꾸려야 합니다. 마지막으로, 높고 안전한 곳으로 이동하여 일기 예보를 계속 들어야 합니다.

2. B: 미나야, 떠날 준비됐니?
   G: 아니, 아직. 가스를 껐는지 확인해야 해.
   B: 만약 우리가 지금 떠나지 않으면, 제 시간에 콘서트에 도착하지 못할 수도 있어.
   G: 알았어. 하지만 나는 우선 가스를 확인해야 해. 잠깐이면 될 거야.

B: 존 삼촌. 제 새로운 자전거 좀 보세요. 어떻게 생각하세요?
M: 아주 멋지구나. 어디를 가고 있니?
B: 친구 만나러 공원에요.
M: 네 헬멧이 어디 있니?
B: 저는 헬멧이 없어요. 그냥 잠깐 타는 거예요.
M: 헬멧을 쓰렴. 다칠 수 있단다.
B: 하지만 저는 헬멧 없이 자전거를 타는 많은 사람들을 봐요.
M: 너는 헬멧을 써야만 한단다. 그것은 사고가 났을 때 네 머리를 보호해 줘.
B: 알았어요. 아빠의 헬멧을 가져올게요.
M: 아니. 너는 네게 맞는 헬멧을 써야 해. 그렇지 않으면 그것은 네 머리를 보호해 줄 수 없어.
B: 저를 위한 헬멧을 사야겠어요.

B: 버스가 온다!
G: 오, 그렇지만 나는 우선 차 마시는 것을 끝내야 해.
B: 그냥 그것을 가지고 타는 것은 어때? 네가 조심한다면 괜찮을 거라고 확신해.
G: 아니, 만약 버스가 갑자기 멈춘다면, 나는 차를 흘릴 수도 있어.
B: 알았어, 그러면 난 네가 음료를 다 마실 때까지 기다릴 수 있어. 곧 다른 버스가 올 것이라고 확신해.
G: 고마워.

※ 다음 우리말과 일치하도록 빈칸에 알맞은 것을 골라 쓰시오.

Safe Camping

1 Although camping trips can _____ sweet _____ for many people, they can also be _____ when bad things _____.

    A. memories   B. happen   C. occasions   D. create

2 If you _____ to go camping with family or friends this summer, you _____ to _____ several things in _____ for your safety.

    A. need   B. mind   C. keep   D. plan

3 _____ to Yumin's family _____ about their _____.

    A. talk   B. trip   C. camping   D. listen

4 They _____ to know _____ to do to _____ their camping trip _____ and fun.

    A. safe   B. what   C. make   D. seem

5 Yumin: Dad, _____ don't we _____ our tent over here _____ this river?

    A. by   B. put   C. why   D. up

6 Dad: I _____ _____ that's a good _____.

    A. idea   B. think   C. don't

7 If it _____ _____ rain, the river _____ _____.

    A. overflow   B. to   C. might   D. starts

8 Yumin: I know, _____ the _____ is _____.

    A. clear   B. but   C. sky

9 I _____ like the _____ of the _____!

    A. sound   B. really   C. water

10 Dad: The _____ can _____ quickly in the _____.

    A. change   B. weather   C. mountains

11 You _____ know _____ it _____ start to _____.

    A. might   B. never   C. rain   D. when

12 Yumin: Okay. _____ first! _____ find _____ place.

    A. another   B. let's   C. safety

13 When you _____ a tent, _____ a _____, sunny area.

    A. up   B. set   C. flat   D. choose

14 _____ places too _____ to big trees that might _____ _____ by lightning.

    A. struck   B. avoid   C. be   D. close

15 Hajun: Mom, I'm _____. What's _____ _____?

    A. hungry   B. lunch   C. for

16 Mom: I'm _____ _____.

    A. Samgyepsal   B. cooking

17 Hajun: Mom, that's not _____ for _____ of us. Can we cook _____ in a _____ pan?

    A. all   B. more   C. enough   D. bigger

안전한 캠핑

1 캠핑 여행이 많은 사람들에게 좋은 추억을 만들어 주기도 하지만, 나쁜 일이 일어나는 때가 될 수도 있습니다.

2 여러분이 이번 여름에 가족이나 친구들과 함께 캠핑을 하려고 계획하고 있다면, 여러분은 여러분의 안전을 위해서 몇 가지 사항을 명심해야 합니다.

3 유민이의 가족이 그들의 캠핑 여행에 대해 이야기하는 것을 들어 보세요.

4 그들은 그들의 캠핑 여행이 안전하고 재미있게 하기 위해 무엇을 해야 하는지 알고 있는 것 같습니다.

5 유민: 아빠, 이 강 근처 이쪽에 텐트를 치면 어때요?

6 아빠: 그건 좋은 생각 같지 않구나.

7 만약 비가 내리기 시작하면, 강이 범람할지도 몰라.

8 유민: 저도 알아요. 하지만 하늘이 맑잖아요.

9 저는 물소리를 정말 좋아한단 말이에요!

10 아빠: 산속의 날씨는 곧 바뀔 수 있어.

11 언제 비가 올지 절대 알 수 없는 일이지.

12 유민: 알겠어요. 안전이 우선이지요! 다른 곳을 찾아봐요.

13 텐트를 칠 때는 평평하고 햇볕이 잘 드는 장소를 고르세요.

14 번개를 맞을지도 모르는 키 큰 나무에 너무 가까운 장소는 피해야 합니다.

15 하준: 엄마, 저 배고파요. 점심이 뭐예요?

16 엄마: 삼겹살을 요리하고 있단다.

17 하준: 엄마, 그건 우리 모두가 먹기에 충분하지 않아요. 우리 더 큰 팬에 더 많이 요리하면 안 돼요?

18 Mom: I'm going to cook _____, but we _____ _____ use this small _____.

    A. to   B. have   C. more   D. pan

19 Hajun: _____ do we _____ to _____ a small pan?

    A. have   B. use   C. why

20 Mom: _____ the pan should _____ be bigger _____ the _____.

    A. burner   B. because   C. not   D. than

21 _____ you use a big pan, it _____ the heat _____ to the burner, and the gas can _____!

    A. sends   B. explode   C. back   D. if

22 Hajun: Oh, I _____ _____ _____.

    A. know   B. didn't   C. that

23 _____ is one more _____ about fire _____ you go camping.

    A. tip   B. here   C. when

24 _____ _____ a gas heater or burner _____ a tent.

    A. inside   B. use   C. never

25 Your tent may catch fire, or you might _____ out because the fire will _____ up the _____ in the tent _____ it burns.

    A. oxygen   B. as   C. use   D. pass

26 Yumin: _____! _____!

    A. mosquitoes   B. ouch

27 Mom: Oh, I _____ _____ tell you to _____ some _____ spray. Here.

    A. bug   B. to   C. apply   D. forgot

28 Yumin: _____, Mom. Oh, you _____ _____?

    A. what   B. know   C. thanks

29 We can _____ orange peels _____ our skin _____ of _____ bug spray.

    A. on   B. applying   C. rub   D. instead

30 It is a nature-friendly _____ _____ _____ mosquitoes _____.

    A. away   B. to   C. way   D. keep

31 Mom: _____ _____!

    A. interesting   B. that's

32 _____ can also _____ bugs _____.

    A. away   B. garlic   C. keep

33 You can place _____ of garlic at the _____ to the tent, and bugs will not _____ _____.

    A. entrance   B. inside   C. pieces   D. come

---

18 엄마: 더 굽긴 할 거야. 하지만 우리는 이 작은 팬을 써야 해.

19 하준: 왜 우리는 작은 팬을 써야 하죠?

20 엄마: 왜냐하면 팬이 버너보다 더 크면 안 되기 때문이야.

21 만약 큰 팬을 사용하면, 팬이 열을 버너로 다시 돌려보내서, 가스가 폭발할 수 있어!

22 하준: 오, 그것은 몰랐어요.

23 캠핑할 때 불을 사용하는 것에 대한 또 하나의 팁이 있습니다.

24 텐트 안에서 가스난로나 버너를 절대 쓰지 마세요.

25 여러분의 텐트에 불이 붙거나, 불이 타면서 텐트 내 산소를 다 써 버려서 여러분이 의식을 잃을 수도 있습니다.

26 유민: 앗! 모기!

27 엄마: 아, 벌레 퇴치 스프레이를 뿌리라고 네게 말하는 걸 잊었구나. 여기 있단다.

28 유민: 고마워요. 엄마. 아, 그거 아세요?

29 벌레 퇴치 스프레이를 뿌리는 것 대신에 오렌지 껍질을 피부에 문질러도 돼요.

30 모기가 접근하지 못하게 하는 자연 친화적인 방법이에요.

31 엄마: 그거 재미있구나!

32 마늘 또한 벌레가 접근하지 못하게 막을 수 있습니다.

33 마늘 조각을 텐트 입구에 놓아두면, 벌레가 안으로 들어오지 않을 것입니다.

※ 다음 우리말과 일치하도록 빈칸에 알맞은 말을 쓰시오.

Safe Camping

1 _____ camping trips can _____ sweet _____ for many people, they can also be occasions _____ bad things _____.

2 If you _____ _____ _____ _____ with family or friends this summer, you _____ to keep several things _____ _____ for your _____.

3 Listen to Yumin's family _____ about their _____ _____.

4 They _____ to know _____ _____ _____ to make their camping trip _____ and fun.

5 Yumin: Dad, _____ _____ we _____ _____ our tent over here _____ this river?

6 Dad: I don't _____ that's a good _____.

7 If it _____ _____ rain, the river _____ _____.

8 Yumin: I know, _____ the sky is _____.

9 I really like the _____ of the water!

10 Dad: The _____ can _____ _____ in the mountains.

11 You _____ know _____ it _____ start _____ _____.

12 Yumin: Okay. _____ first! _____ find _____ place.

13 When you _____ _____ a tent, _____ a flat, sunny area.

14 _____ places too _____ to big trees that might _____ _____ _____ _____.

15 Hajun: Mom, I'm _____. What's _____ lunch?

16 Mom: I'm _____ Samgyepsal.

17 Hajun: Mom, that's not _____ for _____ of us. Can we cook _____ in a _____ _____?

1 캠핑 여행이 많은 사람들에게 좋은 추억을 만들어 주기도 하지만, 나쁜 일이 일어나는 때가 될 수도 있습니다.

2 여러분이 이번 여름에 가족이나 친구들과 함께 캠핑을 하려고 계획하고 있다면, 여러분은 여러분의 안전을 위해서 몇 가지 사항을 명심해야 합니다.

3 유민이의 가족이 그들의 캠핑 여행에 대해 이야기하는 것을 들어 보세요.

4 그들은 그들의 캠핑 여행이 안전하고 재미있게 하기 위해 무엇을 해야 하는지 알고 있는 것 같습니다.

5 유민: 아빠, 이 강 근처 이쪽에 텐트를 치면 어때요?

6 아빠: 그건 좋은 생각 같지 않구나.

7 만약 비가 내리기 시작하면, 강이 범람할지도 몰라.

8 유민: 저도 알아요. 하지만 하늘이 맑잖아요.

9 저는 물소리를 정말 좋아한단 말이에요!

10 아빠: 산속의 날씨는 곧 바뀔 수 있어.

11 언제 비가 올지 절대 알 수 없는 일이지.

12 유민: 알겠어요. 안전이 우선이지요! 다른 곳을 찾아봐요.

13 텐트를 칠 때는 평평하고 햇볕이 잘 드는 장소를 고르세요.

14 번개를 맞을지도 모르는 키 큰 나무에 너무 가까운 장소는 피해야 합니다.

15 하준: 엄마, 저 배고파요. 점심이 뭐예요?

16 엄마: 삼겹살을 요리하고 있단다.

17 하준: 엄마, 그건 우리 모두가 먹기에 충분하지 않아요. 우리 더 큰 팬에 더 많이 요리하면 안 돼요?

18 Mom: I'm _____ _____ cook _____, but we _____ _____ _____ this small pan.

19 Hajun: _____ do we _____ _____ _____ a small pan?

20 Mom: _____ the pan _____ _____ be _____ _____ the burner.

21 _____ you use a big pan, it _____ the heat _____ to the burner, and the gas can _____!

22 Hajun: Oh, I didn't _____ that.

23 _____ is one more _____ about fire _____ you _____.

24 _____ use a gas heater or burner _____ a tent.

25 Your tent _____ _____ _____, _____ you might _____ out because the fire will _____ up the _____ in the tent as it _____.

26 Yumin: Ouch! _____!

27 Mom: Oh, I _____ _____ tell you _____ _____ some bug spray. Here.

28 Yumin: Thanks, Mom. Oh, you know _____?

29 We can _____ orange _____ _____ our skin _____ _____ _____ bug spray.

30 It is a _____ _____ _____ _____ mosquitoes _____.

31 Mom: That's _____!

32 Garlic can also _____ bugs _____.

33 You can place _____ _____ _____ at the _____ to the tent, and bugs will not _____ _____.

---

18 엄마: 더 굽긴 할 거야. 하지만 우리는 이 작은 팬을 써야 해.

19 하준: 왜 우리는 작은 팬을 써야 하죠?

20 엄마: 왜냐하면 팬이 버너보다 더 크면 안 되기 때문이야.

21 만약 큰 팬을 사용하면, 팬이 열을 버너로 다시 돌려보내서, 가스가 폭발할 수 있어!

22 하준: 오, 그것은 몰랐어요.

23 캠핑할 때 불을 사용하는 것에 대한 또 하나의 팁이 있습니다.

24 텐트 안에서 가스난로나 버너를 절대 쓰지 마세요.

25 여러분의 텐트에 불이 붙거나, 불이 타면서 텐트 내 산소를 다 써 버려서 여러분이 의식을 잃을 수도 있습니다.

26 유민: 앗! 모기!

27 엄마: 아, 벌레 퇴치 스프레이를 뿌리라고 네게 말하는 걸 잊었구나. 여기 있단다.

28 유민: 고마워요, 엄마. 아, 그거 아세요?

29 벌레 퇴치 스프레이를 뿌리는 것 대신에 오렌지 껍질을 피부에 문질러도 돼요.

30 모기가 접근하지 못하게 하는 자연 친화적인 방법이에요.

31 엄마: 그거 재미있구나!

32 마늘 또한 벌레가 접근하지 못하게 막을 수 있습니다.

33 마늘 조각을 텐트 입구에 놓아 두면, 벌레가 안으로 들어오지 않을 것입니다.

※ 다음 문장을 우리말로 쓰시오.

Safe Camping

1 Although camping trips can create sweet memories for many people, they can also be occasions when bad things happen.

➡ _____

2 If you plan to go camping with family or friends this summer, you need to keep several things in mind for your safety.

➡ _____

3 Listen to Yumin's family talk about their camping trip.

➡ _____

4 They seem to know what to do to make their camping trip safe and fun.

➡ _____

5 Yumin: Dad, why don't we put up our tent over here by this river?

➡ _____

6 Dad: I don't think that's a good idea.

➡ _____

7 If it starts to rain, the river might overflow.

➡ _____

8 Yumin: I know, but the sky is clear.

➡ _____

9 I really like the sound of the water!

➡ _____

10 Dad: The weather can change quickly in the mountains.

➡ _____

11 You never know when it might start to rain.

➡ _____

12 Yumin: Okay. Safety first! Let's find another place.

➡ _____

13 When you set up a tent, choose a flat, sunny area.

➡ _____

14 Avoid places too close to big trees that might be struck by lightning.

➡ _____

15 Hajun: Mom, I'm hungry. What's for lunch?

➡ _____

16 Mom: I'm cooking Samgyepsal.

➡ _____

17 Hajun: Mom, that's not enough for all of us. Can we cook more in a bigger pan?

➡ _____

18 Mom: I'm going to cook more, but we have to use this small pan.

➡ _____

19 Hajun: Why do we have to use a small pan?

➡ _____

20 Mom: Because the pan should not be bigger than the burner.

➡ _____

21 If you use a big pan, it sends the heat back to the burner, and the gas can explode!

➡ _____

22 Hajun: Oh, I didn't know that.

➡ _____

23 Here is one more tip about fire when you go camping.

➡ _____

24 Never use a gas heater or burner inside a tent.

➡ _____

25 Your tent may catch fire, or you might pass out because the fire will use up the oxygen in the

tent as it burns.

➡ _____

26 Yumin: Ouch! Mosquitoes!

➡ _____

27 Mom: Oh, I forgot to tell you to apply some bug spray. Here.

➡ _____

28 Yumin: Thanks, Mom. Oh, you know what?

➡ _____

29 We can rub orange peels on our skin instead of applying bug spray.

➡ _____

30 It is a nature-friendly way to keep mosquitoes away.

➡ _____

31 Mom: That's interesting!

➡ _____

32 Garlic can also keep bugs away.

➡ _____

33 You can place pieces of garlic at the entrance to the tent, and bugs will not come inside.

➡ _____

※ 다음 괄호 안의 단어들을 우리말에 맞도록 바르게 배열하시오.

1 (camping / although / trips / create / can / memories / sweet / many / for / people, / can / they / be / also / occasions / bad / when / things / happen.)
➡ _____

2 (you / if / to / plan / camping / go / family / with / or / this / friends / summer, / need / you / to / several / keep / things / mind / in / your / for / safety.)
➡ _____

3 (to / listen / family / Yumin's / about / talk / camping / their / trip.)
➡ _____

4 (seem / they / know / to / to / what / do / make / their / trip / camping / safe / fun. / and)
➡ _____

5 (Yumin: / why / dad, / don't / put / we / our / up / tent / here / over / by / river? / this)
➡ _____

6 (Dad: / don't / I / think / a / that's / good / idea.)
➡ _____

7 (it / if / to / starts / rain, / river / the / overflow. / might)
➡ _____

8 (Yumin: / know, / I / but / sky / the / clear. / is)
➡ _____

9 (really / I / the / like / of / sound / water! / the)
➡ _____

10 (Dad: / weather / the / change / can / in / quickly / mountains. / the)
➡ _____

11 (never / you / when / know / might / it / to / start / rain.)
➡ _____

12 (Yumin: / okay. // first! / safety // find / let's / another / place.)
➡ _____

13 (you / when / up / set / tent, / a / choose / flat, / a / area. / sunny)
➡ _____

14 (places / avoid / close / too / big / to / trees / might / that / struck / be / lightning. / by)
➡ _____

15 (Hajun: / I'm / mom, / hungry. // for / what's / lunch?)
➡ _____

16 (mom: / cooking / I'm / Samgyepsal.)
➡ _____

17 (Hajun: / mom, / not / that's / enough / all / for / us. / of // we / can / more / cook / a / in / pan? / bigger)
➡ _____

안전한 캠핑

1 캠핑 여행이 많은 사람들에게 좋은 추억을 만들어 주기도 하지만, 나쁜 일이 일어나는 때가 될 수도 있습니다.

2 여러분이 이번 여름에 가족이나 친구들과 함께 캠핑을 하려고 계획하고 있다면, 여러분은 여러분의 안전을 위해서 몇 가지 사항을 명심해야 합니다.

3 유민이의 가족이 그들의 캠핑 여행에 대해 이야기하는 것을 들어 보세요.

4 그들은 그들의 캠핑 여행이 안전하고 재미있게 하기 위해 무엇을 해야 하는지 알고 있는 것 같습니다.

5 유민: 아빠, 이 강 근처 이쪽에 텐트를 치면 어때요?

6 아빠: 그건 좋은 생각 같지 않구나.

7 만약 비가 내리기 시작하면, 강이 범람할지도 몰라.

8 유민: 저도 알아요. 하지만 하늘이 맑잖아요.

9 저는 물소리를 정말 좋아한단 말이에요!

10 아빠: 산속의 날씨는 곧 바뀔 수 있어.

11 언제 비가 올지 절대 알 수 없는 일이지.

12 유민: 알겠어요. 안전이 우선이지요! 다른 곳을 찾아봐요.

13 텐트를 칠 때는 평평하고 햇볕이 잘 드는 장소를 고르세요.

14 번개를 맞을지도 모르는 키 큰 나무에 너무 가까운 장소는 피해야 합니다.

15 하준: 엄마, 저 배고파요. 점심이 뭐예요?

16 엄마: 삼겹살을 요리하고 있단다.

17 하준: 엄마, 그건 우리 모두가 먹기에 충분하지 않아요. 우리 더 큰 팬에 더 많이 요리하면 안 돼요?

18 (Mom: / going / I'm / cook / to / more, / we / but / to / have / this / use / pan. / small)
➡ _____

19 (Hajun: / do / why / have / we / use / to / small / a / pan?)
➡ _____

20 (Mom: / the / because / pan / not / should / be / than / bigger / burner. / the)
➡ _____

21 (you / if / a / use / pan, / big / sends / it / heat / the / to / back / the / burner, / the / and / gas / explode! / can)
➡ _____
_____

22 (Hajun: / I / oh, / know / didn't / that.)
➡ _____

23 (is / here / more / one / about / tip / when / fire / you / camping. / go)
➡ _____

24 (use / never / gas / a / heater / or / inside / burner / tent. / a)
➡ _____

25 (tent / your / catch / may / fire, / you / or / pass / might / out / the / because / fire / use / will / up / oxygen / the / in / tent / the / it / as / burns.)
➡ _____
_____

26 (Yumin: / mosquitoes! / ouch!)
➡ _____

27 (Mom: / I / oh, / to / forgot / you / tell / apply / to / bug / some / spray. // here.)
➡ _____

28 (Yumin: / Mom. / thanks, // you / oh, / what? / know)
➡ _____

29 (can / we / orange / rub / peels / our / on / skin / of / instead / bug / applying / spray.)
➡ _____

30 (is / it / nature-friendly / a / to / way / mosquitoes / keep / away.)
➡ _____

31 (Mom: / interesting! / that's)
➡ _____

32 (can / garlic / keep / also / away. / bugs)
➡ _____

33 (can / you / pieces / place / garlic / of / the / at / entrance / the / to / tent, / and / will / bugs / come / not / inside.)
➡ _____
_____

18 엄마: 더 굽긴 할 거야. 하지만 우리는 이 작은 팬을 써야 해.

19 하준: 왜 우리는 작은 팬을 써야 하죠?

20 엄마: 왜냐하면 팬이 버너보다 더 크면 안 되기 때문이야.

21 만약 큰 팬을 사용하면, 팬이 열을 버너로 다시 돌려보내서, 가스가 폭발할 수 있어!

22 하준: 오, 그것은 몰랐어요.

23 캠핑할 때 불을 사용하는 것에 대한 또 하나의 팁이 있습니다.

24 텐트 안에서 가스난로나 버너를 절대 쓰지 마세요.

25 여러분의 텐트에 불이 붙거나, 불이 타면서 텐트 내 산소를 다 써 버려서 여러분이 의식을 잃을 수도 있습니다.

26 유민: 앗! 모기!

27 엄마: 아, 벌레 퇴치 스프레이를 뿌리라고 네게 말하는 걸 잊었구나. 여기 있단다.

28 유민: 고마워요, 엄마. 아, 그거 아세요?

29 벌레 퇴치 스프레이를 뿌리는 것 대신에 오렌지 껍질을 피부에 문질러도 돼요.

30 모기가 접근하지 못하게 하는 자연 친화적인 방법이에요.

31 엄마: 그거 재미있구나!

32 마늘 또한 벌레가 접근하지 못하게 막을 수 있습니다.

33 마늘 조각을 텐트 입구에 놓아 두면, 벌레가 안으로 들어오지 않을 것입니다.

※ 다음 우리말을 영어로 쓰시오.

Safe Camping

1 캠핑 여행이 많은 사람들에게 좋은 추억을 만들어 주기도 하지만, 나쁜 일이 일어나는 때가 될 수도 있습니다.
➡ _____
_____

2 여러분이 이번 여름에 가족이나 친구들과 함께 캠핑을 하려고 계획하고 있다면, 여러분은 여러분의 안전을 위해서 몇 가지 사항을 명심해야 합니다.
➡ _____

3 유민이의 가족이 그들의 캠핑 여행에 대해 이야기하는 것을 들어 보세요.
➡ _____

4 그들은 그들의 캠핑 여행이 안전하고 재미있게 하기 위해 무엇을 해야 하는지 알고 있는 것 같습니다.
➡ _____

5 유민: 아빠, 이 강 근처 이쪽에 텐트를 치면 어때요?
➡ _____

6 아빠: 그건 좋은 생각 같지 않구나.
➡ _____

7 만약 비가 내리기 시작하면, 강이 범람할지도 몰라.
➡ _____

8 유민: 저도 알아요. 하지만 하늘이 맑잖아요.
➡ _____

9 저는 물소리를 정말 좋아한단 말이에요!
➡ _____

10 아빠: 산속의 날씨는 곧 바뀔 수 있어.
➡ _____

11 언제 비가 올지 절대 알 수 없는 일이지.
➡ _____

12 유민: 알겠어요. 안전이 우선이지요! 다른 곳을 찾아봐요.
➡ _____

13 텐트를 칠 때는 평평하고 햇볕이 잘 드는 장소를 고르세요.
➡ _____

14 번개를 맞을지도 모르는 키 큰 나무에 너무 가까운 장소는 피해야 합니다.
➡ _____

15 하준: 엄마, 저 배고파요. 점심이 뭐예요?
➡ _____

16 엄마: 삼겹살을 요리하고 있단다.
➡ _____

17 하준: 엄마, 그건 우리 모두가 먹기에 충분하지 않아요. 우리 더 큰 팬에 더 많이 요리하면 안 돼요?
➡ _____

18 엄마: 더 굽긴 할 거야. 하지만 우리는 이 작은 팬을 써야 해.

➡ _____

19 하준: 왜 우리는 작은 팬을 써야 하죠?

➡ _____

20 엄마: 왜냐하면 팬이 버너보다 더 크면 안 되기 때문이야.

➡ _____

21 만약 큰 팬을 사용하면, 팬이 열을 버너로 다시 돌려보내서, 가스가 폭발할 수 있어!

➡ _____

22 하준: 오, 그것은 몰랐어요.

➡ _____

23 캠핑할 때 불을 사용하는 것에 대한 또 하나의 팁이 있습니다.

➡ _____

24 텐트 안에서 가스난로나 버너를 절대 쓰지 마세요.

➡ _____

25 여러분의 텐트에 불이 붙거나, 불이 타면서 텐트 내 산소를 다 써 버려서 여러분이 의식을 잃을 수도 있습니다.

➡ _____

➡ _____

26 유민: 앗! 모기!

➡ _____

27 엄마: 아, 벌레 퇴치 스프레이를 뿌리라고 네게 말하는 걸 잊었구나. 여기 있단다.

➡ _____

28 유민: 고마워요, 엄마. 아, 그거 아세요?

➡ _____

29 벌레 퇴치 스프레이를 뿌리는 것 대신에 오렌지 껍질을 피부에 문질러도 돼요.

➡ _____

30 모기가 접근하지 못하게 하는 자연 친화적인 방법이에요.

➡ _____

31 엄마: 그거 재미있구나!

➡ _____

32 마늘 또한 벌레가 접근하지 못하게 막을 수 있습니다.

➡ _____

33 마늘 조각을 텐트 입구에 놓아두면, 벌레가 안으로 들어오지 않을 것입니다.

➡ _____

※ 다음 우리말과 일치하도록 빈칸에 알맞은 말을 쓰시오.

Before You Read

1. _____ _____ Our Sky Camping Trip!
2. We _____ _____ many activities for _____ _____ _____.
3. _____ we always think about your safety first, we _____ _____ _____ _____ _____ _____ _____ that may happen.
4. We _____ _____ _____ a comfortable stay _____ _____ a can of bug spray in each tent so you can _____ _____ _____ _____.
5. We hope _____ _____ _____ _____ _____ _____ _____ of the trip!

Writing Workshop

1. _____ you would think that you _____ _____ _____ _____ _____, that is not true.
2. Then, what should you do _____ _____ _____?
3. There are _____ _____ you _____ _____ _____ _____ _____.
4. First, _____ _____ and keep informed _____ _____ _____ _____.
5. It _____ _____ _____ _____ to go outside, but something _____ _____ _____ you.
6. Second, _____ _____ the gas and the electricity.
7. Third, _____ _____ the table and _____ _____ _____ _____ _____.
8. _____ is important _____ _____ your head.
9. Finally, if you are outside, try to get as _____ _____ buildings, trees, and streetlights _____ _____.
10. _____ _____ these tips, you _____ _____ _____ from the earthquake.

Wrap Up

1. My Camping _____ _____
2. _____: Yeongwol Date: _____ 12
3. Traveled _____: my family
4. I _____ to Yeongwol _____ my family _____ _____ 12.
5. _____ the trip, we _____ _____ and _____.
6. _____ I _____ _____ _____ _____ rafting _____ _____, it was really fun and exciting.
7. I'll _____ _____ again _____ I _____ _____ _____.

---

1. 스카이 캠핑에 오신 것을 환영합니다!
2. 저희는 이틀간의 캠핑 여행을 위해 많은 활동들을 준비했습니다.
3. 저희는 항상 여러분의 안전을 우선으로 생각하기 때문에, 발생할 수 있는 나쁜 일에 대비하기 위해 최선을 다합니다.
4. 저희는 여러분이 모기에 물리는 것을 피할 수 있도록 각각의 텐트에 벌레 퇴치 스프레이를 한 통씩 비치해 둠으로써 여러분이 편안하게 머물도록 돕습니다.
5. 저희는 모든 분들이 여행의 좋은 추억을 집으로 가져가시기를 바랍니다.

1. 비록 여러분이 지진으로부터 자유롭다고 생각할 수 있지만, 사실은 그렇지 않습니다.
2. 그러면 지진이 발생하면 여러분은 무엇을 해야 할까요?
3. 여러분이 명심해야 할 것이 몇 가지 있습니다.
4. 첫째, 흔들림이 멈출 때까지 안에서 머물며 계속 정보를 받아야 합니다.
5. 밖으로 나가는 게 안전해 보이지만 무언가가 여러분에게 떨어질 수도 있습니다.
6. 둘째, 가스와 전기를 끄십시오.
7. 셋째, 테이블 아래로 들어가서 팔로 머리를 감싸세요.
8. 여러분의 머리를 보호하는 것이 중요합니다.
9. 만일 여러분이 밖에 있다면, 가능한 한 건물이나 나무, 가로등으로부터 멀리 떨어지세요.
10. 이 팁을 따름으로써 여러분은 지진으로부터 안전할 수 있습니다.

1. 나의 캠핑 여행 일기
2. 위치: 영월 날짜: 9월 12일
3. 함께 여행한 사람: 나의 가족
4. 나는 9월 12일에 나의 가족과 함께 영월에 갔다.
5. 여행 중에 우리는 급류 타기와 하이킹을 즐겼다.
6. 나는 처음에 급류 타기를 무서워했지만, 그것은 정말 재미있고 신났다.
7. 기회가 있다면 나는 다시 급류 타기를 하러 갈 것이다.

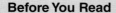

※ 다음 우리말을 영어로 쓰시오.

Before You Read

1. 스카이 캠핑에 오신 것을 환영합니다!
➡ _____

2. 저희는 이틀간의 캠핑 여행을 위해 많은 활동들을 준비했습니다.
➡ _____

3. 저희는 항상 여러분의 안전을 우선으로 생각하기 때문에, 발생할 수 있는 나쁜 일에 대비하기 위해 최선을 다합니다.

4. 저희는 여러분이 모기에 물리는 것을 피할 수 있도록 각각의 텐트에 벌레 퇴치 스프레이를 한 통씩 비치해 둠으로써 여러분이 편안하게 머물도록 돕습니다.
➡ _____

5. 저희는 모든 분들이 여행의 좋은 추억을 집으로 가져가시기를 바랍니다.
➡ _____

Writing Workshop

1. 비록 여러분이 지진으로부터 자유롭다고 생각할 수 있지만, 사실은 그렇지 않습니다.
➡ _____

2. 그러면 지진이 발생하면 여러분은 무엇을 해야 할까요?
➡ _____

3. 여러분이 명심해야 할 것이 몇 가지 있습니다.
➡ _____

4. 첫째, 흔들림이 멈출 때까지 안에서 머물며 계속 정보를 받아야 합니다.
➡ _____

5. 밖으로 나가는 게 안전해 보이지만 무언가가 여러분에게 떨어질 수도 있습니다.
➡ _____

6. 둘째, 가스와 전기를 끄십시오.
➡ _____

7. 셋째, 테이블 아래로 들어가서 팔로 머리를 감싸세요.
➡ _____

8. 여러분의 머리를 보호하는 것이 중요합니다.
➡ _____

9. 마지막으로, 만일 여러분이 밖에 있다면, 가능한 한 건물이나 나무, 가로등으로부터 멀리 떨어지세요.
➡ _____

10. 이 팁을 따름으로써 여러분은 지진으로부터 안전할 수 있습니다.
➡ _____

Wrap Up

1. 나의 캠핑 여행 일기
➡ _____

2. 위치: 영월 날짜: 9월 12일
➡ _____

3. 함께 여행한 사람: 나의 가족
➡ _____

4. 나는 9월 12일에 나의 가족과 함께 영월에 갔다.
➡ _____

5. 여행 중에 우리는 급류 타기와 하이킹을 즐겼다.
➡ _____

6. 나는 처음에 급류 타기를 무서워했지만, 그것은 정말 재미있고 신났다.
➡ _____

7. 기회가 있다면 나는 다시 급류 타기를 하러 갈 것이다.
➡ _____

※ 다음 영어를 우리말로 쓰시오.

01 pack	_____		22 lose	_____
02 reopen	_____		23 demand	_____
03 college	_____		24 either	_____
04 part	_____		25 order	_____
05 contract	_____		26 sign	_____
06 seriously	_____		27 refuse	_____
07 except	_____		28 grade	_____
08 decision	_____		29 follow	_____
09 eventually	_____		30 attend	_____
10 allow	_____		31 care	_____
11 exactly	_____		32 realize	_____
12 famous	_____		33 imagine	_____
13 gym	_____		34 disappointed	_____
14 happen	_____		35 by -ing	_____
15 principal	_____		36 find out	_____
16 improve	_____		37 A as well as B	_____
17 promise	_____		38 pay attention to	_____
18 life	_____		39 carry out	_____
19 lock	_____		40 become used to -ing	_____
20 accept	_____		41 in addition to	_____
21 actually	_____		42 one after anther	_____
			43 to make matters worse	_____

28 ▸ The players did not like it.

➡ _____

29 ▸ They told him that his actions were just for him, not for them.

➡ _____

30 ▸ Worm: We're the basketball team.

➡ _____

31 ▸ All we see is you on TV, getting famous.

➡ _____

32 ▸ Carter: If you think so, go home and ask yourself, "Do I want a better life?"

➡ _____

33 ▸ If the answer is yes, I will do everything in my power to help you.

➡ _____

34 ▸ But you have to do your part.

➡ _____

35 ▸ The players' parents did not like Carter's decision either.

➡ _____

36 ▸ At the parents' demand, the principal ordered Carter to reopen the gym.

➡ _____

37 ▸ Disappointed, Carter decided to leave Richmond High.

➡ _____

38 ▸ When he entered the gym to pack his things, however, all of his players were there.

➡ _____

39 ▸ We want you to enjoy the movie, so we won't tell you what happens next.

➡ _____

40 ▸ Find out for yourself by watching the movie *Coach Carter*.

➡ _____

※ 다음 괄호 안의 단어들을 우리말에 맞도록 바르게 배열하시오.

1 (to / welcome / *Trip*. / *Movie*)
➡ _____

2 (we're / today / to / going / about / talk / the / *Coach* / movie / *Carter*.)
➡ _____

3 (you / can / a / imagine / basketball / who / coach / doesn't / his / allow / players / practice? / to)
➡ _____
_____

4 (exactly / that's / Coach / what / does. / Carter)
➡ _____

5 (movie / this / about / is / coach / a / who / more / cares / his / about / than / students / about / games. / winning)
➡ _____
_____

6 (basketball / the / at / team / High / Richmond / in / School / Richmond, / was / California, / one / having / season / losing / another. / after)
➡ _____
_____

7 (players / the / used / became / losing. / to)
➡ _____

8 (make / to / worse, / matters / had / they / plans / no / the / for / future: / went / they / school / to / to / only / basketball, / play / and / did / they / do / not / very / that / well.)
➡ _____
_____

9 (they / then / a / got / coach, / new / Carter. / Kenny)
➡ _____

10 (Carter / Coach / to / wanted / things. / change)
➡ _____

11 (wanted / he / teach / to / how / kids / play / to / well / basketball / win. / and)
➡ _____

12 (more / but / that, / than / wanted / he / give / to / players / the / future / a / sending / by / them / college. / to)
➡ _____
_____

13 (carry / to / his / out / plan, / Carter / Coach / the / had / players / a / sign / contract.)
➡ _____

1 「영화 여행」에 오신 것을 환영합니다.

2 오늘 우리는 영화 「코치 카터」에 대해 이야기할 것입니다.

3 선수들이 연습하는 것을 허락하지 않는 농구 코치를 상상할 수 있나요?

4 그것이 바로 카터 코치가 한 것입니다.

5 이 영화는 경기에서 이기는 것보다 학생들을 더 걱정하는 코치에 대한 영화입니다.

6 캘리포니아 리치몬드 지역의 리치몬드 고등학교 농구 팀은 연속해서 경기에서 지고 있었습니다.

7 선수들도 지는 것에 익숙하게 되었습니다.

8 설상가상으로 그들은 미래에 대한 계획도 없었습니다. 즉, 그들은 단지 농구하기 위해 학교에 갔고, 그것마저도 잘하지 못했습니다.

9 그때 그들은 케니 카터라는 새로운 코치를 선임했습니다.

10 카터 코치는 몇 가지를 바꾸고자 했습니다.

11 그는 아이들에게 어떻게 농구를 잘하고 이기는지를 가르치기를 원했습니다.

12 그러나 그것보다도, 그는 그들을 대학에 보냄으로써 선수들에게 미래를 주기를 원했습니다.

13 그의 계획을 실행하기 위해서, 카터 코치는 선수들에게 계약서에 서명하게 했습니다.

14 (had / they / promise / to / hard / to / study / in / to / addition / basketball. / playing)

➡ _____

15 (first, / at / students / not / did / his / take / idea / a / for / seriously. / contract)

➡ _____

16 (Carter: / going / I'm / give / to / a / you / contract.)

➡ _____

17 (Cruz: / all / "attend / classes," / a / "get / C$^+$ / higher," / or / be / "don't / late…")

➡ _____

18 (are / what / these / all / about? / rules)

➡ _____

19 (I / do / a / get / bonus / singing / signing / for / contract? / this)

➡ _____

20 (Carter: / yes. // will / you / a / get / bonus / big / you / because / will / a / become / in / winner / the / game / basketball / well / as / as / the / in / game / the / life. / of)

➡ _____

_____

21 (hard / with / and / work / new / a / plan, / game / team / the / to / began / for / win / first / the / in / time / years. / many)

➡ _____

_____

22 (that / from / on, / point / won / they / after / game / game.)

➡ _____

23 (except / everybody, / Carter, / Coach / happy. / was)

➡ _____

24 (players / the / not / did / the / do / part / "study" / of / contract. / their)

➡ _____

25 (of / few / them / believed / actually / could / they / to / go / college, / they / so / little / paid / attention / their / to / grades.)

➡ _____

_____

26 (decided / Carter / take / to / action. / stronger)

➡ _____

27 (locked / he / gym / the / and / to / refused / let / play / them / basketball / their / until / improved, / grades / promised / as / the / contract. / in)

➡ _____

_____

14 그들은 농구를 하는 것뿐만 아니라 열심히 공부할 것도 약속해야만 했습니다.

15 처음에는 학생들이 계약서에 대한 그의 생각을 심각하게 받아들이지 않았습니다.

16 카터: 내가 너희들에게 계약서를 줄 것이다.

17 크루즈: "모든 수업에 출석하라." "C 플러스 또는 그 이상 받아라." "지각하지 말아라."

18 이 모든 규칙들은 무엇이죠?

19 제가 이 계약서에 사인하면 사이닝 보너스를 받나요?

20 카터: 그래. 너는 큰 보너스를 받게 될 거야. 왜냐하면 인생의 게임에서뿐 아니라 농구 경기에서도 승리자가 될 것이기 때문이지.

21 맹연습과 새로운 경기 전략으로 그 팀은 몇 년 만에 처음으로 이기기 시작했습니다.

22 그때 이후로 경기마다 이겼습니다.

23 카터 코치를 제외한 모든 이들이 행복했습니다.

24 선수들은 그들 계약의 '학습' 부분을 하지 않았습니다.

25 그들 중 정말 그들이 대학을 갈 수 있다고 믿는 사람들은 거의 없었습니다. 그래서 그들은 성적에는 거의 관심을 두지 않았습니다.

26 카터는 더 강력한 조치를 취하기로 결심했습니다.

27 그는 체육관 문을 잠그고 계약서에서 약속한 대로 그들의 성적이 좋아질 때까지 농구를 못하게 했습니다.

28 (players / the / not / did / it. / like)

➡ _____

29 (told / they / that / him / actions / his / just / were / him, / for / for / not / them.)

➡ _____

30 (Worm: / the / we're / team. / basketball)

➡ _____

31 (we / all / is / see / on / you / TV, / famous. / getting)

➡ _____

32 (Carter: / you / if / so, / think / home / go / and / yourself, / ask / I / "do / want / better / a / life?")

➡ _____

33 (the / if / is / answer / yes, / will / I / everything / do / my / in / power / help / you. / to)

➡ _____

34 (you / but / to / have / your / do / part.)

➡ _____

35 (players' / the / did / parents / like / not / decision / Carter's / either.)

➡ _____

36 (the / at / demand, / parents' / principal / the / Carter / ordered / reopen / to / gym. / the)

➡ _____

37 (Carter / disappointed, / decided / leave / to / High. / Richmond)

➡ _____

38 (he / when / the / entered / to / gym / pack / things, / his / all / however, / of / playes / his / there. / were)

➡ _____

39 (want / we / to / you / the / enjoy / movie, / we / so / tell / won't / you / happens / what / next.)

➡ _____

40 (out / find / yourself / for / watching / by / movie / the / Carter. / Coach)

➡ _____

---

28 선수들은 그것을 좋아하지 않았습니다.

29 그들은 그에게 그의 행동들이 그들을 위한 것이 아닌 단지 카터 자신을 위한 것이라고 말했습니다.

30 웜: 우리는 농구 팀이에요.

31 우리가 보는 모든 것은 유명세를 타며 TV에 있는 당신이에요.

32 카터: 네가 그렇게 생각한다면, 집으로 가서 너 자신에게 물어봐. "나는 더 나은 삶을 원하는가?"

33 대답이 '맞다'라면, 나는 너를 돕기 위해 내 힘이 닿는 한 모든 것을 할 거야.

34 그러나 너는 네 역할을 해야만 해.

35 선수들의 부모들 역시 카터의 결정을 좋아하지 않았습니다.

36 부모들의 요구에 따라 교장은 카터에게 체육관을 다시 열도록 했습니다.

37 실망한 카터는 리치몬드 고등학교를 떠나기로 결심했습니다.

38 그가 짐을 싸기 위해 체육관으로 들어섰을 때, 그의 선수들 모두가 그곳에 있었습니다.

39 우리는 여러분이 이 영화를 즐기기 원합니다. 그래서 당신에게 다음에 무슨 일이 일어나는지 이야기하지 않을 것입니다.

40 영화 「코치 카터」를 보고 스스로 찾아보세요.

※ 다음 우리말을 영어로 쓰시오.

1 「영화 여행」에 오신 것을 환영합니다.

➡ _____

2 오늘 우리는 영화 「코치 카터」에 대해 이야기할 것입니다.

➡ _____

3 선수들이 연습하는 것을 허락하지 않는 농구 코치를 상상할 수 있나요?

➡ _____

4 그것이 바로 카터 코치가 한 것입니다.

➡ _____

5 이 영화는 경기에서 이기는 것보다 학생들을 더 걱정하는 코치에 대한 영화입니다.

➡ _____

6 캘리포니아 리치몬드 지역의 리치몬드 고등학교 농구 팀은 연속해서 경기에서 지고 있었습니다.

➡ _____
　 _____

7 선수들도 지는 것에 익숙하게 되었습니다.

➡ _____

8 설상가상으로 그들은 미래에 대한 계획도 없었습니다. 즉, 그들은 단지 농구하기 위해 학교에 갔고, 그것마저도 잘하지 못했습니다.

➡ _____
　 _____

9 그때 그들은 케니 카터라는 새로운 코치를 선임했습니다.

➡ _____

10 카터 코치는 몇 가지를 바꾸고자 했습니다.

➡ _____

11 그는 아이들에게 어떻게 농구를 잘하고 이기는지를 가르치기를 원했습니다.

➡ _____

12 그러나 그것보다도, 그는 그들을 대학에 보냄으로써 선수들에게 미래를 주기를 원했습니다.

➡ _____

13 그의 계획을 실행하기 위해서, 카터 코치는 선수들에게 계약서에 서명하게 했습니다.

➡ _____

14 그들은 농구를 하는 것뿐만 아니라 열심히 공부할 것도 약속해야만 했습니다.

➡ _____

15 처음에는 학생들이 계약서에 대한 그의 생각을 심각하게 받아들이지 않았습니다.

➡ _____

16 카터: 내가 너희들에게 계약서를 줄 것이다.

➡ _____

17 크루즈: "모든 수업에 출석하라," "C 플러스 또는 그 이상 받아라," "지각하지 말아라."

➡ _____

18 이 모든 규칙들은 무엇이죠?

➡ _____

19 제가 이 계약서에 사인하면 사이닝 보너스를 받나요?

➡ _____

20 카터: 그래. 너는 큰 보너스를 받게 될 거야. 왜냐하면 인생의 게임에서뿐 아니라 농구 경기에서도 승리자가 될 것이기 때문이지.

➡ _____

➡ _____

21 맹연습과 새로운 경기 전략으로 그 팀은 몇 년 만에 처음으로 이기기 시작했습니다.

➡ _____

22 그때 이후로 경기마다 이겼습니다.

➡ _____

23 카터 코치를 제외한 모든 이들이 행복했습니다.

➡ _____

24 선수들은 그들 계약의 '학습' 부분을 하지 않았습니다.

➡ _____

25 그들 중 정말 그들이 대학을 갈 수 있다고 믿는 사람들은 거의 없었습니다. 그래서 그들은 성적에는 거의 관심을 두지 않았습니다.

➡ _____

➡ _____

26 카터는 더 강력한 조치를 취하기로 결심했습니다.

➡ _____

27 그는 체육관 문을 잠그고 계약서에서 약속한 대로 그들의 성적이 좋아질 때까지 농구를 못하게 했습니다.

➡ _____

➡ _____

28 선수들은 그것을 좋아하지 않았습니다.

➡ _____

29 그들은 그에게 그의 행동들이 그들을 위한 것이 아닌 단지 카터 자신을 위한 것이라고 말했습니다.

➡ _____

30 웜: 우리는 농구 팀이에요.

➡ _____

31 우리가 보는 모든 것은 유명세를 타며 TV에 있는 당신이에요.

➡ _____

32 카터: 네가 그렇게 생각한다면, 집으로 가서 너 자신에게 물어봐. "나는 더 나은 삶을 원하는가?"

➡ _____

33 대답이 '맞다'라면, 나는 너를 돕기 위해 내 힘이 닿는 한 모든 것을 할 거야.

➡ _____

34 그러나 너는 네 역할을 해야만 해.

➡ _____

35 선수들의 부모들 역시 카터의 결정을 좋아하지 않았습니다.

➡ _____

36 부모들의 요구에 따라 교장은 카터에게 체육관을 다시 열도록 했습니다.

➡ _____

37 실망한 카터는 리치몬드 고등학교를 떠나기로 결심했습니다.

➡ _____

38 그가 짐을 싸기 위해 체육관으로 들어섰을 때, 그의 선수들 모두가 그곳에 있었습니다.

➡ _____

39 우리는 여러분이 이 영화를 즐기기 원합니다. 그래서 당신에게 다음에 무슨 일이 일어나는지 이야기하지 않을 것입니다.

➡ _____

40 영화 「코치 카터」를 보고 스스로 찾아보세요.

➡ _____

※ 다음 영어를 우리말로 쓰시오.

01	means	22	annoyed
02	attention	23	useful
03	below	24	various
04	meaning	25	comfortable
05	relax	26	popular
06	closely	27	detail
07	magazine	28	realistic
08	bright	29	imagination
09	drop	30	calm
10	emotion	31	careful
11	cheerful	32	loudly
12	independent	33	peaceful
13	article	34	reduce
14	relate	35	sold out
15	personality	36	deal with
16	protection	37	get along
17	reasonable	38	at the same time
18	difference	39	in other words
19	dependent	40	be related to
20	curious	41	have to do with
21	delay	42	according to
		43	on the other hand

※ 다음 우리말을 영어로 쓰시오.

01 기사	
02 상황, 환경	
03 다름, 차이점	
04 (긴장을) 늦추다, 휴식을 취하다	
05 잡지	
06 창의적인	
07 감정	
08 방울	
09 ~을 관련[연결]시키다	
10 독립적인, 자립심이 강한	
11 발랄한, 쾌활한	
12 편한, 편안한	
13 조리[요리]법	
14 호기심이 있는	
15 합리적인	
16 의존적인	
17 성격	
18 여러 가지의, 다양한	
19 보호	
20 상상, 상상력	
21 차분한	

22 줄이다	
23 인기 있는	
24 세부 사항	
25 현실적인	
26 주의 깊은	
27 평화로운	
28 미루다, 연기하다	
29 표현하다	
30 면밀히, 밀접하게	
31 짜증이 난	
32 의미	
33 수단, 방법	
34 의견	
35 다시 말하면	
36 ~을 다루다, ~을 처리하다	
37 (사람들과) 잘 어울리다	
38 ~와 연관되다	
39 ~에 따르면, ~에 따라	
40 ~와 관련되다	
41 동시에, 함께	
42 반면에, 한편으로는	
43 자신에게 관심을 끌다	

※ 다음 영영풀이에 알맞은 단어를 <보기>에서 골라 쓴 후, 우리말 뜻을 쓰시오.

1 _____ : fair and sensible: _____

2 _____ : feeling or showing fear: _____

3 _____ : a set of instructions for making food: _____

4 _____ : to wait until later to do something: _____

5 _____ : not excited, nervous, or upset: _____

6 _____ : not causing any physically unpleasant feelings: _____

7 _____ : a place where you can sit, for example a chair: _____

8 _____ : to direct your attention or effort at something specific: _____

9 _____ : to make something smaller in size, amount, number, etc.: _____

10 _____ : believing that something you want will happen: _____

11 _____ : the way you think and feel about someone or something: _____

12 _____ : not requiring or relying on other people for help or support:

_____

13 _____ : to show or make known a feeling, an opinion, etc. by words, looks or

actions: _____

14 _____ : something that makes one thing or person not the same as another thing

or person: _____

15 _____ : a piece of writing about a particular subject that is included in a magazine,

newspaper, etc.: _____

16 _____ : the set of emotional qualities, ways of behaving, etc., that makes a

person different from other people: _____

보기			
article	comfortable	focus	seat
independent	frightened	reduce	reasonable
express	calm	difference	recipe
attitude	delay	hopeful	personality

※ 다음 우리말과 일치하도록 빈칸에 알맞은 말을 쓰시오.

Listen & Speak 1 Listen

1. G: What _____ "be in a cold sweat" _____?
    B: It means "to be _____ or _____ before _____ something."
2. B: What _____ "feel blue" _____?
    G: It means "to _____ _____."
3. G: What _____ "have a long face" _____?
    B: It _____ "to _____ _____."
4. B: What _____ "throw up one's hands" _____?
    G: It _____ "to _____ _____."

Listen & Speak 1 A

1. G: Hi, Jack! _____ are you _____?
    B: I'm on cloud nine! I got a concert ticket _____ my favorite band.
    G: What _____ "on cloud nine" _____?
    B: It _____ I'm really _____ and _____.
2. G: I took a _____ _____ today. I _____ _____ _____ a house.
    B: A house?
    G: Yeah. _____ _____ the test, you can tell _____ _____ about a person _____ their drawing. Here's _____.
    B: Interesting. So what _____ these big windows _____?
    G: They _____ I'm _____ to _____ people.

Listen & Speak 2 Listen

1. M: Sorry. The tickets for the blue zone are all _____ _____.
    G: _____ _____ any _____ _____?
    M: Yes, we have _____ _____ for the red zone.
2. W: What would you like on your hot dog? We have _____ sauce and _____ sauce.
    B: Are there any _____ _____?
    W: Sorry. Those are the _____ _____ we have.
3. M: What _____ you _____ _____ drink? A soft drink _____?
    G: Are there _____ _____ drinks? Soft drinks have _____ _____ _____ in them.
    M: We have apple juice _____.
4. W: This is _____ _____ _____ cap in our store.
    B: Are there any _____ _____?
    W: Sure, we have _____ more. They're _____ _____. I'll show you.

1. G: 'be in a cold sweat'가 무엇을 의미하니?
   B: 그것은 '무언가 하기 전에 긴장하거나 겁을 먹는 것'을 의미해.
2. B: 'feel blue'가 무엇을 의미하니?
   G: 그것은 '슬프게 느끼는 것'을 의미해.
3. G: 'have a long face'가 무엇을 의미하니?
   B: 그것은 '슬퍼 보이는 것'을 의미해.
4. B: 'throw up one's hands'가 무엇을 의미하니?
   G: 그것은 '포기하는 것'을 의미해.

1. G: 안녕, 잭! 어떻게 지내니?
   B: 나는 날아갈 것 같아! 내가 가장 좋아하는 밴드의 콘서트 티켓을 얻었어.
   G: 'on cloud nine'이 무엇을 의미하니?
   B: 그것은 내가 아주 기쁘고 들떠 있다는 뜻이야.
2. G: 나 오늘 성격검사를 했어. 나는 집을 그려야 했어.
   B: 집?
   G: 응, 그 시험에 따르면 그림을 통해서 사람의 많은 것을 알 수 있대. 여기 내 것이 있어.
   B: 흥미롭구나. 그러면 이 큰 창문들은 무엇을 의미하니?
   G: 그들은 내가 타인에게 열려 있다는 것을 의미해.

1. M: 죄송합니다. 파란 구역의 표는 매진입니다.
   G: 다른 자리가 있나요?
   M: 네, 빨간 구역의 표가 좀 있습니다.
2. W: 핫도그에 무엇을 올릴까요? 저희에겐 매운 소스와 달콤한 소스가 있습니다.
   B: 다른 소스들도 있나요?
   W: 죄송합니다. 이것들이 저희가 가진 오직 두 가지입니다.
3. M: 무엇을 마시겠습니까? 혹시 탄산음료를 마시겠어요?
   G: 다른 음료가 있나요? 탄산음료에는 지나치게 많은 설탕이 들어 있어요.
   M: 사과 주스도 있습니다.
4. W: 이것은 우리 가게에서 가장 인기 있는 모자예요.
   B: 다른 색도 있나요?
   W: 물론이죠. 우리는 더 많이 가지고 있어요. 그것들은 이쪽에 있어요. 제가 보여드릴게요.

Listen & Speak 2 A

1. **B:** Jane, what are you _____?

   G: I'm reading an interesting magazine. It _____ colors can _____ _____ _____.

   B: That's _____.

   G: Yes. _____ _____, the color red can _____ _____ better.

   B: Are there any other _____ _____?

   G: Yes. The color blue _____ people _____.

2. **M:** EDPI Test Center. Do you want to learn _____ about _____? We have many _____ _____ personality tests. If there are any _____ _____ you want to learn more about, we are here to help you.

   B: Hi, I'm _____ _____ _____ a personality _____. Can I do one this afternoon?

   M: Sure, you can come _____ _____ 5 o'clock.

Real-Life Zone

Hajun: Look! I found this test on an app that tells _____ _____ _____ person you are. Do you want _____ _____ it?

Emma: Sure. Sounds _____ _____.

Hajun: Okay, listen. What are you _____ _____? Choose _____ _____ these: crowds, _____, or dark places.

Emma: I hate _____ _____. I cannot sleep _____ a night light _____. What does that _____?

Hajun: It _____ you are _____ _____ imagination. _____ _____ you _____ dark places _____ all kinds of _____ _____.

Emma: That's very interesting. What _____ you? Is there _____ you are _____ _____?

Hajun: I chose dark places too. But I don't think I have a _____ _____.

Emma: This is fun. I want to do some more. Are there _____ _____ _____ we can _____?

Hajun: Sure. This app has _____ _____ _____ them.

Wrap Up 1~2

B: What's your _____ _____?

G: Type A. Why?

B: I'm reading _____ _____. It _____ that blood type tells something about _____ _____.

G: Wow. Then what does _____ _____ mean?

B: People _____ blood type A are _____. They are good _____, _____.

---

1. **B:** 제인, 무엇을 읽고 있니?
   G: 나는 흥미로운 잡지를 읽고 있어. 이것이 말하길 색깔은 사람들의 기분을 바꿀 수 있대.
   B: 그거 놀랍네.
   G: 응. 예를 들어, 빨간색은 우리가 집중을 더 잘하도록 도와준대.
   B: 다른 유용한 색깔들도 있니?
   G: 응. 파란색은 사람들이 편안하도록 도와줘.

2. **M:** EDPI 검사 센터입니다. 자신에 대해 더 알고 싶으신가요? 우리는 여러 종류의 성격검사를 가지고 있습니다. 당신이 더 알아보고 싶은 검사가 있다면 우리는 이곳에서 당신을 도와드리겠습니다.
   B: 안녕하세요. 성격검사를 받기 위해 전화드렸습니다. 오늘 오후에 하나 해 볼 수 있을까요?
   M: 물론입니다. 5시 전에 아무 때나 오시면 됩니다.

하준: 봐! 네가 어떤 종류의 사람인지 말해주는 앱에서 이 검사를 발견했어. 한 번 해볼래?
Emma: 물론이지. 재미있겠다.
하준: 응, 들어봐. 당신이 두려워하는 것은 무엇입니까? 이들 중 하나를 고르세요. 군중, 거미, 또는 어두운 곳.
Emma: 나는 어두운 곳을 싫어해. 나는 야간등을 켜놓지 않고는 잘 수 없어. 그것은 무엇을 의미하니?
하준: 그것은 네가 상상력이 풍부하다는 것을 말해줘. 그것이 네가 어두운 곳을 온갖 종류의 무서운 것들로 채우는 이유야.
Emma: 매우 흥미롭구나. 너는 어때? 너는 두려워하는 것이 있니?
하준: 나도 어두운 곳을 골랐어. 그렇지만 나는 내가 상상력이 풍부하다고 생각하지 않아.
Emma: 이거 재미있다. 더 하고 싶어. 우리가 할 수 있는 다른 검사들이 있니?
하준: 물론이지. 이 앱에는 많은 검사가 있어.

B: 너의 혈액형은 무엇이니?
G: A형이야. 왜?
B: 내가 기사 하나를 읽고 있어. 거기에서 말하길 혈액형이 너의 성격에 대해 무언가 말해준대.
G: 와, 그러면 A형은 무엇을 의미하니?
B: 혈액형이 A형인 사람들은 차분해. 그들은 또한 남의 말을 잘 들어주는 사람이기도 해.

※ 다음 우리말에 맞도록 대화를 영어로 쓰시오.

Listen & Speak 1 Listen

1. G: _____
   B: _____
2. B: _____
   G: _____
3. G: _____
   B: _____
4. B: _____
   G: _____

Listen & Speak 1 A

1. G: _____
   B: _____
   G: _____
   B: _____
2. G: _____
   B: _____
   G: _____
   B: _____
   G: _____

Listen & Speak 2 Listen

1. M: _____
   G: _____
   M: _____
2. W: _____
   B: _____
   W: _____
3. M: _____
   G: _____
   M: _____
4. W: _____
   B: _____
   W: _____

해석

1. G: 'be in a cold sweat'가 무엇을 의미하니?
   B: 그것은 '무언가 하기 전에 긴장하거나 겁을 먹는 것'을 의미해.
2. B: 'feel blue'가 무엇을 의미하니?
   G: 그것은 '슬프게 느끼는 것'을 의미해.
3. G: 'have a long face'가 무엇을 의미하니?
   B: 그것은 '슬퍼 보이는 것'을 의미해.
4. B: 'throw up one's hands'가 무엇을 의미하니?
   G: 그것은 '포기하는 것'을 의미해.

1. G: 안녕, 잭! 어떻게 지내니?
   B: 나는 날아갈 것 같아! 내가 가장 좋아하는 밴드의 콘서트 티켓을 얻었어.
   G: 'on cloud nine'이 무엇을 의미하니?
   B: 그것은 내가 아주 기쁘고 들떠 있다는 뜻이야.
2. G: 나 오늘 성격검사를 했어. 나는 집을 그려야 했어.
   B: 집?
   G: 응, 그 시험에 따르면 그림을 통해서 사람의 많은 것을 알 수 있대. 여기 내 것이 있어.
   B: 흥미롭구나. 그러면 이 큰 창문들은 무엇을 의미하니?
   G: 그들은 내가 타인에게 열려 있다는 것을 의미해.

1. M: 죄송합니다. 파란 구역의 표는 매진입니다.
   G: 다른 자리가 있나요?
   M: 네, 빨간 구역의 표가 좀 있습니다.
2. W: 핫도그에 무엇을 올릴까요? 저희에겐 매운 소스와 달콤한 소스가 있습니다.
   B: 다른 소스들도 있나요?
   W: 죄송합니다. 이것들이 저희가 가진 오직 두 가지입니다.
3. M: 무엇을 마시겠습니까? 혹시 탄산음료를 마시겠어요?
   G: 다른 음료가 있나요? 탄산음료에는 지나치게 많은 설탕이 들어 있어요.
   M: 사과 주스도 있습니다.
4. W: 이것은 우리 가게에서 가장 인기 있는 모자예요.
   B: 다른 색도 있나요?
   W: 물론이죠. 우리는 더 많이 가지고 있어요. 그것들은 이쪽에 있어요. 제가 보여드릴게요.

Listen & Speak 2 A

1. B: _____

   G: _____

   _____

   B: _____

   G: _____

   B: _____

   G: _____

2. M: _____

   _____

   _____

   B: _____

   M: _____

Real-Life Zone

Hajun: _____

_____

Emma: _____

Hajun: _____

_____

Emma: _____

_____

Hajun: _____

_____

Emma: _____

_____

Hajun: _____

Emma: _____

Hajun: _____

Wrap Up 1~2

B: _____

G: _____

B: _____

_____

G: _____

B: _____

1. B: 제인, 무엇을 읽고 있니?
   G: 나는 흥미로운 잡지를 읽고 있어. 이것이 말하길 색깔은 사람들의 기분을 바꿀 수 있대.
   B: 그거 놀랍네.
   G: 응. 예를 들어, 빨간색은 우리가 집중을 더 잘하도록 도와준대.
   B: 다른 유용한 색깔들도 있니?
   G: 응. 파란색은 사람들이 편안하도록 도와줘.

2. M: EDPI 검사 센터입니다. 자신에 대해 더 알고 싶으신가요? 우리는 여러 종류의 성격검사를 가지고 있습니다. 당신이 더 알아보고 싶은 검사가 있다면 우리는 이곳에서 당신을 도와드리겠습니다.
   B: 안녕하세요. 성격검사를 받기 위해 전화드렸습니다. 오늘 오후에 하나 해 볼 수 있을까요?
   M: 물론입니다. 5시 전에 아무 때나 오시면 됩니다.

하준: 봐! 네가 어떤 종류의 사람인지 말해주는 앱에서 이 검사를 발견했어. 한 번 해볼래?
Emma: 물론이지. 재미있겠다.
하준: 응, 들어봐. 당신이 두려워하는 것은 무엇입니까? 이들 중 하나를 고르세요. 군중, 거미, 또는 어두운 곳.
Emma: 나는 어두운 곳을 싫어해. 나는 야간등을 켜놓지 않고는 잘 수 없어. 그것은 무엇을 의미하니?
하준: 그것은 네가 상상력이 풍부하다는 것을 말해줘. 그것이 네가 어두운 곳을 온갖 종류의 무서운 것들로 채우는 이유야.
Emma: 매우 흥미롭구나. 너는 어때? 너는 두려워하는 것이 있니?
하준: 나도 어두운 곳을 골랐어. 그렇지만 나는 내가 상상력이 풍부하다고 생각하지 않아.
Emma: 이거 재미있다. 더 하고 싶어. 우리가 할 수 있는 다른 검사들이 있니?
하준: 물론이지. 이 앱에는 많은 검사가 있어.

B: 너의 혈액형은 무엇이니?
G: A형이야. 왜?
B: 내가 기사 하나를 읽고 있어. 거기에서 말하길 혈액형이 너의 성격에 대해 무언가 말해준대.
G: 와, 그러면 A형은 무엇을 의미하니?
B: 혈액형이 A형인 사람들은 차분해. 그들은 또한 남의 말을 잘 들어주는 사람이기도 해.

※ 다음 우리말과 일치하도록 빈칸에 알맞은 것을 골라 쓰시오.

Drawing the Mind

1 _____ you _____ _____ _____ about you.
    A. something   B. everything   C. says   D. do

2 The language you use, the clothes you _____, and _____ the pets you _____ somehow show what _____ of person you are.
    A. raise   B. wear   C. kind   D. even

3 The _____ you _____ are not _____ _____.
    A. much   B. things   C. draw   D. different

4 _____ you draw and _____ you draw it are _____ to your _____.
    A. personality   B. how   C. related   D. what

5 Doctors have been _____ _____ drawing tests to _____ _____ people.
    A. better   B. various   C. understand   D. using

6 _____ of _____ _____ is the Draw-a-Person-in-the-Rain (DAPR) _____.
    A. tests   B. test   C. those   D. one

7 _____ the pictures _____.
    A. below   B. study

8 The _____ in Drawing A is _____ an umbrella in a _____ _____.
    A. light   B. holding   C. person   D. rain

9 On the _____ _____, the person in Drawing B is in a _____ rain and has _____ umbrella.
    A. heavy   B. no   C. hand   D. other

10 Also, _____ are _____ clouds _____ the _____ in Drawing B.
    A. above   B. dark   C. person   D. there

11 _____ can these _____ _____?
    A. differences   B. what   C. mean

12 First, the _____ shows the _____ the person _____ drew the picture is _____.
    A. under   B. stress   C. rain   D. who

13 The _____ the _____ are or the more _____ the rain is _____, the bigger the stress is.
    A. heavily   B. bigger   C. drops   D. falling

14 The clouds mean problems _____ to _____, so a big cloud shows the drawer is not very _____ about the _____.
    A. happen   B. future   C. waiting   D. hopeful

마음 그리기

1 당신이 하는 모든 행동은 당신에 대해 말해 줍니다.

2 당신이 사용하는 언어, 당신이 입는 옷, 그리고 당신이 기르는 애완동물까지도 당신이 어떤 종류의 사람인지 보여 줍니다.

3 당신이 그리는 그림도 마찬가지입니다.

4 당신이 무엇을 그리는지 그리고 그것을 어떻게 그리는지는 당신의 성격과 관련이 있습니다.

5 의사들은 사람들을 더 잘 이해하기 위해 다양한 그림 그리기 검사를 사용해 오고 있습니다.

6 이런 검사들 중 하나는 빗속의 사람 그리기 검사입니다.

7 아래의 그림들을 연구해 봅시다.

8 A 그림 속의 사람은 가벼운 빗속에서 우산을 들고 있습니다.

9 반면에, B 그림 속의 사람은 거센 빗속에서 우산을 가지고 있지 않습니다.

10 또한, 검은 구름들이 B 그림의 사람 머리 위에 있습니다.

11 이런 차이는 무엇을 의미하는 걸까요?

12 첫 번째, 비는 그림을 그린 사람이 받고 있는 스트레스를 보여 줍니다.

13 빗방울의 크기가 크면 클수록, 혹은 비가 더 세게 내리면 내릴수록 스트레스는 더 큽니다.

14 구름은 앞으로 벌어질 문제를 의미하기 때문에, 큰 구름은 그림을 그린 사람이 미래에 대해 그다지 희망적이지 않다는 것을 나타냅니다.

15 _____, the umbrella means the _____ the person has in a
_____ _____.

    A. stressful   B. second   C. situation   D. protection

16 A _____ umbrella _____ that the drawer has a lot of _____
or _____.

    A. plans   B. big   C. protection   D. shows

17 If there's no umbrella in the _____, the drawer does not have
any _____ to _____ _____ difficult situations.

    A. drawing   B. with   C. means   D. deal

18 Third, the _____ in the drawing of the person _____ to
do _____ the drawer's _____ under stress.

    A. attitude   B. details   C. have   D. with

19 For _____, someone who _____ a person _____ a face
does not want to draw people's _____ to himself or herself.

    A. attention   B. without   C. example   D. draws

20 Someone who draws the person on the _____ _____ of the
paper is _____ _____ meet the future.

    A. right   B. ready   C. side   D. to

21 On the other _____, someone who draws the person on the
left side _____ be _____ about things that have _____
in the past.

    A. happened   B. may   C. hand   D. worried

22 These are some of the _____ _____ of each _____ of
the _____.

    A. meanings   B. part   C. possible   D. drawings

23 Now, _____ _____ and _____ _____ the two drawings.

    A. at   B. back   C. look   D. go

24 _____ _____ them _____.

    A. yourself   B. reading   C. try

25 Can you understand _____ _____ of person drew _____
_____?

    A. one   B. kind   C. each   D. what

26 What's _____ _____?

    A. opinion   B. your

15 두 번째, 우산은 스트레스를 받는 상황에서 그 사람이 가지고 있는 보호 기제를 의미합니다.

16 큰 우산은 그림을 그린 사람이 많은 계획이나 보호 기제를 가지고 있음을 보여 줍니다.

17 만약 그림에 우산이 없다면, 그 그림을 그린 사람은 어려운 상황을 헤쳐 나갈 어떤 방법도 가지고 있지 않습니다.

18 세 번째, 그림 속 사람의 세부적인 것들은 그 그림을 그린 사람이 스트레스를 받을 때의 태도와 관련이 있습니다.

19 예를 들어, 얼굴이 없는 사람을 그린 사람은 사람들의 관심을 끌기를 원하지 않습니다.

20 사람을 종이의 오른쪽에 그린 사람은 미래를 맞이할 준비가 되어 있습니다.

21 반면에, 사람을 왼쪽에 그린 사람은 과거에 일어났던 일에 대해 걱정하고 있을 수도 있습니다.

22 이것들은 그림 각 부분의 가능한 의미 풀이 중 일부입니다.

23 이제, 돌아가서 두 그림을 보세요.

24 그 그림들을 스스로 읽으려고 시도해 보세요.

25 당신은 각 그림을 그린 사람이 어떤 사람인지 알 수 있나요?

26 당신의 의견은 어떤가요?

Step2

※ 다음 우리말과 일치하도록 빈칸에 알맞은 것을 골라 쓰시오.

Drawing the Mind

1 _____ you do _____ _____ about you.

2 The language you _____, the clothes you _____, and _____ the pets you _____ somehow show _____ _____ _____ _____ _____ _____.

3 The things you _____ are not _____ different.

4 _____ you draw and _____ you draw it _____ _____ your _____.

5 Doctors _____ _____ _____ various drawing tests _____ _____ _____ people.

6 _____ of _____ _____ is the Draw-a-Person-in-the-Rain (DAPR) test.

7 _____ the pictures _____.

8 The person in Drawing A is _____ an umbrella in a _____ rain.

9 _____ _____ _____ _____, the person in Drawing B is in a _____ rain and has _____ umbrella.

10 Also, _____ _____ dark clouds _____ the person in Drawing B.

11 What can these _____ _____?

12 First, the rain shows the _____ the person _____ drew the picture is _____.

13 _____ _____ the drops are or _____ _____ _____ the rain is falling, _____ _____ the stress is.

14 The clouds mean problems _____ to _____, so a big cloud shows the drawer is not very _____ about the _____.

마음 그리기

1 당신이 하는 모든 행동은 당신에 대해 말해 줍니다.

2 당신이 사용하는 언어, 당신이 입는 옷, 그리고 당신이 기르는 애완동물까지도 당신이 어떤 종류의 사람인지 보여 줍니다.

3 당신이 그리는 그림도 마찬가지입니다.

4 당신이 무엇을 그리는지 그리고 그것을 어떻게 그리는지는 당신의 성격과 관련이 있습니다.

5 의사들은 사람들을 더 잘 이해하기 위해 다양한 그림 그리기 검사를 사용해 오고 있습니다.

6 이런 검사들 중 하나는 빗속의 사람 그리기 검사입니다.

7 아래의 그림들을 연구해 봅시다.

8 A 그림 속의 사람은 가벼운 빗속에서 우산을 들고 있습니다.

9 반면에, B 그림 속의 사람은 거센 빗속에서 우산을 가지고 있지 않습니다.

10 또한, 검은 구름들이 B 그림의 사람 머리 위에 있습니다.

11 이런 차이는 무엇을 의미하는 걸까요?

12 첫 번째, 비는 그림을 그린 사람이 받고 있는 스트레스를 보여 줍니다.

13 빗방울의 크기가 크면 클수록, 혹은 비가 더 세게 내리면 내릴수록 스트레스는 더 큽니다.

14 구름은 앞으로 벌어질 문제를 의미하기 때문에, 큰 구름은 그림을 그린 사람이 미래에 대해 그다지 희망적이지 않다는 것을 나타냅니다.

15 _____, the umbrella means the _____ the person has in a _____ _____.

16 A _____ umbrella _____ that the drawer has _____ _____ _____ _____ or _____.

17 If there's no umbrella in the _____, the drawer does not have any _____ to _____ _____ _____ _____.

18 _____, the _____ in the drawing of the person _____ _____ _____ with the drawer's _____ under stress.

19 For _____, someone _____ draws a person _____ a face does not want to draw people's _____ to _____ or _____.

20 Someone _____ draws the person on the _____ side of the paper _____ _____ _____ _____ the future.

21 On the other _____, someone who draws the person on the left side _____ be _____ about things that have _____ in the past.

22 These are some of the _____ _____ of each _____ of the _____.

23 Now, go _____ and _____ _____ the two drawings.

24 Try _____ them _____.

25 Can you understand _____ _____ of person _____ _____ _____?

26 What's your _____?

15 두 번째, 우산은 스트레스를 받는 상황에서 그 사람이 가지고 있는 보호 기제를 의미합니다.

16 큰 우산은 그림을 그린 사람이 많은 계획이나 보호 기제를 가지고 있음을 보여 줍니다.

17 만약 그림에 우산이 없다면, 그 그림을 그린 사람은 어려운 상황을 헤쳐 나갈 어떤 방법도 가지고 있지 않습니다.

18 세 번째, 그림 속 사람의 세부적인 것들은 그 그림을 그린 사람이 스트레스를 받을 때의 태도와 관련이 있습니다.

19 예를 들어, 얼굴이 없는 사람을 그린 사람은 사람들의 관심을 끌기를 원하지 않습니다.

20 사람을 종이의 오른쪽에 그린 사람은 미래를 맞이할 준비가 되어 있습니다.

21 반면에, 사람을 왼쪽에 그린 사람은 과거에 일어났던 일에 대해 걱정하고 있을 수도 있습니다.

22 이것들은 그림 각 부분의 가능한 의미 풀이 중 일부입니다.

23 이제, 돌아가서 두 그림을 보세요.

24 그 그림들을 스스로 읽으려고 시도해 보세요.

25 당신은 각 그림을 그린 사람이 어떤 사람인지 알 수 있나요?

26 당신의 의견은 어떤가요?

※ 다음 문장을 우리말로 쓰시오.

Drawing the Mind

1 Everything you do says something about you.

➡ _____

2 The language you use, the clothes you wear, and even the pets you raise somehow show what kind of person you are.

➡ _____

3 The things you draw are not much different.

➡ _____

4 What you draw and how you draw it are related to your personality.

➡ _____

5 Doctors have been using various drawing tests to better understand people.

➡ _____

6 One of those tests is the Draw-a-Person-in-the-Rain (DAPR) test.

➡ _____

7 Study the pictures below.

➡ _____

8 The person in Drawing A is holding an umbrella in a light rain.

➡ _____

9 On the other hand, the person in Drawing B is in a heavy rain and has no umbrella.

➡ _____

10 Also, there are dark clouds above the person in Drawing B.

➡ _____

11 What can these differences mean?

➡ _____

12 First, the rain shows the stress the person who drew the picture is under.

➡ _____

13 The bigger the drops are or the more heavily the rain is falling, the bigger the stress is.

➡ _____

14 The clouds mean problems waiting to happen, so a big cloud shows the drawer is not very hopeful about the future.

➡ _____

_____

15 Second, the umbrella means the protection the person has in a stressful situation.

➡ _____

16 A big umbrella shows that the drawer has a lot of plans or protection.

➡ _____

17 If there's no umbrella in the drawing, the drawer does not have any means to deal with difficult situations.

➡ _____

18 Third, the details in the drawing of the person have to do with the drawer's attitude under stress.

➡ _____

19 For example, someone who draws a person without a face does not want to draw people's attention to himself or herself.

➡ _____

20 Someone who draws the person on the right side of the paper is ready to meet the future.

➡ _____

21 On the other hand, someone who draws the person on the left side may be worried about things that have happened in the past.

➡ _____

22 These are some of the possible meanings of each part of the drawings.

➡ _____

23 Now, go back and look at the two drawings.

➡ _____

24 Try reading them yourself.

➡ _____

25 Can you understand what kind of person drew each one?

➡ _____

26 What's your opinion?

➡ _____

※ 다음 괄호 안의 단어들을 우리말에 맞도록 바르게 배열하시오.

Drawing the Mind

1 (you / everything / do / something / says / you. / about)
➡ _____

2 (language / the / use, / you / clothes / the / wear, / you / even / and / the / you / pets / somehow / raise / what / show / of / kind / person / are. / you)
➡ _____
_____

3 (things / the / draw / you / not / are / different. / much)
➡ _____

4 (you / what / and / draw / you / how / draw / are / it / to / related / personality. / your)
➡ _____

5 (have / doctors / using / been / drawing / various / tests / better / to / people. / understand)
➡ _____
_____

6 (of / one / tests / those / the / is / / test. / Draw-a-Person-in-the-Rain (DAPR))
➡ _____

7 (the / study / below. / pictures)
➡ _____

8 (person / the / Drawing / in / A / holding / is / an / umbrella / in / light / a / rain.)
➡ _____

9 (the / on / hand, / other / person / the / Drawing / in / B / in / is / heavy / a / rain / and / no / has / umbrella.)
➡ _____
_____

10 (there / also, / are / clouds / dark / the / above / in / person / B. / Drawing)
➡ _____

11 (can / what / differences / these / mean?)
➡ _____

12 (the / first, / rain / the / shows / the / stress / person / drew / who / picture / the / under. / is)
➡ _____

13 (bigger / the / drops / the / or / are / more / the / the / heavily / rain / falling, / is / bigger / the / stress / the / is.)
➡ _____
_____

14 (clouds / the / problems / mean / to / waiting / happen, / a / so / cloud / big / the / shows / drawer / not / is / hopeful / very / the / about / future.)
➡ _____
_____

마음 그리기

1 당신이 하는 모든 행동은 당신에 대해 말해 줍니다.

2 당신이 사용하는 언어, 당신이 입는 옷, 그리고 당신이 기르는 애완동물까지도 당신이 어떤 종류의 사람인지 보여 줍니다.

3 당신이 그리는 그림도 마찬가지입니다.

4 당신이 무엇을 그리는지 그리고 그것을 어떻게 그리는지는 당신의 성격과 관련이 있습니다.

5 의사들은 사람들을 더 잘 이해하기 위해 다양한 그림 그리기 검사를 사용해 오고 있습니다.

6 이런 검사들 중 하나는 빗속의 사람 그리기 검사입니다.

7 아래의 그림들을 연구해 봅시다.

8 A 그림 속의 사람은 가벼운 빗속에서 우산을 들고 있습니다.

9 반면에, B 그림 속의 사람은 거센 빗속에서 우산을 가지고 있지 않습니다.

10 또한, 검은 구름들이 B 그림의 사람 머리 위에 있습니다.

11 이런 차이는 무엇을 의미하는 걸까요?

12 첫 번째, 비는 그림을 그린 사람이 받고 있는 스트레스를 보여 줍니다.

13 빗방울의 크기가 크면 클수록, 혹은 비가 더 세게 내리면 내릴수록 스트레스는 더 큽니다.

14 구름은 앞으로 벌어질 문제를 의미하기 때문에, 큰 구름은 그림을 그린 사람이 미래에 대해 그다지 희망적이지 않다는 것을 나타냅니다.

15 (the / second, / umbrella / the / means / the / protection / person / has / a / in / situation. / stressful)

➡ _____

_____

16 (big / a / shows / umbrella / the / that / has / drawer / a / of / lot / or / plans / protection.)

➡ _____

17 (there's / if / umbrella / no / the / in / drawing, / drawer / the / does / have / not / any / means / to / deal / difficult / with / situations.)

➡ _____

_____

18 (the / third, / details / the / in / drawing / of / person / the / to / have / with / do / drawer's / the / attitude / stress. / under)

➡ _____

_____

19 (example, / for / who / someone / a / draws / without / person / face / a / does / want / not / draw / to / attention / people's / himself / to / herself. / or)

➡ _____

_____

20 (who / someone / the / draws / person / the / on / side / right / of / paper / the / ready / is / meet / to / future. / the)

➡ _____

_____

21 (the / on / hand, / other / who / someone / draws / person / the / on / left / the / may / side / be / worried / things / about / have / that / in / happened / past. / the)

➡ _____

_____

22 (are / these / of / some / possible / the / of / meanings / part / each / the / of / drawings.)

➡ _____

23 (go / now, / back / look / and / the / at / drawings. / two)

➡ _____

24 (reading / try / yourself. / them)

➡ _____

25 (you / can / what / understand / of / kind / drew / person / one? / each)

➡ _____

26 (your / what's / opinion?)

➡ _____

15 두 번째, 우산은 스트레스를 받는 상황에서 그 사람이 가지고 있는 보호 기제를 의미합니다.

16 큰 우산은 그림을 그린 사람이 많은 계획이나 보호 기제를 가지고 있음을 보여 줍니다.

17 만약 그림에 우산이 없다면, 그 그림을 그린 사람은 어려운 상황을 헤쳐 나갈 어떤 방법도 가지고 있지 않습니다.

18 세 번째, 그림 속 사람의 세부적인 것들은 그 그림을 그린 사람이 스트레스를 받을 때의 태도와 관련이 있습니다.

19 예를 들어, 얼굴이 없는 사람을 그린 사람은 사람들의 관심을 끌기를 원하지 않습니다.

20 사람을 종이의 오른쪽에 그린 사람은 미래를 맞이할 준비가 되어 있습니다.

21 반면에, 사람을 왼쪽에 그린 사람은 과거에 일어났던 일에 대해 걱정하고 있을 수도 있습니다.

22 이것들은 그림 각 부분의 가능한 의미 풀이 중 일부입니다.

23 이제, 돌아가서 두 그림을 보세요.

24 그 그림들을 스스로 읽으려고 시도해 보세요.

25 당신은 각 그림을 그린 사람이 어떤 사람인지 알 수 있나요?

26 당신의 의견은 어떤가요?

※ 다음 우리말을 영어로 쓰시오.

Drawing the Mind

1 당신이 하는 모든 행동은 당신에 대해 말해 줍니다.

➡ _____

2 당신이 사용하는 언어, 당신이 입는 옷, 그리고 당신이 기르는 애완동물까지도 당신이 어떤 종류의 사람인지 보여 줍니다.

➡ _____

_____

3 당신이 그리는 그림도 마찬가지입니다.

➡ _____

4 당신이 무엇을 그리는지 그리고 그것을 어떻게 그리는지는 당신의 성격과 관련이 있습니다.

➡ _____

5 의사들은 사람들을 더 잘 이해하기 위해 다양한 그림 그리기 검사를 사용해 오고 있습니다.

➡ _____

6 이런 검사들 중 하나는 빗속의 사람 그리기 검사입니다.

➡ _____

7 아래의 그림들을 연구해 봅시다.

➡ _____

8 A 그림 속의 사람은 가벼운 빗속에서 우산을 들고 있습니다.

➡ _____

9 반면에, B 그림 속의 사람은 거센 빗속에서 우산을 가지고 있지 않습니다.

➡ _____

10 또한, 검은 구름들이 B 그림의 사람 머리 위에 있습니다.

➡ _____

11 이런 차이는 무엇을 의미하는 걸까요?

➡ _____

12 첫 번째, 비는 그림을 그린 사람이 받고 있는 스트레스를 보여줍니다.

➡ _____

13 빗방울의 크기가 크면 클수록, 혹은 비가 더 세게 내리면 내릴수록 스트레스는 더 큽니다.

➡ _____

14 구름은 앞으로 벌어질 문제를 의미하기 때문에, 큰 구름은 그림을 그린 사람이 미래에 대해 그다지 희망적이지 않다는 것을 나타냅니다.

➡ _____

_____

15 두 번째, 우산은 스트레스를 받는 상황에서 그 사람이 가지고 있는 보호 기제를 의미합니다.

➡ _____

16 큰 우산은 그림을 그린 사람이 많은 계획이나 보호 기제를 가지고 있음을 보여 줍니다.

➡ _____

17 만약 그림에 우산이 없다면, 그 그림을 그린 사람은 어려운 상황을 헤쳐 나갈 어떤 방법도 가지고 있지 않습니다.

➡ _____

_____

18 세 번째, 그림 속 사람의 세부적인 것들은 그 그림을 그린 사람이 스트레스를 받을 때의 태도와 관련이 있습니다.

➡ _____

19 예를 들어, 얼굴이 없는 사람을 그린 사람은 사람들의 관심을 끌기를 원하지 않습니다.

➡ _____

_____

20 사람을 종이의 오른쪽에 그린 사람은 미래를 맞이할 준비가 되어 있습니다.

➡ _____

21 반면에, 사람을 왼쪽에 그린 사람은 과거에 일어났던 일에 대해 걱정하고 있을 수도 있습니다.

➡ _____

_____

22 이것들은 그림 각 부분의 가능한 의미 풀이 중 일부입니다.

➡ _____

23 이제, 돌아가서 두 그림을 보세요.

➡ _____

24 그 그림들을 스스로 읽으려고 시도해 보세요.

➡ _____

25 당신은 각 그림을 그린 사람이 어떤 사람인지 알 수 있나요?

➡ _____

26 당신의 의견은 어떤가요?

➡ _____

※ 다음 우리말과 일치하도록 빈칸에 알맞은 말을 쓰시오.

Before You Read

1. A picture is often _____ _____ _____ _____ you're feeling in your mind.
2. _____ you _____ a picture, it _____ _____ _____.
3. _____ _____ _____, your various feelings _____ _____ _____ through pictures.
4. _____, you can _____ _____ other people's feelings if you _____ _____ _____ _____ their drawings.

1. 그림은 네 마음속에 느끼고 있는 것과 밀접한 관계가 있다.
2. 네가 그림을 그릴 때, 그것은 너의 감정들을 나타낸다.
3. 다시 말해서, 너의 다양한 감정들은 그림을 통해 표현될 수 있다.
4. 그러므로 너는 다른 사람들의 그림에 주의 깊게 관심을 기울인다면 그들의 감정을 이해할 수 있다.

Writing Workshop

1. This year, we _____ _____ _____ a lot of _____ _____ _____ activities at school.
2. Today, we _____ _____ _____ _____ our _____ _____ and then talk about a friend's personality.
3. I _____ _____ as _____ and _____.
4. _____ my friend _____ about me was _____ _____.
5. She said I am _____ and _____ because I _____ _____ _____ _____ others and am in _____ _____ _____.

1. 올해, 우리는 학교에서 많은 다양한 종류의 활동들을 해 오고 있다.
2. 오늘 우리는 우리 자신의 성격과 친구의 성격에 대해 말해야 했다.
3. 나는 내 자신이 수줍음이 많고 친절하다고 생각했다.
4. 나에 대해 내 친구가 말한 것은 매우 달랐다.
5. 그녀는 내가 활동적이고 호기심이 많다고 말했는데, 그 이유는 내가 다른 사람들과 잘 지내고 많은 동아리에 속해 있기 때문이라고 했다.

Wrap Up 3~4

1. G: I _____ _____ _____ to Daegu today, but there are _____ _____ _____ _____.
2. Are there _____ _____ _____ to get there?
3. B: You can _____ _____ _____. It's fast and _____.
4. G: That's a great idea. I'll _____ _____.

1. G: 나는 오늘 대구에 가야 하지만 남아 있는 기차표가 없어.
2. 거기로 가는 다른 방법이 있을까?
3. B: 버스를 탈 수 있어. 그것은 빠르고 편해.
4. G: 좋은 생각이야. 그렇게 할게.

※ 다음 우리말을 영어로 쓰시오.

Before You Read

1. 그림은 네 마음속에 느끼고 있는 것과 밀접한 관계가 있다.

   ➡ _____

2. 네가 그림을 그릴 때, 그것은 너의 감정들을 나타낸다.

   ➡ _____

3. 다시 말해서, 너의 다양한 감정들은 그림을 통해 표현될 수 있다.

   ➡ _____

4. 그러므로 너는 다른 사람들의 그림에 주의 깊게 관심을 기울인다면 그들의 감정을 이해할 수 있다.

   ➡ _____

Writing Workshop

1. 올해, 우리는 학교에서 많은 다양한 종류의 활동들을 해 오고 있다.

   ➡ _____

2. 오늘 우리는 우리 자신의 성격과 친구의 성격에 대해 말해야 했다.

   ➡ _____

3. 나는 내 자신이 수줍음이 많고 친절하다고 생각했다.

   ➡ _____

4. 나에 대해 내 친구가 말한 것은 매우 달랐다.

   ➡ _____

5. 그녀는 내가 활동적이고 호기심이 많다고 말했는데, 그 이유는 내가 다른 사람들과 잘 지내고 많은 동아리에 속해 있기 때문이라고 했다.

   ➡ _____

Wrap Up 3~4

1. G: 나는 오늘 대구에 가야 하지만 남아 있는 기차표가 없어.

   ➡ _____

2. 거기로 가는 다른 방법이 있을까?

   ➡ _____

3. B: 버스를 탈 수 있어. 그것은 빠르고 편해.

   ➡ _____

4. G: 좋은 생각이야. 그렇게 할게.

   ➡ _____

4. write down, spend, on / think

1. What, do, weekend / played, decided, exercise, for / you, important, regularly / Right, about, with

2. late / took, bus / think, leave, earlier / too, won't / arrive, on

Listen & Speak 2

1. too / should, brought, one
2. cold / have
3. missed / have, earlier
4. Look, should, put on / right

Listen & Speak 2 A

1. how, movie / enjoy, was / What, about / knew, have, before / sorry, like

2. still, minutes, before, top, down, and, snack / brought, brought / okay, share / keep, mind, some, time

Real-Life Zone

look, energy / because, got, last / usually, enough / know, important, night's, always, up, surfing, playing, phone / sometimes, me / After, regret, morning, have, earlier / different / climbed, dad, tired, home, sleep, after / Outdoor, are, way, get

Wrap Up

blanket, wet, checked / rwash / put, sun / Why, wash / blanket, way, keep, clean / know, remember / important, remember, regularly

시험대비 기본평가   p.16

01 ①   02 ⑤   03 ④

01 소년이 규칙적으로 운동하는 것이 중요하다고 한 말과 빈칸 뒤에 이어지는 대답이 "Why not?"이라고 하는 것으로 보아 함께 테니스를 치자는 제안이 있었다고 생각할 수 있다.

02 또 다시 지각했다고 야단치는 것에 대하여 미안하다는 말에 이어서 버스를 잘못 타서 지각하게 되었다는 이유를 덧붙이는 것이 자연스럽다.

03 영화를 즐기지 못했다는 말에 (C) 무엇이 나빠서 영화를 즐기지 못했는지 이유를 묻자 (A) 이미 결말을 알았기 때문이라고 대답하고, 그것에 대해 읽어본 것을 후회한다. (B) 상대의 말에 공감하는 의미로 유감을 표시한다.

시험대비 실력평가   p.17~18

01 ③   02 ④   03 ②   04 ③
05 ④   06 ③   07 ①   08 ④

09 ⑤   10 I should have brought some snacks.
11 ①   12 ③

01 "too"가 나타내는 것은 앞에 나온 말에 대한 동의의 의미라고 볼 수 있기 때문에, 앞에서 강조하는 의미에 동의하는 말에 해당하는 ③이 적절하다.

02 "It's important to exercise regularly"가 앞의 빈칸에 나온 말에 대한 반응이기 때문에 운동에 대한 언급이 있는 ④가 적절하다.

03 앞에 나온 내용을 보면 소녀가 테니스를 친 것은 주말이기 때문에 "weekday 평일"이라고 할 수는 없다.

04 밤에 늦게 잔 것을 후회한다는 것으로 보아 빈칸에는 밤에 잠을 자지 않고 깨어 있는 것을 나타내는 ③이 적절하다.

05 주어진 문장은 산에 다녀온 이후의 상황을 나타내는 것이기 때문에 (D)가 적절한 곳이다.

06 Ben은 밤늦게 인터넷 서핑을 하면서 보낸 것을 후회하기 때문에 인터넷 서핑을 밤늦게까지 계속하지는 않을 것이다.

07 이어지는 대화를 보았을 때 소녀는 결말을 알고 있어서 영화가 지루했다는 것을 알 수 있으므로 ①이 적절하다.

08 대화의 흐름상 앞에 있었던 일에 대한 유감의 내용이 되어야 하기 때문에 ④"I shouldn't have read about it before seeing it."이 옳다.

09 미나가 본 영화에 대하여 두 사람이 이야기하고 있다. 영화에 대한 미나의 반응은 있지만 소년이 영화를 좋아하는지 싫어하는지는 알 수 없다.

10 간식을 가져오지 않은 것에 대한 후회를 나타내야 하므로 should bring을 should have brought로 고쳐야 한다.

11 (B) 한 사람이 가지고 온 것을 함께 먹는 것은 share에 해당한다. (C) "명심하다, 염두에 두다"는 "keep in mind"이다.

12 두 사람이 등산 중에 휴식을 취하려는 상황에서 소녀가 간식을 가지고 오지 않았다고 하니까 소년이 자기가 많이 가지고 와서 나눠먹을 수 있다고 하는 것으로 보아 간식이 충분하지 않다는 것은 본문의 내용과 일치하지 않는다.

서술형 시험대비   p.19

01 I should have worn a jacket.
02 (B) – (C) – (A)   03 exercise
04 It's important to exercise regularly.
05 playing
06 I shouldn't have read about it before seeing it.
07 I'm sorry   08 good → bad

01 춥지 않은지 묻는 말에 춥다고 하는 것으로 보아 재킷을 입지 않은 것을 후회하는 의미의 "should have+과거분사" 형태가 들어가야 한다.

3

02 어젯밤 잠을 못 잤다는 말에 (B) 이유를 묻자 (C) TV로 영화를 봤다고 말하고, (A) 그것에 대해 유감을 나타내는 말을 한다.

03 "자신을 더 강하고 건강하게 만들기 위해서 신체 활동을 하다"에 해당하는 단어는 "exercise 운동하다"이다.

04 강조하는 의미의 "~하는 것이 중요하다"는 "It's important to ~"이다.

05 권유나 제안의 표현은 "How about -ing?"이다.

06 유감을 나타내는 의미의 "should have+과거분사"를 써야 한다. before 다음에는 적절한 주어로 쓰일 말이 없으므로 seeing을 쓰도록 한다.

07 내용상 상대의 후회에 대한 유감을 나타내는 "I am sorry"가 적절하다.

08 소녀가 영화를 즐기지 못했다고 했으므로 무엇이 좋지 않은지 묻는 "What was bad about it?"이 적절하다.

교과서 Grammar

핵심 Check
p.20~21

1 (1) longer　(2) less
2 (1) that　(2) It　(3) whom

시험대비 기본평가
p.22

01 ④　　**02** ③　　**03** ②

04 (1) It is you that I love.
　(2) It is calcium that builds strong bones and teeth.
　(3) The more I exercise, the stronger I get.
　(4) The more, the better.

01 'It ~ that 강조 구문'은 'It is/was ~ that ...'의 형태로, 강조하고자 하는 부분을 'It is/was'와 that 사이에 넣고, 나머지 부분을 that 뒤에 써서 주어, 목적어인 명사, 부사(구/절) 등을 강조한다. 공통으로 that이 들어가는 것이 적절하다.

02 the 비교급+주어+동사 ~, the 비교급+주어+동사 …: ~하면 할수록 더 …하다

03 It was John who[that] loved her. 강조되는 어구가 사람일 때는 that 대신에 who를 쓸 수 있다.

04 (1), (2) 'It is/was 강조어(구) that ...'의 형태로 특정 부분을 강조하여 나타낼 때 사용한다. (3), (4) 'the 비교급+주어+동사 ~, the 비교급+주어+동사 …'의 형태로 '~하면 할수록 더 …하다'라는 뜻이며, 점점 더해지거나 덜해지는 것을 표현할 때 사용한다.

시험대비 실력평가
p.23~25

01 ②　　**02** ①　　**03** ④　　**04** ⑤
05 ③, ⑤　**06** ③　　**07** ④　　**08** ②
09 ①　　**10** ①, ④

11 (1) The higher I went up, the fresher the air was.
　(2) The more you walk, the more tired you will get.

12 ②

13 (1) This red dress looks the prettier of the two.
　(2) The more water we use, the drier our well will become.
　(3) The more stress I get, the more emotional I become.

14 ⑤　　　　**15** ③

16 (1) why → that　(2) who → that[which]
　(3) July 26 → on July 26

17 (1) The spicier, the more
　(2) The more, the more　(3) when　(4) where
　(5) whom

18 ②　　　　**19** ①

01 the 비교급+주어+동사 ~, the 비교급+주어+동사 …: ~할수록 더 …하다 The hotter it gets, the harder it is to work.

02 ② which → that[who] ③ where → that[when] ④ 두 개의 much → more ⑤ wise → wiser

03 'the 비교급+주어+동사 ~, the 비교급+주어+동사 …: ~할수록 …하다' 구문은 'As+주어+동사+비교급 ~, 주어+동사+비교급 …'으로 바꿔 쓸 수 있다.

04 'It ~ that ...' 강조구문에서 강조하는 대상이 사람일 경우 that 대신에 관계대명사 who로 바꿔 쓸 수 있다.

05 the 비교급+주어+동사 ~, the 비교급+주어+동사 … = As+주어+동사+비교급 ~, 주어+동사+비교급 …: ~할수록 …하다

06 'an apple'을 강조하므로 which나 that을 써야 한다.

07 the 비교급+주어+동사 ~, the 비교급+주어+동사 …: ~할수록 …하다

08 <보기>와 ②번은 강조 용법의 that이다. ① 지시부사 ③ 지시대명사 ④ 접속사 ⑤ 지시형용사

09 the 비교급+주어+동사 ~, the 비교급+주어+동사 …: ~할수록 …하다

10 'It ~ that …' 강조구문에서 강조하는 대상이 사물일 경우 that 대신에 관계대명사 which로 바꿔 쓸 수 있다.

11 the 비교급+주어+동사 ~, the 비교급+주어+동사 … = As+주어+동사+비교급 ~, 주어+동사+비교급 …: ~할수록 …하다
(2) '많이 걸으면 피곤해질 것이다.'라는 의미이므로 비교급을 이용하여 바꿔 쓰면, '더 많이 걸을수록 더 피곤해질 것이다.'라고 쓸 수 있다.

12 ②번은 'It: 가주어, that절: 진주어'이고 나머지는 모두 It ~

that 강조 용법으로 쓰였다.

13 (1) 비교급에는 the를 사용하지 않는 것이 원칙이지만 문장 속에 'of the two'와 같이 비교의 대상이 명확히 둘인 경우 'the+비교급'으로 쓴다. (2), (3) the 비교급+주어+동사 ~, the 비교급+주어+동사 …: ~할수록 …하다

14 ① That → It ②, ③ 'It ~ that …' 강조구문에서 형용사나 동사는 강조할 수 없다. ④ make → makes

15 ① ugly → uglier ② more safe → safer ④ good and good → better and better ⑤ nicer → the nicer

16 (1) why를 that으로 고치는 것이 적절하다. (2) 강조되는 것이 'a good breakfast'이므로 who를 that[which]로 고치는 것이 적절하다. (3) 태어난 날을 강조하는 것이므로 전치사 on을 붙여야 한다.

17 (1), (2) the 비교급+주어+동사 ~, the 비교급+주어+동사 …: ~할수록 …하다 (3), (4) 강조하는 대상이 시간 또는 장소의 부사(구/절)일 경우, when(시간) 또는 where(장소)로 바꿔 쓸 수 있다. (5) 강조하는 대상이 사람으로 목적격이므로 that 대신에 whom으로 바꿔 쓸 수 있다.

18 'the movie'를 강조하는 것이므로 'It was the movie that[which] …'가 적절하다.

19 the gloomier로 쓰는 것이 적절하다.

 서술형 시험대비 p.26~27

01 (1) The higher a bird flies, the farther it can see.
   (2) The more they have, the more they want.

02 (1) The more stress I get, the more emotional I become.
   (2) Ryan thinks the more slowly he eats, the fuller he gets.
   (3) The younger you are, the easier it is to learn.
   (4) This country is the better of the two.
   (5) It was Hamin that[who] played basketball with Eric last Saturday.
   (6) It is on Saturdays that[when] there are lots of weddings.
   (7) It was in Hangang Park that[where] Ms. Jones was at 2 p.m. last Saturday.
   (8) It was Amy's house that[which] James visited last Friday.

03 (1) It was Jenny's family that[who] went to the beach last summer.
   (2) It was to the beach that[where] Jenny's family went last summer.
   (3) It was last summer that[when] Jenny's family went to the beach.

04 (1) The more I like her, the more I miss her.
   (2) The earlier you leave, the earlier you will arrive there.
   (3) The harder you study for the exam, the better you will do.
   (4) The more careful you are, the fewer mistakes you will make.

05 (1) It was Anna who bought the dress on the Internet last Sunday.
   (2) Anna did buy the dress on the Internet last Sunday.
   (3) It was the dress which Anna bought on the Internet last Sunday.
   (4) It was on the Internet where Anna bought the dress last Sunday.
   (5) It was last Sunday when Anna bought the dress on the Internet.

06 (1) the healthier you will feel
   (2) the harder doing outdoor activities is
   (3) the more dangerous you will be

07 (1) The more you study, the smarter you will become.
   (2) The less money you spend, the more money you will have in your account.
   (3) It was five years ago that[when] Mr. Smith moved to our apartment.
   (4) It was at the Italian restaurant that[where] I learned this recipe.
   (5) It was his book that[which] Jack lost at the market.

01 the 비교급+주어+동사 ~, the 비교급+주어+동사 …: ~할수록 …하다

02 (1)~(3) the 비교급+주어+동사 ~, the 비교급+주어+동사 …: ~할수록 …하다 (4) 비교급에는 the를 사용하지 않는 것이 원칙이지만 문장 속에 'of the two'와 같이 비교의 대상이 명확히 둘인 경우 'the+비교급'으로 쓴다. (5) 강조하는 것이 'Hamin'이므로 that이나 who를 쓰는 것이 적절하다. (6) 강조하는 것이 'on Saturdays'이므로 that이나 when을 쓰는 것이 적절하다. (7) which 다음에 완전한 절이 나오므로 Hangang Park를 강조하는 것으로 볼 수 없다. 'in Hangang Park'를 강조하는 것으로 that이나 where를 쓰는 것이 적절하다. (8) 강조하는 것이 'Amy's house'이므로 that이나 which를 쓰는 것이 적절하다..

03 It was와 that 사이에 강조하고자 하는 부분을 넣고, that 대신에 사람이면 who, 장소일 경우 where, 시간이면 when을 쓸 수도 있다.

04 (1) '많이 좋아하면, 많이 그리워할 것이다.'를 비교급을 이용하

5

여 '더 많이 좋아할수록 더 그리워할 것이다.'라고 쓸 수 있다. (2) '일찍 출발하면, 일찍 도착할 것이다.'를 비교급을 이용하여 '더 일찍 출발할수록 더 일찍 도착할 것이다.'라고 쓸 수 있다. (3), (4) the 비교급+주어+동사 ~, the 비교급+주어+동사 … = As+주어+동사+비교급 ~, 주어+동사+비교급 …: ~할수록 …하다

05 과거시제이므로 강조하고자 하는 부분을 It was와 that 사이에 넣고, 나머지 부분을 that 뒤에 쓴다. 이때 that을 사용하지 말라고 하였으므로 that 대신에 사람이면 who, 사물이면 which, 장소일 경우 where, 시간일 경우 when을 사용한다. 또한 'It is[was] ~ that ...' 구문은 동사를 강조할 수 없으므로 동사를 동사 앞에 did를 사용하여 강조한다.

06 the 비교급+주어+동사 ~, the 비교급+주어+동사 …: ~할수록 …하다

07 (1), (2) the 비교급+주어+동사 ~, the 비교급+주어+동사 …: ~할수록 …하다 (3)~(5) 강조하고자 하는 부분을 It was와 that 사이에 넣고, 나머지 부분을 that 뒤에 쓴다. 이때 that 대신에 시간일 경우 when, 장소일 경우 where, 사물이면 which를 사용할 수 있다.

교과서 Reading

확인문제   p.28

1 T   2 F   3 T   4 F   5 T   6 F

확인문제   p.29

1 T   2 F   3 T   4 F   5 T   6 F

교과서 확인학습 A   p.30~31

01 Sunshine   02 out in the sun
03 Not much
04 too busy, to spend, outdoors
05 plays an important role   06 stay healthy
07 feels happier
08 the body's happy hormone
09 The more sun, the more, happy hormone
10 goes up   11 fight everyday stress
12 calming effect, what you are doing
13 Moreover, a good night's sleep
14 not just
15 also, build strong bones   16 As you all know
17 for the body to use

18 when sunlight shines   19 to go outside
20 As you can see, enjoy its benefits safely
21 getting direct sunlight, to benefit from it
22 Try to go out into, get sunshine on
23 for just a few minutes every day
24 to protect your face and neck
25 a little sunshine, make a world of difference

교과서 확인학습 B   p.32~33

1 Enjoy the Sunshine
2 How much time do you spend every day out in the sun?
3 Not much, right?
4 Most people are too busy at school or at work to spend much time outdoors.
5 However, the sun plays an important role in your health.
6 It helps you stay healthy.
7 Everyone feels happier when the sun shines.
8 This is because of serotonin, the body's happy hormone.
9 The more sun you get, the more "happy hormone" the brain produces.
10 When your serotonin level goes up, you feel happier and stronger.
11 This helps you fight everyday stress.
12 Serotonin also has a calming effect, helping you focus better on what you are doing.
13 Moreover, serotonin helps you get a good night's sleep because it helps the brain produce a sleep hormone.
14 Sunshine does not just make you feel and sleep better.
15 It also helps build strong bones.
16 As you all know, it is calcium that builds strong bones and teeth.
17 However, for the body to use calcium properly, it needs vitamin D.
18 Interestingly, the skin creates vitamin D when sunlight shines on it.
19 The easiest way to make strong bones is to go outside and enjoy the sun.
20 As you can see, sunshine has many benefits, but how can you enjoy its benefits safely?
21 Fortunately, getting direct sunlight on your skin for 10 to 20 minutes a day is enough to benefit from it.

22 Try to go out into the sun between classes or during lunch breaks and get sunshine on your arms and hands.

23 A walk in the sun, for just a few minutes every day, is good for both your mind and your body.

24 However, avoid the sun during peak summer hours, between 11 and 3, and use sunscreen to protect your face and neck.

25 Enjoy the sun safely and see how a little sunshine can make a world of difference in your health and your mood.

시험대비 실력평가
p.34~37

01 ⑤　　　　　02 (A) Most　(B) outdoors　(C) healthy
03 part　　　04 spend → can't spend　　05 ②
06 sunscreen 또는 sunblock
07 it is calcium that builds strong bones and teeth
08 ③　　　　09 ⑤　　　　10 Vitamin D　11 ③
12 ④　　　　13 ④　　　　14 ①, ④
15 serotonin　　　　16 ③
17 (A) serotonin　(B) sleep hormone
18 Sunshine helps build strong bones as well as makes you feel and sleep better.
19 ①, ④　　　　　　20 the body
21 As you can see　　22 ①
23 and it helps you focus better on what you are doing
24 ④

---

01 앞에 나오는 내용과 상반되는 내용이 뒤에 이어지므로 However가 가장 적절하다. ① 따라서, 그러므로, ② 게다가, 더욱이, ③ 예를 들면, ④ 다시 말해서

02 (A) '대부분의' 사람들이라고 해야 하므로 Most가 적절하다. almost: 거의, most: 대부분(의), (B) outdoor: 옥외[야외]의(형용사) [주로 명사 앞에만 씀], outdoors: 옥외[야외]에서(부사), (C) stay 뒤에 형용사 보어를 써야 하므로, healthy가 적절하다.

03 play a role = play a part: 역할을 맡다, 한몫을 하다

04 대부분의 사람들은 학교와 직장에서 너무 바빠서 많은 시간을 야외에서 '보내지 못한다.' spend를 can't spend로 고치는 것이 적절하다. too ~ to부정사 = so ~ that 주어 cannot ...(너무 ~해서 …할 수 없다), Almost all the people = Most people, outdoors = outside a building or in the open air

05 이 글은 '햇빛의 많은 이점을 안전하게 즐길 수 있는 방법을 소개하고 있는 글'이므로, 제목으로는 ②번 '햇빛의 많은 이점을

안전하게 즐길 수 있는 법'이 적절하다. ④ spare time: 자투리 시간, 여가 시간, ⑤ make a difference: 변화를 가져오다, 차이를 낳다, 영향을 주다, 중요하다

06 sunscreen = sunblock: 자외선 차단제, 특히 더운 날씨에 태양 광선으로부터 당신의 피부를 보호해 주는 크림

07 it ~ that 강조 구문: 강조하고자 하는 부분을 it과 that 사이에 쓰고, it 뒤에 오는 be동사는 문장의 시제에 맞춰 is나 was를 사용한다.

08 ⓑ와 ②, ⑤: 부사적 용법, ①, ④: 명사적 용법, ③: 형 용사적 용법

09 이 글은 '칼슘은 튼튼한 뼈를 만들어 주는데, 그 칼슘을 몸이 적절하게 사용하기 위해서는 비타민 D가 필요하고 햇빛이 피부에 비칠 때 비타민 D를 만들어 내므로 튼튼한 뼈를 만드는 가장 쉬운 방법은 밖으로 나가서 햇빛을 즐기는 것'이라는 내용의 글이므로, 주제로는 ⑤번 '햇빛은 튼튼한 뼈를 만드는 가장 쉬운 방법이다'가 적절하다.

10 '비타민 D'가 필요하다.

11 ⓐ for+숫자: ~ 동안, ⓑ in the sun: 햇빛을 쬐며

12 주어진 문장의 However에 주목한다. ④번 앞 문장의 내용과 상반되는 내용이 뒤에 이어지므로 ④번이 적절하다.

13 ⓐ와 ④: (작업 중의) 휴식 (시간)(명사), lunch breaks: 점심시간, ① 부수다(동사), ② (~ 사이의) 틈[구멍](명사), ③ (법·약속 등을) 어기다(동사), ⑤ (무엇을 갑자기) 중단시키다 (동사)

14 ⓐ와 ①, ④: 현재분사, ②, ③, ⑤: 동명사

15 '세로토닌'을 가리킨다.

16 여러분의 세로토닌 수치가 '높아지면', 여러분은 더 행복하고 더 건강하게 느낀다.

17 '세로토닌' 덕분에 여러분은 숙면을 취할 수 있는데, 세로토닌이 뇌가 '수면 호르몬'을 생성하도록 도와주기 때문이다. get a good night's sleep = have a good night's sleep: 충분히 숙면을 취하다

18 본문에서는 ⓐ와 ⓑ가 각각의 문장이라서 접속사가 필요하지 않지만, 한 문장일 경우는 접속사를 써야 하므로, not just[only] A but also B = B as well as A(A 뿐만 아니라 B도) 구문을 사용하여 고치는 것이 적절하다.

19 ⓒ와 ②, ③, ⑤: 'It is[was] ~ that ...'의 형태의 강조 구문, ① so ~ that ...: 너무 ~해서 …하다(부사절을 이끄는 접속사), ④ 진주어를 이끄는 접속사

20 '몸'을 가리킨다.

21 as: ~한 것처럼, ~하다시피(접속사)

22 다행히도, 하루에 10분에서 20분 동안 피부에 직사광선을 쪼이는 것은 햇빛으로부터 이점을 얻는 데 충분하다고 했으므로, '햇빛의 이점들을 안전하게 즐길 수 있는 방법은 찾기 어렵다'는 말은 옳지 않다.

23 helping 이하는 분사구문으로 앞 절에 대한 추가 설명을 제공

한다.

24 이 글은 '세로토닌의 이로운 점들'에 관한 글이므로, 제목으로는 ④번 '세로토닌의 여러 가지 이로운 점들'이 적절하다. benefit: 이익; 편의, 이로움

01 Most people are so busy at school or at work that they cannot spend much time outdoors.
02 the sun   03 (A) health   (B) healthy
04 As you get more sun, the brain produces more "happy hormone".
05 helping you focus better on what you are doing
06 (A) the brain   (B) happy hormone
07 (1) It[Sunshine] makes you feel better.
    (2) It[Sunshine] makes you sleep better.
    (3) It[Sunshine] helps build strong bones.
08 Therefore → However   09 the skin
10 (A) vitamin D   (B) sunlight   (C) enjoy the sun
11 does not make → does not just[only/merely/simply] make
12 (A) during   (B) protect   (C) a world of
13 10 to 20

01 too ~ to부정사: so ~ that 주어 cannot ...(너무 ~해서 …할 수 없다)
02 '해[햇빛]'를 가리킨다.
03 햇빛은 여러분이 '건강'을 유지하는 데 도움을 주며 여러분의 '건강'에 중요한 영향을 미친다(역할을 한다). play a role(part) in = have an effect on
04 the 비교급 ~, the 비교급 …: '~할수록 …하다', As를 이용하여 고칠 때는 the를 생략하고 비교급을 원래의 자리에 쓰는 것이 적절하다.
05 'on'을 보충하면 된다. focus on: ~에 주력하다, 초점을 맞추다
06 여러분이 햇살을 받을 때 '뇌'는 세로토닌을 만들어 내고, 세로토닌 수치에 비례하여 여러분은 더 행복하게 느낄 수 있다. 그래서 여러분은 세로토닌을 '행복 호르몬'이라고 부를 수 있다. be in the sun: 햇살을 받다
07 (1) 햇빛은 여러분이 더 기분 좋게 느끼게 해준다. (2) 햇빛은 여러분이 잠을 더 잘 자게 해 준다. (3) 햇빛은 튼튼한 뼈를 만드는 것을 돕는다.
08 튼튼한 뼈와 치아를 만드는 것은 칼슘'이지만', 몸이 칼슘을 적절하게 사용하기 위해서는 비타민 D가 필요하다고 하는 것이 적절하므로 'However'나 'But' 등으로 고치는 것이 적절하다.
09 '피부'를 가리킨다.
10 몸이 튼튼한 뼈를 만들어 주는 칼슘을 적절하게 사용하기 위해

서는 '비타민 D'가 필요하다. 피부는 '햇빛'이 피부에 비칠 때 비타민 D를 만들어 내므로, 튼튼한 뼈를 만드는 가장 쉬운 방법은 밖으로 나가서 '햇볕을 즐기는 것'이다.
11 '햇빛은 단지 여러분이 더 기분 좋게 느끼고 잠을 더 잘 자게 하는 것만은 아니다.'라고 해야 하므로 does not just[only/merely/simply] make로 고치는 것이 적절하다.
12 (A) '여름의 절정 시간 동안'이라고 해야 하므로 during이 적절하다. during+기간을 나타내는 명사, for+숫자, (B) 얼굴과 목을 '보호하기 위해'라고 해야 하므로 protect가 적절하다. prevent: 막다, 예방하다, protect: 보호하다, (C) '큰 차이'라고 해야 하므로 a world of가 적절하다. a world of: 산더미 같은, 막대한, a number of+복수명사: 많은
13 햇빛으로부터 이점을 얻으려면 하루에 '10분에서 20분' 동안 피부에 직사광선을 쪼이는 것이 필요하다.

01 ①   02 ④   03 ⑤   04 ④
05 It's important to arrive at school on time.
06 I shouldn't have read about it
07 ⑤   08 (A) boring   (B) like   09 ⑤
10 ③   11 ②   12 ⑤   13 ①
14 (1) It was Tina that[who] bought a camera at the shop yesterday.
    (2) Tina did buy a camera at the shop yesterday.
    (3) It was a camera that[which] Tina bought at the shop yesterday.
    (4) It was at the shop that[where] Tina bought a camera yesterday.
    (5) It was yesterday that[when] Tina bought a camera at the shop.
15 ③   16 ④
17 (1) The healthier, the healthier
    (2) the more, the sadder   (3) darker and darker
    (4) where   (5) which
18 It was, that[where]
19 ④   20 ⑤   21 ①, ②   22 ①
23 for 10 to 20 minutes a day
24 between   25 ②
26 As you get more sunlight, you feel happier and stronger.
27 wash your hands   28 ⑤
29 good breakfast

01 그것은 그녀 평생의 가장 어려운 결정이었다. be동사의 보어로 명사 decision이 적절하다.
02 "사람이나 동물 신체의 표피층"은 "피부 skin"를 가리킨다.

03 버스는 정확히 제시간에 왔다. 제시간에 = on time / 너는 이 추운 날씨에 코트를 입는 것이 낫다. 입다 = put on

04 건강을 유지하기 위해 뭘 하니? stay healthy = 건강을 유지하다, stay = ~한 상태를 유지하다

05 "~하는 것이 중요하다"는 "It's important to ~"이다.

06 "~하지 말았어야 했는데"의 의미로 유감이나 후회를 나타내는 표현은 "shouldn't[should not] have+과거분사"이다.

07 타야 할 비행기를 놓쳤기 때문에 일찍 오지 않은 것에 대한 유감을 나타내는 표현이 적절하다.

08 (A) 영화를 즐기지 못했다는 말에 이어지므로 영화에 대한 부정적인 단어가 적절하다. (B) 상대가 영화를 즐기지 못했다는 말에 대한 유감의 의미가 되는 단어가 적절하다.

09 영화를 보기 전에 읽지 말았어야 했다는 의미이다. 전치사 before 뒤에 오기 때문에 동명사 seeing이 되어야 한다.

10 위 대화에서 미나는 영화를 즐기지 못한 것은 미리 읽은 것 때문이라고 생각하면서 유감스럽게 생각하고 있다.

11 'It is[was] ~ that ...' 강조구문에서 that 대신에 강조하는 것이 사람이면 who, 사물이면 which, 장소일 경우에는 where, 시간일 경우에는 when을 쓸 수 있다.

12 the 비교급+주어+동사 ~, the 비교급+주어+동사 …: ~할수록 …하다

13 ① of the two로 수식을 받는 경우 비교급이라도 the를 붙인다. ② The higher the top of a mountain, the better the view. ③ The more I got to know her, the more I liked her. ④ The angrier she got, the more loudly she yelled. ⑤ The older David gets, the wiser he becomes.

14 강조하고자 하는 부분을 It is[was]와 that 사이에 넣고, 나머지 부분을 that 뒤에 쓴다. that 대신에 강조하는 것이 사람이면 who, 사물이면 which, 장소일 경우에는 where, 시간일 경우에는 when을 쓸 수 있다. 하지만 'It is[was] ~ that ...' 구문은 동사를 강조할 수는 없고 동사는 동사 앞에 do/does/did를 사용하여 강조한다.

15 ① It was my uncle that[who] bought this smartphone for me on my birthday. ② It is Brian that[who] broke the door. ④ It is the new car that my son wants to buy. ⑤ It was on the day that[when] I met her.

16 the 비교급+주어+동사 ~, the 비교급+주어+동사 …: ~할수록 …하다

17 (1), (2) the 비교급+주어+동사 ~, the 비교급+주어+동사 …: ~할수록 …하다 (3) '비교급 and 비교급'은 '점점 더 …하다'의 뜻이다. (4)~(5) 'It is[was] ~ that ...' 구문에서 that 대신에 강조하는 것이 사람이면 who, 사물이나 동물이면 which, 시간이면 when, 장소이면 where를 쓸 수 있다.

18 'It is[was] ~ that ...' 구문은 강조하고자 하는 부분을 It is[was]와 that 사이에 넣고, 나머지 부분을 that 뒤에 쓰며, 강

19 앞에 나오는 내용에 추가하는 내용이 뒤에 이어지므로 Moreover가 가장 적절하다. Moreover 게다가, 더욱이, ② 즉[말하자면], ③ 그러므로

20 세로토닌은 뇌가 수면 호르몬을 생성하도록 도와주기 때문에 여러분이 숙면을 취하도록 해 준다고 했으므로, 세로토닌이 숙면과 아무 관계가 없다는 말은 옳지 않다. have nothing to do with: ~와는 전혀 관계가 없다

21 ⓐ와 ①, ②: 명사적 용법, ③, ⑤: 부사적 용법, ④: 형용사적 용법

22 이 글은 '칼슘은 튼튼한 뼈를 만들어 주는데, 그 칼슘을 몸이 적절하게 사용하기 위해서는 비타민 D가 필요하고, 햇빛이 피부에 비칠 때 비타민 D를 만들어 내므로, 튼튼한 뼈를 만드는 가장 쉬운 방법은 밖으로 나가서 햇빛을 즐기는 것'이라는 내용의 글이므로, 제목으로는 ①번 '햇빛을 즐기기, 튼튼한 뼈를 만드는 가장 쉬운 방법!'이 적절하다.

23 10 to 20 minutes: 10분에서 20분

24 between A and B: A와 B 사이에

25 ② '무슨 근거로 하루에 10분에서 20분 동안 피부에 직사광선을 쪼이는 것이 햇빛으로부터 이점을 얻는 데 충분한 것인지'는 대답할 수 없다. on what ground: 무슨 까닭으로, 무슨 근거로, ① Yes. ③ Between classes or during lunch breaks. ④ During peak summer hours, between 11 and 3. ⑤ By using sunscreen.

26 the 비교급 ~, the 비교급 …: '~할수록 …하다', As를 이용하여 고칠 때는 the를 생략하고 비교급을 원래의 자리에 쓰는 것이 적절하다.

27 외출한 다음에 '손을 잘 씻으면' 감기에 쉽게 걸리지 않을 것이다. catch[take, get, have] a cold: 감기에 걸리다

28 ⑤ 아침 식사를 잘하면 당신의 일에 더 잘 집중할 수 있고 사물들을 더 잘 기억할 수 있다.

29 '좋은 아침 식사'는 당신의 일에 더 잘 집중할 수 있고 사물들을 더 잘 기억할 수 있도록 도와준다.

단원별 예상문제   p.46~49

01 irregularly   02 ③   03 ④
04 ⑤   05 ③   06 ②   07 ①
08 ①   09 ⑤

10 (1) It is the whole thing that[which] we are pretty much unsure about.

(2) It was with her friends that[who, whom] she went to the movies last Sunday.

(3) It was yesterday that[when] a friend of mine bought a luxurious car.

9

11 ④　　　　　　12 ③, ⑤

13 (1) The more careful we are, the fewer mistakes
　　　 we make.

　　 (2) It is sunscreen that you should put on before
　　　 you go out.

14 ②

15 Everyone feels happier when the sun shines.

16 ③　　　　17 ③　　　　18 ④

19 safe → safely

20 (A) peak summer hours　　　　21 ⑤

22 ③　　　　　23 sunscreen → umbrella　　24 ④

01 주어진 단어는 반의어 관계이다. wet 젖은, dry 건조한,
　 regularly 규칙적으로, irregularly 불규칙하게

02 태양을 안전하게 즐기고 적은 양의 햇빛이 여러분의 건강과 기
　 분에 얼마나 큰 차이를 만들어 내는지 보세요. / make a world
　 of difference 큰 차이를 만들다

03 나는 여가 시간이 있을 때 보통 인터넷 서핑을 한다. surf the
　 Internet 인터넷 서핑을 하다 / 햇빛은 여러분의 건강에 중요한
　 역할을 합니다. play an important role 중요한 역할을 하다

04 ① effect 효과 ② flight 항공편 ③ grade 성적 ④ journal
　 일기, 일지 ⑤ regret 후회하다

05 산꼭대기에 도달하다는 의미의 타동사로 쓰이는 것은 reach이
　 다.

06 "~했어야 했는데"는 "should have+과거분사"의 형태로 과거
　 에 하지 못한 일에 대한 유감이나 후회를 나타낸다.

07 두 사람은 산을 오르는 중이고 꼭대기까지는 30분 정도 남은 지
　 점에 도착했지만 지금까지 얼마나 시간이 걸렸는지는 알 수 없
　 다.

08 stay up late: 늦게까지 자지 않고 있다

09 일찍 잠자리에 들었어야 했다는 의미가 적절하므로 "should
　 have+과거분사"가 와야 한다.

10 강조하고자 하는 부분을 'It is[was]'와 that 사이에 넣고, 나머
　 지 부분을 that 뒤에 쓴다.

11 ④ The redder the apples are, the sweeter they taste.

12 ① The higher I went up, the foggier it became. ②
　 Of the two boys, Simon is the taller. ④ Buying new
　 furniture may prove too costly. 강조되는 부분에 형용사
　 나 동사는 사용할 수 없다. ⑥ He played basketball at the
　 playground. ⑦ last Friday를 강조하는 것이므로 that이나
　 when을 써야 한다.

13 (1) the 비교급+주어+동사 ~, the 비교급+주어+동사 …: ~할
　 수록 …하다 (2) 강조하고자 하는 부분을 'It is[was]'와 that
　 사이에 넣고, 나머지 부분을 that 뒤에 쓴다.

14 ②번 다음 문장의 This에 주목한다. 주어진 문장의 내용을 받고
　 있으므로 ②번이 적절하다.

15 앞 문장 전체를 가리킨다.

16 이 글은 '세로토닌의 이로운 점들'에 관한 글이므로, 주제
　 로는 ③번 '유익한 호르몬인 세로토닌의 역할'이 적절하다.
　 beneficial: 유익한, 이로운

17 ⓐ와 ③: ~한 것처럼, ~하다시피(접속사), 녹이 쇠를 좀먹듯이
　 근심은 마음을 좀먹는다. ① [보통 'as ~ as …'로 형용사·부사
　 앞에서] ~와 같은 정도로, ('as ~ as …'에서, 앞의 as가 지시부
　 사, 뒤의 as는 접속사), ② 때(접속사), ④ 이유(접속사), ⑤ [비
　 례] ~함에 따라, ~할수록(접속사)

18 몸이 '칼슘'을 적절하게 사용하기 위해서는 '비타민 D'가 필요하
　 다.

19 동사 enjoy를 수식하는 것이기 때문에, 부사로 고치는 것이 적
　 절하다.

20 '여름의 절정 시간'인 11시에서 3시 사이에는 햇빛을 피하는 것
　 이 좋다.

21 매일 '적은' 양의 햇빛이라도 쬐면 자신의 건강과 기분에 큰 차이
　 를 만들어 낼 수 있다.

22 위 글은 '일기 예보'이다. ① book report: 독후감, ② article:
　 (신문·잡지의) 글, 기사, ④ review: (책·연극·영화 등에 대한)
　 논평[비평], 감상문, ⑤ travel essay: 기행문

23 서울과 파리는 비가 예보되고 있기 때문에 '우산'을 가지고 가라
　 고 하는 것이 적절하다. sunscreen 자외선 차단제

24 뉴욕은 현재 날씨가 흐리다.

서술형 실전문제
p.50~51

01 ④, How was yesterday different?

02 I finally got a good night's sleep last night

03 Outdoor

04 (1) I think the older Sue gets, the wiser she
　　　 becomes.

　 (2) The fewer the words, the better the prayer.

　 (3) It was in the library that he lent me the book
　　　 yesterday.

　 (4) It was last year that[when] my family traveled
　　　 to Busan.

　 (5) It was because she lost her mother that the girl
　　　 was confused.

05 It, she is waiting for in the rain

06 (A) up　(B) calming　(C) helping

07 (A) everyday stress　(B) serotonin level

08 sunlight

10 정답 및 해설

09 see how a little sunshine can make a world of difference in your health and your mood

10 (A) many benefits   (B) safe   (C) sunscreen

02 "하룻밤을 잘 자다"는 "get a good night's sleep"이다.

03 앞에서 언급한 등산을 지칭하는 의미로 "Outdoor activities"가 되도록 해야 한다.

04 (1), (2) the 비교급+주어+동사 ~, the 비교급+주어+동사 …: ~할수록 …하다 (3) that 다음에 이어지는 절이 완전하므로 'the library'를 'in the library'로 고쳐야 한다. (4) last year를 강조하고 있으므로 that[when]을 써야 한다. (5) who 다음에 나오는 절이 완전하므로 who를 that으로 고쳐 'because she lost her mother'라는 부사절을 강조하는 문장으로 만들어야 한다.

05 빗속에서 버스를 기다리고 있는 그림이므로 'It is'와 that 사이에 the bus를 넣어 강조한다. be동사가 주어졌으므로 'is waiting for'로 현재진행형으로 쓴다.

06 (A) 세로토닌 수치가 '높아지면' 더 행복하고 더 건강하게 느끼는 것이므로 up이 적절하다. (B) '진정시키는' 효과라고 해야 하므로 calming이 적절하다. (C) and it helps나 분사구문으로 써야 하므로 helping이 적절하다.

07 여러분이 '매일의 스트레스'를 이겨낼 필요가 있다면 여러분의 '세로토닌 수치'를 높이는 편이 낫겠다. 왜냐하면 그것이 여러분을 더 행복하고 더 건강하게 느끼도록 도와줄 수 있기 때문이다. may as well ~: ~하는 편이 낫다

08 '햇빛'을 가리킨다.

09 see의 목적어로 간접의문문(의문사+주어+동사) 순서로 쓰는 것이 적절하다.

10 여러분은 여름의 절정 시간인 11시에서 3시 사이에는 햇빛을 피하고 얼굴과 목을 보호하기 위해 '자외선 차단제'를 사용하면서, 하루에 10분에서 20분 동안 피부에 직사광선을 쪼임으로써 그것의 '많은 이점'을 '안전하게' 즐길 수 있다.

창의사고력 서술형 문제   p.52

|모범답안|

01 1. stress, happier   2. focus   3. sleep
   4. vitamin D, bones

02 (1) It is Paul that[who] is having breakfast.
   (2) It was Susan that[who] prepared breakfast.
   (3) It is ham and egg that[which] Paul is having.
   (4) It is in the kitchen that[where] they are.

03 (A) after going out   (B) wash your hands
   (C) direct sunlight   (D) 10 to 20 minutes
   (E) a good breakfast

01 deal with 처리하다, 해결하다 focus on 집중하다

02 강조하고자 하는 부분을 'It is[was]'와 that 사이에 넣고, 나머지 부분을 that 뒤에 쓴다.

단원별 모의고사   p.53~56

01 unhealthy   02 ③   03 ⑤

04 (1) mood   (2) outdoors   (3) peak   (4) properly

05 ②   06 ④   07 ③   08 ①

09 ②   10 ⑤

11 (1) I become richer, I am happier
   (2) the magnet is bigger, it is stronger
   (3) you practice more, your English speaking skills are better

12 (1) It is your smartphone that[which] you should put away.
   (2) It was not until I came to Korea that[when] I learned Hangeul.
   (3) It was for dessert that Jina had a chocolate cake.
   (4) It is Minji and Jian that[who] want to join the art club.

13 ④   14 ②, ④, ⑥, ⑦

15 (1) The longer I boil the soup, the better it tastes.
   (2) The better the weather is, the better I feel.
   (3) It was at school that[where] Layla met Jinho.
   (4) It is her father that[who/whom] Ella respects the most.

16 ②

17 The more sun you get, the more "happy hormone" the brain produces.

18 (When your serotonin level goes up,) you feel happier and stronger.

19 ①, ②, ④   20 ③   21 ②

22 Benefits   23 ③

01 두 단어의 관계는 반의어 관계이다. wide 넓은, narrow 좁은, healthy 건강한, unhealthy 건강하지 못한

02 "자신들에게 일어난 일을 규칙적으로 기록하는 책"은 "journal 일지, 일기"이다.

03 라일라는 외출 전에 항상 자외선 차단제를 바른다. / sunscreen 자외선 차단제 apply 바르다

04 (1) 그는 늘 기분이 안 좋다. (mood 기분) (2) 비 때문에 그들은 야외에서 식사를 하지 못했다. (outdoors 야외에서) (3) 호텔들이 성수기에는 항상 만원이 된다. (peak 최고조의) (4) 텔

레비전이 제대로 작동이 안 된다. (properly 제대로, 적절하게)

05 앞에서 담요가 비에 젖었다는 것으로 볼 때 날씨에 관해서 주의를 기울이지 않은 것에 대한 유감의 의미가 적절하다.

06 주어진 문장은 상대가 알려주는 새로운 사실에 대한 응답이므로 자연친화적인 방법에 대한 설명 다음인 (D)에 들어가는 것이 적절하다.

07 "Did you wash it?"이라는 질문에 No라고 대답하는 것으로 보아 여자는 담요를 빨지 않았다.

08 "you look full of energy today"에 대한 대답이기 때문에 잠을 잘 잤다는 내용이 적절하다. 밤에 잠을 잘 자는 것을 나타내는 표현이 "get a good night's sleep"이다.

09 ② 접속사 or로 이어지는 동사 "play"는 surfing과 병렬 관계에 있기 때문에 playing이 되어야 한다.

10 Ben이 등산을 다녀온 뒤에 잠을 잘 잤다는 말은 있지만, 어떤 야외 활동을 좋아하는지에 대한 언급은 없다.

11 'the 비교급, the 비교급' 구문은 'As+주어+동사+비교급 ~, 주어+동사+비교급 …'으로 바꿔 쓸 수 있다.

12 강조하고자 하는 부분을 시제에 맞춰 'It is[was]'와 that 사이에 넣고, 나머지 부분을 that 뒤에 쓴다. 이때 that 대신에 사람이면 who, 사물이면 which, 장소일 경우 where, 시간일 경우 when을 쓸 수 있다.

13 the 비교급+주어+동사 ~, the 비교급+주어+동사 …: ~할수록 …하다 bitter는 형용사로 '맛이 쓴, 격렬한'의 뜻이며 비교급은 'more bitter'이다.

14 ② The faster you go, the earlier you will reach your grandma's house. ④ It was the window that John broke. ⑥, ⑦ 'It ~ that …' 강조 구문은 동사나 양태부사를 강조하는 데 쓰이지 않는다.

15 (1), (2) the 비교급+주어+동사 ~, the 비교급+주어+동사 …: ~할수록 …하다 (3), (4) 강조하고자 하는 부분을 시제에 맞춰 'It is[was]'와 that 사이에 넣고, 나머지 부분을 that 뒤에 쓴다. 이때 that 대신에 사람이면 who, 사물이면 which, 장소일 경우 where, 시간일 경우 when을 쓸 수 있다.

16 선행사를 포함하는 관계대명사 'what'을 쓰는 것이 적절하다.

17 the 비교급 ~, the 비교급 …: ~할수록 …하다

18 '(여러분의 세로토닌 수치가 높아지면,) 여러분은 더 행복하고 더 건강하게 느끼는 것'을 가리킨다.

19 ⓐ와 ①, ②, ④: 동명사, ① get ahead of: [경쟁자 따위]를 앞지르다, 능가하다, ③, ⑤: 현재분사

20 이 글은 '햇빛의 많은 이점을 안전하게 즐길 수 있는 방법을 소개하고 있는 글'이므로, 주제로는 ③번 '햇빛의 많은 이점을 안전하게 즐길 수 있는 방법'이 적절하다.

21 하루에 10분에서 20분 동안 피부에 직사광선을 쪼이는 것은 햇빛으로부터 이점을 얻는 데 '충분하다.'

22 benefits: 혜택들, 이득들, 좋은 점들, 여러분이 어떤 것으로부터 얻는 도움이 되는 것들 또는 어떤 것의 결과로 나오는 이점들, helps: 도움이 되는[요긴한] 것들

23 햇빛을 충분히 쪼이면 밤에 잠을 '더 잘 잘 것이다.'

Safety First

시험대비 실력평가   p.60

01 exit   02 ⑤   03 put up   04 ②

05 ②   06 ③

07 (1) overeat   (2) exploded   (3) attention

01 주어진 관계는 반의어 관계이다. 젖은 : 마른 = 입구 : 출구

02 '강물이나 빗물이 넓은 땅을 덮고 있는 상황'을 가리키는 말은 flooding(홍수, 범람)이다.

03 put up: 설치하다, 세우다

04 place는 명사로는 '(경주•대회에서 입상권에 드는) 등위'를 의미하지만, 동사로는 '놓다, 두다'를 의미한다.

05 ②번 문장에서 apply는 '(크림 등을) 바르다'를 의미한다.

06 pass out: 의식을 잃다, 기절하다 / use up: ~을 다 써버리다

교과서 대화문 익히기

Check(√) True or False   p.64

1 F   2 T   3 F   4 T

교과서 확인학습   p.66~67

Listen & Speak 1 Listen

1. have to watch out

2. looks nice / to get to

3. wet / have to walk down

4. Let's climb, top / have to check, going to rain, should

Listen & Speak 1 A

1. play outside / Don't forget to / cloudy, have to put on / wear, every day / put, on

2. go bowling / go see a doctor / wrong / hurts

Listen & Speak 2 Listen

1. may fall / won't run

2. into, without warming up

3. to swim / how deep the water is, deeper than

4. right / with, uncomfortable

Listen & Speak 2 A

1. can cause, what to do, have to do, have to turn off, pack, Finally, safe place, keep listening to

2. ready to / yet, if, turned off / may not get to, in time / have to check

Real-Life Zone

look at, What, think / are, going / to meet / one, short ride / Put on, yourself / riding, without / have to wear, protects / fits, not / have to buy

Wrap Up

finish drinking / Why don't, sure that / suddenly, may spill / wait for, another bus

서술형 시험대비   p.61

01 irregularly

02 (1) earthquake   (2) memory   (3) lightning

03 (1) apply   (2) safety   (3) overflow   (4) entrance

04 Keep in mind what I told you.

05 rub

06 (1) keep away   (2) passed out   (3) put on
   (4) instead of

01 주어진 관계는 반의어 관계이다. 규칙적으로 : 불규칙적으로

02 (1) 지구 표면의 갑작스럽고 격렬한 흔들림: 지진 (2) 기억하고 있는 것: 기억 (3) 폭풍우가 몰아칠 때 여러분이 하늘에서 보는 밝은 빛: 번개

03 (1) 우리는 밖에 나가기 전에 자외선 차단제를 피부에 발라야 한다. (2) 우리는 다른 어떤 것보다 안전을 우선시해야 한다. (3) 비가 많이 오기 때문에 그 강은 범람할 수 있다. (4) 많은 사람들이 야구 경기장 입구에서 기다리고 있었다.

04 keep in mind: ~을 명심하다

05 손이나 물체를 어떤 표면 위로 누르고 움직이다 / rub: 비비다, 문지르다

06 (1) keep away: ~을 접근하지 못하게 하다 (2) pass out: 기절하다 (3) put on: ~을 바르다 (4) instead of: ~ 대신에

13

01 ③   02 (B) → (D) → (A) → (C)   03 ②

04 we may not get to the concert in time

01 have to는 '~해야 한다'는 의미로 의무를 나타내는 표현이다.

02 (B) 제안 → (D) 거절 → (A) 증상 묻기 → (C) 증상 말하기

03 if: ~인지 아닌지

04 may not: ~하지 못할 수도 있다, get to: ~에 도착하다, in time: 제 시간에, 늦지 않게

01 ④   02 Put on   03 ②, ④, ⑤   04 ⑤

05 ③   06 Do I have to put on sunscreen?

07 some sunscreen   08 ①

09 spill   10 ③   11 ②

12 Why don't we

13 I have to go see a doctor.

14 Because her stomach hurts.

01 주어진 문장의 It은 a helmet을 가리키므로 ④가 적절하다.

02 put on: ~을 쓰다

03 '~해야 한다'는 의미의 should, need to, have to 등이 들어가야 한다.

04 소년이 헬멧을 언제 살 것인지는 알 수 없다.

05 밖에 나가기 전에 선크림을 바르라는 당부의 말이 적절하다. Don't forget to+동사원형 ~.: ~할 것을 잊지 마라.

06 Do I have to ~?: 제가 ~해야 하나요?, put on: ~을 바르다, sunscreen: 선크림

07 some은 부정대명사로 some sunscreen을 가리킨다.

08 may는 '~할 수도 있다'는 의미로 추측을 나타낸다.

09 대개 실수로 용기의 가장자리로 어떤 것이 넘치거나 흐르거나 나오게 하다: spill(흘리다, 엎지르다, 쏟다)

10 소녀는 차를 다 마시고 버스를 탈 것이다.

11 식사 후 배부른 상태에서 수영하는 것이 편하다는 대답은 어색하다.

12 Let's ~.(~합시다)는 제안을 나타내는 표현으로 Why don't we ~?, How[What] about -ing? 등으로 바꿔 쓸 수 있다.

13 go see a doctor: 병원에 가다

14 소녀는 배가 아프기 때문에 병원에 가야 한다.

01 (A) → (D) → (B) → (C)

02 I have to finish drinking my tea

03 (A) if   (B) stops   (C) another

04 wait, drinks   05 (A) To   (B) on

06 You have to wear a helmet that fits you.

07 a helmet

01 (A) 떠날 준비를 했는지 묻자 → (D) 아직 준비가 안 되었다고 대답한다. → (B) 콘서트에 늦을까봐 걱정하자 → (C) 알겠다고 답하는 순서가 적절하다.

02 have to: ~해야 한다, finish+동명사: ~하는 것을 끝내다

03 (A) if: ~인지 아닌지 (B) 조건을 나타내는 if절에서는 미래시제 대신 현재시제를 쓴다. (C) another+단수명사

04 소년은 소녀가 그녀의 차를 다 마실 때까지 기다릴 수 있다고 했다.

05 (A) To: ~에, ~로 (B) put on: ~을 쓰다, ~을 입다

06 have to: ~해야 한다, a helmet that fits you: 너에게 맞는 헬멧

07 one은 부정대명사로 앞에 나온 a helmet을 가리킨다.

Grammar

1 (1) although   (2) eats

2 (1) It seems that you dance very well.

   (2) It seems that Sara likes you.

   (3) It seems that you are angry.

01 (1) Besides → Although[Even though, Though]

   (2) is → be

   (3) enjoying → enjoy

   (4) to → that

02 Even though I have a lot to do, I am doing nothing.
/ I am doing nothing even though I have a lot to do.

03 ③

04 (1) Even though this cup is beautiful, it has a crack on the side. / This cup has a crack on the side even though it is beautiful.

   (2) Rose seemed to go to bed late. / It seemed that Rose went to bed late.

   (3) Alex seems to be depressed these days. / It seems that Alex is depressed these days.

01 (1) 종속절과 주절이 서로 대조적인 의미를 나타내므로 Besides가 아니라 Although가 적절하다. (2), (3) 'seem to 부정사' 구문. (4) seem to부정사 = It seems that 주어 동사

02 부사절 접속사 even though를 활용하여 연결한다.

03 'seem to부정사'이므로 ③이 적절하다.

04 (1) Even though 주어 동사, 주어 동사: 비록 ~하더라도 …하다 (2), (3) seem+to부정사 = seem that 주어 동사: ~인 것처럼 보이다

01 Despite → Although[Though]   02 ⑤

03 (1) He seems to be lonely. / It seems that he is lonely.

  (2) She seems to be happy. / It seems that she is happy.

  (3) Sally seems to be in a hurry. / It seems that Sally is in a hurry.

  (4) It seemed that the computer didn't work at all.

04 ③   05 ①   06 ①   07 ①

08 (1) Although there was a loud noise, the baby did not wake up.

  (2) Although he disliked movies, he went to the movies with his girlfriend to please her.

09 ④   10 (1) to be (2) that   11 ③

12 (1) she is three years old / she can read and write

  (2) they haven't won any games this season / they're fantastic

  (3) you put on two or three jumpers / You're still going to be cold

13 ①   14 ①, ②   15 ③   16 ①, ③

17 (1) rich, not 또는 him, he (2) have

  (3) have (4) despite 또는 day

01 문제에서 Despite 뒤에 주어와 동사가 나와 있으므로 접속사가 필요하다는 것을 알 수 있다. 그러므로 Despite 대신 Although[Though]가 적절하다.

02 'seem to부정사' 구문을 'It seems/seemed that' 구문으로 바꾼 것이다. 각 빈칸에 that이 들어가는 것이 적절하다. • Jay는 대답을 알고 있는 것처럼 보인다. • 그는 곧 떠날 것처럼 보인다.

03 seem to부정사 = It seems/seemed 주어 동사

04 ① 아빠는 화나 보이신다. ② 그들은 곧 돌아올 것처럼 보인다. ③ Kidson은 그녀의 헤어스타일을 맘에 들어 하지 않는 것 같다. seem → seem to ④ 그는 아무런 계획이 없는 것 같다. ⑤ 그녀는 가족을 그리워하고 있는 것 같다.

05 그는 아주 바빴던 것처럼 보인다. 'It seems[seemed] that 주어 과거동사'는 '주어 seem(s/ed) to have been'으로 바꿔 쓸 수 있다.

06 그는 90세인데도 정신적인 기능이 아직 약화되지 않았다. 빈칸 뒤에 절이 있고, 이어서 주절이 나왔으므로 빈칸에는 접속사가 들어가야 한다. 종속절과 주절이 의미상 대조를 이루므로 although가 적절하다.

07 • 뛰어가도 너는 여전히 늦을 거야. • 이상하게 들릴지 모르겠지만, 나는 게임이 끝나서 기뻤다. 단독으로 또는 even과 함께 양보의 뜻으로 쓰이는 접속사는 though이다.

08 'although 주어 동사, 주어 동사' 구문으로 쓰는 것이 적절하다.

09 ④ It seemed that they had known what to do to make their camping trip safe. 완료부정사가 나왔으므로 주절의 시제보다 하나 앞선 시제가 되어야 한다.

10 ' 주어 seem(s/ed) to부정사' 또는 'It seems[seemed] that 주어+동사'의 형태로 쓴다.

11 '주어 seem(s/ed) to부정사'의 형태로 쓰며 주어가 Harry and Catherine으로 복수이므로 seem이 적절하다.

12 (1) 비록 그녀는 3살이지만 읽고 쓸 줄 안다. (2) 나는 그들이 이번 시즌에 어떤 경기도 이기지 못했음에도 불구하고 그들이 환상적이라고 생각한다. (3) 너는 점퍼를 두세 벌 입어도 여전히 추울 거다.

13 그는 정직한 사람처럼 보인다. 'seem to부정사' 구문으로 be가 적절하다.

14 Although 주어+동사 ~, 주어+동사. / Though 주어+동사, 주어+동사 ~: 비록 ~하지만 …한다.

15 • 그녀는 모든 것에 대해 걱정하는 것처럼 보인다. • Kevin은 그의 새 학교를 마음에 들어 하는 것 같아 보인다. • 아이들은 배고파 보였다.

16 ① 그 재킷은 숨겨진 주머니가 있는 것 같다. It seems that the jacket has a hidden pocket.이 적절하다. ② 너 열나는 것 같아. ③ 나는 열쇠 꾸러미를 잘 못 들고 나온 것 같았다. It seems that I picked up the wrong set of keys.가 절적하다. ④ 너는 이런 소문에 대해 많이 알고 있는 것 같다. ⑤ 그는 이 제안에 동의할 것 같지 않다.

17 어법에 맞게 배열하면, (1) Even though he is rich, I will not marry him. 또는 I will not marry him even though he is rich. (2) I seem to have a cold. (3) I seem to have forgotten something. (4) They enjoyed their day at the zoo, despite the bad weather. 또는 Despite the bad weather, they enjoyed their day at the zoo.

01 (1) seem to cry all the time / seems that they cry all the time

  (2) seems to get along with bad guys / seems that she gets along with bad guys

  (3) didn't seem to enjoy the movie

(4) seemed that nothing could stop the team this year

(5) seemed that she was disappointed

02 (1) He seems to be ill. / It seems that he is ill.

(2) They seem to know everything. / It seems that they know everything.

(3) It seems that he was not there.

(4) It seems that he was poisoned.

03 Although cars crashed(또는 Altough there was a car crash), no lives were lost.

04 seem to enjoy themselves

05 (1) seems to be

(2) seem to have

(3) seem to know

(4) seem to have

06 (1) It seems that

(2) It seems that

07 (1) It seems that she was angry last night.

(2) He seems to have fallen in love with the girl.

08 seems to be cold

09 (1) Although it rained, they played soccer outside. 또는 They played soccer outside although it rained.

(2) Although my younger brother ate food, he was still hungry. 또는 My younger brother was still hungry although he ate food.

(3) Although I didn't sleep much last night, I'm not tired. 또는 I'm not tired although I didn't sleep much last night.

(4) Although she was busy, she would never ask for help. 또는 She would never ask for help although she was busy.

10 Though, don't like, agree, agree, though, don't like

01 '~인 것처럼 보인다.'는 '주어 seem(s/ed) to부정사' 또는 'It seems(ed) that 주어 동사'이다.

02 '~인 것처럼 보인다'는 '주어 seem(s/ed) to부정사' 또는 'It seems(ed) that 주어 동사'이다.

03 although가 이끄는 부사절과 주절이 서로 상반된 내용이다.

04 주어+seem+to부정사

05 to부정사를 활용한 '~인 것처럼 보인다.'는 '주어 seem to부정사'로 쓴다.

06 주어와 동사가 있는 절이 나와 있으므로 'It seems(ed) that 주어 동사'로 쓴다.

07 (1) 어젯밤 그녀는 매우 화가 났던 것처럼 보인다. (2) 그는 그녀와 사랑에 빠졌던 것처럼 보인다.

08 날씨가 매우 추워 보인다.

09 Although+주어+동사 ~, 주어+동사: 비록 ~이지만 …하다.

10 Though가 이끄는 부사절과 주절의 내용은 서로 상반된다.

Reading

확인문제   p.80

1 F   2 T   3 T   4 F   5 T

확인문제   p.81

1 T   2 F   3 T   4 T   5 F   6 T

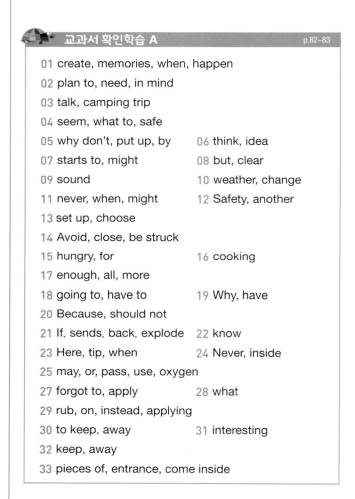

교과서 확인학습 A p.82-83

01 create, memories, when, happen

02 plan to, need, in mind

03 talk, camping trip

04 seem, what to, safe

05 why don't, put up, by   06 think, idea

07 starts to, might   08 but, clear

09 sound   10 weather, change

11 never, when, might   12 Safety, another

13 set up, choose

14 Avoid, close, be struck

15 hungry, for   16 cooking

17 enough, all, more

18 going to, have to   19 Why, have

20 Because, should not

21 If, sends, back, explode   22 know

23 Here, tip, when   24 Never, inside

25 may, or, pass, use, oxygen

27 forgot to, apply   28 what

29 rub, on, instead, applying

30 to keep, away   31 interesting

32 keep, away

33 pieces of, entrance, come inside

교과서 확인학습 B p.84-85

1 Although camping trips can create sweet memories for many people, they can also be occasions when bad things happen.

2 If you plan to go camping with family or friends

this summer, you need to keep several things in mind for your safety.

3 Listen to Yumin's family talk about their camping trip.

4 They seem to know what to do to make their camping trip safe and fun.

5 Yumin: Dad, why don't we put up our tent over here by this river?

6 Dad: I don't think that's a good idea.

7 If it starts to rain, the river might overflow.

8 Yumin: I know, but the sky is clear.

9 I really like the sound of the water!

10 Dad: The weather can change quickly in the mountains.

11 You never know when it might start to rain.

12 Yumin: Okay. Safety first! Let's find another place.

13 When you set up a tent, choose a flat, sunny area.

14 Avoid places too close to big trees that might be struck by lightning.

15 Hajun: Mom, I'm hungry. What's for lunch?

16 Mom: I'm cooking Samgyepsal.

17 Hajun: Mom, that's not enough for all of us. Can we cook more in a bigger pan?

18 Mom: I'm going to cook more, but we have to use this small pan.

19 Hajun: Why do we have to use a small pan?

20 Mom: Because the pan should not be bigger than the burner.

21 If you use a big pan, it sends the heat back to the burner, and the gas can explode!

22 Hajun: Oh, I didn't know that.

23 Here is one more tip about fire when you go camping.

24 Never use a gas heater or burner inside a tent.

25 Your tent may catch fire, or you might pass out because the fire will use up the oxygen in the tent as it burns.

26 Yumin: Ouch! Mosquitoes!

27 Mom: Oh, I forgot to tell you to apply some bug spray. Here.

28 Yumin: Thanks, Mom. Oh, you know what?

29 We can rub orange peels on our skin instead of applying bug spray.

30 It is a nature-friendly way to keep mosquitoes away.

31 Mom: That's interesting!

32 Garlic can also keep bugs away.

33 You can place pieces of garlic at the entrance to the tent, and bugs will not come inside.

---

01 선행사가 occasions이므로 관계부사 when이 적절하다.

02 keep ~ in mind: ~을 명심하다

03 유민의 가족이 자주 캠핑을 가는지는 알 수 없다.

04 주어진 문장은 산에서는 날씨가 급격히 변할 수 있다는 뜻이므로 언제 비가 올지도 모른다는 문장 앞에 와야 한다.

05 that은 지시대명사로 앞에 나온 문장의 내용을 받을 수 있다.

06 강 옆은 비가 올지 몰라 위험하다는 내용이므로 '안전이 우선이다!'라는 문장이 가장 적절하다.

07 enough for ~: ~에게 충분한

08 어떤 것이 요란하게 그리고 맹렬한 기세로 터져 종종 손실이나 부상을 입히는 것은 '폭발하다(explode)'이다.

09 접속사 앞뒤의 문장이 상반되는 내용이므로 (A)는 but이 적절하다. (B)는 문맥상 작은 팬이 적절하고, (C)는 조건을 나타내는 접속사가 적절하다.

10 하준이가 왜 배가 고픈지는 알 수 없다.

11 go camping: 캠핑하러 가다

12 ⓑ, ①, ③, ⑤는 추측을 나타내고, ②, ④는 허가를 나타낸다.

13 use up: ~을 다 써버리다

14 '~할 것을 잊다'는 'forget+to부정사'가 알맞다.

15 '그거 알아요?, 있잖아요.'라고 상대방이 모르는 새로운 주제를 꺼낼 때에는 You know what?의 표현을 쓴다.

16 ⓐ, ② 형용사적 용법 ①, ⑤ 명사적 용법 ③, ④ 부사적 용법

17 유민이의 엄마가 벌레 퇴치 스프레이를 뿌렸는지는 알 수 없다.

19 빈칸 (A)와 ①, ②, ③, ⑤번에는 although가 적절하다. ④번에는 조건의 접속사 if가 알맞다.

20 keep ~ in mind: ~을 명심하다

21 safe의 명사형으로 고쳐야 한다.

22 '의문사+to부정사'는 '의문사+주어+should+동사원형'으로 바꿔 쓸 수 있다.

23 ⑤ 유민이의 가족은 안전하고 재미있는 캠핑을 할 수 있는 법을 아는 것 같다고 위 글에서 언급되었다.

24 주어진 문장은 상대방의 의견에 반대하는 내용이므로 강가에 텐트를 치자는 문장의 대답인 ②에 와야 한다.

25 ⓓ other 뒤에는 복수명사가 오므로 another로 고쳐야 한다.

26 ④ 산에서 왜 날씨가 갑자기 변하는 지는 알 수 없다.

17

01 hungry

02 I'm going to cook more, but we have to use this small pan.

03 Because

04 버너보다 더 큰 팬을 사용하면 팬이 버너로 열을 도로 보내서 가스가 폭발할 수 있는 것

05 Here is one more tip about fire when you go camping.

06 catch   07 of

08 벌레 퇴치 스프레이를 뿌리는 대신에 오렌지 껍질을 피부에 문지르는 것

09 She forgot to tell Yumin to apply some bug spray.

10 memories

11 in which   12 seems that, know

13 유민이의 가족은 캠핑 여행을 안전하고 재미있게 하는 방법을 아는 것처럼 보인다.

01 얼마 동안 먹지 않아서 위에 불편하거나 고통스러운 느낌이 있어서 음식을 먹기를 원하는: hungry(배가 고픈)

02 be going to와 have to, 그리고 much의 비교급 more를 이용한다.

03 이유를 나타내는 접속사 Because가 알맞다.

04 that은 지시대명사로 앞에 나온 문장을 받을 수 있다.

05 조언이 하나 더: one more tip

06 catch fire: 불이 붙다

07 instead of ~ing: ~하는 대신에 pieces of garlic: 몇 조각의 마늘

08 That은 지시대명사로 앞 문장의 내용을 받는다.

09 유민이의 어머니는 유민에게 벌레 퇴치 스프레이를 뿌리라고 말하는 것을 잊었다.

10 과거로부터 기억하는 어떤 것: memory(추억)

11 관계부사 when을 '전치사+관계대명사 which'로 바꿔 쓴다. 선행사가 occasions이므로 전치사는 in을 쓴다.

12 'seem to부정사'는 'It seems that ~' 구문으로 바꿔 쓸 수 있다.

01 ④   02 garlic   03 keep

04 (1) out (2) up (3) away (4) on

05 (1) overuse (2) overwork (3) overeat

06 Remember 07 ⑤   08 wear

09 a helmet 10 ⑤   11 ⑤   12 ④

13 (1) The tickets seemed to have got lost.

  (2) Although[Though] the sun was shining, it wasn't very warm.

(3) The children always seem to be hungry.

(4) Although[Though] he's nearly 80, he is still very active.

14 ①   15 I don't mind even if she doesn't come.

16 Although the kitchen is small, it is well designed.
또는 Although small, the kitchen is well designed.

17 (1) didn't love him, though

  (2) is coming to stay next week although

18 is very young / acts like an old man

19 seems to be happy / seems to be sad

20 (1) millionaire, lives in

  (2) went out, was raining

21 despite   22 let's   23 ②, ④   24 ②

25 비가 내리기 시작하면 강이 범람할 위험이 있기 때문이다.

26 여러분이 지진으로부터 자유롭다고 생각하는 것

27 ③   28 ③   29 ②

30 Location 31 ①   32 exciting   33 ⑤

01 폭탄이 폭발하는 소리를 들었을 때 나는 경찰에게 전화를 걸었다. explode: 폭발하다

02 강한 맛을 내기 위해 요리에 사용되는 작은 양파 같은 식물에 해당하는 단어는 garlic(마늘)이다.

03 keep ~ in mind: ~을 명심하다 / 케이트, 이 교훈을 명심해라. keep 동사ing: ~을 계속하다, 반복하다 / 그녀가 그에게 설거지하라고 말해서 그는 계속해서 TV를 볼 수 없었다.

04 (1) hang out: 어울려 놀다 / 난 방과 후에 친구들이랑 자주 어울려 논다. (2) use up: ~을 다 써 버리다 / 불이 타면서 텐트 내 산소를 다 써 버릴 것입니다. (3) keep away: ~을 접근하지 못하게 하다 / 그는 Billy에게 자신의 딸에게 접근하지 말라고 경고했다. (4) put on: ~을 바르다 / 밖에 나가기 전에, 선크림을 바르는 것을 잊지 마세요.

05 (1) overuse: 너무 많이 사용하다 / 컴퓨터를 너무 많이 사용하는 것은 좋지 않다. (2) overwork: 과로하다 / 건강에 유념하시고, 너무 과로하지 마세요. (3) overeat: 과식하다 / 아침을 거르면 점심에 과식하기 쉽다.

06 Don't forget to+동사원형 ~.은 Remember to+동사원형 ~.으로 바꿔 쓸 수 있다.

07 ⑤를 제외한 나머지는 의무를 나타내는 표현이다. ⑤ 제가 선크림을 발라도 될까요?

08 wear: ~을 바르다

09 one은 부정대명사로 앞에 나온 'a+단수명사'를 받는다.

10 주어진 문장의 If not은 If you don't wear a helmet that fits you를 대신하는 말이므로 ⑤가 적절하다.

11 for의 목적어가 주어 자신이므로 재귀대명사를 쓴다.

12 소년이 자전거를 타다가 다쳤다는 내용은 언급되지 않았다.

13 (1), (3) 주어 seem to부정사 (2) 주어와 동사가 이어지므

로 Despite를 Although[Though]로 고쳐야 한다. (4) 부사절과 주절의 내용이 상반되므로 Because가 아니라 Although[Though]가 적절하다.

14 ① 그는 비록 경험은 가장 적지만 가장 훌륭한 선생님이다. ② 그녀는 여유가 될 때에도 절대 택시를 타지 않았다. even → even though ③ 나는 슬프지만 그들 앞에서 울 수는 없지. Because → Even though ④ 그건 거저 줘도 싫어. Even → Even if ⑤ 비록 갈 수 있다 하더라도 난 안 갈 것이다. if → even if

15 '그녀가 오지 않더라도'라는 가정이 들어가기 때문에 even if가 사용된 문장이다.

16 although가 이끄는 부사절과 주절의 내용은 상반된 의미를 갖는다.

17 although, though가 이끄는 부사절과 주절의 내용은 상반된 의미를 갖는다.

18 although가 쓰인 문장은 부사절과 주절 간 상반된 의미의 내용이 온다.

19 거북은 경기에 이겨서 행복해 보인다. 토끼는 경기에 져서 슬퍼 보인다.

20 although와 even though는 '~임에도 불구하고'라는 뜻으로 부사절과 주절 간에 상반된 내용이 온다.

21 despite는 전치사이므로 뒤에 명사가 오고 although는 '주어+동사'가 온다.

22 Why don't we ~?는 제안을 나타내는 말로 Let's ~로 시작하는 표현으로 바꿔 쓸 수 있다.

23 ⓑ, ①, ③, ⑤는 추측을 나타내고, ②, ④는 허가를 나타낸다.

24 ② 유민이의 아빠는 위험하다고 유민이의 의견에 반대한다.

26 that은 지시대명사로 앞 문장의 내용을 받는다.

27 문맥상 '흔들림이 멈출 때까지'이므로 until이 알맞다.

28 문맥상 가스와 전기를 끄라고 해야 하므로 turn on을 turn off로 고쳐야 한다.

29 ② 흔들림이 멈출 때까지 집안에 머물고, 또 밖으로 나갈 때는 무엇인가 떨어질지도 모르므로 주의하라고 언급되었다.

30 어떤 것이 일어나거나 위치하는 장소: location(장소, 위치)

31 문맥상 '처음에는 급류 타기가 무서웠다'이므로 at last가 알맞다.

32 사물이 사람을 흥미진진하게 하는 것이므로 현재분사형의 형용사가 알맞다.

33 ⑤ 기회가 있다면 다시 가겠다고 하였다.

단원별 예상문제 p.98~101

01 shallow   02 (1) up (2) keep
03 overflow   04 ③
05 (1) try (2) stay (3) put (4) close
06 ④   07 ⑤   08 ①

---

09 drinking   10 ③
11 I'm sure that another bus will come soon.
12 (F)looding 13 ③
14 There are several things you have to do.
15 (1) Although (2) Despite (3) Although
(4) Although (5) Despite (6) Despite
16 Although Jamin studied hard, he didn't do well on the test.
17 ①
18 (1) He seems to know the test result.
(2) It seems that they are satisfied with the test result.
(3) It seems that everyone is looking at my face.
(4) Suji seems to have breakfast every day.
19 ②   20 (A) more (B) bigger
21 버너보다 더 큰 팬을 사용하면 팬이 열을 버너로 다시 보내어 가스가 폭발하는 것
22 ④   23 ③   24 ③
25 an earthquake   26 you can

01 주어진 단어는 반의어 관계이다. 안전 : 위험, 깊은 : 얕은
02 (1) use up: ~을 다 써버리다, put up: ~을 설치하다 (2) keep in mind: ~을 명심하다, keep ~ away: ~을 접근하지 못하게 하다
03 어떤 것의 언저리나 꼭대기 너머로 흐르다: overflow: 넘쳐흐르다, 범람하다
04 (A) instead of: ~ 대신에 (B) although: ~임에도 불구하고, 비록 ~이지만 / Despite와 In spite of는 전치사이므로 뒤에 명사나 동명사가 올 수 있다.
05 (1) try to 동사원형: ~하려고 애쓰다 (2) stay up late: 늦게까지 자지 않고 있다 (3) put on: ~을 바르다 (4) close to: ~에 가까운
06 flooding: 홍수
07 turn off: [가스·라디오·텔레비전을] 끄다
08 get to: ~에 도착하다
09 finish는 동명사를 목적어로 취한다.
10 차를 가지고 버스를 탔을 때 주의하면 괜찮을 거라고 확신한다는 내용이 적절하므로 careful(주의 깊은)이 알맞다.
11 I'm sure that ~.은 '나는 ~라고 확신해.'라는 의미이다. another+단수명사
12 위 글은 홍수가 발생했을 때의 행동 요령에 관한 글이다.
13 unpack → pack / 집을 떠날 때 물과 음식을 꾸려야 한다는 내용이 적절하다. unpack: (짐을) 풀다
14 There are ~. ~들이 있다, have to: ~해야 한다

15 although와 despite는 모두 '~임에도 불구하고'라는 의미를 가지지만, although는 부사절 접속사로 뒤에 '주어+동사'가 이어지고 despite는 전치사로 뒤에 명사가 이어진다. (1) 나는 열심히 공부했지만 시험에 떨어졌다. (2) 나쁜 날씨에도 불구하고, 우리는 소풍을 가기로 했던 계획을 이행하기로 결정했다 .(3) Jay는 일찍 일어났지만 평소보다 집에서 늦게 출발했다. (4) Jay는 우산을 가지고 왔지만, 여전히 비를 맞았다. (5) 우리의 염려에도 불구하고 모든 것이 잘 해결됐다. (6) 그의 울부 짖음에도 불구하고 아무도 그를 도우러 오지 않았다.

16 Although 주어 동사, 주어 동사

17 ① 비록 비싸더라도 난 그것을 사고 말 거야. although로 이끌리는 부사절과 주절 간에는 상반된 내용이 나오므로 '그것을 사고 말 것이다'와 상반되는 '못사는 상황의 내용'이 나오는 것이 적절하므로 cheap을 expensive로 고치는 것이 적절하다. ② 시험은 비록 떨어졌지만 포기하지 않을 거야. ③ 더운 날씨인데도 코트를 입고 있구나. ④ 비록 그는 모든 것을 잃었지만 난 여전히 그를 사랑합니다. ⑤ 불경기에도 불구하고 수요가 늘고 있다.

18 '~인 것처럼 보인다'는 '주어 seem(s/ed) that 주어 동사' 또는 'It seems(ed) that 주어 동사'로 나타낸다.

19 음식이 우리 모두에게 충분하지 않다는 말 다음인 ②에 와야 한다.

20 각각 much와 big의 비교급이 와야 한다.

21 that은 지시대명사로 앞에 나온 문장의 내용을 받는다.

22 ④ 하준의 엄마는 더 요리할 것이라고 말했다.

23 (A) although: 비록 ~이지만 (B) but: 그러나

24 문맥상 지진으로부터 '안전할' 수 있다가 자연스럽다.

25 it은 인칭대명사로 앞에 나온 단수명사를 받는다.

26 'as ~ as possible'은 'as ~ as 주어+can'으로 바꿔 쓸 수 있다.

01 Put on

02 I see a lot of people riding bikes without helmets

03 He is going to the park to meet a friend.

04 Because it protects our head in an accident.

05 (1) It seems that they love each other. /
   They seem to love each other.
   (2) It seems that they loved each other. /
   They seem to have loved each other.
   (3) It seems that Reina raises a cat at home. /
   Reina seems to raise a cat at home.
   (4) It seems that Reina raised a cat at home.
   Reina seems to have raised a cat at home.

06 (1) Although, has a headache / has a headache, although

(2) seem to prepare / seems that they prepare

07 During   08 up

09 I will never forget how much fun we had.

10 They baked potatoes.   11 to tell

12 applying   13 entrance

01 어떤 것을 옷, 장식 또는 보호로써 몸에 지니고 있다: put up(입다, 쓰다, 신다)

02 see+목적어+목적격보어: ~가 …하는 것을 보다

03 소년은 친구를 만나러 공원에 가고 있다.

04 사고가 났을 때 머리를 보호해 주기 때문이다.

05 (1)과 (3)은 문장 내에서 시제의 차이가 없으므로 '주어 seem(s/ed) to부정사' 또는 'It seems that 주어 동사'로 쓴다. (2)와 (4)는 문장 내에서 시제의 차이가 있으므로 완료부정사를 써야 한다.

06 (1) 그는 어젯밤 잘 잤지만 머리가 아프다. (2) 그들은 음식을 준비하는 것처럼 보인다.

07 기간을 나타내는 특정한 명사가 오므로 during이 알맞다. while 뒤에는 주어와 동사를 포함하는 부사절이 온다.

08 stay up: 깨어 있다

09 how much fun we had: 우리가 얼마나 즐겁게 지냈는지

11 forget+~ing: ~한 것을 잊다(과거의 일) forget+to부정사: ~할 것을 잊다(미래의 일)

12 전치사의 목적어이므로 동명사형이 되어야 한다.

13 어떤 장소로 들어가는 길, 예를 들면 문이나 정문: entrance(출입구)

|모범답안|

01 what I like about the product / They are very comfortable, so I wear them often / what I don't like about the product / The color of the shoes is white, so they get dirty easily / satisfied with / four stars

02 (2) → (1) → (4) → (6) → (5) → (7) → (3) → (8)

01 put   02 overuse   03 peel   04 ③
05 (C) – (B) – (D) – (A)   06 (c)ause
07 listening

08 첫째, 수도와 전기를 꺼야 한다. 둘째, 집을 떠날 때 물과 음식을 꾸려야 한다. 마지막으로, 높고 안전한 곳으로

이동하여 일기 예보를 계속 들어야 한다.

09 ④　　　　　　　10 ①

11 (1) seem to　(2) seems to

　　(3) Although 또는 Even though

　　(4) Although 또는 Even though

12 Even if he gets accepted to Harvard, he won't be able to afford the tuition. / You should always exercise even if it's only 10 minutes a day. / Even if the government survives this crisis, they still face big problems. / He's going to buy the farm even if the government raises the price.

13 ④

14 Even though he was born in America, he is a Korean son.

15 tried to, to have been

16 ②　　　　　17 ①　　　　　18 sunny

19 Because they might be struck by lightning.

20 ③　　　　　21 of　　　　　22 ②

23 벌레 퇴치 스프레이를 뿌리는 대신에 오렌지 껍질을 피부에 문지르는 것

24 ①　　　　　25 ③　　　　　26 ④

01 put up: 설치하다, put on: ~을 바르다

02 '어떤 것을 너무 많이 또는 자주 사용하다'는 'overuse (남용하다, 너무 많이 사용하다)'가 적절하다. 약을 남용하지 않도록 해라.

03 '과일의 껍질'은 peel이 적절하다. 나는 바나나 껍질을 밟고 미끄러졌다.

04 ① flat: 평평한 ② pan: 냄비 ③ overflow: 흘러넘치다, 범람하다 ④ memory: 기억, 추억 ⑤ avoid: 피하다

05 밖에 나가 놀아도 되는지 묻자 - (C) 허락하며 선크림을 바를 것을 당부한다. (B) 선크림을 발라야만 하는지 묻자 - (D) 매일 발라야 한다고 대답한다. - (A) 알겠다며 선크림을 바르겠다는 순서가 적절하다.

06 어떤 것이 발생하거나 존재하게 하다: cause(야기하다)

07 keep -ing: 계속해서 ~하다

09 • 걸어가야 한다 해도 나는 거기에 갈 것이다. • 비록 그는 나에게 거짓말을 했지만 난 그를 믿어.

10 미국에 살고 있지만 영어를 말하는 데에 어려움을 겪고 있다. even though 부사절과 주절 간의 내용은 서로 상반되므로 주절의 '영어를 말하는 데 어려움을 겪고 있다'는 내용과 반대 의미를 지니려면 live가 적절하다.

11 (1), (2) '~인 것 같다', '~처럼 보인다'는 'seem to'를 사용한다. (3), (4) '비록 ~이지만'은 although[though] 또는 even though 등을 쓴다.

12 • 하버드에서 그를 받아주더라도, 그는 수업료를 감당하지 못할 것이다. • 하루에 10분이라도 넌 운동해야 한다. • 정부가 간신히 위기를 넘기더라도 그들은 여전히 수 많은 문제에 직면해 있다. • 정부가 가격을 올리더라도 그는 농장을 살 것이다.

13 ④ '주어+동사'가 이어지므로 Despite를 Although 또는 Even though로 바꿔야 한다.

14 부사절의 내용은 '태어났지만'이고 주절은 '대한민국의 아들이다'이므로 even though를 사용하여 '미국에서 태어났지만'을 쓰고, 주절에는 '그는 대한민국의 아들이다'를 쓴다.

15 엄마는 다림질을 시도했지만 잘 되지 않았다. 다리미는 고장 난 것처럼 보인다. 시제가 앞서므로 완료부정사를 이용한다.

16 ② make의 목적보어이므로 형용사 safe가 적절하다.

17 (A) '무엇을 해야 할지'이므로 what to do가 알맞다. (B) '우리 ~하는 게 어때요?'이므로 Why don't we ~?가 알맞다.

18 sun의 형용사형은 sunny이다.

19 큰 나무들은 번개를 맞을지도 모르므로 피하라고 하였다.

20 주어진 문장은 '아, 그거 아세요?'의 뜻으로 새로운 사실을 언급할 때 흔히 쓰이므로 ③에 와야 한다.

21 instead of: ~하는 대신에 pieces of garlic: 마늘 몇 조각

22 ⑧, ② 형용사적 용법 ①, ④ 명사적 용법 ③, ⑤ 부사적 용법

23 that은 지시대명사로 앞에 나온 문장의 내용을 받는다.

24 ① '이틀간의 캠핑 여행'이란 뜻으로 two-day가 camping trip을 수식하는 것이므로 단수형인 two-day가 적절하다.

25 (A)와 ③의 may는 '~일지도 모르다'의 뜻으로 약한 추측을 나타낸다.

26 so (that) 주어+can ~: ~하기 위해서

Coach Carter

교과서
Reading

확인문제   p.112

1 T   2 F   3 T   4 F   5 T   6 F

확인문제   p.113

1 T   2 F   3 F   4 T   5 T

확인문제   p.114

1 T   2 T   3 F   4 F   5 F

교과서 확인학습 A   p.115~117

01 Welcome to
02 going to talk
03 imagine, allow, to practice
04 what, does
05 cares, about, about winning games
06 one, after another
07 became used to losing
08 To make, worse, only to play
09 new coach
10 to change
11 how to play
12 more than, by sending
13 To carry out, contract
14 had to, in addition to
15 At first, seriously
16 give you a contract
17 Attend, be late
18 all these rules
19 signing bonus
20 because, as well as
21 With, in many years
22 From, point on, after
23 except
24 part of
25 Few of, paid little attention to
26 take, action
27 let, play, until, improved, as
28 it
29 that, just, not
30 basketball team
31 All we see
32 If, yourself, better life
33 to help
34 have to
35 either
36 demand, ordered, to reopen

37 Disappointed, decided to
38 When, to pack, were
39 what happens next
40 Find out, by watching

교과서 확인학습 B   p.118~120

1 Welcome to *Movie Trip*.
2 Today we're going to talk about the movie *Coach Carter*.
3 Can you imagine a basketball coach who doesn't allow his players to practice?
4 That's exactly what Coach Carter does.
5 This movie is about a coach who cares more about his students than about winning games.
6 The basketball team at Richmond High School in Richmond, California, was having one losing season after another.
7 The players became used to losing.
8 To make matters worse, they had no plans for the future; they went to school only to play basketball, and they did not do that very well.
9 Then they got a new coach, Kenny Carter.
10 Coach Carter wanted to change things.
11 He wanted to teach kids how to play basketball well and win.
12 But more than that, he wanted to give the players a future by sending them to college.
13 To carry out his plan, Coach Carter had the players sign a contract.
14 They had to promise to study hard in addition to playing basketball.
15 At first, students did not take his idea for a contract seriously.
16 Carter: I'm going to give you a contract.
17 Cruz: "Attend all classes," "Get a C⁺ or higher," "Don't be late...."
18 What are all these rules about?
19 Do I get a signing bonus for signing this contract?
20 Carter: Yes. You will get a big bonus because you will become a winner in the game of basketball as well as in the game of life.
21 With hard work and a new game plan, the team began to win for the first time in many years.
22 From that point on, they won game after game.
23 Everybody, except Coach Carter, was happy.
24 The players did not do the "study" part of their contract.

25 Few of them actually believed they could go to college, so they paid little attention to their grades.

26 Carter decided to take stronger action.

27 He locked the gym and refused to let them play basketball until their grades improved, as promised in the contract.

28 The players did not like it.

29 They told him that his actions were just for him, not for them.

30 Worm: We're the basketball team.

31 All we see is you on TV, getting famous.

32 Carter: If you think so, go home and ask yourself, "Do I want a better life?"

33 If the answer is yes, I will do everything in my power to help you.

34 But you have to do your part.

35 The players' parents did not like Carter's decision either.

36 At the parents' demand, the principal ordered Carter to reopen the gym.

37 Disappointed, Carter decided to leave Richmond High.

38 When he entered the gym to pack his things, however, all of his players were there.

39 We want you to enjoy the movie, so we won't tell you what happens next.

40 Find out for yourself by watching the movie *Coach Carter*.

서술형 실전문제

p.121~123

01 unlock

02 (1) for the first time (2) carry out (3) take action
    (4) one after another

03 (1) sign (2) contract (3) except

04 (1) improve (2) attend (3) order (4) pack

05 (1) when (2) to wash (3) too

06 (1) Mr. Brown let his son go to the party.
    (2) The project manager had us meet at 9 a.m.
    (3) They made me repeat the whole story.
    (4) She helped me to complete this assignment.

07 (1) What I want to do for the community is to pick up trash.
    (2) I liked what Yuna gave to me last month.
    (3) Did you enjoy what we saw at the movie theater last night?

08 He has experience as well as knowledge.

09 ⓐ out ⓑ to   10 seriously

11 what   12 winning

13 To make matters worse

14 그들은 농구를 별로 잘하지 못했다

15 how

16 (1) 아이들에게 농구를 잘해서 이기는 법을 가르치기를 원했다.
    (2) 아이들을 대학에 보내서 그들에게 미래를 주기를 원했다.

17 after   18 little

19 Because the players did not do the "study" part of their contract.

20 Carter는 체육관을 잠그고 선수들의 성적이 향상될 때까지 농구를 못하게 했다.

01 주어진 관계는 반의어 관계이다. lock: 잠그다 : unlock: 열다

02 (1) for the first time: 처음으로 (2) carry out: 이행하다 (3) take action: 조치를 취하다 (4) one after another: 잇따라서

03 (1) sign: 서명하다 (2) contract: 계약서 (3) except: ~을 제외하고

04 (1) 어떤 것을 더 나아지게 하다: improve(향상시키다) (2) 행사, 모임 등에 참석하다: attend(참석하다) (3) 권위를 사용하여 누군가에게 어떤 일을 하라고 시키다: order(명령하다) (4) 어떤 것을 가져갈 수 있도록 가방, 여행 가방 등에 넣다: pack((짐을) 꾸리다)

05 (1) '너는 언제 이곳에 다시 올지 아니?'의 뜻이므로 when이 알맞다. (2) order는 목적보어로 to부정사를 취한다. (3) too ... to ~: 너무 …해서 ~하지 못하다

06 (1) let+목적어+원형부정사(go) (2) have+목적어+원형부정사(meet) (3) make+목적어+원형부정사(repeat) (4) help+목적어+to부정사[원형부정사](to complete) 등에 유의하여 영작한다.

07 what은 선행사를 포함한 관계대명사로 '~하는 것'으로 해석하며, the thing(s) which[that]를 나타낸다.

08 not only A but also B = B as well as A: A뿐만 아니라 B도. B에 강조의 초점이 맞춰져 있다.

09 carry out: ~을 실행하다 in addition to: ~ 외에도

10 동사 take를 수식하는 부사형으로 고친다.

11 선행사를 포함하는 관계대명사 what이 알맞다.

12 전치사의 목적어이므로 동명사 winning이 알맞다.

13 to make matters worse: 설상가상으로

14 do that은 앞에 언급된 play basketball을 받는다.

15 how to play basketball well: 농구를 어떻게 하면 잘하는지

16 위 글의 마지막 두 문장의 내용을 쓰면 된다.

17 win game after game: 경기를 연달아 이기다

23

18 '주의를 거의 기울이지 않았다'는 부정의 의미이므로 little이 알맞다. a little은 긍정의 의미이다.

p.124~128
단원별 예상문제

01 (1) exactly (2) lock (3) college (4) coach
   (5) imagine
02 ④   03 ④   04 refusal   05 ③
06 (1) carry (2) make (3) pay (4) take
07 demand   08 ③   09 ②   10 ④
11 (1) I will wait here until you come back.
   (2) He spoke clearly so (that) we might hear him
       well.
   (3) I want to know if[whether] she can sleep in this
       noisy place.
   (4) He has not been practicing dancing since last
       Friday.
   (5) She felt too hungry to keep walking.
   (6) He danced so well that he won (the) first
       prize.
12 ④   13 ③
14 (1) I should do (2) I should[could] open
   (3) he should[can] get
15 ③   16 losing   17 play basketball
18 ②   19 ①   20 Attend at → Attend
21 rules   22 ④   23 ④
24 From that point on, they won game after game.
25 ③
26 Carter 코치가 체육관에 자물쇠를 채우고 선수들의 성적이
    향상될 때까지 농구 경기를 하도록 허락하지 않은 것
27 ②   28 getting
29 우리가 보는 것은 오직 유명해져서 TV에 나오는 당신을
    보는 것
30 ④   31 decision   32 Disappointed
33 (A) to reopen   (B) entered   (C) yourself
34 ④

01 (1) exactly: 정확히 (2) lock: 잠그다 (3) college: 대학 (4)
   coach (스포츠 팀의) 코치 (5) imagine: 상상하다
02 계약의 내용을 적은 서류를 의미하는 단어는 'contract(계약
   서)'이다.
03 except: ~을 제외하고
04 주어진 단어는 동사와 명사의 관계이다. refuse는 뒤에 -al
   을 붙여 명사형을 만든다. decide: 결정하다 decision: 결정,
   refuse: 거절하다 refusal: 거절
05 order: 명령하다, 주문하다
06 (1) carry out: 이행하다 (2) to make matters worse: 설

상가상으로 (3) pay attention to: ~에 주의를 기울이다 (4)
take action: 조치를 취하다
07 어떤 것을 해야 한다거나 또는 받아야 한다는 강력한 주장을 의
   미하는 단어는 'demand(요구)'이다.
08 ③ That he says의 선행사가 없으므로 That을 선행사를 포함
   하는 관계대명사 What으로 고쳐야 한다.
09 ② make는 사역동사이므로 원형부정사를 목적보어로 취한다.
10 ① what → that[which] ② That → What ③ what →
   that[which] ⑤ that → what
11 (1) until이 이끄는 부사절에서는 미래의 일이라도 현재형을 쓴
   다. (2) 목적을 나타내는 so that 주어+may[can] ~ 구문에서
   구어체에서는 that을 생략할 수 있다. (3) 명사절을 이끄는 접속
   사 if[whether]를 이용한다. (4) 현재완료진행의 부정문을 이
   용한다. (5) 'so ~ that 주어+can't … = too ~ to …: 너무 ~
   해서 …할 수 없다' 구문을 이용한다. (6) 'so ~ that ... 구문을
   이용한다.
12 have 대신에 get을 쓸 수 있다. have는 사역동사이므로 원형부
   정사를 목적보어로 취하지만, get은 to부정사를 목적보어로 취
   한다.
13 let 대신에 allow를 쓸 수 있다. let은 사역동사이므로 원형부정
   사를 목적보어로 취하지만, allow는 to부정사를 목적보어로 취
   한다.
14 '의문사+to부정사'는 '의문사+주어+should[can] ~'으로 바꿔
   쓸 수 있다.
15 hear는 지각동사이므로 원형부정사를 목적보어로 취한다.
   allow는 to부정사를 목적보어로 취한다.
16 become used to ~ing: ~하는 데 익숙해지다
17 do that은 앞에 언급된 play basketball을 받는다.
18 문맥상 '아이들에게 어떻게 하면 농구를 잘하고 이기는지 가르
   쳐 주고 싶었다'라고 하는 것이 적절하다.
19 ① 왜 그 농구팀이 연달아 경기에 졌는지는 위 글의 내용으로 보
   아 알 수 없다.
20 attend는 타동사이므로 목적어 앞에 전치사가 필요없다.
21 당신에게 어떤 것은 할 수 있고 어떤 것은 할 수 없다고 말해 주
   는 지시들: rules(규칙, 원칙)
22 문맥상 이유를 나타내는 접속사가 알맞다.
23 let은 사역동사이므로 목적보어로 원형부정사를 취한다.
24 '경기를 연달아 이겼다'의 뜻으로 전치사 after에 연결되어 관용
   적으로 쓰일 때는 부정관사 a를 붙이지 않는다.
25 문맥상 결과를 나타내는 접속사가 알맞다.
26 it은 인칭대명사로 앞에 나온 문장을 받는다.
27 ② Carter를 제외한 모든 사람이 행복해 했다고 언급되었다.
28 '유명해지면서'의 뜻으로 능동의 의미를 나타내므로 현재분사형
   이 알맞다.
29 so는 지시대명사로 앞에 나온 내용을 받는다.

30 ⓒ, ④ 부사적 용법 ①, ⑤ 형용사적 용법 ②, ③ 명사적 용법

31 decide의 명사형이 와야 한다.

32 분사구문으로 수동의 의미이므로 과거분사로 고쳐야 한다.

33 (A) order는 to부정사를 목적보어로 취한다. (B) enter가 '~에 들어가다'의 뜻일 때는 전치사 없이 목적어를 취한다. (C) 전치사 for의 목적어가 주어 자신이므로 재귀대명사를 취한다.

34 선수들이 Carter가 리치몬드 고등학교를 떠나는 것을 환영했는지는 알 수 없다.

Look Inside You

시험대비 실력평가   p.132

01 independent   02 ⑤   03 ④
04 sold out   05 (a)ttitude   06 ④
07 (1) protection   (2) situation   (3) difference

01 주어진 관계는 반의어 관계이다. dependent: 의존적인, independent: 독립적인

02 '어떤 사람을 다른 사람과 구별시켜 주는 일련의 감정적인 특성, 행동 방식 따위'를 가리키는 말은 personality(성격)이다.

03 ④번 문장에서 means는 '수단'을 의미한다.

04 sold out: 매진된, 다 팔린

05 '사람이나 사물에 대해 생각하거나 느끼는 방식'을 가리키는 단어는 attitude(태도)이다.

06 주어진 문장과 나머지는 '표현하다'를 나타내지만 ④번은 '급행'을 나타낸다.

서술형 시험대비   p.133

01 (s)imilarity
02 (1) details   (2) opinion   (3) raise   (4) focus
03 (1) at the same time   (2) According to
    (3) participate in
04 (r)easonable, (f)rightened, (r)educe
    (1) frightened   (2) reasonable   (3) reduce
05 various
06 (1) Jake is not ready to live on his own.
    (2) Jane knows how to deal with angry dogs.
    (3) It may have to do with culture.

01 주어진 관계는 반의어 관계이다. difference: 차이, 다름 / similarity: 유사, 비슷함

02 (1) detail: 세부 사항 / 그의 상사는 회의 전에 세부 사항들을 확인했다. (2) opinion: 의견 / 이 상황에서 내 개인적인 의견은 중요하지 않다. (3) raise: 기르다 / 너는 개를 키울 때 책임감을 가져야 한다. (4) focus: 집중하다 / 너는 공부에 더 집중하는 게 좋겠다.

03 (1) at the same time: 동시에 (2) according to: ~에 따르면 (3) participate in: ~에 참여하다

04 reasonable: 합리적인, 타당하고 분별 있는 / frightened: 겁먹은, 두려워하는, 두려움을 느끼거나 드러내는 / reduce: 줄이

다, 어떤 것의 크기, 양, 수 등이 작아지게 하다 (1) Ellen은 대중 앞에서 말하는 것을 두려워했다. (2) 그는 아주 합리적인 사람이다. (3) 우리는 그 무게를 절반으로 줄여야 할 것이다.

05 various: 다양한, 여러 가지의 / 이제 환경 친화적인 다양한 자동차들이 있다.

06 (1) be ready to: ~할 준비가 되다 (2) deal with: ~을 다루다 (3) have to do with: ~와 관련이 있다

교과서
Conversation

핵심 Check   p.134~135

1 (B) – (C) – (A)

2 ④

3 are there any other ways to get there?

교과서 대화문 익히기

Check(√) True or False   p.136

1 F   2 T   3 T   4 F

교과서 확인학습   p.138~139

Listen and Speak 1 Listen

1. mean / nervous, frightened, doing
2. does, mean / feel sad
3. does, mean / means, look sad
4. does, mean / means, give up

Listen and Speak 1 A

1. How, doing / for / does, mean / means, happy, excited
2. personality test, had to / According to, a lot, by, mine / do, mean / mean, other

Listen and Speak 2 Listen

1. sold out / other seats / some tickets
2. spicy, sweet / other sauces / only
3. would, like to, maybe / too much sugar / too
4. the most popluar / other colors / lots, over here

Listen and Speak 2 A

1. reading, says, people's feelings / surprising / For example, help us focus / useful colors / helps,

relax

2. more, yourself, kinds of, other tests / take, test / before

Real-Life Zone

what kind of, to try / like / afraid of, one of / dark places, without, on, mean / says, full of, That's why, fill, with, scary things / about, anything, afraid of / big imagination / any other tests / a lot of

Wrap Up 1~2

blood type / an article, says / your personality / type A / with, calm, too

시험대비 기본평가   p.140

01 ②   02 spicy sauce and sweet sauce

03 ③   04 (D) – (B) – (E) – (C) – (A)

01 Are there any other ~?는 '다른 ~가 있나요?'라는 의미로 대안을 묻는 표현이다.

02 Those는 앞에 나온 것을 지칭하는 지시대명사로 spicy sauce and sweet sauce를 가리킨다.

03 What does ~ mean?은 의미를 설명해 달라고 요청하는 말이므로 그에 대한 대답은 It means ~.(그것은 ~을 의미해.)가 적절하다.

시험대비 실력평가   p.141~142

01 ④   02 ②   03 meaning

04 these big windows   05 open   06 ⑤

07 (A) → (D) → (C) → (B)   08 ①

09 Are there any other useful colors?   10 ③

11 ④   12 a personality test   13 ③

01 그것이 무슨 뜻인지 묻는 질문에 '그는 너를 이해하는 것 같아.' 라는 대답은 어색하다.

02 by: ~에 따르면, ~로 보아

03 What does ~ mean?은 What is the meaning of ~?로 바꿔 쓸 수 있다.

04 인칭대명사 They는 앞에 나온 these big windows를 가리킨다.

05 '생각과 감정을 직접적이고 정직하게 표현하는'을 가리키는 말은 open(솔직한, 숨김없는)이다.

06 큰 창문들은 다른 사람에게 솔직하다는 것을 의미한다.

07 (A) 안부 묻기 → (D) 안부에 답하기 → (C) 'on cloud nine' 의 의미 묻기 → (B) 의미 설명

08 주어진 문장의 It은 an interesting magazine을 가리키므로 ①번이 적절하다.

09 Are there any other ～?: 다른 어떤 ～가 있니?

10 Jane은 잡지를 통해서 색깔이 사람의 감정에 영향을 미치는 것을 알게 되었다.

11 (A) There are any other ～.: 다른 어떤 ～이 있습니다. (C) any time: 언제든지

12 부정대명사 one은 앞에 나온 a personality test를 가리킨다.

13 B는 적성검사를 받기 위해 전화를 했다.

01 this test

02 (A) these (B) on (C) with

03 Are there any other tests we can take?

04 It means that we are full of imagination.

05 They are talking about blood type and personality.

06 Her blood type is A.

07 A형은 차분하며 남의 말을 잘 들어주는 사람이다.

08 Then what does type A means?

01 인칭대명사 it은 앞에 나온 this test를 가리킨다.

02 (A) one of+복수명사: ～ 중 하나 (B) 어두운 밤을 싫어한다고 했으므로 불을 켜야만 잠을 잘 수 있다는 내용이 자연스럽다. (C) fill A with B: A를 B로 채우다

03 Are there any other ～?: 다른 어떤 ～가 있니? / take a test: 검사를 받다

04 어두운 곳을 싫어한다면 상상력이 풍부한 사람이라는 의미이다.

05 그들은 혈액형과 성격에 관해 이야기하고 있다.

06 소녀의 혈액형은 무엇인가?

07 A형은 차분하며 남의 말을 잘 들어주는 사람이다.

08 what does ～ means?: ～은 무슨 뜻이니?

교과서
Grammar

핵심 Check p.144~145

1 (1) what (2) What

2 (1) have been living (2) has been drawing

시험대비 기본평가 p.146

01 (1) have been knowing → have known

  (2) am learning → have been learning

  (3) Which → What

  (4) which → what

02 You can tell me what you need.

03 (1) It has been raining since lunch time.

  (2) They have been running for one hour.

  (3) What Paul cooked was a pizza.

  (4) I bought my son what he really needed.

  (5) Suji has been studying English for a year.

01 (1) 인식, 소유, 감정 등을 나타내는 동사는 현재완료진행형으로 쓰지 않는다. (2) 4개월째 공부해 온 것이므로 현재완료진행형으로 쓰는 것이 적절하다. (3) 관계대명사 what은 명사절을 이끌며 선행사를 포함한다. 주격 관계대명사로 쓰였다. (4) 관계대명사 what은 명사절을 이끌며 선행사를 포함한다. 목적격 관계대명사로 쓰였다.

02 관계대명사 what은 명사절을 이끌며 선행사를 포함한다.

03 (1) 점심시간 이후로 비가 쭉 내리고 있는 것이므로 현재완료진행형을 쓰는 것이 적절하다. (2) 그들이 한 시간 동안 계속 달리고 있는 것이므로 현재완료진행형으로 쓰는 것이 적절하다. (3) 관계대명사 what은 명사절을 이끌며 선행사를 포함한다. 주격 관계대명사로 쓰였다. (4) 관계대명사 what은 명사절을 이끌며 선행사를 포함한다. 목적격 관계대명사로 쓰였다. (5) 1년 동안 쭉 공부하고 있는 중이므로 현재완료진행형으로 쓰는 것이 적절하다.

시험대비 실력평가 p.147~149

01 has cooking → has been cooking 02 What

03 have been studying

04 ④ 05 ② 06 ①

07 She bought a luxurious house that[which] has a huge pool.

08 ② 09 have been doing

10 It has been raining for three days. 11 ③

12 ⑤ 13 ①, ③ 14 ③ 15 is

16 (1) have been doing (2) What my friend said

  (3) have been raising (4) has been snowing

  (5) What I want

  (6) What Jane and Jay will see

17 ④ 18 ②, ⑤ 19 ①

20 has been playing

01 엄마는 두 시간 동안 부엌에서 소고기 스튜를 요리하고 계신다. 두 시간 동안 요리를 하고 있으므로 현재완료진행형을 쓰는 것이 적절하다.

02 done의 목적어와 is의 주어 역할을 할 수 있는 What이 적절하다.

03 하루에 적어도 1시간씩 지속적으로 해오고 있는 것이므로 현재완료진행형이 들어가는 것이 적절하고 have been studying으로 쓴다.

04 ④ 내가 아는 모든 것을 너에게 말했다. 선행사 everything이 있으므로 what이 아닌 that이 적절하다. ① 그는 내가 신뢰할 수 있는 유일한 사람이다. ② Sam과 Son은 물에 대한 저항을 최소화할 수 있는 수영복을 샀다. ③ 나는 사람들이 말하는 것에 신경 쓰지 않는다. ⑤ 그 미술가들은 그들이 보는 것을 그리고 있다.

05 그가 말한 것은 사실이다. The thing which를 What이 대신할 수 있으므로 ②가 적절하다.

06 Jay는 내가 가르친 가장 똑똑한 학생입니다. 선행사 the most brilliant student가 있고 빈칸 뒤에 taught의 목적어가 없으므로 that이 적절하다.

07 • 그녀는 호화로운 집을 샀다 • 그것은 큰 수영장을 가지고 있다. 두 문장을 한 문장으로 만들고자 할 때 중복된 단어는 a luxurious house이고 이것을 선행사로 하고 관계대명사는 that이나 which로 한다.

08 do의 목적어와 is의 주어 역할을 할 수 있는 What이 적절하다.

09 지난달 이후로 지금까지 사용한 방법이므로 현재완료진행형이 들어가야 적절하다.

10 3일 동안 지속해서 비가 오고 있으므로 현재완료진행형을 쓰는 것이 적절하다.

11 3시간 동안 계속해서 페인트칠을 하고 있는 중이므로 현재완료진행으로 쓰며 painted를 has been painting으로 고치는 것이 적절하다.

12 과거에 시작되어 현재도 지속되는 일을 표현할 때 쓰고, 기간을 나타내기 위해 'for, how long, since' 등을 함께 쓸 수 있다.

13 관계대명사 What은 The thing which로 쓸 수 있고 '내가 필요하다'라는 불완전한 절인 주절을 이끌기 위해 선행사를 포함한 what을 쓰는 것이 적절하다.

14 • 나를 기쁘게 만드는 것은 축구를 하는 것이다. • 그가 썼던 책은 큰 히트를 쳤다. 첫 번째 문장은 선행사를 포함하며 주절을 이끄는 관계대명사 What이 나오는 것이 적절하다. 두 번째 문장은 선행사가 있고 wrote의 목적어가 없으므로 that이 나오는 것이 적절하다.

15 어법에 맞게 배열하면 What John and Paul want to eat is fried chicken.

16 (1), (3), (4)는 현재완료진행형을 쓰는 문제이므로 'have[has]+been+~ing'로 쓰고, (2), (5), (6)은 선행사를 포함하고 명사절을 이끄는 관계대명사를 쓰는 문제이므로 관계대명사 what을 쓰는 것이 적절하다.

17 ④ 그녀는 최근에 매우 열심히 일을 하고 있었다. 부사 recently와 과거진행형과는 어울리지 않는다. ① 나는 내 친구들과 그 이후로 나무를 심고 있다. ② 나는 20년 동안 호주에서 살고 있다. ③ Jason은 오늘 아침부터 기분이 별로 좋지 않다. ⑤ 나는 이것을 찾고 있었다.

18 ② Harry는 30분째 버스를 기다리고 있다. ⑤ 그녀는 20살부터 운전을 했습니다. ①은 have planting을 have been

planting으로 쓰는 것이 적절하다. 우리는 거기에 정기적으로 꽃을 심고 있다. ③ since로 보아 2019년 이래로 쭉 프로젝트를 진행한 것이므로 worked를 has been working으로 쓰는 것이 적절하다. ④ since로 보아 그가 오늘 아침부터 계속해서 TV를 보고 있는 것이므로 has been watched를 has been watching으로 쓰는 것이 적절하다. since는 보통 완료형과 함께 쓰이는 것에 주의한다.

19 ① 내가 말했던 것을 잊지 마세요. that → what ② 그녀는 그녀가 해야 했던 것을 했다. ③ 나는 딸에게 먹고 싶어 하는 것을 요리해 줄 것이다. ④ 그들이 필요했던 것은 단지 한 병의 물이었다. ⑤ 그 소녀는 그녀를 흥미진진하게 하는 영화를 보고 있다.

20 현재완료진행 형태로 has been playing으로 쓰는 것이 적절하다.

서술형 시험대비
p.150~151

01 what you're feeling
02 What
03 (1) I know what you want.
   (2) This is what I mean.
   (3) Do what I do.
   (4) What Suji will take to the theater is a bus.
04 They have been eating chicken for thirty minutes.
05 I know what you did last summer.
06 (1) I don't care what people say.
   (2) I don't care the thing[things] which people say.
07 (1) John has been singing for two hours.
   (2) They have been playing darts for one[an] hour.
   (3) What they want is to talk and play.
08 (1) I know the thing which you're doing these days.
   (2) I know what you're doing these days.
09 What I have to finish, I have been writing
10 What John wants to do with Sally is to see a movie.
11 (1) have been doing
   (2) what the company will become

01 빈칸에 '당신이 느끼고 있는 것'이 들어가야 하므로 'what you're feeling'으로 쓰는 것이 적절하다.

02 내가 갖고 싶은 것은 컴퓨터이다. The thing which 대신 들어갈 수 있는 것으로 관계대명사 What이 적절하다.

03 (1) '나는 안다'의 의미로 I know가 오고 '내가 원하는 것'이라는 의미가 know 뒤에 이어져야 하므로 선행사를 포함한 what을 쓰는 것이 적절하다. 관계대명사 what절에서는 want에 대한 목적어를 what이 대신한다. (2) '이것은 ~이다'의 의미가 먼저 와야 하므로 This is로 시작하고 '바로 내가 의미하는 것이다'라는

의미가 뒤에 이어져야 하므로 is에 대한 보어로 선행사를 포함한 what을 쓰는 것이 적절하다. 관계대명사 절 안에서 mean의 목적어를 what이 대신한다. (3) 명령문 '~해 봐'의 의미를 쓰기 위해 do가 문장 맨 앞에 오고, '내가 하는 것'이란 의미가 뒤에 이어져야하므로 what I do를 쓰는 것이 적절하다. (4) 'Suji가 영화관에 타고 갈 것'이란 내용이 먼저 와야 하므로 'What Suji will take to the theater'를 쓰고 이어 '버스이다'가 와야 하므로 'is a bus'를 쓰는 것이 적절하다.

04 30분 동안 계속해서 먹고 있으므로 8 단어에 맞추어 현재완료진행형으로 쓰는 것이 적절하다.

05 '나는 알고 있다'+'네가 지난여름에 한 일'. 한 문장 안에 두 절이 있으므로 선행사를 포함하는 관계대명사 what으로 연결시키는 것이 적절하다.

06 관계대명사 what은 선행사를 포함하고 명사절을 이끄는 관계대명사이므로 'I don't care what people say.'로 쓰는 것이 적절하고, which는 선행사가 필요하므로 the thing[things]를 넣어 'I don't care the thing[things] which people say.'로 쓰는 것이 적절하다.

07 (1), (2)는 몇 시간 동안 계속해서 노래를 부르거나 게임을 하고 있는 것이므로 현재완료진행 시제를 쓰는 것이 적절하다. (3) 주어 자리에 쓰인 명사절로 관계대명사 what을 쓰는 것이 적절하고 what 뒤에는 주어가 빠진 불완전한 절이 이어져야 한다.

08 the thing which = what. what을 중심으로 '나는 안다'는 의미를 갖는 말이 앞에 오고 '요즘 네가 무엇을 하는지'라는 말이 what에 뒤이어 오는 것이 적절하다.

09 3시까지 내가 끝내야 하는 것은 에세이 숙제다. 그러나 나는 그것을 끝내기에 충분한 시간이 없다. 나는 한 시간 동안 에세이를 쓰고 있는데, 단지 두 문장밖에 적지 못했다. 나는 시간이 더 필요하다!

10 주어 자리에 쓰인 명사절로 관계대명사 What을 쓰는 것이 적절하다.

11 (1) 전치사 since가 힌트가 되어 아침부터 쭉 지금까지 숙제로 해오고 있는 중이므로 현재완료진행형을 쓰는 것이 적절하다. (2) 관계대명사 what은 know의 목적절을 이끄는 역할을 하면서, become의 보어 역할을 한다.

Reading

확인문제   p.152

1 T   2 F   3 F

확인문제   p.153

1 F   2 T   3 F   4 T

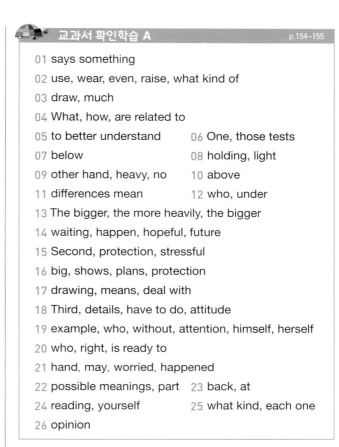

교과서 확인학습 A   p.154~155

01 says something
02 use, wear, even, raise, what kind of
03 draw, much
04 What, how, are related to
05 to better understand
06 One, those tests
07 below
08 holding, light
09 other hand, heavy, no
10 above
11 differences mean
12 who, under
13 The bigger, the more heavily, the bigger
14 waiting, happen, hopeful, future
15 Second, protection, stressful
16 big, shows, plans, protection
17 drawing, means, deal with
18 Third, details, have to do, attitude
19 example, who, without, attention, himself, herself
20 who, right, is ready to
21 hand, may, worried, happened
22 possible meanings, part
23 back, at
24 reading, yourself
25 what kind, each one
26 opinion

교과서 확인학습 B   p.156~157

1 Everything you do says something about you.
2 The language you use, the clothes you wear, and even the pets you raise somehow show what kind of person you are.
3 The things you draw are not much different.
4 What you draw and how you draw it are related to your personality.
5 Doctors have been using various drawing tests to better understand people.
6 One of those tests is the Draw-a-Person-in-the-Rain (DAPR) test.
7 Study the pictures below.
8 The person in Drawing A is holding an umbrella in a light rain.
9 On the other hand, the person in Drawing B is in a heavy rain and has no umbrella.
10 Also, there are dark clouds above the person in Drawing B.
11 What can these differences mean?
12 First, the rain shows the stress the person who drew the picture is under.
13 The bigger the drops are or the more heavily the rain is falling, the bigger the stress is.

14 The clouds mean problems waiting to happen, so a big cloud shows the drawer is not very hopeful about the future.

15 Second, the umbrella means the protection the person has in a stressful situation.

16 A big umbrella shows that the drawer has a lot of plans or protection.

17 If there's no umbrella in the drawing, the drawer does not have any means to deal with difficult situations.

18 Third, the details in the drawing of the person have to do with the drawer's attitude under stress.

19 For example, someone who draws a person without a face does not want to draw people's attention to himself or herself.

20 Someone who draws the person on the right side of the paper is ready to meet the future.

21 On the other hand, someone who draws the person on the left side may be worried about things that have happened in the past.

22 These are some of the possible meanings of each part of the drawings.

23 Now, go back and look at the two drawings.

24 Try reading them yourself.

25 Can you understand what kind of person drew each one?

26 What's your opinion?

시험대비 실력평가
p.158~161

01 ③　　　02 ⓐ What ⓑ how　　　03 ⑤
04 ⑤　　　05 ③　　　06 waiting　　　07 ⑤
08 stressful　　09 ②
10 그림을 그린 사람이 많은 계획이나 보호 기제를 가지고 있음을 보여 준다.
11 ③
12 (A) For example (B) On the other hand
13 future　　　14 ③　　　15 ④
16 drawing　　17 ②
18 what kind of person you are　　　19 ①
20 personality 21 ②
22 As, bigger or the rain is falling more heavily, the stress is bigger
23 ①　　　24 many　　　25 ⑤　　　26 ⑤
27 two drawings
28 당신은 어떤 종류의 사람이 각각의 그림을 그렸는지 이해할 수 있나요?

01 여러분이 그리는 그림이 성격과 관련이 있다는 문장 앞에 와야 한다.

02 글의 흐름상 '당신이 무엇을 그리는지 그리고 그것을 어떻게 그리는지'가 되어야 한다.

03 의사들이 사람들을 더 잘 이해하기 위해 그림 그리기 검사를 사용해 오고 있다고 언급되었으므로 ⑤가 알맞다.

04 문맥상 '반면에'의 뜻을 가진 On the other hand가 적절하다.

05 be under the stress: 스트레스를 받다

06 능동의 의미이므로 현재분사가 알맞다.

07 ⑤ 큰 구름은 그림을 그린 사람이 미래에 희망적이지 않다는 것을 보여준다고 언급되었다.

08 stressful: 스트레스를 주는 / stressed: 스트레스를 받는

09 ⓑ, ② 형용사적 용법 ①, ③, ④ 명사적 용법 ⑤ 부사적 용법

10 A big umbrella shows that the drawer has a lot of plans or protection.을 참고할 것.

11 draw one's attention to: ~에게 주의를 끌다

12 for example: 예를 들면 / on the other hand: 한편

13 future: 미래 / past: 과거

14 ⓑ와 ③의 may는 '~일지도 모르다'의 뜻으로 약한 추측을 나타낸다.

15 문맥상 '그 그림들을 스스로 읽으려고 시도해 보세요'가 알맞으므로 try+-ing 형이 되어야 한다.

16 one은 부정대명사로 앞에 나온 단수 명사를 받는다.

17 문맥상 '당신이 하는 모든 행동은 당신에 대해 무엇인가를 말해준다'가 알맞다.

18 what kind of: 어떤 종류의

19 문맥상 '당신이 그리는 것'이라는 뜻으로 draw의 목적어이므로 What이 알맞다. which는 특정하게 주어진 것 중에서 선택을 나타내므로 알맞지 않다.

20 personal: 개인의, 개인적인 / personality: 성격, 개성

21 선행사가 사람이고 주격이므로 who가 알맞다.

22 'the+비교급 ~, the+비교급 …' 구문은 접속사 as를 써서 바꿔 쓸 수 있다. as 구문에서는 비교급 앞에 정관사 the를 붙이지 않는다.

23 문맥상 '그래서'의 뜻을 가진 so가 알맞다.

24 a lot of 뒤에 셀 수 있는 명사의 복수형이 오므로 many가 알맞다.

25 deal with: ~을 처리하다, ~을 다루다

26 ⑤ 큰 우산은 그림을 그린 사람이 많은 계획을 가지고 있음을 보여 준다고 언급되었다.

27 them은 앞에 나온 복수 명사를 받는다.

28 what kind of person 이하는 간접의문문으로 understand의 목적어이다.

01 hand   02 heavy   03 differences

04 There are dark clouds.

05 with   06 himself or herself

07 have happened

08 미래를 맞이할 준비가 되었다.

09 Everything you do says something about you.

10 당신이 그리는 그림을 통해서 당신이 어떤 종류의 사람인지 알 수 있다.

11 당신이 그리는 것

12 They have been using various drawing tests to better understand people.

13 The bigger the drops are or the more heavily the rain is falling, the bigger the stress is.

14 waiting   15 stressful

01 on the other hand: 반면에

02 문맥상 light의 반의어 heavy가 알맞다.

03 different의 명사형 difference의 복수형이 알맞다.

04 Also, there are dark clouds above the person in Drawing B.를 참고할 것

05 have to do with: ~와 관계가 있다

06 전치사 to의 목적어가 주어 자신이므로 재귀대명사로 고쳐야 한다.

07 happen은 자동사이므로 수동태로 쓸 수 없다.

09 you do 앞에 관계대명사 that이 생략되었다.

11 it은 인칭대명사로 앞에 나온 What you draw를 받는다.

13 'the+비교급 ~, the+비교급 ...' 구문이므로 bigger the stress is 앞에도 the를 붙인다.

14 능동의 의미로 problems를 수식하므로 현재분사가 알맞다.

15 stressed: 스트레스를 받는 / stressful: 스트레스를 주는

01 below   02 ⑤   03 ⑤   04 ⑤

05 ②   06 ②

07 (1) gets along with

   (2) In other words

   (3) has to do with

08 ①

09 what is the meaning of / what do you mean by

10 Are there any other ways to get there?

11 She will take a bus.

12 ②   13 is → are

14 He wants to take a personality test this afternoon.

15 (A) to help (B) to take

16 소년은 성격 검사 일정을 잡기 위해서 전화를 걸고 있다.

17 (1) have been using

(2) what makes me happy

(3) has been living

(4) what I can do

18 ①   19 What they want is some food.

20 what I am going to say

21 (1) what they wanted

(2) have known

(3) have been working

(4) what I say

22 don't know

23 (1) what he says

(2) I knew what

24 Henry couldn't understand what the teacher said.

25 ③   26 light   27 hopeful   28 ⑤

29 ⑤   30 ④   31 past

32 He or she is ready to meet the future.   33 ③

34 ④   35 curious

01 주어진 관계는 반의어 관계이다. above: ~ 위에 : below: ~ 아래에

02 '다른 사람에게 도움이나 지원을 구하거나 의지하지 않는'을 뜻하는 말은 independent(독립적인)이다.

03 be covered with: ~로 덮여 있다 / deal with: ~을 다루다

04 against: ~에 반대하는, for: ~에 찬성하는

05 personality: 성격 / 내 친구는 잘생기고 성격도 좋다.

06 raise: 기르다, 들다 / • 나는 애완동물로 햄스터를 기른다. • 답을 알면 손을 드세요.

07 (1) get along with ~: ~와 잘 어울리다 (2) in other words: 다시 말하면 (3) have to do with: ~와 관련이 있다

08 소녀가 집을 그려야 했다고 말하자 소년이 A house?라고 묻고 있으므로 ①번이 적절하다.

09 what do ~ mean?은 what is the meaning of ~?, what do you mean by ~? 등으로 바꿔 쓸 수 있다.

10 Are there any other ~?: 다른 ~이 있나요?

11 소녀는 버스를 타고 갈 것이다.

12 혈액형이 무엇인지 묻자 - (B) 대답하고 이유 묻기 - (D) 이유 설명 - (A) A형에 대한 의미 묻기 (C) A형에 대한 특징 설명

13 주어가 People이므로 복수동사 are가 되어야 한다.

14 소년은 오늘 오후에 성격검사를 받고 싶어 한다.

15 목적을 나타내는 to부정사 형태가 되어야 한다.

17 (1) 사용하고 있는 중이므로 have been using이 적절하다. (2) 괄호 안의 what이 보어 자리에 '나를 행복하게 한다'는 명사절을 이끌어야 하므로 what makes me happy가 나오는 것이 적절하다. (3) 2010년 이후로 지금까지 쭉 서울에서 살고 있는 것이므로 현재완료진행형이 나오는 것이 적절하다. (4) '내가 할 수 있는 일'이란 의미가 들어가야 하므로 'what I can do'가

18 ① 사람들이 보고 싶은 것은 고흐가 쓴 편지이다. ② what → who 또는 that ③ the thing 삭제 ④,⑤ that → what

19 '괄호 안에 what이 있고 동사 want의 목적어가 없으므로 관계 대명사 what절을 쓰는 것이 적절하다.

20 '내가 말하려고 하던 것'을 what을 이용하여 6 단어로 'what I am going to say'로 쓴다.

21 (1) 보어 자리에 들어갈 명사절이 와야 하므로 'what they wanted'가 나오는 것이 적절하다. (2) know, like, believe 동사는 진행형으로 쓰지 않으므로 현재완료로 쓰는 것이 적절하다. (3) 작년부터 지금까지 진행되어 온 것이므로 현재완료진행 형을 쓰는 것이 적절하다. (4) 목적어 자리에 들어갈 명사절이 와야 하므로 'what I say'가 나오는 것이 적절하다.

22 내가 뭘 먼저 할 수 있을지 모르겠어.

23 (1) 나는 믿을 수 없다+그가 말했던 것 (2) 나는 알고 있었다+ 네가 발견했던 것

24 헨리는 선생님이 말씀하신 것을 이해하지 못했다. 문장에서 understand에 대한 목적어와 said에 대한 목적어가 없으므로 두 개의 목적어 대신 관계대명사 what을 써서 한 문장으로 만드 는 것이 적절하다.

25 Also에 주목한다. 처음 그림 B에 있는 사람을 언급한 문장 다음인 ③에 와야 한다.

26 heavy: 무거운, 심한 / light: 가벼운

27 hope의 형용사형이 와야 한다.

28 큰 구름은 그림을 그린 사람이 미래에 대해 희망적이지 않다고 언급되었다.

29 under stress: 스트레스를 받을 때

30 for example: 예를 들면, on the other hand: 반면에

31 문맥상 future의 반의어인 past(과거)가 알맞다.

32 그림의 오른쪽에 있는 사람은 미래를 맞이할 준비가 되어 있다 고 하였다.

33 나와 친구의 성격에 대해 말해야 했다는 문장 다음인 ③에 와야 한다.

34 선행사를 포함하는 관계대명사 what이 알맞다.

35 '어떤 것에 흥미를 가지고 그것에 관해 더 많이 알기를 원하는'은 curious(호기심이 있는)이다.

단원별 예상문제 p.170~173

01 ③	02 ⑤	03 (d)rops	04 ⑤
05 ①	06 relax	07 to look sad	
08 ④	09 According to		

10 큰 창문들은 그녀가 타인에게 개방되어 있다는 것을 의미한다.

11 (1) that (2) what

12 It has been raining heavily for three hours.

13 ①

14 (1) that they wanted
   (2) what she needed
   (3) have been working

15 have been discussing

16 These are some of the possible meanings of each part of the drawings.

17 ⑤	18 ④	19 ③	20 ④

21 Because he gets along well with others and is in lots of clubs.

22 The bigger the drops are or the more heavily the rain is falling, the bigger the stress is.

23 ③	24 ②	25 ①	26 ⑤

27 큰 우산은 그림을 그린 사람이 많은 계획이나 보호 기제를 가지고 있음을 보여 준다.

01 ③은 동의어 관계이지만 나머지는 반의어 관계이다. ① heavy(무거운) - light(가벼운) ② future(미래) - past(과거) ③ various(다양한) - diverse(다양한) ④ calm(차분한) - excited(흥분한) ⑤ carefully: 조심스럽게 - carelessly: 부 주의하게

02 see A as B: A를 B로 보다, 나는 내 자신이 수줍음이 많고 친 절하다고 생각했다. / deal with: ~을 다루다, 난 다른 두 가지 문제를 다루고 싶다.

03 drop: 방울 / 하늘이 어두워지더니 비가 몇 방울 떨어졌다. / 동 그란 모양으로 떨어지는 매우 적은 양의 액체

04 at the same time: 동시에(=simultaneously)

05 주어진 문장은 잡지에 대한 보충 설명이므로 ①에 오는 것이 적 절하다.

06 누군가 더 차분해지고 덜 걱정하게 되거나 되게 하다: relax(안 심[진정]하다)

07 have a long face는 '슬퍼 보이는 것'을 의미한다.

08 (A) take a personality test: 성격 검사를 받다 (C) what does ~ mean?: ~는 무엇을 의미하니?

09 according to: ~에 따르면

11 (1) 내가 아는 모든 사람은 정직하고 친절하다. (2) 그는 내가 원하는 것을 주었다.

12 현재완료진행은 과거에서부터 지금까지 진행되고 있는 의미를 표현할 때 사용한다.

13 ① know, like, believe 등은 진행형으로 사용 불가하므로 I have known him since my childhood.가 적절하다. ② 그 녀는 어젯밤부터 계속해서 울고 있다. ③ 난 5년 동안 스페인어 를 공부하고 있다. ④ 나는 네가 빌려준 책을 읽고 있다. ⑤ 그

는 8살부터 우표를 모으는 중이다.

14 (1) 선행사 the house가 있으므로 관계대명사 that을 쓰는 것이 적절하다. (2) 선행사를 포함하는 관계대명사 what을 쓰는 것이 적절하다. (3) 지난해부터 여기에서 일하고 있으므로 현재완료진행을 쓰는 것이 적절하다.

15 우리는 1시간 동안 그 문제들에 대해 의논해 왔다.

16 these를 문장의 주어로 한다.

17 both 뒤에는 복수형이 오므로 each로 고쳐야 한다.

18 kinds가 복수 명사이므로 much는 쓸 수 없다.

19 필자의 성격에 대한 판단이 필자 본인과 친구가 각각 달랐다는 내용이 적절하므로 different가 들어가야 한다.

20 민수의 친구는 민수가 적극적이라고 말했다.

22 이때의 as는 '~함에 따라서'의 뜻으로 'the+비교급 ~, the+비교급 ...' 구문을 써서 바꿔 쓸 수 있다.

23 구름들은 앞으로 벌어질 문제들을 의미하므로 큰 구름은 그림을 그린 사람이 미래에 대해 희망적이지 않다는 것이 문맥상 자연스럽다.

24 (C), ② 동사의 목적어가 되는 명사절을 이끄는 접속사이다. ① 진주어 ③, ⑤ 관계대명사 ④ It ... that 강조 구문

25 문맥상 조건을 나타내는 접속사 if가 알맞다.

26 우산이 없는 그림을 그리는 사람은 어려운 상황을 대처할 수단이 없다고 하였다.

서술형 실전문제
p.174~175

01 (1) to feel sad (2) to give up

02 It is about colors and people's feelings.

03 색깔이 사람들의 기분을 바꿀 수 있다는 것

04 (1) He is the very man that loves music.

　(2) pick what you want

　(3) It is the very music that he loves.

　(4) what you brought

05 I have been doing the course for six months.

06 He has been taking a bus for two hours.

07 ④번 → is　08 clothes

09 여러분이 그리는 그림을 통해서 여러분이 어떤 종류의 사람 인지 알 수 있다.

10 그림 A의 인물은 가벼운 빗속에 우산을 가지고 있고, 그림 B의 인물은 심한 빗속에 우산도 없고 또한 그 인물의 위에 어두운 구름들이 있는 것

11 그 그림을 그린 사람이 스트레스를 받을 때의 태도를 알 수 있다.

12 worried

---

01 (1) feel blue는 to feel sad(슬프게 느끼는 것)을 의미한다. (2) throw up one's hands는 to give up(포기하는 것)을 의미한다.

02 잡지는 색깔과 사람의 기분에 관한 내용이다.

04 (1)과 (3)은 선행사 the very man, the very music이 있으므로 관계대명사 that을 써서 문장을 완성하는 것이 적절하다. (2)와 (4)는 선행사를 포함하고 각 동사의 목적어가 되는 명사절이 나와야 하므로 관계대명사 what을 써서 문장을 완성하는 것이 적절하다.

05 6개월 동안 지속되고 있는 것이므로 현재완료진행형이 오는 것이 적절하므로 have been doing으로 써야 한다.

06 그는 버스를 2시간 동안 타고 있는 것이므로 'he has been taking a bus'가 오고 2시간 동안이라는 정확한 숫자 표현이 나왔으므로 전치사 for를 사용하여 'for two hours'를 쓴다.

07 주어가 One이므로 단수로 받아야 한다.

08 셔츠, 상의, 바지, 드레스와 같이 사람들이 입는 것들: clothes(옷, 의복)

12 사람이 걱정하는 것이므로 과거분사형이 알맞다.

창의사고력 서술형 문제
p.176

|모범답안|

01 (2) → (3) → (1)

02 (2) What I like to do is watching movies.

　(3) What I have to do is (to) do my homework.

　(4) What I have in my pocket is the doll.

03 (A) street dancing

　(B) taking modern dance lessons for three months

　(C) want is to post wonderful video clips of me dancing someday

02 선행사를 쓰지 않고 '~하는 것'으로 해석되는 관계대명사 what을 쓴다.

단원별 모의고사
p.177~180

01 ⑤　　02 ②　　03 (1) out　(2) in　(3) to

04 ④　　05 (1) detail　(2) attention　(3) attitude

06 ①, ③　　07 ④

08 Is there anything you are afraid of?

09 (A) why (B) too (C) other

10 imagination　　11 ③

33

01 frightened: 두려워하는 scared: 무서워하는, 겁먹은

02 draw attention to oneself: 자신에게 관심을 끌다 / 그녀는 밝은 색의 옷을 입어 이목을 끌려고 한다.

03 (1) sold out: 매진된 / 모든 콘서트 표가 매진되었다. participate in: ~에 참가하다 / 그녀는 회의에 참가하지 않았다. (3) according to: ~에 따라 / 모든 것이 계획대로 되어 갔다.

04 '지원, 도움 등을 얻기 위해 다른 사람이나 사물이 필요한'을 뜻하는 단어는 dependent(의존하는)이다.

05 (1) detail: 세부 사항 (2) attention: 주의, 집중 (3) attitude: 태도

06 '어떻게 지내니?'라는 뜻으로 How have you been?, How's it going? 등으로 바꿔 쓸 수 있다.

07 on cloud nine은 더할 나위 없이 기분이 좋은 상태를 의미한다.

08 Is there ~?: ~이 있니? / be afraid of: ~을 두려워하다

09 (A) That why ~.: 그것이 ~한 이유이다. (B) 긍정문이므로 too를 쓴다. (C) Are there any other ~?: 다른 어떤 ~가 있니?

10 '보거나 경험해 보지 못한 것을 마음속으로 그려 볼 수 있는 능력'을 나타내는 단어는 imagination(상상력)이다.

11 ③ Emma는 불을 켜놓지 않고는 잠을 잘 수 없다고 했다.

12 what = the thing which

13 2012년 이후 현재까지 영어를 가르치고 있기 때문에 현재완료진행형이 나오는 것이 적절하다.

14 ④ 네가 하는 말을 못 알아듣겠어. that을 what으로 바꾸는 것이 적절하다. ① 이것이 너를 돕기 위해 내가 할 수 있는 것이다. ② 나는 내가 해야 하는 일을 잘하기를 원한다. ③ 그가 좋아하는 것

을 말해줄게. ⑤ 그녀가 그를 사랑한다는 것이 나를 놀라게 만들었다.

15 • 그들은 민수를 30분 동안 기다리고 있다. 30분 전부터 지금까지 계속 민수를 기다리고 있는 것이고 숫자 앞에 '~ 동안'이라는 의미를 담고 있는 전치사가 와야 하므로 for가 나오는 것이 적절하다.

16 know, like, believe 등의 동사는 진행형으로 쓰이지 않으므로 현재완료진행형이 아닌 현재완료가 적절하다.

17 요리사가 휴가 중이므로 'the cook has been taking a vacation'이 나오고 '그래서 음식점이 문을 닫았다'는 의미가 뒤에 이어져야 하므로 'so the restaurant is closed'를 쓴다.

18 the thing which[that] = what

19 내가 주문한 것은 사과 주스 한 잔이다.

20 2시간째 피구를 하고 있는 것이므로 현재완료진행형을 쓴다.

21 오늘 아침부터 쭉 몸이 안 좋았던 것이므로 has been feeling sick이 나오는 것이 적절하다.

22 문맥상 '다른 사람들'의 뜻이 되어야 하므로 others로 고쳐야 한다.

23 명사 friend의 형용사형으로 고친다.

24 get along well with: ~와 잘 지내다

26 ⓐ, ① …도[조차] ② 한층, 훨씬 ③ 짝수의 ④ 동일한 ⑤ 평평한

27 be related to: ~와 관계가 있다

28 ⓒ, ④ 부사적 용법 ①, ③, ⑤ 명사적 용법 ② 형용사적 용법

29 여러분이 먹는 음식은 언급되지 않았다.

교과서 파헤치기

Lesson 3

단어 TEST Step 1   p.02

01 이득; 이득을 보다   02 게다가   03 진정시키는
04 자연친화적인   05 후회하다   06 만들어 내다
07 피하다   08 마침내   09 이불, 담요
10 항공편, 비행   11 성적   12 규칙적으로
13 뇌   14 다행스럽게도   15 칼슘
16 일지, 일기   17 세로토닌   18 젖은
19 자외선 차단제   20 기분, 감정   21 제대로
22 빛나다   23 보호하다   24 이미
25 피부   26 날씨   27 야외에서
28 절정의, 최고조의; 절정, 최고조   29 복습하다
30 안전하게   31 직접적인, (열기나 빛이) 직접 닿는
32 효과   33 뼈   34 건강한
35 착용하다, 바르다
36 ~을 명심하다   37 A와 B 둘 다   38 ~로 가득 찬
39 깨어 있다   40 ~했어야 했는데   41 내놓다
42 너무 ~해서 …할 수 없다   43 ~에 유익하다

단어 TEST Step 2   p.03

01 already   02 interestingly   03 benefit
04 moreover   05 healthy   06 calming
07 sunlight   08 nature-friendly   09 outdoors
10 skin   11 avoid   12 flight
13 blanket   14 fortunately   15 check
16 hang   17 review   18 brain
19 finally   20 sunshine   21 effect
22 weather   23 journal   24 bone
25 mood   26 peak   27 produce
28 regret   29 regularly   30 role
31 wet   32 properly   33 protect
34 safely   35 full of   36 put on
37 be good for   38 on time   39 both A and B
40 put out   41 stay up   42 keep ~ in mind
43 surf the Internet

단어 TEST Step 3   p.04

1 peak, 절정, 최고조   2 mood, 기분, 감정
3 sunshine, 햇빛   4 benefit, 이득을 보다
5 go up, 올라가다   6 review, 복습하다   7 role, 역할
8 skin, 피부   9 wet, 젖은   10 blanket, 이불, 담요
11 shine, 빛나다   12 regularly, 규칙적으로
13 brain, 뇌   14 bone, 뼈   15 journal, 일지, 일기

16 protect, 보호하다

대화문 TEST Step 1   p.05~06

Listen & Speak 1 Listen

1. can, stay healthy / Well, important to eat, breakfast
2. What, do to get, grades / important, review
3. think, write, journal
4. to write down, spend, on / think, too

Listen & Speak 1 A

1. What, do, weekend / played, decided to exercise, for / you, important, exercise regularly / Right, about playing, with / not
2. late / took, wrong bus / think, leave, earlier / too, won't be late / arrive, on time

Listen & Speak 2

1. too / should have brought, one
2. cold / should have worn
3. missed, flight / have, earlier
4. Look at, should have put on / right

Listen & Speak 2 A

1. how, movie / enjoy, was boring / What, about / knew, ending, have, before seeing / sorry, like
2. still, minutes, before, top, sit down, and, snack / brought, brought / okay, brought, share / keep, mind, some, time

Real-Life Zone

look, energy / because, got, last / usually, enough sleep / know, important, night's, always stay up, surfing, playing, with, phone / sometimes happens, me / After, regret, morning, have, earlier / different / climbed, dad, tired, home, sleep, after, went to bed / Outdoor, are, way to help, get

Wrap Up 1

blanket, wet, should have checked / wash / put, out, sun / Why, wash / blanket, way, keep, clean / know, remember / important, remember, regularly

대화문 TEST Step 2   p.07~08

Listen & Speak 1 Listen

1. G: How can we stay healthy?
   B: Well, it's important to eat a good breakfast.
2. B: What can we do to get good grades?
   G: It's important to review every day.
3. B: I think it's important to write a journal after reading.
   G: I agree.

4. B: It's important to write down what you spend your money on.

G: I think so, too.

1. B: What did you do on the weekend?

G: I played tennis. I have decided to exercise on the weekend for my health.

B: Good for you. It's important to exercise regularly.

G: Right. How about playing tennis with me?

B: Why not?

2. M: John, you are late again.

B: I'm sorry. I took the wrong bus.

M: I think you need to leave home a little earlier.

B: I think so, too. Next time I won't be late.

M: It's important to arrive at school on time.

1. G: Your bag is too small.

B: Yes. I should have brought a bigger one.

2. G: Aren't you cold?

B: Yes. I should have worn a jacket.

3. B: We missed our flight.

G: Oh, no. We should have come earlier.

4. G: Look at my face. I should have put on some sunscreen.

B: Yes. You're right.

1. B: Mina, how was the movie?

G: I didn't enjoy it. It was boring.

B: What was bad about it?

G: I already knew the ending. I shouldn't have read about it before seeing it.

B: Oh, I'm sorry you didn't like it.

2. B: We still have 30 minutes to go before we reach the top of the mountain. Let's sit down over there and have a snack.

G: Oh, I brought only water. I should have brought some snacks.

B: That's okay. I brought a lot. We can share.

G: I'll keep it in mind to bring some snacks next time.

G: Ben, you look full of energy today!

B: Do I? Maybe that's because I finally got a good night's sleep last night.

G: Why? Don't you usually get enough sleep?

B: No, I know it's really important to get a good night's sleep, but I always stay up late surfing the Internet or playing with my phone.

G: That sometimes happens to me too.

B: After I do that, I regret it the next morning and say, "I should have gone to bed earlier last night."

G: How was yesterday different?

B: Well, yesterday afternoon I climbed the mountain with my dad. I was really tired when I got home. I went to sleep right after I went to bed.

G: Outdoor activities are a great way to help you get a good night's sleep.

W: Oh, your blanket is wet from the rain! I should have checked the weather.

B: Did you wash it?

W: No. I just put it out in the sun this morning.

B: Why didn't you wash it?

W: Hanging a blanket in the sun is a nature-friendly way to keep the blanket clean.

B: Oh, I didn't know that. I'll remember that.

W: And it's also important to remember to do it regularly.

01 Enjoy, Sunshine   02 much, spend, out in

03 Not much

04 too busy, spend, outdoors

05 However, plays, role, health

06 helps, stay healthy   07 feels happier, shines

08 because, body's happy hormone

09 more, hormone, brain produces

10 When, goes up, stronger   11 fight everyday stress

12 calming effect, what, doing

13 Moreover, night's sleep, produce

14 not just, feel, better

15 also, build strong bones

16 As, builds, bones, teeth

17 for, body, use, properly

18 creates, when sunlight shines

19 easiest, bones, go outside

20 As, see, benefits safely

21 direct sunlight, skin, benefit

22 classes, breaks, sunshine, arms

23 walk, few minutes, mind

24 peak, protect, face, neck

25 safely, little, difference, mood

01 Enjoy, Sunshine

02 spend, out in the sun

03 Not much

04 too busy, at work to spend, outdoors

05 However, plays an important role

06 helps, stay healthy   07 feels happier, shines

08 because of, the body's happy hormone

09 The more sun, the more, happy hormone, produces

10 goes up, feel happier, stronger

11 helps, fight everyday stress

12 calming effect, focus, what you are doing

13 Moreover, a good night's sleep, helps, produce

14 not just, sleep better

15 also, build strong bones

16 As you all know, bones, teeth

17 for the body to use, properly

18 Interestingly, creates, when sunlight shines

19 The easiest way, to go outside

20 As you can see, enjoy its benefits safely

21 getting direct sunlight, to benefit from it

22 Try to go out into, between, during, get sunshine on

23 for just a few minutes every day, both, and

24 avoid, peak, to protect your face and neck

25 a little sunshine, make a world of difference, health, mood

1 햇빛을 즐기세요

2 여러분은 매일 햇빛 속에서 얼마나 많은 시간을 보내나요?

3 많지 않죠, 그렇죠?

4 대부분의 사람들은 학교와 직장에서 너무 바빠서 많은 시간을 야외에서 보내지 못합니다.

5 그러나 햇빛은 여러분의 건강에 중요한 역할을 합니다.

6 그것은 여러분이 건강을 유지하는 데 도움을 줍니다.

7 모든 사람들은 해가 비칠 때 더 행복하게 느낍니다.

8 이것은 몸의 행복 호르몬인 세로토닌 때문입니다.

9 여러분이 햇빛을 쬘수록 뇌는 행복 호르몬을 더 만들어 냅니다.

10 여러분의 세로토닌 수치가 높아지면, 여러분은 더 행복하고 더 건강하게 느낍니다.

11 이것은 여러분이 매일의 스트레스를 이겨 내는 데 도움을 줍니다.

12 세로토닌은 또한 진정 효과가 있고, 여러분이 하는 일에 더 잘 집중할 수 있도록 도와줍니다.

13 게다가, 세로토닌은 뇌가 수면 호르몬을 생성하도록 도와주기 때문에 여러분이 숙면을 취하도록 해 줍니다.

14 햇빛은 단지 여러분이 더 기분 좋게 느끼고 잠을 더 잘 자게 하는 것만은 아닙니다.

15 그것은 또한 튼튼한 뼈를 만드는 것을 돕습니다.

16 여러분 모두가 알다시피, 튼튼한 뼈와 치아를 만드는 것은 칼슘입니다.

17 그러나 몸이 칼슘을 적절하게 사용하기 위해서는 비타민 D가 필요합니다.

18 흥미롭게도, 피부는 햇빛이 피부에 비칠 때 비타민 D를 만들어 냅니다.

19 튼튼한 뼈를 만드는 가장 쉬운 방법은 밖으로 나가서 햇빛을 즐기는 겁니다.

20 보시다시피, 햇빛은 많은 이점이 있지만, 어떻게 그것의 이점을 안전하게 즐길 수 있을까요?

21 다행히도, 하루에 10분에서 20분 동안 피부에 직사광선을 쬐는 것은 햇빛으로부터 이점을 얻는 데 충분합니다.

22 수업 시간 사이나 점심시간에 햇빛을 쬐러 밖으로 나가서 팔과 손에 햇빛을 쬐어 보세요.

23 매일 단 몇 분 동안 햇살을 쬐며 걷는 것은 여러분의 마음과 몸 모두에 좋습니다.

24 그러나 여름 절정 시간인 11시에서 3시 사이에는 햇빛을 피하고, 얼굴과 목을 보호하기 위해 자외선 차단제를 사용하세요.

25 태양을 안전하게 즐기고 적은 양의 햇빛이 여러분의 건강과 기분에 얼마나 큰 차이를 만들어 내는지 보세요.

1 Enjoy the Sunshine

2 How much time do you spend every day out in the sun?

3 Not much, right?

4 Most people are too busy at school or at work to spend much time outdoors.

5 However, the sun plays an important role in your health.

6 It helps you stay healthy.

7 Everyone feels happier when the sun shines.

8 This is because of serotonin, the body's happy hormone.

9 The more sun you get, the more "happy hormone" the brain produces.

10 When your serotonin level goes up, you feel happier and stronger.

11 This helps you fight everyday stress.

12 Serotonin also has a calming effect, helping you focus better on what you are doing.

13 Moreover, serotonin helps you get a good night's sleep because it helps the brain produce a sleep

hormone.

14 Sunshine does not just make you feel and sleep better.

15 It also helps build strong bones.

16 As you all know, it is calcium that builds strong bones and teeth.

17 However, for the body to use calcium properly, it needs vitamin D.

18 Interestingly, the skin creates vitamin D when sunlight shines on it.

19 The easiest way to make strong bones is to go outside and enjoy the sun.

20 As you can see, sunshine has many benefits, but how can you enjoy its benefits safely?

21 Fortunately, getting direct sunlight on your skin for 10 to 20 minutes a day is enough to benefit from it.

22 Try to go out into the sun between classes or during lunch breaks and get sunshine on your arms and hands.

23 A walk in the sun, for just a few minutes every day, is good for both your mind and your body.

24 However, avoid the sun during peak summer hours, between 11 and 3, and use sunscreen to protect your face and neck.

25 Enjoy the sun safely and see how a little sunshine can make a world of difference in your health and your mood.

구석구석지문 TEST Step 1

Communication Task

1. it's important to exercise, exercise every day

2. No, don't, try

3. Okay

After You Read A

1. Benefits, Sunshine

2. helps, deal with, feel happier

3. helps you focus better on what

4. get enough sunshine, will sleep better

5. When, sun shines on your skin, which is needed

Writing Workshop

1. Health, First

2. Wash, after going out, will not catch a cold, if

3. direct sunlight, every day

4. The more, that, happier, stonger you feel

5. It, that, brain work properly

6. When, focus more clearly on your work, remember, better

구석구석지문 TEST Step 2

Communication Task

1. A: I think it's important to exercise every day. Do you exercise every day?

2. B: No, I don't. But I'll try.

3. A: Okay.

After You Read A

1. The Benefits of Sunshine

2. Sunshine helps you deal with stress and feel happier.

3. Sunshine helps you focus better on what you are doing.

4. If you get enough sunshine, you will sleep better at night.

5. When the sun shines on your skin, your skin produces vitamin D, which is needed for strong bones.

Writing Workshop

1. Health Comes First!

2. Wash your hands after going out. You will not catch a cold easily if you wash your hands well.

3. Get direct sunlight for 10 to 20 minutes every day.

4. The more sunlight you get, the happier and stonger you feel.

5. It is a good breakfast that helps the brain work properly.

6. When you eat a good breakfast, you can focus more clearly on your work and remember things better.

38 정답 및 해설

단어 TEST Step 1 · p.21

01 사고	02 남용하다, 너무 많이 사용하다
03 비록 ~이긴 하지만	04 길, 통로
05 불편한	06 (과일 또는 채소의) 껍질
07 규칙적으로	08 과로하다, 혹사하다
09 지진	10 ~을 야기하다　11 전기
12 과식하다	13 (짐을) 꾸리다　14 폭발하다
15 먹이를 주다	16 산소　17 마늘
18 번개	19 장소　20 기억, 추억
21 피하다	22 흘러넘치다, 범람하다
23 모기	24 자연 친화적인　25 (특정한) 때, 경우
26 준비하다, 대비하다	27 보호하다
28 (출)입구, 문	29 자외선 차단제, 선크림
30 (크림 등을) 바르다	31 주의, 집중
32 홍수, 범람	33 ~에 맞다　34 안전, 안전성
35 ~을 다 써버리다	36 의식을 잃다, 기절하다
37 어울리다	38 ~을 접근하지 못하게 하다
39 설치하다, 세우다	40 ~함으로써　41 ~을 명심하다
42 ~을 바르다	43 최선을 다하다

단어 TEST Step 2 · p.22

01 uncomfortable		02 accident
03 overflow	04 garlic	05 fit
06 mosquito	07 peel	08 although
09 apply	10 lightning	11 regularly
12 entrance	13 location	14 explode
15 overeat	16 earthquake	17 overwork
18 protect	19 oxygen	20 safety
21 overuse	22 flat	23 attention
24 flooding	25 hang	26 nature-friendly
27 spill	28 occasion	29 pack
30 prepare	31 rub	32 strike
33 electricity	34 avoid	35 put on
36 use up	37 keep ~ in mind	
38 hang out	39 keep away	40 stay up
41 instead of	42 pass out	43 do one's best

단어 TEST Step 3 · p.23

1 memory, 기억, 추억　2 feed, 먹이를 주다

3 earthquake, 지진　4 peel, (과일 또는 채소의) 껍질

5 lightning, 번개　6 strike, (세게) 치다

7 rub, 문지르다, 비비다　8 entrance, (출)입구, 문

9 location, 장소　10 flooding, 홍수, 범람

11 pack, (짐을) 꾸리다　12 explode, 폭발하다

13 apply, (크림 등을) 바르다　14 mosquito, 모기

15 sunscreen, 자외선 차단제, 선크림　16 garlic, 마늘

대화문 TEST Step 1 · p.24~25

Listen & Speak 1 Listen

1. have to watch out
2. this way, looks nice / go straight, to get to
3. stairs, wet / have to walk down
4. Let's climb, top / have to check, going to rain, should go down

Listen & Speak 1 A

1. play outside / Don't forget to, go out / cloudy, have to put on / wear, every day / put, on
2. go bowling / go see a doctor / wrong / stomach hurts

Listen & Speak 2 Listen

1. Don't, may fall / won't run
2. into, without warming up, be dangerous
3. to swim / how deep the water is, deeper than
4. right after eating / with, uncomfortable

Listen & Speak 2 A

1. can cause, what to do, have to do, have to turn off, pack, Finally, safe place, keep listening to
2. ready to leave / yet, have to, if, turned off / may not get to, in time / have to check, minute

Real-Life Zone

look at, What, think / are, going / to meet / don't have one, short ride / Put on, hurt yourself / lot, riding, without / have to wear, protects / have to wear, fits, not / have to buy

Wrap Up

comes / finish drinking / Why don't, sure that / careful / suddenly, may spill / wait for, to finish, another bus

대화문 TEST Step 2 · p.26~27

Listen & Speak 1 Listen

1. B: We have to watch out for bees.

   G: Oh, there are bees. Run!

2. G: Can we go this way? It looks nice.

   B: No. We have to go straight if we want to get to the top.

3. B: Oh, the stairs are wet.

G: Then we have to walk down the stairs slowly.

4. G: Let's climb some more. I want to reach the top of the mountain.

B: First we have to check the weather. Oh, it says it's going to rain. We should go down.

Listen & Speak 1 A

1. G: Mom, can I play outside this afternoon?

W: Sure. Don't forget to put on sunscreen before you go out.

G: But it's cloudy today. Do I have to put on sunscreen?

W: Yes, you have to wear sunscreen every day.

G: Okay. Then I'll put some on now.

2. B: Let's go bowling.

G: I'm sorry, I can't. I have to go see a doctor.

B: Oh, what's wrong?

G: I don't know, but my stomach hurts.

Listen & Speak 2 Listen

1. M: Don't run. You may fall.

B: Okay, I won't run.

2. B: Jumping into cold water without warming up can be dangerous.

G: Oh, okay. I will warm up.

3. G: Mom, I want to swim here.

W: Okay, but first you should check how deep the water is. It may be deeper than you think.

4. B: Can I swim right after eating?

G: Swimming with a full stomach can be uncomfortable.

Listen & Speak 2 A

1. M: Flooding can cause big problems. However, you may not know what to do when it happens. There are several things you have to do. First, you have to turn off the water and the electricity. Second, pack water and food when you leave the house. Finally, you have to move to a high and safe place and keep listening to the weather report.

2. B: Mina, are you ready to leave?

G: No, not yet. I have to check if I turned off the gas.

B: If we don't leave now, we may not get to the concert in time.

G: Okay, but I have to check the gas first. It will only take a minute.

Real-Life Zone

B: Uncle John, look at my new bike. What do you think?

M: It's really nice. Where are you going?

B: To the park to meet a friend.

M: Where's your helmet?

B: I don't have one. It's just a short ride.

M: Put on your helmet. You may hurt yourself.

B: But I see a lot of people riding bikes without helmets.

M: You have to wear a helmet. It protects your head in an accident.

B: Okay. I'll get my dad's helmet.

M: No. You have to wear a helmet that fits you. If not, it cannot protect your head.

B: I guess I'll have to buy one for myself.

Wrap Up

B: Here comes the bus!

G: Oh, but first I have to finish drinking my tea.

B: Why don't you just take it with you? I'm sure that it will be okay if you are careful.

G: No. If the bus stops suddenly, I may spill it.

B: Okay, then I can just wait for you to finish your drink. I'm sure another bus will come soon.

G: Thanks.

본문 TEST Step 1   p.28~29

01 create, memories, occasions, happen

02 plan, need, keep, mind

03 Listen, talk, camping trip

04 seem, what, make, safe

05 why, put up, by   06 don't think, idea

07 starts to, might overflow   08 but, sky, clear

09 really, sound, water

10 weather, change, mountains

11 never, when, might, rain

12 Safety, Let's, another   13 set up, choose, flat

14 Avoid, close, be struck

15 hungry, for lunch

16 cooking Samgyepsal

17 enough, all, more, bigger

18 more, going to, pan   19 Why, have, use

20 Because, not, than, burner

21 If, sends, back, explode   22 didn't know that

23 Here, tip, when   24 Never use, inside

25 pass, use, oxygen, as   26 Ouch! Mosquitoes

27 forgot to, apply, bug   28 Thanks, know what

29 rub, on, instead, applying

30 way to keep, away   31 That's interesting

9 저는 물소리를 정말 좋아한단 말이에요!

10 아빠: 산속의 날씨는 곧 바뀔 수 있어.

11 언제 비가 올지 절대 알 수 없는 일이지.

12 유민: 알겠어요. 안전이 우선이지요! 다른 곳을 찾아봐요.

13 텐트를 칠 때는 평평하고 햇볕이 잘 드는 장소를 고르세요.

14 번개를 맞을지도 모르는 키 큰 나무에 너무 가까운 장소는 피해야 합니다.

15 하준: 엄마, 저 배고파요. 점심이 뭐예요?

16 엄마: 삼겹살을 요리하고 있단다.

17 하준: 엄마, 그건 우리 모두가 먹기에 충분하지 않아요. 우리 더 큰 팬에 더 많이 요리하면 안 돼요?

18 엄마: 더 굽긴 할 거야. 하지만 우리는 이 작은 팬을 써야 해.

19 하준: 왜 우리는 작은 팬을 써야 하죠?

20 엄마: 왜냐하면 팬이 버너보다 더 크면 안 되기 때문이야.

21 만약 큰 팬을 사용하면, 팬이 열을 버너로 다시 돌려보내서, 가스가 폭발할 수 있어!

22 하준: 오, 그것은 몰랐어요.

23 캠핑할 때 불을 사용하는 것에 대한 또 하나의 팁이 있습니다.

24 텐트 안에서 가스난로나 버너를 절대 쓰지 마세요.

25 여러분의 텐트에 불이 붙거나, 불이 타면서 텐트 내 산소를 다 써 버려서 여러분이 의식을 잃을 수도 있습니다.

26 유민: 앗! 모기!

27 엄마: 아, 벌레 퇴치 스프레이를 뿌리라고 네게 말하는 걸 잊었구나. 여기 있단다.

28 유민: 고마워요, 엄마. 아, 그거 아세요?

29 벌레 퇴치 스프레이를 뿌리는 것 대신에 오렌지 껍질을 피부에 문질러도 돼요.

30 모기가 접근하지 못하게 하는 자연 친화적인 방법이에요.

31 엄마: 그거 재미있구나!

32 마늘 또한 벌레가 접근하지 못하게 막을 수 있습니다.

33 마늘 조각을 텐트 입구에 놓아두면, 벌레가 안으로 들어오지 않을 것입니다.

본문 TEST Step 2 p.30~31

01 Although, create, memories, when, happen
02 plan to go camping, need, in mind, safety
03 talk, camping trip
04 seem, what to do, safe
05 why don't, put up, by　　06 think, idea
07 starts to, might overflow　08 but, clear
09 sound
10 weather, change quickly
11 never, when, might, to rain
12 Safety, Let's, another　　13 set up, choose
14 Avoid, close, be struck by lightning
15 hungry, for　　　　　　16 cooking
17 enough, all, more, bigger pan
18 going to, more, have to use
19 Why, have to use
20 Because, should not, bigger than
21 If, sends, back, explode　22 know
23 Here, tip, when, go camping
24 Never, inside
25 may catch fire, or, pass, use, oxygen, burns
26 Mosquitoes　　　　　27 forgot to, to apply
28 what
29 rub, peels on, instead of applying
30 nature-friendly way to keep, away
31 interesting　　　　　　32 keep, away
33 pieces of garlic, entrance, come inside

본문 TEST Step 3 p.32~33

1 캠핑 여행이 많은 사람들에게 좋은 추억을 만들어 주기도 하지만, 나쁜 일이 일어나는 때가 될 수도 있습니다.

2 여러분이 이번 여름에 가족이나 친구들과 함께 캠핑을 하려고 계획하고 있다면, 여러분은 여러분의 안전을 위해서 몇 가지 사항을 명심해야 합니다.

3 유민이의 가족이 그들의 캠핑 여행에 대해 이야기하는 것을 들어 보세요.

4 그들은 그들의 캠핑 여행이 안전하고 재미있게 하기 위해 무엇을 해야 하는지 알고 있는 것 같습니다.

5 유민: 아빠, 이 강 근처 이쪽에 텐트를 치면 어때요?

6 아빠: 그건 좋은 생각 같지 않구나.

7 만약 비가 내리기 시작하면, 강이 범람할지도 몰라.

8 유민: 저도 알아요. 하지만 하늘이 맑잖아요.

본문 TEST Step 4-Step 5 p.34~37

1 Although camping trips can create sweet memories for many people, they can also be occasions when bad things happen.

2 If you plan to go camping with family or friends this summer, you need to keep several things in mind for your safety.

3 Listen to Yumin's family talk about their camping trip.

4 They seem to know what to do to make their camping trip safe and fun.

5 Yumin: Dad, why don't we put up our tent over here by this river?

6 Dad: I don't think that's a good idea.

7 If it starts to rain, the river might overflow.

8 Yumin: I know, but the sky is clear.

9 I really like the sound of the water!

10 Dad: The weather can change quickly in the mountains.

11 You never know when it might start to rain.

12 Yumin: Okay. Safety first! Let's find another place.

13 When you set up a tent, choose a flat, sunny area.

14 Avoid places too close to big trees that might be struck by lightning.

15 Hajun: Mom, I'm hungry. What's for lunch?

16 Mom: I'm cooking Samgyepsal.

17 Hajun: Mom, that's not enough for all of us. Can we cook more in a bigger pan?

18 Mom: I'm going to cook more, but we have to use this small pan.

19 Hajun: Why do we have to use a small pan?

20 Mom: Because the pan should not be bigger than the burner.

21 If you use a big pan, it sends the heat back to the burner, and the gas can explode!

22 Hajun: Oh, I didn't know that.

23 Here is one more tip about fire when you go camping.

24 Never use a gas heater or burner inside a tent.

25 Your tent may catch fire, or you might pass out because the fire will use up the oxygen in the tent as it burns.

26 Yumin: Ouch! Mosquitoes!

27 Mom: Oh, I forgot to tell you to apply some bug spray. Here.

28 Yumin: Thanks, Mom. Oh, you know what?

29 We can rub orange peels on our skin instead of applying bug spray.

30 It is a nature-friendly way to keep mosquitoes away.

31 Mom: That's interesting!

32 Garlic can also keep bugs away.

33 You can place pieces of garlic at the entrance to the tent, and bugs will not come inside.

구석구석지문 TEST Step 1 p.38

Before You Read

1. Welcome to

2. have prepared, the two-day camping trip

3. Because, do our best to prepare for anything bad

4. help people have, by placing, avoid getting bitten

by mosquitoes

5. everyone tales home good memories

Writing Workshop

1. Although, are free from an earthquake

2. when it strikes

3. several things, need to keep in mind

4. stay inside, until the shaking stops

5. seems to be safe, might fall on

6. turn off

7. get under, cover your head with your arms

8. It, to protect

9. far away from, as possible

10. By following, can be safe

Wrap Up

1. Trip Diary

2. Location, September

3. with

4. went, with, on September

5. During, enjoyed rafting, hiking

6. Although, was afraid of doing, at first

7. go rafting, if, have a chance

구석구석지문 TEST Step 2 p.39

Before You Read

1. Welcome to Our Sky Camping Trip!

2. We have prepared many activities for the two-day camping trip.

3. Because we always think about your safety first, we do our best to prepare for anything bad that may happen.

4. We help people have a comfortable stay by placing a can of bug spray in each tent so you can avoid getting bitten by mosquitoes.

5. We hope everyone tales home good memories of the trip!

Writing Workshop

1. Although you would think that you are free from an earthquake, that is not true.

2. Then, what should you do when it strikes?

3. There are several things you need to keep in mind.

4. First, stay inside and keep informed until the shaking stops.

5. It seems to be safe to go outside, but something might fall on you.

6. Second, turn off the gas and the electricity.

7. Third, get under the table and cover your head with your arms.

8. It is important to protect your head.

9. Finally, if you are outside, try to get as far away from buildings, trees, and streetlights as possible.

10. By following these tips, you can be safe from the earthquake.

Wrap Up

1. My Camping Trip Diary

2. Location: Yeongwol Date: September 12

3. Traveled with: my family

4. I went to Yeongwol with my family on September 12.

5. During the trip, we enjoyed rafting and hiking.

6. Although I was afraid of doing rafting at first, it was really fun and exciting.

7. I'll go rafting again if I have a chance.

단어 TEST Step 1　　　　　　　　　p.40

01 (짐을) 싸다, 꾸리다

02 다시 문을 열다, 다시 시작하다　　03 대학

04 역할, 부분　　05 계약, 계약서　　06 심각하게

07 ~을 제외하고　　08 결정, 판단　　09 결국, 마침내

10 허락하다　　11 정확히　　12 유명한

13 체육관　　14 일어나다, 발생하다

15 교장　　16 향상하다, 향상시키다

17 약속하다　　18 인생, 삶　　19 잠그다

20 받아들이다　　21 실제로, 정말로

22 지다, 패하다　　23 요구

24 (부정문에서) 역시, 또한　　25 명령하다

26 서명하다　　27 거절하다　　28 성적

29 (충고·지시 등을) 따르다　　30 참석하다

31 마음을 쓰다, 걱정하다

32 깨닫다, 알아차리다　　33 상상하다

34 실망한, 낙담한　　35 ~함으로써　　36 ~을 찾아보다

37 B뿐만 아니라 A도

38 ~에 유의하다, ~에 관심을 갖다

39 이행하다, 수행하다　　40 ~하는 데 익숙해지다

41 게다가, ~에 더하여　　42 잇따라서

43 설상가상으로

단어 TEST Step 2　　　　　　　　　p.41

01 sign　　02 accept　　03 gym

04 happen　　05 attend　　06 college

07 decision　　08 improve　　09 care

10 follow　　11 pack　　12 contract

13 disappointed　14 future　　15 principal

16 seriously　　17 lose　　18 decide

19 eventually　　20 exactly　　21 except

22 actually　　23 order　　24 either

25 grade　　26 realize　　27 imagine

28 practice　　29 lock　　30 demand

31 refuse　　32 winner　　33 allow

34 reopen　　35 in addition to　　36 A as well as B

37 carry out　　38 take action　　39 find out

40 pay attention to

41 one after another

42 to make matters worse

43 become used to -ing

1 sign, 서명하다　2 win, 이기다　3 improve, 향상시키다
4 principal, 교장　5 coach, (스포츠 팀의) 코치
6 order, 명령하다　7 contract, 계약서　8 attend, 참석하다
9 bonus, 상여금, 보너스　10 refuse, 거절하다
11 pack, (짐을) 꾸리다　12 gym, 체육관
13 demand, 요구　14 rule, 규칙　15 imagine, 상상하다
16 college, 대학

01 Welcome to　　　　　02 going to talk
03 imagine, allow, to practice　04 exactly what, does
05 cares, about, than, winning
06 having, losing, after another
07 became used to losing
08 To make, worse, only　09 get, new coach
10 wanted to change things　11 how to play, win
12 more than, by sending
13 To carry out, contract
14 had, in addition to
15 At first, contract seriously
16 give you a contract
17 Attend, classes, be late　18 all these rules
19 signing bonus, contract
20 because, winner, well, life　21 With, in many years
22 From, point on, after
23 Everybody, except, happy
24 do, part of, contract
25 Few, paid little attention
26 decided, take, action
27 let, until, improved, as　28 players, not, it
29 that, actions, just, not
30 the basketball team
31 All, on, getting famous
32 If, yourself, better life
33 answer, everything, to help
34 have to do, part
35 parents, like, decision either
36 demand, ordered, to reopen
37 Disappointed, decided to leave
38 When, to pack, were
39 won't, what happens next
40 Find out, by watching

01 Welcome to　　　　　02 going to talk
03 imagine, doesn't allow, to practice
04 exactly what, does
05 cares, about, than about winning games
06 one, after another
07 became used to losing
08 To make, worse, had no plans, only to play
09 new coach　　　　　10 wanted to change
11 how to play, win
12 more than, by sending, to college
13 To carry out, sign a contract
14 had to promise, in addition to playing
15 At first, take his idea, seriously
16 give you a contract
17 Attend, classes, be late　18 all these rules
19 signing bonus, contract
20 because, become a winner, as well as
21 With, began to win, in many years
22 From, point on, after　23 except
24 part of
25 Few of, paid little attention to
26 take stronger action
27 refused to let, play, until, improved, as
28 it
29 that, actions, just, not
30 basketball team
31 All we see, getting famous
32 If, yourself, better life
33 If, everything, to help
34 have to, part　　　　35 decision either
36 demand, principal ordered, to reopen
37 Disappointed, decided to
38 When, to pack, however, all of, were
39 what happens next
40 Find out, by watching

1 「영화 여행」에 오신 것을 환영합니다.
2 오늘 우리는 영화 「코치 카터」에 대해 이야기할 것입니다.
3 선수들이 연습하는 것을 허락하지 않는 농구 코치를 상상할 수 있나요?
4 그것이 바로 카터 코치가 한 것입니다.
5 이 영화는 경기에서 이기는 것보다 학생들을 더 걱정하는 코치에 대한 영화입니다.
6 캘리포니아 리치몬드 지역의 리치몬드 고등학교 농구 팀은 연속해서 경기에서 지고 있었습니다.

7 선수들도 지는 것에 익숙하게 되었습니다.

8 설상가상으로 그들은 미래에 대한 계획도 없었습니다. 즉, 그들은 단지 농구하기 위해 학교에 갔고, 그것마저도 잘하지 못했습니다.

9 그때 그들은 케니 카터라는 새로운 코치를 선임했습니다.

10 카터 코치는 몇 가지를 바꾸고자 했습니다.

11 그는 아이들에게 어떻게 농구를 잘하고 이기는지를 가르치기를 원했습니다.

12 그러나 그것보다도, 그는 그들을 대학에 보냄으로써 선수들에게 미래를 주기를 원했습니다.

13 그의 계획을 실행하기 위해서, 카터 코치는 선수들에게 계약서에 서명하게 했습니다.

14 그들은 농구를 하는 것뿐만 아니라 열심히 공부할 것도 약속해야만 했습니다.

15 처음에는 학생들이 계약서에 대한 그의 생각을 심각하게 받아들이지 않았습니다.

16 카터: 내가 너희들에게 계약서를 줄 것이다.

17 크루즈: "모든 수업에 출석하라," "C 플러스 또는 그 이상 받아라," "지각하지 말아라."

18 이 모든 규칙들은 무엇이죠?

19 제가 이 계약서에 사인하면 사이닝 보너스를 받나요?

20 카터: 그래. 너는 큰 보너스를 받게 될 거야. 왜냐하면 인생의 게임에서뿐 아니라 농구 경기에 서도 승리자가 될 것이기 때문이지.

21 맹연습과 새로운 경기 전략으로 그 팀은 몇 년 만에 처음으로 이기기 시작했습니다.

22 그때 이후로 경기마다 이겼습니다.

23 카터 코치를 제외한 모든 이들이 행복했습니다.

24 선수들은 그들 계약의 '학습' 부분을 하지 않았습니다.

25 그들 중 정말 그들이 대학을 갈 수 있다고 믿는 사람들은 거의 없었습니다. 그래서 그들은 성적에는 거의 관심을 두지 않았습니다.

26 카터는 더 강력한 조치를 취하기로 결심했습니다.

27 그는 체육관 문을 잠그고 계약서에서 약속한 대로 그들의 성적이 좋아질 때까지 농구를 못하게 했습니다.

28 선수들은 그것을 좋아하지 않았습니다.

29 그들은 그에게 그의 행동들이 그들을 위한 것이 아닌 단지 카터 자신을 위한 것이라고 말했습니다.

30 웜: 우리는 농구 팀이에요.

31 우리가 보는 모든 것은 유명세를 타며 TV에 있는 당신이에요.

32 카터: 네가 그렇게 생각한다면, 집으로 가서 너 자신에게 물어봐. "나는 더 나은 삶을 원하는가?"

33 대답이 '맞다'라면, 나는 너를 돕기 위해 내 힘이 닿는 한 모든 것을 할 거야.

34 그러나 너는 네 역할을 해야만 해.

35 선수들의 부모들 역시 카터의 결정을 좋아하지 않았습니다.

36 부모들의 요구에 따라 교장은 카터에게 체육관을 다시 열도록 했습니다.

37 실망한 카터는 리치몬드 고등학교를 떠나기로 결심했습니다.

38 그가 짐을 싸기 위해 체육관으로 들어섰을 때, 그의 선수들 모두가 그곳에 있었습니다.

39 우리는 여러분이 이 영화를 즐기기 원합니다. 그래서 당신에게 다음에 무슨 일이 일어나는지 이야기하지 않을 것입니다.

40 영화 「코치 카터」를 보고 스스로 찾아보세요.

---

1 Welcome to *Movie Trip*.

2 Today we're going to talk about the movie *Coach Carter*.

3 Can you imagine a basketball coach who doesn't allow his players to practice?

4 That's exactly what Coach Carter does.

5 This movie is about a coach who cares more about his students than about winning games.

6 The basketball team at Richmond High School in Richmond, California, was having one losing season after another.

7 The players became used to losing.

8 To make matters worse, they had no plans for the future; they went to school only to play basketball, and they did not do that very well.

9 Then they got a new coach, Kenny Carter.

10 Coach Carter wanted to change things.

11 He wanted to teach kids how to play basketball well and win.

12 But more than that, he wanted to give the players a future by sending them to college.

13 To carry out his plan, Coach Carter had the players sign a contract.

14 They had to promise to study hard in addition to playing basketball.

15 At first, students did not take his idea for a contract seriously.

16 Carter: I'm going to give you a contract.

17 Cruz: "Attend all classes," "Get a C⁺ or higher," "Don't be late…."

18 What are all these rules about?

19 Do I get a signing bonus for signing this contract?

20 Carter: Yes. You will get a big bonus because you will become a winner in the game of basketball as well as in the game of life.

21 With hard work and a new game plan, the team began to win for the first time in many years.

22 From that point on, they won game after game.

23 Everybody, except Coach Carter, was happy.

24 The players did not do the "study" part of their contract.

25 Few of them actually believed they could go to college, so they paid little attention to their grades.

26 Carter decided to take stronger action.

27 He locked the gym and refused to let them play basketball until their grades improved, as promised in the contract.

28 The players did not like it.

29 They told him that his actions were just for him, not for them.

30 Worm: We're the basketball team.

31 All we see is you on TV, getting famous.

32 Carter: If you think so, go home and ask yourself, "Do I want a better life?"

33 If the answer is yes, I will do everything in my power to help you.

34 But you have to do your part.

35 The players' parents did not like Carter's decision either.

36 At the parents' demand, the principal ordered Carter to reopen the gym.

37 Disappointed, Carter decided to leave Richmond High.

38 When he entered the gym to pack his things, however, all of his players were there.

39 We want you to enjoy the movie, so we won't tell you what happens next.

40 Find out for yourself by watching the movie *Coach Carter*.

Lesson 5

01 수단, 방법	02 주의, 집중	03 ~ 아래에
04 의미	05 (긴장을) 늦추다, 휴식을 취하다	
06 면밀히, 밀접하게	07 잡지	08 밝은, 긍정적인
09 방울	10 감정	11 발랄한, 쾌활한
12 독립적인, 자립심이 강한		13 기사
14 ~을 관련[연결]시키다		15 성격
16 보호	17 합리적인	18 다름, 차이점
19 의존적인	20 호기심이 있는	21 미루다, 연기하다
22 짜증이 난	23 유용한, 도움이 되는	
24 여러 가지의, 다양한		25 편한, 편안한
26 인기 있는	27 세부 사항	28 현실적인
29 상상, 상상력	30 차분한	31 주의 깊은
32 큰 소리로	33 평화로운	34 줄이다
35 매진된, 다 팔린	36 ~을 다루다, ~을 처리하다	
37 (사람들과) 잘 어울리다		38 동시에, 함께
39 다시 말하면	40 ~와 연관되다	41 ~와 관련되다
42 ~에 따르면, ~에 따라		
43 반면에, 한편으로는		

01 article	02 situation	03 difference
04 relax	05 magazine	06 creative
07 emotion	08 drop	09 relate
10 independent	11 cheerful	12 comfortable
13 recipe	14 curious	15 reasonable
16 dependent	17 personality	18 various
19 protection	20 imagination	21 calm
22 reduce	23 popular	24 detail
25 realistic	26 careful	27 peaceful
28 delay	29 express	30 closely
31 annoyed	32 meaning	33 means
34 opinion	35 in other words	36 deal with
37 get along	38 be related to	39 according to
40 have to do with		41 at the same time
42 on the other hand		
43 draw attention to oneself		

단어 TEST Step 3

1 reasonable, 합리적인　2 frightened, 겁먹은, 두려워하는
3 recipe, 조리[요리]법　4 delay, 미루다, 연기하다
5 calm, 차분한　6 comfortable, 편안한
7 seat, 자리, 좌석　8 focus, 집중하다　9 reduce, 줄이다
10 hopeful, 희망찬　11 attitude, 태도
12 independent, 독립적인, 자립심이 강한
13 express, 표현하다　14 difference, 다름, 차이점
15 article, 기사　16 personality, 성격

대화문 TEST Step 1　p.61~62

Listen and Speak 1 Listen

1. does, mean / nervous, frightened, doing
2. does, mean / feel sad
3. does, mean / means, look sad
4. does, mean / means, give up

Listen and Speak 1 A

1. How, doing / for / does, mean / means, happy, excited
2. personality test, had to draw / According to, a lot, by, mine / do, mean / mean, open, other

Listen and Speak 2 Listen

1. sold out / Are there, other seats / some tickets
2. spicy, sweet / other sauces / only two
3. would, like to, maybe / any other, too much sugar / too
4. the most popluar / other colors / lots, over here

Listen and Speak 2 A

1. reading / says, change people's feelings / surprising / For example, help us focus / useful colors / helps,　relax
2. more, yourself, kinds of, other tests / calling to take, test / any time before

Real-Life Zone

what kind of, to try / like fun / afraid of, one of, spiders / dark places, without, on, mean / says, full of, That's why, fill, with, scary things / about, anything, afraid of / big imagination / any other tests, take / a lot of

Wrap Up 1~2

blood type / an article, says / your personality / type A / with, calm, listeners, too

대화문 TEST Step 2　p.63~64

Listen and Speak 1 Listen

1. G: What does "be in a cold sweat" mean?

B: It means "to be nervous or frightened before doing something."
2. B: What does "feel blue" mean?

G: It means "to feel sad."
3. G: What does "have a long face" mean?

B: It means "to look sad."
4. B: What does "throw up one's hands" mean?

G: It means "to give up."

Listen and Speak 1 A

1. G: Hi, Jack! How are you doing?

B: I'm on cloud nine! I got a concert ticket for my favorite band.

G: What does "on cloud nine" mean?

B: It means I'm really happy and excited.
2. G: I took a personality test today. I had to draw a house.

B: A house?

G: Yeah. According to the test, you can tell a lot about a person by their drawing. Here's mine.

B: Interesting. So what do these big windows mean?

G: They mean I'm open to other people.

Listen and Speak 2 Listen

1. M: Sorry. The tickets for the blue zone are all sold out.

G: Are there any other seats?

M: Yes, we have some tickets for the red zone.
2. W: What would you like on your hot dog? We have spicy sauce and sweet sauce.

B: Are there any other sauces?

W: Sorry. Those are the only two we have.
3. M: What would you like to drink? A soft drink maybe?

G: Are there any other drinks? Soft drinks have too much sugar in them.

M: We have apple juice too.
4. W: This is the most popluar cap in our store.

B: Are there any other colors?

W: Sure, we have lots more. They're over here. I'll show you.

Listen and Speak 2 A

1. B: Jane, what are you reading?

G: I'm reading an interesting magazine. It says colors can change people's feelings.

B: That's surprising.

G: Yes. For example, the color red can help us focus better.

B: Are there any other useful colors?

G: Yes. The color blue helps people relax.

2. M: EDPI Test Center. Do you want to learn more about yourself? We have many kinds of personality tests. If there are any other tests you want to learn more about, we are here to help you.

B: Hi, I'm calling to take a personality test. Can I do one this afternoon?

M: Sure, you can come any time before 5 o'clock.

Real-Life Zone

Hajun: Look! I found this test on an app that tells what kind of person you are. Do you want to try it?

Emma: Sure. Sounds like fun.

Hajun: Okay, listen. What are you afraid of? Choose one of these: crowds, spiders, or dark places.

Emma: I hate dark places. I cannot sleep without a night light on. What does that mean?

Hajun: It says you are full of imagination. That's why you fill dark places with all kinds of scary things.

Emma: That's very interesting. What about you? Is there anything you are afraid of?

Hajun: I chose dark places too. But I don't think I have a big imagination.

Emma: This is fun. I want to do some more. Are there any other tests we can take?

Hajun: Sure. This app has a lot of them.

Wrap Up 1~2

B: What's your blood type?

G: Type A. Why?

B: I'm reading an article. It says that blood type tells something about your personality.

G: Wow. Then what does type A mean?

B: People with blood type A are calm. They are good listeners, too.

본문 TEST Step 1　　　　　　　　　　　　p.65~66

01 Everything, do says something

02 wear, even, raise, kind

03 things, draw, much different

04 What, how, related, personality

05 using various, better understand

06 One, those tests, test　　　07 Study, below

08 person, holding, light rain

09 other hand, heavy, no

---

10 there, dark, above, person

11 What, differences mean

12 rain, stress, who, under

13 bigger, drops, heavily, falling

14 waiting, happen, hopeful, future

15 Second, protection, stressful situation

16 big, shows, plans, protection

17 drawing, means, deal with

18 details, have, with, attitude

19 example, draws, without, attention

20 right side, ready to

21 hand, may, worried, happened

22 possible meanings, part, drawings

23 go back, at look　　　24 Try reading, yourself

25 what kind, each one　　26 your opinion

본문 TEST Step 2　　　　　　　　　　　　p.67~68

01 Everything, says something

02 use, wear, even, raise, what kind of person you are

03 draw, much

04 What, how, are related to, personality

05 have been using, to better understand

06 One, those tests　　　07 Study, below

08 holding, light

09 On the other hand, heavy, no

10 there are, above　　　11 differences mean

12 stress, who, under

13 The bigger, the more heavily, the bigger

14 waiting, happen, hopeful, future

15 Second, protection, stressful situation

16 big, shows, a lot of plans, protection

17 drawing, means, deal with difficult situations

18 Third, details, have to do, attitude

19 example, who, without, attention, himself, herself

20 who, right, is ready to meet

21 hand, may, worried, happened

22 possible meanings, part, drawings

23 back, look at　　　24 reading, yourself

25 what kind, drew each one　26 opinion

본문 TEST Step 3　　　　　　　　　　　　p.69~70

1 당신이 하는 모든 행동은 당신에 대해 말해 줍니다.

2 당신이 사용하는 언어, 당신이 입는 옷, 그리고 당신이 기르는 애완동물까지도 당신이 어떤 종류의 사람인지 보여 줍니다.

---

3 당신이 그리는 그림도 마찬가지입니다.

4 당신이 무엇을 그리는지 그리고 그것을 어떻게 그리는지는 당신의 성격과 관련이 있습니다.

5 의사들은 사람들을 더 잘 이해하기 위해 다양한 그림 그리기 검사를 사용해 오고 있습니다.

6 이런 검사들 중 하나는 빗속의 사람 그리기 검사입니다.

7 아래의 그림들을 연구해 봅시다.

8 A 그림 속의 사람은 가벼운 빗속에서 우산을 들고 있습니다.

9 반면에, B 그림 속의 사람은 거센 빗속에서 우산을 가지고 있지 않습니다.

10 또한, 검은 구름들이 B 그림의 사람 머리 위에 있습니다.

11 이런 차이는 무엇을 의미하는 걸까요?

12 첫 번째, 비는 그림을 그린 사람이 받고 있는 스트레스를 보여줍니다.

13 빗방울의 크기가 크면 클수록, 혹은 비가 더 세게 내리면 내릴수록 스트레스는 더 큽니다.

14 구름은 앞으로 벌어질 문제를 의미하기 때문에, 큰 구름은 그림을 그린 사람이 미래에 대해 그다지 희망적이지 않다는 것을 나타냅니다.

15 두 번째, 우산은 스트레스를 받는 상황에서 그 사람이 가지고 있는 보호 기제를 의미합니다.

16 큰 우산은 그림을 그린 사람이 많은 계획이나 보호 기제를 가지고 있음을 보여 줍니다.

17 만약 그림에 우산이 없다면, 그 그림을 그린 사람은 어려운 상황을 헤쳐 나갈 어떤 방법도 가지고 있지 않습니다.

18 세 번째, 그림 속 사람의 세부적인 것들은 그 그림을 그린 사람이 스트레스를 받을 때의 태도와 관련이 있습니다.

19 예를 들어, 얼굴이 없는 사람을 그린 사람은 사람들의 관심을 끌기를 원하지 않습니다.

20 사람을 종이의 오른쪽에 그린 사람은 미래를 맞이할 준비가 되어 있습니다.

21 반면에, 사람을 왼쪽에 그린 사람은 과거에 일어났던 일에 대해 걱정하고 있을 수도 있습니다.

22 이것들은 그림 각 부분의 가능한 의미 풀이 중 일부입니다.

23 이제, 돌아가서 두 그림을 보세요.

24 그 그림들을 스스로 읽으려고 시도해 보세요.

25 당신은 각 그림을 그린 사람이 어떤 사람인지 알 수 있나요?

26 당신의 의견은 어떤가요?

본문 TEST Step 4~Step 5

p.71~74

1 Everything you do says something about you.

2 The language you use, the clothes you wear, and even the pets you raise somehow show what kind of person you are.

3 The things you draw are not much different.

4 What you draw and how you draw it are related to your personality.

5 Doctors have been using various drawing tests to better understand people.

6 One of those tests is the Draw-a-Person-in-the-Rain (DAPR) test.

7 Study the pictures below.

8 The person in Drawing A is holding an umbrella in a light rain.

9 On the other hand, the person in Drawing B is in a heavy rain and has no umbrella.

10 Also, there are dark clouds above the person in Drawing B.

11 What can these differences mean?

12 First, the rain shows the stress the person who drew the picture is under.

13 The bigger the drops are or the more heavily the rain is falling, the bigger the stress is.

14 The clouds mean problems waiting to happen, so a big cloud shows the drawer is not very hopeful about the future.

15 Second, the umbrella means the protection the person has in a stressful situation.

16 A big umbrella shows that the drawer has a lot of plans or protection.

17 If there's no umbrella in the drawing, the drawer does not have any means to deal with difficult situations.

18 Third, the details in the drawing of the person have to do with the drawer's attitude under stress.

19 For example, someone who draws a person without a face does not want to draw people's attention to himself or herself.

20 Someone who draws the person on the right side of the paper is ready to meet the future.

21 On the other hand, someone who draws the person on the left side may be worried about things that have happened in the past.

22 These are some of the possible meanings of each part of the drawings.

23 Now, go back and look at the two drawings.

24 Try reading them yourself.

25 Can you understand what kind of person drew each one?

26 What's your opinion?

Before You Read

1. closely related to what
2. When, draw, shows your feelings
3. In other words, can be expressed
4. Therefore, find out, pay careful attention to

Writing Workshop

1. have been doing, different kinds of
2. had to talk about, own personalities
3. saw myself, shy, friendly
4. What, said, quite different
5. active, curious, get along well with, lots of clubs

Wrap Up 3~4

1. need to go, no train tickets left
2. any other ways
3. take a bus, comfortable
4. do that

Before You Read

1. A picture is often closely related to what you're feeling in your mind.
2. When you draw a picture, it shows your feelings.
3. In other words, your various feelings can be expressed through pictures.
4. Therefore, you can find out other people's feelings if you pay careful attention to their drawings.

Writing Workshop

1. This year, we have been doing a lot of different kinds of activities at school.
2. Today, we had to talk about our own personalities and then talk about a friend's personality.
3. I saw myself as shy and friendly.
4. What my friend said about me was quite different.
5. She said I am active and curious because I get along well with others and am in lots of clubs.

Wrap Up 3~4

1. G: I need to go to Daegu today, but there are no train tickets left.
2. Are there any other ways to get there?
3. B: You can take a bus. It's fast and comfortable.
4. G: That's a great idea. I'll do that.